C000265001

The Battle of the Catalaunian Fields, AD 451

The Battle of the Catalaunian Fields, AD 451

Flavius Aetius, Attila the Hun and the Transformation of Gaul

Evan Michael Schultheis

Pen & Sword
MILITARY

AN IMPRINT OF PEN & SWORD BOOKS LTD.
YORKSHIRE – PHILADELPHIA

First published in Great Britain in 2019 by
Pen & Sword Military
An imprint of
Pen & Sword Books Ltd
Yorkshire – Philadelphia

Copyright © Evan Michael Schultheis 2019

ISBN 978 1 52674 565 1

The right of Evan Michael Schultheis to be identified as Author of this work
has been asserted by him in accordance with the Copyright, Designs and Patents
Act 1988.

A CIP catalogue record for this book is
available from the British Library.

All rights reserved. No part of this book may be reproduced or transmitted in any
form or by any means, electronic or mechanical including photocopying, recording
or by any information storage and retrieval system, without permission from the
Publisher in writing.

Printed and bound in the UK by TJ International Ltd, Padstow, Cornwall.

Pen & Sword Books Limited incorporates the imprints of Atlas, Archaeology,
Aviation, Discovery, Family History, Fiction, History, Maritime, Military, Military
Classics, Politics, Select, Transport, True Crime, Air World, Frontline Publishing,
Leo Cooper, Remember When, Seaforth Publishing, The Praetorian Press,
Wharncliffe Local History, Wharncliffe Transport, Wharncliffe True Crime and
White Owl.

For a complete list of Pen & Sword titles please contact

PEN & SWORD BOOKS LIMITED
47 Church Street, Barnsley, South Yorkshire, S70 2AS, England
E-mail: enquiries@pen-and-sword.co.uk
Website: www.pen-and-sword.co.uk

or

PEN AND SWORD BOOKS
1950 Lawrence Rd, Havertown, PA 19083, USA
E-mail: Uspen-and-sword@casematepublishers.com
Website: www.penandswordbooks.com

Contents

List of Plates

Maps

Acknowledgements

This work has been the culmination of more than ten years of research since I first became interested in Roman history at the age of 11 in 2006, after watching the admittedly cheesy 'Barbarians II' series on the *History Channel*. It began as an attempt to submit an article to the *Journal of Late Antiquity*, which was rejected, but I had constructive feedback provided to me because of this attempt, which inspired me to continue in my endeavour by seeking out dozens of volumes of modern scholarship. It has since then been an on and off crusade of research, interrupted only by university coursework, which has spurred many of my side projects on the obscure fifth-century Roman Army. As a result, my knowledge of the era has dramatically transformed over the past few years: this is the culmination of that knowledge.

Without the internet, I could not have acquired most of the scholarly books and journals that were used to build this volume. Indeed, this work could be considered a result of the digitization of classics and history. I would like to thank the members of *RomanArmyTalk.com* for providing references, copies of primary or secondary sources, reviews and discussion which have helped me generate many of my arguments here. I would like to give special commendations to Michael Kerr and Marko Jelusic for taking their time to scan dozens of articles, and Mr Hays of the Ida Jane Dacus Library at Winthrop University, who provided many books which would have otherwise been inaccessible to me. Secondly, I would like to thank various members participating in the re-enactment community, like Robert Vermaat, Matthew Bunker, Seb Herzynia, Nadeem Ahmad and many others, who have a knowledge of the history and archaeology that more than qualifies them for the title of 'expert'. Many of them also gave me permission to use photos of their reconstructions for this work. Thirdly, I must thank Pavel Simak for providing the fantastic cover art for this volume.

I would like to thank some of the academics who have encouraged and influenced me and this work, including my Latin teachers and professors Dr Tracy Seiler and Dr Joseph Tipton; authors who have written on the battle, including Ian Hughes, MA, and Dr Hyun Jin Kim, who constantly engaged me in lively discussion and agreed to review this work; and other authors, such as Dr Guy Halsall, Dr Roger Blockley, Dr Ralph Mathisen and Simon MacDowall, for pointing me towards books, answering my persistent questions and allowing me to use photos. It would be impossible to name all the academics, enthusiasts, and re-enactors who have uploaded their works to the internet, an ever-expanding database of source material, but general thanks I give to them. Sadly, I cannot possibly name everyone who deserves recognition; but it is on that particular note that I would also like to give special thanks to the unnamed reviewer who gave such constructive criticism of my rejected article. I literally could not have done it without you.

I would like to dedicate this work to my friend Rusty Myers, *Primus Pilus* of *Legio VI Ferrata Fidelis Constans,* our re-enactment group. Rusty brought me into re-enactment and continued to encourage me throughout the composition of this work, and I cannot thank him enough.

Introduction

Sidonius Apollinaris describes the events surrounding what has long been considered one of the most pivotal battles in late antiquity with the single phrase 'the barbarian world, rent by a mighty upheaval, poured the whole north into Gaul'.[1] A battle with a plethora of names, the Battle of the Catalaunian Fields (or Plains), deriving from *Campus Catalauniensis*, or Battle of the Mauriac Plains, deriving from *Campus Mauriacus*, was fought on 20 June AD 451, and is one of the few fifth-century battles that was fortunate enough to receive both detailed primary source accounts and have them passed down to the modern day. It is now commonly referred to by the name of the chief town in the region, being the Battle of Chalons.[2] Traditionally, the battle is considered one of the major highlights of the fifth century, or even of world history. It is infamous for being the engagement where 'Attila the Hun was defeated' and for the second time 'western civilization was saved'. Although both of these assertions are dated, having been offered in the nineteenth century, since the mid-twentieth century great strides have been made in historiographical analysis, the understanding of *topoi* in late antique history, but study of the battle has been rather neglected. Because of its over-prescribed historical significance, the battle still appears in most modern scholarship regarding the middle of the fifth century. Modern historians typically ascribe a brief mention to the Battle of the Catalaunian Fields, often stating that it has been detailed enough elsewhere, although a handful of authors have chosen to offer new perspectives on the battle.[3]

The Battle of the Catalaunian Fields was recounted for the first time in almost a millennium by none other than Sir Edward Gibbon. Gibbon's long-outdated but comprehensive work, *The History of the Decline and Fall of the Roman Empire*, called the battle 'the last victory which was achieved in the name of the Western Roman Empire'.[4] Following partially in his footsteps, the next and probably most widely known historical survey of the Battle of the Catalaunian Fields was given by Sir Edward Creasy. He listed it in his *Fifteen Decisive Battles of the World* and heralded it as the triumph of Christian Europe over the pagan savages of central Asia, saving the classical heritage of Greece and Rome.[5] These works of the eighteenth and nineteenth centuries set premises that have shadowed the battle since then, often appearing in abridgements of Creasy. Some of the biases of these authors have also remained widespread to this day, with authors as recent as Arther Ferrill and John Julius Norwich also perpetuating the notion that the battle prevented Europe from being turned into a cultural desert.[6] On the other hand, authors like Samuel Barnish are among the most recent in a line of scholars who have brought the decisiveness of the battle into question, and in comparison his work is a central example of how the modern view has changed significantly from that of Gibbon or Creasy.[7] Despite the perpetuation of the traditional nineteenth-century views, twentieth-century scholarship has greatly advanced our understanding of the battle, its context and the context in which the primary sources were written.

The commentary by J.B. Bury in the early twentieth century could be considered the first serious attempt at a discussion of the real historical importance of the Battle of the Catalaunian Fields. Bury offered what would become the traditionally accepted date of the battle, while expressing views against a macro-historical importance of the battle. He dedicates a small section of his book to the campaign of 451, arguing that the siege of Orleans just before the engagement was the real turning point in Attila's invasion, and that the Battle of the River Nedao in 454 was more instrumental in European history.[8] Ulf Tackholm, in the latter half of the twentieth century, used the immense strides that had been made in late antique history to offer many new thoughts about the Gothic sources that record the battle, and on the battle itself, which have since been widely accepted and reiterated.[9] Samuel Barnish, in his work 'Old Kaspars', advances and expounds upon many of Tackholm's views, and also discusses potential political and literary biases of the primary source narratives in the context of the Gothic and Frankish kingdoms.[10] Arne Søby Christiensen, in his historiographic analysis on Cassiodorus and Jordanes, dedicates almost eighteen pages to a comprehensive discussion of the literature and historiography of Jordanes' writing on the battle.[11] Conor Whately's recent paper, 'Jordanes, the Battle of the Catalaunian Fields, and Constantinople', takes a look at the writing of Jordanes in contemporary political terms, attempting to discuss how the battle served as a climax of Jordanes' work and as a political commentary on the sixth-century policy of Justinian.[12] With a count of sixteen pages dedicated to the battle, Hyun Jin Kim's recent work on the Huns advances the controversial opinion that it was a Hunnish victory and discusses its repercussions on Gaul in the late fifth century.[13] Kim's work, however, has received heavy criticism from his peers, and his proposal of a Hunnic victory is considered a fringe theory.[14] More admissible is Kim's argument that the Hun invasions effectively crippled the Roman Empire for more than a decade, and created 'military impotency'. He also provides a comprehensive historiographical analysis of the battle, as his background is in Herodotus. His paper, 'Herodotean Allusions in Late Antiquity', goes into far more detail on the historiography of the sources Priscus, Cassiodorus and Jordanes and elaborates on the allusions and formatting of history in these late antique authors.[15]

On the tactical side, Arther Ferrill, in his *The Fall of the Roman Empire: The Military Explanation*, gives roughly a two-page overview, mixing up some of the standard assumptions taken from Jordanes, but still assuming Jordanes' account is correct.[16] Phillipe Richardot gives a comprehensive overview of the campaign and tactics of the battle in his work *La Fin de l'Armee Romaine*, dedicating a whole chapter to the battle, but his historiographic treatment of the primary sources does not extend beyond Tackholm. However, he gives a multi-page overview based on the account of Jordanes, again with some slight deviation from the original, like Ferrill before him.[17] Richardot's overview is repeated in the 2011 work *La campagne d'Attila en Gaule 451 apr. J.-C.* by Iaroslav Lebedynsky, which numbers about 100 pages in length, but at the same time offers a very modern overview of the battle and campaign.[18] Ian Hughes, in his recent book *Aetius: Attila's Nemesis*, dedicates a couple of chapters to the war in 451, but focuses mostly on the military engagement itself and neglects many possible influences the authors recording it may have been affected by.[19] Simon MacDowall's Osprey publication is the lengthiest English work on the battle, and he makes effective use of his prior military experience to discuss the campaign and retreat of Attila while advancing M. Girard's proposal of its location. However, this book is written for a more general reader and lacks a comprehensive analysis of the sources, and his analysis of the course of the battle itself fails to offer new interpretations, differing very little from prior authors' outlines such as Ferrill's or Richardot's.[20] Both of the widely available general histories on Attila, John Man's *Attila: The Barbarian King who Challenged Rome* and Christopher Kelly's *The End of Empire: Attila the Hun & the Fall of Rome*, generally follow ancient source format without much consideration of the historiography of the primary sources, although Man does put forth a few interesting ideas.[21] Their conclusions elsewhere in the books about the Huns and Attila are, however, varied and useful. It should be noted that Istvan Bona, whose works focus primarily on Hun archaeology, also has much to say about the motivations of the Huns and the battle.[22]

The problem with prior works is that none of them have provided a complete analysis. Although individual works have discussed different aspects of the battle, historiography of the battle has never been combined with a tactical or ethnographic analysis of the battle. Furthermore, tactical overviews have been lacking, partially because of not considering the historiography of the battle, nor considering Roman military treatises and strategy. An ethnographic reconsideration of its participants has not been performed for some time, despite the significant modern advances of ethnogenesis and new archaeological evidence. Therefore, I am putting forward a new, comprehensive evaluation of the battle using prior historiography, modern ethnographic interpretations, critical analysis and an incorporation of Roman military theory, while proposing new interpretations and drawing new conclusions. Much of this book's interpretation and reconstruction is conjectural, but it will nevertheless piece together the holes in our understanding of the events leading up to and surrounding the battle, and attempt to rectify the errors of past centuries of interpretation of the battle. It will finally show that the Battle of the Catalaunian Fields did have a long-lasting, regional impact on western Europe, particularly with the Goths and to a lesser extent among the Romans and Franks. However, it will also show that the battle does not necessarily constitute one of the 'decisive battles of history', a title that for the fifth century may be more appropriately held by the Battle of the River Utus or the Battle of the River Nedao. All of this will be discussed while considering the advances made in historiography and critical analysis of the primary and secondary sources that discuss the battle.

Cassiodorus-Jordanes: About the Origin and Deeds of the Goths

In the sixth century AD, Jordanes put together his piece the *De Origine Actibusque Getarum* ('About the Origins and Deeds of the Goths').[23] In it, he provided the only detailed account of the Battle of the Catalaunian Fields in existence, taking up a tenth of the entirety of his work and a third of his section on the Visigoths, yet it is not included in his other work, the *De Summa Temporum vel Origine Actibusque Gentis Romanorum*.[24] Jordanes himself claimed to be a Goth, and he may have been a descendant of the *Sadages/Sadagarii*, who seem to have been a Gothic group. Many historians consider Jordanes to have been biased towards the Goths because both he and his patron, Castalius, were of Gothic ancestry, but modern historians note that much of his writing was from a Roman point of view.[25] Jordanes also manages to garble or omit huge portions of Gothic history, which Walter Goffart argues that Jordanes' glaring description of the Battle of Catalaunian Fields and Attila the Hun are subject to.[26] Barnish, however, believes that the Catalaunian Fields passage is not garbled, but rather more eloquent than Jordanes' usual writing, and its stylistic parallels of the *Variae* suggest it was abridged directly from Cassiodorus.[27] Many scholars have taken Jordanes' or Cassiodorus' description of the Battle of the Catalaunian Fields to have been drawn from Priscus.[28] However, Tackholm largely suspects that it was not: he argues that the writing style of the two parts of the battle and the speech do not express any similarities to that of Priscus, and also states that Priscus concerned himself with cultural and political matters and took little interest in military affairs.[29] Barnish, on the other hand, believes that his citations of Priscus are indirect, as Cassiodorus reworked Priscus for his own usage.[30] Christiensen believes the battle narrative is of Cassiodorus' hand as well.[31] It is known that Priscus did write an account of the Hunnish campaign in the west, but given the information Priscus conveys about the recent Battle of the River Utus, a disastrous affair in which a large Roman army was annihilated, to many authors it seems unlikely that he presented any exceptional amount of information regarding the Catalaunian Fields.[32] Christiensen points out that his description of the battlefield in Gallic measurements points to either Jordanes, Cassiodorus or Priscus having access to a Gallic source, possibly the lost Visigothic History of Ablabius.[33] It could be possible that Cassiodorus' or Jordanes' account could be drawn from the history of Renatus Profuturus Frigeridus or the unfinished history of the war by Sidonius Apollinaris.[34] However, both of these particular possibilities have in the past been seen as unlikely, and it is therefore entirely possible that Cassiodorus/Jordanes' description of the battle might be fabricated.[35]

Altheim was the first to notice the similarities between Jordanes and Herodotus, and argued that Jordanes' entire account was written in the style of the Battle of Salamis and completely fabricated.[36] Wallace-Hadrill also drew a parallel, noting the similarities between the tale of Themistocles' and Aetius' alleged subterfuge after the battle.[37] Hyun Jin Kim is also highly sceptical of the battle's account and suggests that Jordanes uses the narrative to create an allusion to the Battle of Marathon, borrowing the format of Herodotus from intermediary authors.[38] Kim compares the Romans to the Plataeans, who receive little mention throughout the account in Jordanes and in Marathon, while the Alans are the Athenian centre, facing the Persians. The Visigoths are portrayed as the Athenian regulars, who save the day at Marathon, with Thorismund as Militiades and Theodoric as Callimachus, who perishes. Whether or not this stems back to the writings of Cassiodorus himself is uncertain, as Brodka argues it goes all the way back to Priscus; however, in his recent paper on Herodotean allusions in Jordanes and Priscus, Kim suggests that Jordanes may have completely mangled the actual narrative to fit the format of Herodotus, while Priscus does not.[39] On the other hand, Samuel Barnish notes that Jordanes' echoes may also parallel later authors and not Herodotus, arguing that they stem instead from Claudian, Lucan and Livy.[40] Christiensen argues that the battle format is a Roman historiographic tradition that stems from a literary model to which authors were expected to conform, and its elements can be found in virtually any description of a Roman battle.[41]

However, some authors have pointed out that the battle narrative is also a commentary on Jordanes' contemporary time. Barnish notes that the battle narrative was written to portray Theodoric as the new Aetius and Clovis as the new Attila. Barnish believes Jordanes may have also been expressing his discontent of Justinian's handling of the Antes, Slavs and Hunno-Bulgars, as well as Theodoric's defence of the Danube being shattered by the Gothic wars.[42] Conor Whately argues that Jordanes uses it in an epic fashion like the *Aeneid* of Virgil, and suggests that the battle is to be considered the climax of Jordanes' writing.[43] Whately makes several more interesting points, suggesting that it is a clever political commentary by Jordanes on his contemporaries, expressing his disdain for how Belisarius handled the second half of the Gothic war, pointing out both the Roman reliance on coalitions and the responsibility of Justinian for bringing much of Europe into the conflict.[44] Jordanes significantly underplays the role of the other nations in the battle, possibly as a result of his commentary on coalitions. This bias is particularly focused against the Alans, shown extensively by Bernard Bachrach, who are portrayed as devious and cowardly during the battle.[45] The scholarship showing Jordanes' political commentary and classicizing themes casts doubt on the credulity of his retelling of the battle. However, as Barnish notes, the fact that Jordanes' narrative of the battle may be a section of his abridgement which is truer to Cassiodorus' original writing, suggests that some of these difficulties may be inherent to Cassiodorus' Gothic history itself. That Cassiodorus also wrote in the tradition of garbling or formatting history to Herodotus' style only complicates Jordanes' inaccuracies.[46] As a result, the works of authors contemporary to the battle, or drawing on other lost sources that were contemporary to the battle, must also be utilized in order to provide a basis from which to draw reliable interpretations from Jordanes.

The Fragmentary History of Priscus

Priscus of Panium is the principal source for the history of Attila the Hun, but his work survives only in fragments passed down through the works of other authors by medieval copyists. Unlike many historians of the era, Priscus took an interest in political events and ethnography, rather than religious events. Priscus has been extensively studied, most notably by Blockley, but also in specific regards to his parallels of Herodotus and Thucydides by Baldwin and Kim.[47] Many authors of Priscus' time wrote in the style of Herodotus, Thucidydes and other Greek authors in order to show their learning, and Priscus belonged to this school.[48] However, unlike Jordanes, who mangles history to fit the format, Priscus writes events in a Herodotean fashion without severely distorting or fabricating facts to fit the narrative.[49] Priscus was personally involved in state affairs, first possibly as a *scrinus* of Maximinus, with whom he travelled to Attila's court, and then to Florus, governor of Alexandria, and then as an *assesor* to Euphemius, *magister officiorum*. Therefore, he wrote in the Sophist tradition of using eyewitness sources, and for those events he did not personally witness he had access to officials of all ranks and official documents, including treaties, to ensure accuracy in his writings.[50] He also wrote in the Attic tradition, using classicizing terminology such as *hypaspistai* instead of *protectores* or *scholae*, or *Galatia* instead of *Gallia*.[51] Priscus published his books using an annalistic format, but did not adhere rigidly to this structure. His eight books were divided into two sets, the first four covering probably from the death of Rua between 434–39 to the death of Theodosius II in 450, while the second covered events from 450–74.[52] The invasion of Gaul, the Battle of the Catalaunian Fields and the invasion of Italy were probably recounted in his fifth book, with most of the precursor events having been covered in his first four.[53]

Priscus was known to dedicate significantly more space to certain topics, particularly those surrounding Attila.[54] Likewise, many details surrounding Aetius' career may have been preserved in his mortuary epitaph which Priscus wrote, again in a now lost fragment.[55] As shown by Tackholm, Priscus did not take particular interest in military events, and as a result his account of the war of 451 and 452 may have been mostly political and ethnographic.[56] His view of military actions was simplistic, politicized and classicized, with the few surviving examples of his records of military events giving little detail. This is the result of a trend in historiography of the period, not specific to Priscus, that shifted away from a view of international relations focusing on fighting to one of negotiation and diplomacy.[57] He surely would have taken interest in the peoples who participated, the agreements between Aetius and his *foederati* that allowed his coalition to be formed, and the treaties between the western empire and the Huns, as well as the diplomatic envoys that established them. Certainly, the tale of Leo's envoy in 452 would have been preserved and elaborated upon by Priscus as a literary aside, much like his account of the western Roman embassy in 449.[58] In fact Kim argues that the Italian campaign was the climax of Priscus' work on Attila, at the effective height of his career, who is then struck down by divine intervention.[59] However, there remains the possibility that his description of the campaign was rather meagre in its content, which is why excerpts of it do not survive.[60] Priscus' information on the West primarily came through the East's involvement in dealings with the Vandals since his contacts were all in the eastern court, which is likely why his description of events surrounding Aetius and Bonifatius are so detailed.

However, again as Tackholm notes, Priscus did not typically give detailed descriptions or outlines of battles, sieges or similar military phenomenon. On the rare occasion he did, as there is one such example from his work that survives, the format and writing belongs to a literary *topos*. The siege of Naissus is shown by Blockley to match the writing of the siege of Platea so closely that he argues the only detail which can be preserved from it is that Naissus was besieged by the Huns.[61] Kim believes otherwise, stating that Priscus' and Jordanes' format indicate they did not have direct access to Herodotus or Thucydides, but only to authors who had likewise copied their writing, from whom Priscus and Jordanes then borrowed Herodotus' format indirectly.[62] The Catalaunian Fields narrative is not exempt from this: as already shown, it is a clear parallel of the Battle of Marathon, but the question remains whether or not that distortion translates back to Priscus or is an invention of Cassiodorus/Jordanes. Dariusz Brodka believes it is the former, while Kim thinks it is the latter.[63] Kim argues that Priscus' writing does not directly parallel Jordanes' style, but rather fits contemporary information into Herodotus' format where it is convenient: e.g. the steppe sword cult and the sword of Mars from Herodotus, his list of the central Asian peoples pushing into Europe or the deception of Kunchas by Peroz.[64] It is possible that all of Priscus/Jordanes' military writings were written as *topoi*, but this cannot be said with certainty.

Priscus' political persuasions also played into his description of military events, and much like Jordanes, Priscus enjoyed elaborating on those which fell in line with his opinions. His description of Apollonius who stood up to Attila's face and lived to tell the tale, and of the defenders of Asemus who defied the Huns and defeated them, indicate Priscus enjoyed and described tales of successful resistance, unlike the disastrous Battle of the River Utus which he does not describe in detail. Priscus was defining his observations in moral terms, contrasting the strong and decisive Huns with the craven Romans.[65] It is for this reason that there could be a substantial argument for his writing a detailed account of the campaign of 451. Priscus saw Aetius as the strong, moral leader who opposed Attila and did so successfully, at least in Gaul. Priscus' detailed mortuary epitaph of Aetius' achievements could provide evidence to support this, despite the fact only a fraction of it survives via John of Antioch.[66] Likewise, Priscus' account of the war in 452 probably covered Italy, but focused primarily on Marcian, whose expedition under a different Aetius saw some success on the frontiers against the Huns while Attila was away.[67] Therefore, despite what some authors have suggested, it seems likely that in this particular instance the political bias of Priscus works in our favour. Because the Gallic campaign was an example of a successful military policy and fitted with Priscus' moral persuasions, he likely dedicated a significant amount of his fifth book to it.

The Lost History of Sidonius

Sidonius Apollinaris, a contemporary of the battle, publicly published a collection of his letters in several volumes, as well as a myriad of Panegyrics, including dedications to emperors Eparchius Avitus and Flavius Majorianus, both also contemporaries of the battle. In his fifth panegyric, dedicated to Majorian, Sidonius describes his service under and his later loss of favour by Aetius, but makes no mention of the battle, likely indicating Majorian was not present.[68] Indeed, Majorian probably had fallen out of favour with Aetius at this time, to be replaced by Agrippinus in 452.[69] However, Sidonius' panegyric on Avitus dedicates a few pages to his involvement in the affair. His surviving poetic description is useful for discussing Jordanes, and of the battle itself Sidonius' panegyric has much to say. The primary focus of Sidonius' description is the glorification of Avitus as an envoy, whose close relationship with the Goths is reflected in the account as part of a theme of growing influence over Toulouse.[70] Sidonius, however, is not without his own issues: some of his writings are based on earlier authors much like those of Jordanes or Priscus. The Panegyric follows the standard late antique rhetorical model, but is clearly based on the work of Claudian.[71] It is also entangled with literary *topoi*: for example, his tale of Avitus' enagement with a band of renegade Hunnish *foederati* is probably based on the battle between Achilles and Patroclus in the *Iliad*.[72] But most prominent throughout his works is that of the 'fourth Punic war', a theme also found in Merobaudes and Procopius.[73] As disastrous as the fall of Carthage was for the Western Roman Empire, for rhetoricians it was a treasure trove with which to showcase their knowledge. Luckily, the Battle of the Catalaunian Fields primarily avoids this trope, and his showcase of his 'fourth Punic war' is of no consequence to interpretation of that part of the literature. What is of consequence, however, is his contrast of military solutions to diplomatic ones, which makes some of his statements unreliable.[74]

Sidonius' account of the battle begins by somewhat accurately listing the peoples who crossed the Rhine with the Huns, intermixed with classicized or fictitious peoples, as well as even describing the crossing itself.[75] He mentions that Aetius then crossed the Alps with his forces, and that, like Prosper and Jordanes both describe, Theodoric was the last to join the coalition, having to be persuaded by Avitus, after which the Gothic people march with the Romans into battle out of honour.[76] This part is probably a literary trope in the same manner as the authors of the late Republic, who glorified the figure by showing how he was recalled from an idealized farming life to lead the empire, such as Cincinnatus.[77] Interestingly enough, in Sidonius' fictional speech by Aetius to Avitus, he states:

> 'bring it to pass, O noble hero, that the Huns, whose flight aforetime shook us, shall by a second defeat be made to do me service.'
>
> (Sid. Apol. Carmen 7.344–46)[78]

Although the latin of Jordanes is by no means the same, this reference could very well be the influence for which he and other late authors draw the concept that Aetius conspired with Attila after the battle, suggesting Cassiodorus had access to Sidonius' work.[79]

Later, Sidonius was asked to write a complete account of the war of 451 for Prosper of Orleans, Anianus' successor. It appears to have been the only semi-contemporary, local and comprehensive account of the campaign, at least in comparison to Hydatius, Prosper and the *Chronica Gallica* 452, which are not comprehensive, descriptive accounts like those of Priscus or Frigeridus. Unfortunately, Sidonius did not deem it worthy of publishing, and never finished the volume. It is thought that part of his incomplete history survives via a lost panegyric to Anianus, which was then abbreviated and preserved through the *Vita Aniani*.[80] Sidonius seems to have personally known Anianus, as well as other important figures of the time, particularly the emperors Avitus and Majorian, as well as Tonantius Ferreolus, and possibly may have been a friend of Aetius himself.[81] His father had probably held office under Aetius' regime some time before AD 449, and Sidonius was probably at least exposed to the man since he was educated in Arles.[82] Sidonius refrains from criticizing Aetius in both Majorian's and Avitus' panegyrics, although Sidonius was well known for his political prudence in his writing as a whole, and praises him greatly in his letter to Tonantius Ferreolus.[83] Sidonius held a place of honour at the side of Astyrius, one of Aetius' generals, in 449, and was married to Avitus' daughter Papianilla in 450, suggesting that before the battle began he was probably already in the entourage of Avitus. Harries goes so far as to suggest that the Apollinares may have been a 'client house' to the Aviti.[84] As an accoutrement to Avitus and therefore Aetius' entourage, Sidonius may have actually travelled with the Roman coalition in AD 451, and may have witnessed both the siege of Aurelianum and the Battle of the Catalaunian Fields first-hand. Being an eyewitness of the battle would have provided him the first-hand knowledge that qualified him for Prosper's commission, and enabled him to flesh out the panegyric he may have written. However, since these works do not survive, and he does not mention his personal presence at these events himself, this cannot be proven. Nevertheless, no other contemporary source preserved the notion that Aetius allowed the Huns to retreat so that they might serve again as federates.[85] It is also clear that Cassiodorus/Jordanes had access to a Gallic source from his terminology in the battlefield description.[86] As such, his panegyric on Avitus may therefore be the source for Cassiodorus' and Jordanes' version of this event. If the unfinished fragment of his history survived into the sixth century, it may have been a major source for both Cassiodorus and Gregory of Tours, the latter of whom recounts Anianus' version of the siege of Aurelianum.[87]

The Fragmentary Descriptions

Most of the chronicles of the fifth century are continuations of the chronicle of Jerome, and have heavy ecclesiastical focuses or undertones. Prosper Tiro of Aquitaine, a scholar who primarily associated himself and his works with ecclesiastical affairs but pays great attention to the relations between the empire and the new barbarian federates, provides his account of the battle which was probably written in 451, just after word of it reached northern Aquitaine.[88] Unlike Cassiodorus or Jordanes, Prosper displays no real bias for the Goths as a whole, although he does voice his opinion on Aetius' policies in some specific circumstances. His views on Aetius are as a whole neutral, being critical in some places and laudatory in others.[89] In the entry of his *Epitoma Chronicon* for AD 451, Prosper writes:

> 'Attila, after the death of his brother, augmented by the power [of his brother], collects many thousands of peoples neighbouring to him into war, which he was announcing that he was inflicting upon only the Goths as the guardian of Roman friendship. But having crossed the Rhine the many Gallic cities experienced the fiercest attacks of his; quickly it pleased both our generals and the Goths that the fury of the haughty enemy would be repulsed by united armies, and so great was the foresight of the patrician Aetius that he engaged on equal terms the enemy multitude having hurriedly collected warriors from all parts. In this conflict although inestimable casualties were inflicted, because neither side yielded, it is accepted that the Huns were defeated, because those who survived returned to their own lands having lost the will to fight.'

(Prosper, *Epitoma Chronicon*, s.a. 451)[90]

Prosper's perspective on the battle seems to be that Aetius acted swiftly and rightfully in joining forces with the Aquitanian Goths, and by that time Aetius had already collected, through said foresight, other federates with which to form a coalition. Prosper notes the battle immediately became famous for the sheer slaughter inflicted, and he states both sides fought until they were completely unable to continue, after which the Huns returned home with their morale in tatters. Although Prosper does not always agree with Aetius' policy and politics, here he casts Aetius in a favourable light, and the Goths receive a noteworthy mention.[91] Prosper's work would be used by Jordanes in the sixth century, and presumably by Cassiodorus as well. Mingarelli notes that Cassiodorus likely copied Prosper's account of the Battle of Nedao, which was then appended into Jordanes' manuscript.[92]

The other two fifth-century sources who recount the battle, and from whom Cassiodorus, Jordanes or other later authors could have drawn, are stored in the accounts of chroniclers: namely Hydatius, the *Gallic Chronicle* of 452, its continuation in the *Chronicle* of 511 and finally the letters of Cassiodorus. The first of these, Hydatius, is probably near-contemporary, having likely compiled his work in two parts: once in 456 and again in or after 468.[93] Hydatius states:

> '[Item 460] The people of the Huns, by the peace having been disrupted, are ravaging the provinces of the Gauls. Many cities have been sacked: on the Catalaunian Fields not far away from the city of Mettis, which they had sacked, *dux* Aetius and king Theodor[ic], who were in a coalition, [clashed with the Huns] who ... are cut down and overpowered with divine aid: the dead of night interrupted the battle. King Theodor[ic], having been struck down in that place, fell dead: nearly three hundred thousand men are said to have fallen in this conflict.'
>
> (Hydatius, *Continuatio Chronicorum*, 150)[94]

Hydatius says nothing particularly special, but attributes the battle to Aetius and Theodoric, placing it on the Catalaunian Fields near Metz. Hydatius' information on events in Spain, southern Gaul and Gallaecia is typically reliable, but his awareness of the West outside of these regions is sporadic.[95] Hydatius likely received his information on these events from multiple sources, possibly eastern, like his later commentary on Attila's invasion of Italy.[96] He usually had access to eastern Roman sources via the ports, which carried news of events when merchants and military vessels docked in places such as Hispalis, hence why he records the activities of Marcian in 452.[97] As a result, much of his information ends up being a synthesis of eastern and western versions of events, including entry 154 on the Huns in Italy.[98]

Alongside the works of Hydatius and Prosper, two *Gallic Chronicles* were also written, again as continuations of Jerome and Eusebius. The first of these, the *Chronicle* of 452, was written probably in Massilia and actually ended in 455, as the copyist sought to copy one of the continuations to Prosper that began in 456 and tacked on entries from Prosper to fill in the gap, while other entries from Prosper were tacked on to the beginning.[99] The *Chronicle* of 511, compiled in 733, drew from Hydatius, Orosius, the Italian Fasti, an unidentified emperor list and possibly the *Annali Arelatenses*, which includes the *Chronicle*'s entry 60: the passage on the

Catalaunian Fields.[100] The *Gallic Chronicles* have a bit more to add on the battle, including the mention of a Hunnic casualty:

'Attila, having invaded the Gauls, demands a wife as though owed to him by law: where having inflicted and received a grave setback, he retreated to his own lands.'

(Chronica Gallica Anno 452, s.a. 451)[101]

'Patrician Aetius with Theodoric king of the Goths fight against Attila king of the Huns at Tricasses on the Catalaunian Fields, where Theodoric was slain, by whom it is uncertain, and Laudaricus the brother of Attila: and the bodies were countless.'

(Chronica Gallica Anno 511, s.a. 451)[102]

What is interesting to note about these early accounts is that they do not share the same bias found in sixth-century desciptions of the battle, where the role of the Goths is continuously inflated over time. Ulf Tackholm makes detailed note of this, arguing that being the victors over Attila became a focal point of Gothic pride and identity, while before Cassiodorus the 'victory' is attributed equally to the Goths and Romans.[103] This first becomes apparent in the letters of Cassiodorus, compiled sometime in the late 530s, but the dates of the letters stretch from 501– 34, many of which coincide with the writing of the Gothic history.[104] Although there is a significant amount of embellishment and formality drowning the various correspondences, one of the letters does make a direct mention of the battle, while another provides vital information about an otherwise unattested embassy to Attila's court.[105] The reference is an obscure and indirect mention of the battle from Theodoric the Great to the King of the Visigoths, Alaric II, in 506 or 507, where he mentions that they 'famously halted the Huns of Attila'.[106] Unfortunately, the details of Cassiodorus' version of events were contained in the now lost Gothic history of Cassiodorus, only partially preserved through Jordanes. Nevertheless, the battle remained highly influential in Gothic eyes, and Cassiodorus' version of events would be reiterated by both Jordanes and Isidore of Seville. As time wears on, the role of Aetius is nearly completely forgotten in favour of the deeds of the Goths. Isidore, in the seventh century, attributes the battle's leadership and victory to Theodoric and Thorismund, stating Aetius merely helped the Goths.[107]

Later Accounts

Despite the important role of the Franks in the war and the battle itself, it seems little of Priscus' account of Frankish happenings survived to reach Gregory of Tours, who writes a late sixth-century account of the battle.[108] His quotation of Frigeridus, who describes a noble Aetius, is contrasted with his opinion of his actions, where Gregory of Tours casts Aetius as a schemer who tricks Thorismund and the Frankish king into returning home in order to collect all the battlefield treasure for himself.[109] This may be based on Jordanes, as Banniard suggests Gregory used Jordanes' text for his description of the Battle of the Catalaunian Fields, although Goffart believes that Gregory drew on Frigeridus for his account of the clash.[110] Gregory also casts Metz effectively as a new 'Sodom and Gomorrah', being punished for its wickedness; Tongres is also cast in this manner. Such allegories are also a persistent theme in hagiographies, which can make it difficult to distinguish actual events from biblical ones. Barnish suggests that there were two dominating viewpoints of secular and religious seen in the battle and the war, where Gregory, Paul the Deacon and the later Fredegar attribute the outcome to divine relics, saints and intervention, while Prosper, Cassiodorus, Jordanes, Isidore and Victor Tonnenensis all give parts to Aetius, Valentinian III, Marcian and both Italian and Gallic affairs.[111] In fact, the role Victor and Procopius give to Aetius attribute the battle entirely to him, showing a divergence in viewpoint between the post-Roman West and the Roman East, where it is co-opted to fit their own people's identities. Aetius in Procopius, Victor Tonnenensis and other sixth-century sources is often cast as a 'true Roman', all probably based on Priscus' mortuary epitaph to the man, which no longer survives but through John of Antioch.[112] In the writings of later Romans, Aetius was a model used in political and social commentary and a focal point of Roman identity, just as much as the battle was for Gothic identity.

The Franks ultimately co-opted Cassiodorus' principle, beginning with Gregory, who recounts the battle as a series of divine interventions, where the intercessions of Servatius, Stephen, Anianus and Aetius' wife Pelagia tell the narrative.[113] Gregory's tales of divine intercession and destruction are believed to be a commentary on contemporary military plundering of church properties. In Gregory, Attila's invasion brings the Franks onto the stage of world history, and is a reflection of the contemporary nomadic enemy of the Merovingians: the Avars. However, the Avars rarely threatened Gaul, and defeat by them was not catastrophic. Other than these, Barnish argues there are few moral or political lessons to be found otherwise.[114] Fredegar conflates this perception, and blatantly, in showing the Franks as 'seeing off' the Huns and reaping the rewards of Aetius' duplicity.[115] The hagiographers of the sixth century have a slightly different perspective to add through the tales of Anianus and Genevieve. Barnish argues that the Merovingians of the sixth century saw their leaders as defenders similar to how Cassiodorus saw Theodoric. He states the Merovingian connections and status of Martin, Anianus and Genevieve owe their repute to the connection to the Hunnic invasion.[116] Servatius, Stephen, Anianus and Lupus, meanwhile, can also all be seen as part of the 'saint as envoy' tradition that is reflected in Pope Leo, Germanus and others.[117] Likewise, he argues that Paul the Deacon uses the Hun invasion as a political tool for the Carolingians, whose home was Metz, and Saint

Stephen.[118] To Paul's readers, the Hun invasion had contemporary resonances, with Pippin III as a new Aetius and Charlemagne as vanquisher of the Avars, head of his own contemporary coalition of Germanic peoples.[119] Paul uses the Hun invasion and the history of Metz as a tool to affirm familial connections and reinforce the relationship between the Gallic churchmen and the aristocracy. Just as much as Cassiodorus and Jordanes intended to make Gothic history Roman, Paul and Gregory made Frankish history Roman.[120]

Maurice's *Strategikon* and the *Epitoma Rei Militaris*

It may seem surprising to include the *Strategikon* in this discussion, as although it utilizes examples of prior conflicts in its work, it makes no reference to the Battle of the Catalaunian Fields. This book is not the first attempt to utilize the *Strategikon* as a resource for the reconstruction of fifth-century military tactics, as Laura Fyfe has recently made forays with tactical analysis based on this concept.[121] However, the *Strategikon* is a valuable resource that will be used often throughout this book, so it is necessary to touch on its background and influences first. It was written under the reign of Maurice in the late sixth-century AD, and can probably be prescribed to one of his Armenian generals.[122] Unlike the works of Vegetius or earlier classical military authors, the *Strategikon* claims to be a handbook of military drill, tactics and day-to-day operations, rather than one of grand strategy or conflated with classical *topoi* and moralisms.[123] However, it is not completely unbiased: for example, in the context of Hun motivations it shares the stereotypical view of many authors that steppe nomads were deceitful, avaracious and operated purely for plunder.[124] It also still fits a certain format of rhetoric found in these military treatises, even if it is far more practical and rudimentary than other known works like Vegetius. Rance points out many parallels with the works of Aelian and Arrian in its format and rhetoric, as well as places where it directly borrows from them.[125] Although Maurice's work is comprehensive and relatively straightforward, it focuses primarily on cavalry warfare. However, it does preserve a section on infantry based on earlier Roman military manuals.[126] Unfortunately, most of the earlier manuals that serve as its basis have been lost to time. They were also probably significantly more convoluted by classicizing terminology and other literary tropes, which made them somewhat impractical for real warfare. It is conjectured that the direct predecessor works to the *Strategikon* are those of Urbicius, who wrote his *Taktikon* based on the *Ars Taktika* of Arrian during the reign of Anastasius, and a second work called the *Epitedemna* or 'invention'.[127] The surviving fragments of Urbicius are now believed to be an amalgam of both his *Taktikon* and the *Onomasticon*, along with other classical sources, compiled by an unknown author in the twelfth century.[128] The problem with such treatises is that this amalgamation characterizes the surviving ones in general: they were both clogged with literary tropes and were designed to generate prestige in the court by the presentation of 'victory through innovation' as much as they were to offer practical advice to emperors.[129] This is a problem that plagues a second, possibly contemporary source.

Vegetius' *Epitoma Rei Militaris* was written at some point between the late fourth and mid-fifth centuries, and falls under this 'victory through innovation' phenomenon through his presentation of an 'ideal legion'. Vegetius is thought to have authored two works: the *Epitoma Rei Militaris* and the *Digesta Artis Mulomedicinae*, based on his familiarity with Gallic terminology found in both works.[130] He is also sometimes suggested to have written under Valentinian III, since his work is dedicated to a Valentinian, although authors have argued against this on many points, notably the lack of any reference to the sacking of Rome.[131] Milner states it can be at earliest dated to about AD 383 and believes it was written under Theodosius, but nevertheless it seems an attribution to the reign of Valentinian III remains likely for a number of reasons. To Vegetius, barbarian *foederati* in the army is anathema, specifically in the way they were incorporated into the army as professional units and not mercenaries; this is indicative that it was written after the beginning of the *Hospitalitas* system in the 410s. Furthermore, Huns were not employed in significant enough numbers to attribute to them resulting military reforms until the 400s, with the heavy usage of Huns and Alans under Stilicho, Constantius III and especially Aetius. Vegetius also regards the Huns and Alans as one body, not separate groups, which seems more in line with Aetius' employment of steppe cavalry than the presence of steppe nomads among the Gothic army.[132] Finally, he mentions that the presiding emperor was adept in horseback archery, a skill noted of Valentinian III in the details of his assassination in 455.[133] Vegetius is mentioned as both *vir inlustris* and *comes primi ordinis*, and may have been a *comes sacri stabuli*.[134] If he did write for Valentinian III, his work may have been presented after Aetius' military successes in the 430s, possibly alongside his triumph in 446. It also may have been delivered upon one of the important occasions of Valentinian III's reign, such as his marriage or the adoption of the Theodosian Code. However, Milner's argument for a Theodosian date remains very strong, so no definitive answer can yet be given.

Vegetius' work was written as a systemized remedy for military and logistical failures of the late fourth or early fifth centuries, and as a need to restore the professional Roman Army. His work does not reflect the actual organization of the late Roman Army either, as Vegetius focuses on the field army, not the defence-in-depth strategy of late Rome.[135] It is largely based on a 'scissors and paste model' of excerpts from Celsus, Paternus and Frontinus, as well as other authors, heavily augmented and interpreted by Vegetius.[136] His approach was mostly theoretical, not practical, as his objective was to adapt the revered ancient legion to the modern-day.[137] Vegetius' confusion and intermixing of the Roman Army was done with a specific political objective, and therefore in order to utilize him as a source on the contemporary Roman Army requires careful navigation and consideration of his text. Unfortunately, Vegetius completely skips over cavalry tactics in his work, on top of both glossing over and classicizing infantry tactics. This makes the *Strategikon* more useful in the discussion of actual battlefield tactics, despite being of later date. Luckily, the tactics mentioned by Vegetius coincide with those of the *Strategikon*, which reinforces its use for conjectural tactical appraisals in this time period.[138]

Conclusions

The main problem with the literary accounts of the battle is that the primary accounts are lost, leaving only secondary abridgements for modern scholars. The surviving narrative via Jordanes is plagued by his formatting and bias, and the accounts of contemporary chroniclers are vague at best. However, a few of these sources, particularly the fragments of Priscus, provide enough information that allow for an effective comparison of the evidence between Jordanes, Priscus and other sources. Sources like Sidonius and Gregory, or even the less reliable ones such as Fredegar, also provide details that are not attested elsewhere, but may still stem from accurate information. Thus, the modern Catalaunian Fields narrative is essentially built on circumstantial evidence and an assumption of truth. Admittedly, this results in much of this work being, at best, conjecture, although it should be noted that most prior attempts to detail the battle narrative have also been built either on conjecture or, worse still, flawed assumptions. Nevertheless, conjecture provokes discussion, which is one aim this volume hopes to achieve.

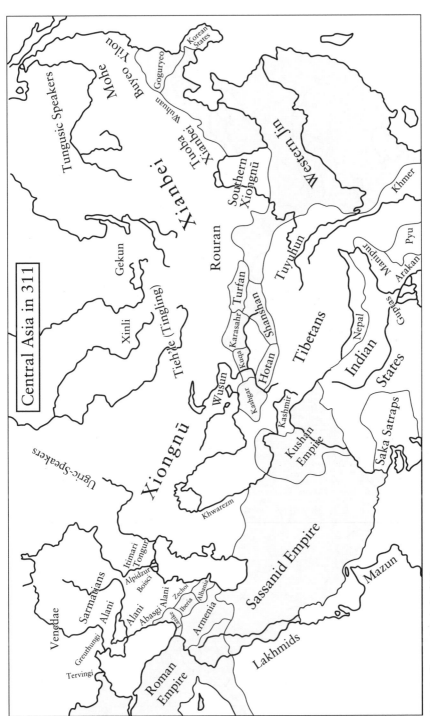

Map 1. Central Asia in 311.

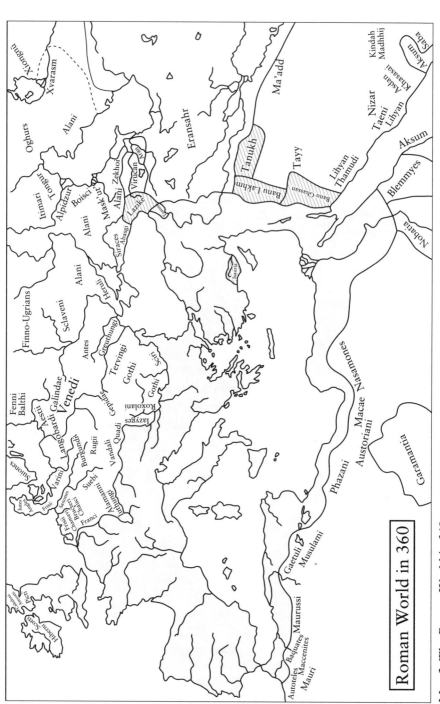

Map 2. The Roman World in 360.

Chapter 1

Background and Prelude to the War of 451

Any discussion of the Huns, their history and their impact on the migration period seems to require an introductory piece concerning their origins and language. Therefore, a brief overview will be presented in order to conform to this trope, and more importantly to clarify what is meant by the term 'Hun' in this volume. The name *Hunni*, pronounced 'On:ni' in Latin, most likely derives from the late old Chinese or early middle Chinese pronunciation of *Xiongnū*, spelled *Xoŋa*, pronounced 'Hoŋ:na'.[1] *Xoŋa* ultimately derives from the older form of *Xiōngnú/Xoŋai* (pronounced 'Hoŋ:gai'), which may originate from a combination of the pronunciation of the old Turkic name for the Ongi River in modern Mongolia (most likely spelled Hoŋï and pronounced 'Hoŋ:gi'), and the pronunciation of the original *Xiongnū* dynastic family name.[2] The Hunnish emperors at least claimed to be descended from this ruling dynasty of the *Xiongnū*, and the Bulgarian *Dulo* and Khazar *Tü-lü* dynasties have been put forward as being etymologically the same as the *Xiongnū* 'T'u-ko', although no dynastic continuity can be conclusively proven. This ultimately goes back to Omeljin Pritsak, in his *The Hunnish Language of the Attila Clan*, who argues that *Dulo* and *Tü-lü* are etymologically similar based on the assumption that they derive from a river of the same name which demarcated the boundary between the western and eastern Turkish qaganates. The royal dynasty of the Xiongnu is variously called '*Xiōngnú*', '*T'u-ko*' (*D'uo'klo*), '*Luandi*' or '*Xulianiti*', of which the latter two's etymological form is unknown.[3]

Otherwise, archaeologically and etymologically, the Huns have been proven to descend from at least part of the former *Xiongnū* and have been identified as a continuation of the *Xiongnū* imperial body. It is also widely accepted that the Hunnish ruling and aristocratic bodies spoke a dialect of Turkic called Oghur, characterized by the use of '-r' rather than '-z' endings, although they may have originally spoken Yeniseian.[4] Despite recent advances, mainstream scholarship, due in part to the conclusions of Maenchen-Helfen, is only slowly reverting back to De Guignes' hypothesis of *Xiongnū* continuity.[5] However, scholars are correct in stating that the Huns who entered Europe were not one homogeneous ethnicity, but the ruling class of a heterogeneous body of various Oghur and Iranic-speaking nomads who made up an organized steppe confederation based on the *Xiongnū* political model. The Huns also conquered or incorporated new Iranic, Tocharian,

Oghur and Germanic-speaking vassal peoples into this confederation over the course of their migration and settlement.[6] This brings up an important concern: the usage of the ethnonym 'Hun'. Steppe identity was highly fluid and it seems likely that all Oghur-speaking nomads of the fifth century either adopted the name or were generally labelled as 'Huns'. It was an advantageous title because it carried with it association to the feared dynasty that had once ruled from Turkmenistan to Manchuria, regardless of whether these peoples were part of the Hun ruling body. This view is confirmed by Procopius, who calls the Hepthaltites 'of the stock and the name of the Huns', indicating that there was a Roman concept of a Hunnish 'stock' or *gens* alongside a specific group or polity that bore the name.[7] It is in this generic context of the term under which we see the Oghur-speaking peoples and the Hun Empire enter Europe, and from this point forward this book will attempt to make distinctions, some conjectural, between the different Oghur speakers labelled 'Huns'.

In the early fourth century AD, the Huns could be found ruling the area from the Minusinsk Basin in the north-west Altai to the Kazakh steppes north-east of Sogdia.[8] In the third and fourth centuries AD, the various Oghur-speaking nomads were slowly precipitating down from the Altai mountains, displacing the Iranic-dominated population, many of whom were under the rule of the Huns.[9] The fall of Kangju and the decline of the Kushans was a direct result of the establishment of a Hun power, likely centred near the Syr Darya, who engaged in trade with Bactrian merchants.[10] These merchants transmitted their name west to the Kuban region, although the Hun Empire itself had not expanded to the north Caspian to reach the fringes of Roman knowledge.[11] However, their Oghur-speaking relatives had, with *Alpidzur* and *Tongur* 'Huns' ruling over two Iranic groups, the *Itimari* and *Boisci* (*Rhoboisci*), all living around the mouth of the Volga in the early fourth century AD.[12] The actual account of the Hun entry into the Roman known world was probably preserved in Priscus, and now lost.[13] Ammianus' tale is now widely discredited, seen as a *topos* of Herodotus' description of the Scythians, but he describes the Huns as being from the 'ice bound ocean'.[14] In the sixth century, Jordanes bungles and conflates what may have been originally preserved in Priscus regarding Hunnish origins, telling a strange story of Goths breeding with witches and Huns following a stag across the Maetoic marshes. Jordanes somewhat amalgams his geography in this passage, but if one assumes that he does not differentiate between the north Caspian Sea where the Oghurs were situated and the Sea of Azov, he then preserves a tale of the Huns coming from beyond the Volga, which preserves some truth.[15] They emigrated across the Turgai Plateau to the Volga, and according to Heather the Huns probably began fighting the local Oghurs and the Alan kingdom around AD 360.[16] This would also coincide with recent studies suggesting high humidity, falling temperatures and glacial expansion at that time, interrupted by severe droughts that reached their peaks in about 360, 460 and 550, which would have spurred nomadic expansion west and south.[17] The Huns had subdued the Alans and *Greuthungi*, and were harassing the *Tervingi* before 376, sparking a series of events leading to the infamous Battle of Adrianople.[18]

Hun Military Actions before Attila

In 395, the Hun position was consolidated enough to launch a massive raid down the Roman oriental *limes*: coming down through the Dariel Pass in the centre of the Caucasus range, they passed along the Cahya mountains near Amida, penetrating as far into Anatolia as Cappadocia and slaughtering the inhabitants of Cilicia, before reaching as far south as Syria Coele via the province of Euphratensis.[19] The leaders of these two operations may have been Kursik and Basik, the first known pair of Hun 'kings', although the exact date of the campaign mentioned to Priscus is uncertain, and Blockley believes their raid to date to about 422.[20] Jerome remarks that the Huns had reached the Euphrates and, having ravaged the countryside near Antioch, he feared they would sack Jerusalem.[21] After this, they proceeded not to return to their own lands with the captives they had taken, but instead invaded the Sassanid Empire, reaching as far as Ctesiphon and ravaging the countryside before retreating from the advancing Persian army. The Huns were caught and defeated in Mesopotamia by the Persians, who freed an alleged 18,000 captives they had taken and resettled them near Ardashir and Ctesiphon.[22] The invasion would have a lasting impact in the minds of the locals, and have severe repercussions on the career of Rufinus.[23] In 397, the Huns would launch a second raid, which was successfully repelled by Eutropius.[24]

In 400, a Gothic *magister militum* named Gainas revolted and laid siege to Constantinople, but he was defeated and fled over the Danube, only to be decapitated by a Hun named Uldin (*Ultzin*), who sent his head to Arcadius. Arcadius then returned the favour with gifts and a treaty between the two parties.[25] At this time, it seems the Huns may have begun to move west again, arriving on the Dniester or maybe as far as the Wallachian plain. Their movements would result in another knock-on effect, spurring the invasion of Radagasius in 405, the Rhine crossing in 406 and the establishment of the Burgundians on the Rhine in 411. In 404 and 405, Uldin crossed the Danube and attacked northern Thrace, and simultaneous Hun campaigning in the Carpathian basin that escaped Roman eyes may have triggered the migrations of Radagasius and the Vandals. Uldin seems to have won concessions from the Romans, and in 405–06 is found campaigning with Stilicho against Radagasius, participating at the Battle of Faesulae.[26] However, he again reneged on his treaty and in 408 he crossed the Danube with a force of Huns and newly vassalized Sciri, seizing the border market of Castra Martis. After some persuasion and gifts, some of these newly vassalized Germanics turned on him, seeking favourable Roman concessions, and forced him back across the Danube.[27] By the 410s, the Huns seem to have begun to settle in the Pannonian basin, and in 409 the Romans sought to hire 10,000 Huns to attack Alaric, who was loose in Italy after defecting Germanic recruits had crippled the Roman Army.[28] Two years later, Olympiodorus, in an envoy to the succeeding king Charaton (*Qaraton*), recounts the deception and illegal execution of Donatus and the Roman attempt to appease Charaton.[29] Although Donatus' execution is usually attributed to an internal rebellion, what is often overlooked here is that, whomever Donatus was, this passage implies that the Romans had been tricked into believing he violated Roman law and Donatus was executed not by his own Huns, but by the Romans. This also implies that Donatus may have been campaigning in Roman service, possibly at the command of the Huns requested by Honorius in 409. Regardless, this seems to have been a diplomatic disaster and may have been the reason for Olympiodorus' envoy. Charaton's reign after these events remains somewhat obscure. In 422, the Huns again raid Thrace, likely due to a withdrawal of the field armies for Theodosius II's war with Persia in 421.[30]

Octar and Rua may have come into power at different times, or at the same time, but they did succeed Charaton. It seems likely that Aetius was sent back from the Hun court after Charaton's death, which must have been several years before 423, and thus Theodoret's statement that Rua was in power during the raid of 422 seems likely.[31] The treaty established after the raid in Thrace includes demands for the refugees and leaders of the *Alpidzur*, *Tongur*, *Itimari* and *Boisci* who were settled on the Danube, suggesting that this raid may have been against this small rival confederation in order to secure his legitimacy.[32] The majority of Rua's reign after 422 seems to express a state of amicable relations between the Romans and Huns, where the Huns again served as *foederati* for the Romans. Octar himself would campaign to secure further vassals in Germania, reaching as far as an independent group of Burgundians on the Neckar and Main rivers. However, he died in his sleep in 430, and his army was ambushed by the Burgundians, resulting in a setback for Hun expansion in Europe.[33] This left Rua as the sole ruler, at least as far as Roman sources indicate. When Bonifatius' son Sebastianus took the post of *comes et magister utriusque militiae* and attempted to have Aetius assassinated, Aetius fled to the court of Rua.[34] This brief stay at Rua's court prior to his return to Ravenna may have been the first and only meeting of Aetius and Attila before the battle in 451.

The Rise of Attila

Like the Huns themselves, not much is known about the origins of Attila the Hun. His name seems to be a title in Gothic meaning 'dear father', or in Oghur meaning maybe 'universal ruler'.[35] When he was born is not recorded, although by modern standards he was young when he came to power. Unlike earlier Hunnish rulers who maintained cordial relations with Aetius or at least the Western Roman Empire, Attila does not seem to have been old enough to have befriended Aetius during his time as *hostes* with Uldin and Charaton. Attila must not have been much older than his 20s or 30s when he came to power. His father, Mundzuk, was a member of the Hunnish royal line and held a high position, but evidently was not a king of left or right (the two principal kingdoms of the Hunnish Empire), nor an appointed successor.[36] His sons, however, were Bleda and Attila, probably half-brothers, who would be appointed kings of left and right when Rua died. Bleda was the older of the two, but whether this guaranteed him the position of senior king is uncertain.[37] It is hard to discern exactly when Attila himself came to power, but it is stated to be upon the death of Rua, which likely occurred sometime between AD 434 and 439. Authors have suggested that there was another brief war with the Romans in 433, after which the treaty of Margus was signed when Rua died, but there is no indication of any actual military campaign. It was the flight of the *Alpidzur*, *Tongur*, *Itimari* and *Boisci* that prompted Rua to send Eslas to the Romans, suggesting he was more concerned about his legitimacy, and this seems to have coincided with the report of raids on Thrace in 422.[38] It seems probable, based on Theodoret's information suggesting Rua likely died after 435, that Bleda and Attila most likely succeeded in 438.[39]

Contrary to what has previously been suggested, the treaty of Margus does not seem to have been a conclusion of an armed conflict, but rather one of succession. Treaties in barbarian societies often lasted only as long as the leaders were both alive and had to be renewed when one of them died. It was signed after 438 when Epigenes was quaestor and Plinthas had been promoted from *magister militum per Thracias* to *magister militum praesentalis*.[40] These men met with Attila and Bleda: two new kings looking to secure their power, in need of rewards from demands of the Roman state to show their authority and in need of a secure southern frontier. The treaty of Margus was a significant step up for the Huns in comparison to the treaty of 422, and its terms were seemingly more imposing:

> 'They reached an agreement that in the future the Romans not only not admit Scythian fugitives but also give back past fugitives together with Roman prisoners of war who had returned home without paying ransom, unless for each escapee eight gold coins were paid to his captors; that the Romans would not form alliances with any barbarian nation if that nation was stirring up war against the Huns; that the marketplaces be havens with equal rights, safe for both Romans and Huns; that the treaty be kept and remain in effect so long as seven hundred pounds of gold be paid each year by the Romans to the royal scythians. (Previously this payment had been three hundred and fifty pounds.)'
>
> (*Priscus*, fr. 1.1)[41]

The first point concedes that this was a treaty of succession, as Attila and Bleda did not want the Romans interfering in their campaigns to secure their thrones. Two Huns of the royal line were received, named Mamas and Atakam, who were immediately crucified near the Roman fortress of Karso.[42] Immediately after the treaty of Margus they campaigned against the *Sorosgi* in 440, which, based on the primary source accounts, seems to have been the only interruption in the turnover from Rua to the Hunnish brothers.[43] This was also at about the time a second megadrought cycle was starting, and this war may alternatively have been caused by inner Asian steppe movements: *Sorosgi* could very well be a corruption of the later *Saragur* Huns, mentioned by Priscus, who were driven to migrate by this cycle.[44] The relative uneventfulness of their parade through their own empire suggests that the majority of Rua's reign had been focused on establishing strong and loyal vassals in Germania, including the Gepids and the Amal Goths: a power base which would provide the launching point for Attila to achieve his infamy.[45]

The Hun Invasions of the Balkans

The cause of the Hun invasion of the Balkans is often overlooked, but there may have been several contributing factors to it. The first of these, and the one most widely reiterated, was the claim that the Bishop of Margus had looted a Hun tomb across the Danube from the town.[46] Unfortunately for modern archaeologists, looting of Hun tombs by the Church does seem to have been a common occurrence, as Theodosius II had to pass a law ordering Christian clergymen to put a stop to it in 437.[47] Hun tombs were usually filled with gold, silver and cloisonné-encrusted artefacts that would have attracted grave robbers, and Christians looking to adorn their basilicas seem to have dominated the business. However, these pretexts, as will also be seen with the invasion of Gaul, made for popular gossip and were a common façade for Attila's actual motives for invasion. In the case of 441, the sacking of Sirmium (Mitrovica) reveals the true reason for Attila's invasion: the land granted to him by Aetius. Sometime in the 430s, presumably in 439 based on Maenchen-Helfen's argument that Priscus 'the barbarian' refers specifically to Attila, Aetius granted the Huns land in Pannonia 'along the River Sava'.[48] This cannot have been the province of Pannonia Savia, as that was too deep in the empire and was surrounded by the other Pannonian provinces; but the city of Sirmium lies on the Danube in Pannonia Secunda, through the heart of which the River Sava passes. Bona's distribution map of Hun burials shows that by this period the Huns had also largely taken over Pannonia Valeria and were edging into Pannonia Prima. Aetius' land grant likely cannot be confined to a single province.[49] Nevertheless, Sirmium was part of the disputed region of Illyricum, which had come under Constantinople's jurisdiction in 437, and the granting of land not actually controlled by the West would have caused a territorial dispute and a pretext for war. The Eastern Roman Empire claimed as far as Noricum, but Priscus records that Noricum Ripense, Noricum Mediterraneum, Pannonia Prima and Pannonia Savia were under Western control, with representatives to Attila from those regions all being associated with Ravenna, not Constantinople.[50]

Furthermore, had it been part of the West and Aetius' domain, Attila likely would not have sacked it, as he was a shrewd politician and must have been aware of the presupposed boundaries near his empire. However, Aetius may have also been playing a political game with Attila, knowing Theodosius would not likely completely forfeit the region.

Attila's invasion in 441 was an exploitation of the Roman preoccupation with the recent loss of Carthage to Gaiseric, which had imperiled the Western Roman Empire.[51] Attila took this opportune moment to strike, since as many as 1,100 ships and possibly 70,000 men were stationed in Sicily for the Vandal campaign.[52] With the three Roman armies in the Balkans away, he utilized this opening to attack over the Danube, beginning with the fortified crossing point near the Morava at the fortress of Constantia, which protected the bridge over the Danube to the Roman walled city of Viminacium (Kastolacz).[53] Attila overwhelmed both, razing Viminacium to the ground; this was a tactic most famously employed by the Mongols, in which they would annihilate one city in order to encourage others to surrender out of fear, allowing their armies to campaign with rapidity.[54] A highly effective form of psychological warfare, and an excellent way to compensate for a limited chain of logistics, this strategy would also be essential in his coming invasion of the West. Having razed Viminacium to the ground, the nearby city of Margus was quickly surrendered by its bishop and looted in exchange for clemency.[55] However, the fortresses of Singidunum (Belgrade) and Sirmium did not surrender, but succumbed instead to Attila's siege assault.[56] Meanwhile, the cost of the African expedition in Sicily had become taxing: if it was anything like the later expedition in 468, it must have cost over 64,000lb of gold and 700,000lb of silver to finance, and that investment had yet to see any dividends.[57] With Attila's capture and devastation of a former Roman capital, Theodosius was prompted to negotiate a treaty with the Vandals and recall the Balkans armies. As a result, Attila withdrew and negotiated a truce in the face of their return.[58] When the truce came to an end in early 443, Attila gave his demands: the return of Hun fugitives and the prompt payment of the overdue tribute he had been afforded in the treaty of Margus.[59] Instead of conceding, Theodosiuis' confidants advised him to talk the Huns into a more mutually beneficial settlement, and in response Attila again crossed, probably at Constantia, and moved east, this time sacking the arms manufacturing centre of Ratiaria (Archar) and then moving south towards Naissus (Nis).[60] Priscus gives a detailed account of this siege, in which he describes the use of advanced siege equipment by the Huns, including covered battering rams, covered towers as firing platforms and ladders:

'The Scythians were besieging Naissus, an Illyrian city on the Danube river … As the town's inhabitants lacked the courage for going out to battle, the barbarians bridged the river to the southern side, just where it flows past the city, so that a large number could easily cross. At this spot, they brought machines up to the city wall. First, since the approach was easy, they brought up beams laid on wheels. Men standing on the beams shot arrows at the defenders on the ramparts. Other men stationed at each of the two ends pushed the wheels with their feet and brought the machines up to wherever they were needed, to make it possible to shoot with good aim through the embrasures in the coverings. For the machines were covered with braided chaste-tree withes, which held hides and leather as a protection against whatever fire-bearing missiles or other projectiles were launched against them. The battle was thus without danger for the men on the beam.

'After many similar engines had been constructed for use against the city, scores of their projectiles caused the rampart defenders to give up and retreat. Now the machines called rams were brought up. This machine, also very large, consisted of a beam hanging down by slack chains from wooden posts inclining toward each other. It had spearheads and protective coverings, in the way already described, to ensure the operators' safety. From the rear, men vigorously drew back the beam with small cords at a spot opposite their target and let it go so that, by its force, the whole part of the wall would collapse and disappear.'

(*Priscus*, fr. 1B)[61]

The defenders, meanwhile, seem to have prepared large stones to crush the rams and may have also utilized onagers and ballistae:

'The defenders on the walls were throwing stones large as wagons, which had already been prepared for this purpose, whenever the engines were brought up to the city wall. They crushed one machine together with its men, but they were no match for the whole number of them. In fact, the attackers also brought up ladders. Here the wall lay destroyed by the rams, there the defenders on the ramparts were overwhelmed by the number of machines. And so the city was taken, with the barbarians gaining access through the part of the wall shattered by the ram's blow, and also via the ladders that were brought up to the parts of the wall not yet falling.'

(*Priscus*, fr. 1B)[62]

After a very long, costly assault, the Huns stormed and sacked Naissus, razing it to the ground and annihilating the population. However, it should be noted that this siege account is based on the siege of Platea in Thucidydes, and much like Jordanes' tale of Chalons, may be distorted beyond reliability.[63] The sack of Naissus appears to have been the end of the campaign and Attila's decisive victory, as no field battle is recorded in this period. The account of the siege was likely the high point of the Roman defensive strategy in the campaign, which utilized the

Map 3. The Campaigns of 441–43 and 446–48.

extensive fourth-century defences of places like Naissus, Viminacium, Singidunum and Sirmium, which prevented the Huns from campaigning over a wide range by bogging them down in long sieges. This strategy of attrition would also prove decisive in the upcoming war in the West. Field army battles against the Huns and the later Hunno-Bulgars were costly, as we shall see, and when the Romans reverted back to this method of defence under Anastasius they saw poor results.[64] Following Naissus, Kelly thinks that Serdica (Sofia) was also sacked in 441/43, while Williams and Friell think he reached as far as Philippopolis (Plovdiv), but there is no object statement that either were attacked in Priscus or the other sources.[65] After the success of the Hunnish siege of Naissus they renegotiated the tribute with Constantinople, and modern authors suggest it may have been doubled to 1,400lb of gold annually, as well as what was owed in arrears. Many of the terms of the treaty of Margus were likely also enforced.[66] It is also possible that the provinces of Pannonia Valeria and Pannonia Secunda were informally ceded to Attila, and the approximately 19,392 men (on paper) in these provinces were either withdrawn or destroyed.[67]

Kim and Jones both point out that historians who have tried to downplay Attila's success in 441–43, attributing them to Roman preoccupation with Persian affairs, are faced with a critical flaw: that Persia had its own concerns, with its own Huns in the far East.[68] With a breach in the Danubian defences, the Huns having taken Pannonia Secunda and ravaged Moesia, Theodosius II needed to take a more active approach towards the Huns in preparation for the next war. In 443 a law was passed in both halves of the empire increasing the punishment for *limitanei* who worked farmland at their garrisons, and Theodosius II retrofitted the entire Danubian defensive system and rebuilt the patrol fleets, probably along with the rest of the empire's *limitanei* in the Orient.[69] Likewise, Attila had his own politics and ambitions to fulfill in this same timeframe, and his brother Bleda was killed in either a hunting accident or by Attila's own hand, possibly both. This left Attila as the new emperor of the Huns and he moved the centre of Hunnish control to the west, the consequences of which would be foreshadowed by the revolt of the previously dominant *Akatir* Huns in his reign. Otto Maenchen-Helfen dates the revolt of the *Akatir* Huns to 445, just after Bleda is killed, which supports the conclusion that Bleda was the ruler of the *Akatir* Huns. After putting down the *Akatir* Huns, installing a puppet ruler named Kuridach and appointing his eldest son as king of the east and heir, Attila again moved against the Roman Empire.[70]

Attila was preparing for another campaign in 446, and probably launched it in response to news of the collapse of a fifty-seven-tower long stretch of the Theodosian land walls in January 447. The terrified Romans quickly resorted to restoring the city's defences: the *magister militum per orientem* Zeno was recalled with a significant force, probably of Isaurian troops, while the race factions were mobilized to restore the walls in a competition.[71] In response to the imminent danger, Theodosius II ordered Arnegisclus, Aspar and Areobindus to march out and meet Attila on the River Vid, in modern Bulgaria. Theodosius, with no other options, had reasoned it necessary to conduct a set-piece battle, which was atypical of the usual strategy. Under these three commanders were the combined forces of the *praesentalis I*, Thracian and Illyrian field armies, totalling on paper about 71,232 men, and likely whatever local forces they could meet en-route.[72] The Battle of the River Utus would be the event that inaugurated Attila's infamous legacy. The combined Roman field armies were annihilated, with Arnegisclus killed in battle. The defeat was so catastrophic that in 478, after thirty years of recovery, the Thracian army still numbered less than half its former strength.[73] Attila pursued the retreating Aspar and Areobindus to their headquarters at Marcianopolis, arriving at and sacking the city while the Romans retreated south.[74]

At this point a man named Senator was sent to negotiate with Attila near Odessos, where the general Theodoulos was campaigning, but he failed and was turned away.[75] While Aspar and Areobindus retreated to the Thracian Chersonese to join with the *praesentalis II* field army, and maybe some of Zeno's forces, Attila turned east and marched straight to Constantinople. However, when he arrived he was confronted by the fully restored land walls, manned by Zeno's forces and bristling with artillery and supplies for a lengthy siege.[76] Attila then turned back and met Aspar, Areobindus and probably Apollonius at the Chersonese, annihilating the remaining forces of the Balkans armies, along with an additional 22,144 men from the *praesentalis II* army.[77] Attila let his army loose on the Balkans, allegedly annihilating seventy cities and fortresses, another 27,008 men along the Danubian *limes* at least as far as Novae (Svishtov) and raiding as far as Thermopylae.[78] Evidence for this is substantial, including destruction layers at Iatrus, Sucidava, Nicopolis ad Istrum and Philippopolis, the latter of which suggests Danubian Germanics took the city.[79] The Balkans was devastated until the turn of the sixth century, resulting in deurbanization, depopulation and the abandonment of significant swathes of inhabited cities.[80] As a result, a significant portion of the East's manpower and tax base went along with it, which, coupled with the Battle of the River Utus and the Battle of the Chersonese, meant the East would be unable to assist the West for the next two decades. It should be noted though, as Williams and Friell point out, that military factionalism in the eastern court may also have played a significant part in their impotency.[81] Whitby argues that Attila's invasions in 441, 443 and 447 had a far greater impact than that of Adrianopolis decades before, and were a serious crisis for the Eastern Roman Empire.[82] Even the Thracian saint Hypatius stated: 'They so devastated Thrace that it will never rise again and be as it was before.'[83] Williams and Friell state that the majority of Balkans reoccupation occurred after the collapse of the Hun threat, partially under Marcian through Zeno but namely under Anastasius.[84]

As a result of his decisive victory over the combined military strength of the Balkans, Attila's new demands were far more imposing: the tribute was to be increased to 2,100lb of gold, 6,000lb was to be paid in arrears, the ransom for prisoners was to be increased to 12 *solidi* per man and a section of the Balkans along the Danube five days' march from Pannonia to Novae was to be evacuated. Bona's distribution maps support this abandonment, with late phase D2 burials being widespread from parts of Pannonia Prima to Moesia Secunda.[85] Additionally, a marketplace was to be set up on the bank of the Danube for the Romans and Huns to trade, which was later moved to Naissus.[86] This was to be expected, as it is previously seen in the Treaty of Margus and was a common feature of *Xiongnū* treaties with the Han.[87] Alongside these conditions came the request that the Hun and Roman prisoners residing in Asemus on the Danube were all to be surrendered for having intercepted and ambushed one of Attila's baggage trains; however, the people of the city managed to slink their way around this demand.[88] Anatolius, Theodosius II's negotiator, informed him that they were in no position to refuse any of the demands when Scottas brought them to the Romans, and he reluctantly agreed.[89] Allegedly, the wealthy landowners of Constantinople were forced to sell their jewellery and furniture in order to meet the contributions demanded by Theodosius to pay Attila, while those who could not meet the demands committed suicide. The severity of these conditions on the eastern treasury, as well as Priscus' account, has oft been called into question, but assessment of the eastern budget suggests that when all factors of expenditure are considered, it may have indeed pushed the breaking point.[90] Attila had received sums of tribute from the empire on a comparable level to that which they paid the Persians, elevating him to immense status. With Zeno and Constantinus in the spotlight for their able restoration of Constantinople's walls, Chrysaphius' position over Theodosius II was now challenged and he in turn sponsored an embassy and plot to restore his fortunes and control over Theodosius in one fell swoop.[91]

The Embassy of Priscus and the Prelude to War

In 449 the Hunnic representatives, a Roman *notararius* from 'Pannonia along the Sava river' named Orestes and one of Attila's vassals, the king of the *Sciri*, Edeco, arrived at Constantinople to emphasize the fulfillment of Attila's demands.[92] Chrysaphius, needing leverage to hold his control over Theodosius II, persuaded Edeco to partake in a plot to assassinate Attila the Hun, since Edeco was commander of Attila's bodyguard and had uninhibited access to him.[93] With the approval of Theodosius II, an embassy was dispatched to return to Attila's court with Edeco, consisting of the translator Bigilas, Theodosius' advisor Maximianus and Priscus, of which the latter two were not involved in the plot.[94] They travelled first to Serdica and then to Naissus, where they picked up some of the fugitives to be returned from the *magister militum per Illyricum*, Agintheus, before crossing the Danube and eventually arriving at Attila's court.[95] Priscus unfortunately does not record the geographic details of this voyage, as the Herodotean tradition preferred to skip such minutiae, so it is impossible to ascertain the location of his court with precise certainty.[96]

Priscus first encountered the western Roman envoy to Attila at a village on the way to the Hunnish palace, where he met the *comes* Romulus, the *praeses norici mediterranei* of Noricum Promotus, and Romanus, who was probably a regimental commander.[97] With them were Constantius, who was a replacement secretary for the prior secretary of the same name, as well as Tatulus, who was Orestes' father, journeying under the same pretexts as Priscus: as friends of the ambassadors.[98] Romulus may have been part of a new command based in the Alpine and sub-Alpine defence-in-depth strategy of the empire, as evidenced in the *Notitia*: the *comes Italiae*, which was likely later held by Bruco.[99] Romanus was probably attached to Romulus, maybe as commander of one of the three Alpine legions in the *Notitia Dignitatum*, making him a *praefectus*.[100] These men had met in Italy, probably at the court of Ravenna, and taken the route through Poetovio to Siscia and ultimately probably Sirmium, and from there across the Danube and into the Hun empire.[101] Romulus was the key member of this embassy, since he had connections both within the court at Ravenna as well as with Attila's secretary and ambassador, Orestes. Romanus and Promotus were present because their administrative and military districts directly concerned the defence of Italy, and thus their expertise in the field was needed for negotiation. Finally, Constantius was Aetius' hand-picked advisor to Attila, and ultimately his informant, while Tatulus and Orestes were native Pannonians (likely also chosen by Aetius) with insight on both the situation on the Danube and the politics of Attila's court.[102]

The mission of the ambassadors was to assuage Attila in his demand to be handed over the banker Silvanus, who had come into possession of some golden dinnerware from Constantius, the secretary of Attila before the current Constantius, who had probably arrived with Cassiodorus and Carpilio in 439.[103] Constantius had been handed these bowls by the Bishop of Sirmium in 441 in order to pay his ransom or the ransom of citizens who could not afford it should he die. Instead, Constantius pawned them upon his return to Rome, but when he returned to Attila's court they suspected him of treachery, likely accused of spying for Aetius, and had him crucified.[104] When Attila learned of these bowls, Valentinian III and Aetius sent the envoy to inform Attila that the bowls had been sold to priests as they were only for use of men of God, and that Silvanus was not accountable for their theft. If he would not listen, they were to recompense him with a payment of gold and return to the emperor.[105] When he met the men again outside Onegesius' manor, they told Priscus they had not had any success and that Attila threatened war unless Silvanus or the golden bowls were turned over to him. They recounted how he planned to invade Persia, and the route which Basik and Kursik had taken before. One of the Pannonians, named Constantiolus, commented that even if he did invade Persia, it would still not better the situation for the Romans.[106] Eventually, Attila likely accepted the compensation for the dinnerware as part of his strategy to maintain pressure on the western empire.[107]

It is in this passage that Attila's relationship with the West is elaborated upon by Priscus. In 439 Carpilio, much like his father, had ventured to Attila's court to spend time as a hostage, although he returned before Priscus' envoy. With this envoy, Attila was granted the title of *magister militum* in order to disguise the tribute as the simple payment of an officer.[108] However, Constantiolus in Priscus makes it clear that Attila was not satisfied with the title, and sought to be treated on equal terms as an emperor.[109] This brings to mind Gaiseric, the first sovereign recognized as *socius et amicus* by the Romans within their own borders, which may have influenced Attila's demands to some degree.[110] The fact that the embassy was required to appear at Attila's palace over a matter so trivial shows that relations had deteriorated, so Romulus had chosen to describe how Attila would attack Persia in order to deflect the conversation from Attila's relationship with Ravenna.[111] The relationship between the two embassies remained within the limits of courtesy, but the western and eastern Romans both had clear concerns about the future of Attila's plans.

The account of Attila's invasion never seems to be complete without a mention of the infamous affair of Iusta Grata Honoria, the sister of Valentinian III, to which has been ascribed the cause of the invasion of Gaul time and time again. Early in Valentinian's rule she had been granted the title of *Augusta* in order that she might serve as regent if Placidia was to die, but like Theodosius' sisters, she was ascribed to a life of chastity in order to protect the throne from a potential competitor.[112] As a result, in 434 she rebelled and had an affair with her *procurator*, Eugenius, and was ferried off to Constantinople to cover up the resulting pregnancy.[113] Honoria was not deprived of her title and the scandal was probably kept confined to the imperial family and the most influential at the courts, like Aetius and Chrysaphius. Eugenius was executed and Honoria was eventually allowed to return to the court, probably in 437 upon Valentinian III's marriage to Licinia Eudoxia. Valentinian III eventually discovered her political scheming and betrothed her to a eunuch named Flavius Bassius Herculanus, and she was divested of the title of *Augusta* before 450.[114] At the time of Priscus' embassy, the matter was not widely known outside the inner circles of the western Roman court, but by 450 it had become common gossip, which is likely how Priscus acquired the tale.[115]

Attila became involved when Honoria, upset at her situation, decided to take advantage of the same strategy that had brought Aetius to power. Kos proposes that Attila received the title of *magister militum* when Pannonia Secunda was granted to him, entering into an official *foedus* with Ravenna. Hughes proposes that Honoria appealed to Attila, leveraging his title of honorary *magister militum* in order to have him exert pressure at the Roman court, so that she would not be forced to marry Herculanus and be restored her title.[116] She sent a missive to him containing her signet ring as proof, and a sum of gold as payment. Attila likely received this message in the spring of 449, and allegedly interpreted it as a proposal for marriage, but bided his time until in 450 he addressed the senior emperor Theodosius II, demanding he persuade Valentinian III to surrender Honoria to him, to which the eastern emperor recommended Valentinian III comply.[117] Allegedly the emperor became furious, and ordered Hyacinthus mutilated and beheaded, with Honoria only escaping punishment by the intercession of Galla Placidia.[118] Contrary to Gracanin's suggestion, who believes Attila wished to see the peaceful fulfillment of these demands, it seems more likely that his embassies in 450 were a test of the waters, and of how pliable the western and eastern courts were.[119] He quickly discovered that the East would cave under his pressure, having no viable military defence in the Balkans, while the West remained defiant.

Other than the case of Honoria, the other commonly referenced *casus belli* was that Attila was making an attack on the Goths for Gaiseric, king of the Vandals in Africa.[120] As both Maenchen-Helfen and Bona point out, it would be absurd for the Huns to conduct a war purely for a king with whom they had no association, and that Gaiseric could somehow send tribute across the Mediterranean and through the Roman Empire to his court seems implausible at best.[121] This entire passage is a conflation and inflation of the power of the Goths by Cassiodorus/Jordanes purely for propaganda and political purposes. Christiensen points out that this fragment, usually attributed to Priscus, is clearly of the language of Cassiodorus/Jordanes, and likely can be attributed to one of them. Christiensen suggests that the tale is a fabrication: Huneric was never betrothed to a daughter of Theodoric, whom the Vandals blinded upon his betrothal to Eudocia, for which the Vandals would fear retaliation. Instead, Jordanes has fabricated the tale in reference to Amalafrida, wife of Thrasamund, king of the Vandals, who was imprisoned and murdered by Hilderic after Thrasamund died in 523.[122] The story of the daughter of Theodoric is instead a commentary on contemporary soured relations between the Goths and Vandals.

Despite the fact that both the tale of Honoria and that of Silvanus' dinnerware are legitimate *casus bellorum*, they may have served as a convenient front to divert attention from the real issue at hand. Priscus maintains that in 449 Chlodio, the king of the federated Franks in Germania Secunda, had died. In response, Aetius quickly moved to adopt the younger son, who was an ambassador to Rome, and appoint him as king. Aetius' choice was likely due to the younger son's perceived amity towards the Roman state as a diplomat, as much as his probable inexperience and pliancy. However, by this time Attila and the Hun Empire had gained enough clout from their success against the Romans that the older son was willing to risk seeking his aid, likely with the objective of breaking free of Roman dominance or at least gaining more control in northern Gaul as his father had envisioned.[123] It has been suggested by Thomas Hodgkin and Istvan Bona that these two sons were Merovech and Childeric, respectively, although the validity of such claims is sourced purely from speculation based upon Gregory of Tours and the garbled

Chronicle of Fredegar.[124] If this is to be believed, according to Fredegar, Childeric had fled to Attila and joined the court of the Thuringians, while Merovech was supported by Aetius. Certainly, it was a common tactic for Attila to involve himself in such affairs, as the revolt by the *Akatir* Huns had been in response to Attila's interference in their succession.[125] Gregory and Fredegar both state that Childeric fled to the Thuringians and remained in exile for eight years, which is a convenient coincidence between the death of Chlodio in probably 449 or 450 and Childeric's attestation as being king of the Franks in approximately 457 or 458. Allegedly, he was restored to power by Wiomad, who made war against Aegidius. This could very well be a garbling of Aetius, considering Fredegar renders his name Aegecius, and thus the figure of Wiomad could possibly represent Attila.[126] It is impossible to prove that either Childeric or Merovech were the sons of Chlodio, but due to the sparcity of material it cannot be ruled out. It could very well be that Merovech was the elder brother, not Childeric, and Childeric was the son of Merovech who fled with him to Thuringia; but this is not attested in the sources. Merovech could also have been a competitor to Chlodio, as the Franks were not united at the time, and there could be no relationship between Chlodio and Childeric, or to the battle. Penny MacGeorge thinks it to be quite the opposite, where Childeric was the ally of Aetius. Any conclusions as to their identities remain controversial at best.[127] Nevertheless, two sons of Chlodio did divide themselves between the Romans and Attila seeking support for their claim to their father's position, and both parties obliged.

As a result, Attila stepped up his pressure on the West. Priscus provides two major pieces of information: that Attila demanded Honoria and 'half of the empire' be handed over as his dowry, and that Attila realized his invasion could potentially be foiled by Aetius, so sought to have him removed.[128] Brodka believes that Jordanes' portrayal of obsession is over Aetius in the reported claim that Attila sought to have Aetius removed before the battle, but Kim believes that Brodka's assessment would be ignoring Jordanes' Gothic propaganda in making the Aquitanian Goths his primary target if that were the case.[129] That Attila attempted to have Aetius removed actually may be somewhat reinforced by Gregory of Tours' tale of Aetius' wife, Pelagia, who prayed for his safe return. In this tale, it is mentioned that if the homeless man who overheard the conversation of the guard with the messenger to Aetius divulged the information, Aetius would likely not return home alive. Despite its clear association with attributing Aetius' survival to an act of God, Gregory may also be referencing that there were known assassination plots against Aetius, and his activities and whereabouts were being kept on a need-to-know basis.[130] The other detail, that half the empire was to be forfeited to Attila, reveals Attila's goal for the success of his invasion. It is an inflated representation of Attila's real demand: the evacuation of the Rhine, Danubian and Sambre-Meuse *limes*, in the same manner that Attila had demanded the East evacuate the *limes* from *Pannonia Secunda* to Novae. Attila, like his *Xiongnū* predecessors, wished to vassalize the peoples on these rivers as buffer states, and wished the authority to shuffle vassals much like the Romans used to do to confederations outside their empire.[131] Attila chose to invade Gaul as a precursor to a campaign in Italy, which would be more easily stopped by a formidable Roman army where he had less room to manoeuvre and retreat.[132]

Jordanes tells how Attila prepared for his invasion of the West by sending out a series of missives claiming to Valentinian III that he wished to only attack the Goths, having meanwhile claimed to Theodoric that he wished to vanquish the Romans.[133] This claim is part of the Roman literary tradition, as most Roman tales of conflict involve a series of letter exchanges before the campaign. In the case of Jordanes, he additionally added 'verbatim' speeches to enhance it, much like Attila's speech in the centre of the battle.[134] It actually is quite likely Attila did send missives for his demands to Valentinian III, despite Jordanes' motivation of portraying a dysfunctional alliance between the Goths and Romans, in which he intended to depict Theodoric as an improvement on Aetius.[135] However, whether Attila sent one to the Gothic court is uncertain: Sidonius, who records the Roman attempt to persuade the Goths to join Aetius, makes no mention of any messengers or dispatches from the Huns circulating through Theodoric's court. Interactions with the Franks in the Rhine region seem to be likely, as Attila would have been seeking supporters of the elder brother, and he also might have sent a message to the Armoricans as one of their leaders had fled to his court in 448.[136] However, the claim that he sent missives to Theodoric and Sangiban is suspect. Any Hunnish activities in Gaul would have certainly come into the knowledge of Aetius' diplomatic and military intelligence networks in the region, as diplomatic envoys still had to go through much of the same aristocratic patron–client system as other messengers, and Aetius had spent his career making aristocratic connections to hold the province together. The coalition he assembled for the battle has often been attributed to his foresight, or more accurately to his diplomatic abilities in establishing treaties and relationships that provisioned for a variety of imperial favours.[137]

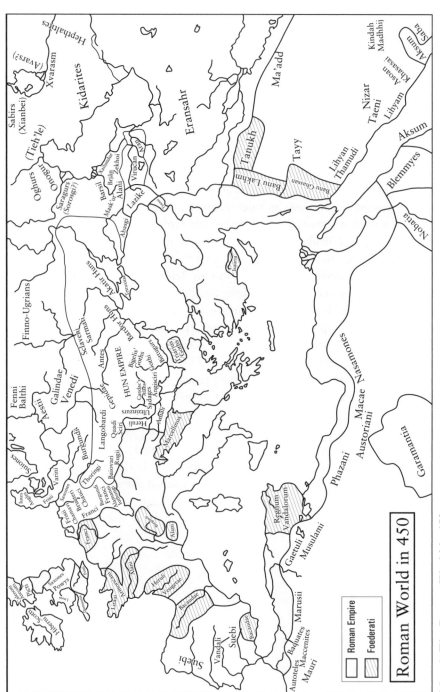

Map 4. The Roman World in 450.

Chapter 2

The Roman Coalition

Aetius was born about 391 in Durostorum (Silistra) to an Italic aristocratic mother and his possibly Gothic father, Gaudentius.[1] Gaudentius' life initially entailed a lacklustre career serving in the eastern and then western courts until he was appointed as *comes Africae* under Stilicho from 399–401. He was later appointed *comes et magister militum per Gallias* under Castinus, serving until he died in about 425.[2] This gave Aetius an opening to rise to high rank in the western administration. He served first as a member of the *protectores domestici*, which was a placeholder unit for those earmarked for political and military careers at the time, and then as *tribunus praetorianus partis militaris*, probably in his early teens.[3] In 405, at the age of 14, he was sent as a *hostes* to the court of Alaric as part of a treaty arrangement and would stay until 408. In 408 he was then sent to the court of the Hun Uldin, where he would stay until an unknown date, but probably through the reign of Charaton, returning home in the early 420s.[4] When Ioannes usurped in 424, both Aetius and his father Gaudentius supported him, with Aetius being granted the post of *cura palatii*, probably serving as commander of the palace guard. He was dispatched to the court of Octar and Rua to request military aid for the usurper, while in the meantime his father, being *magister militum per Gallias*, was killed in one of the revolts against Ioannes' usurpation. It was relatively clear that the Roman Army did not support Ioannes' usurpation and as a result he looked to its lower echelons, and to men like Gaudentius, to replace those who had served under Honorius.[5] In 425 Aetius returned three days after Ioannes had been beheaded, unaware of his execution, and after a brief skirmish with Aspar's army he was granted his late father's position as *comes et magister militum per Gallias*.[6]

Aetius would quickly surpass his father's reputation, defeating the Aquitanian Goths during the siege of Arelate (Arles) in 426 and then Chlodio and the Franks in 428.[7] Germanus of Auxerre's military actions in Britain may have also been at the behest of Aetius, although because Germanus' miracles are modelled after Martin of Tours, it is uncertain whether or not his 'Alleluia victory' actually occurred. Gildas records that the Romans did defeat the Picts at this time, so in any regard it seems that Aetius may have been invested with Britain.[8] Around this same time, in 427, the *comes et magister utriusque militiae*, Flavius Constantius Felix, who had been appointed probably by Theodosius II, framed Bonifatius and started a civil war for control of North Africa. Felix sent two expeditionary forces against Bonifatius, the first of which failed after the Huns under Sanoeces turned on the

Roman commanders, the second resulting in a two-year deadlock between the Gothic *foederati* of Sigisvultus (who was probably recruited in the treaty of 426) and Bonifatius' *bucellarii* alongside the African field army.[9] In this interval the Vandals under Gaiseric exploited the civil war to cross into Africa. When news of this action reached Ravenna, a truce was called and Bonifatius was quickly restored to Placidia's favour.[10] In turn Felix allegedly began plotting against Aetius, but Aetius and the Roman army quickly had Felix hanged in what was probably a premeditated assassination, and Aetius was promoted to his post in 430.[11]

Aetius then set out across the empire once more, defeating a force of marauding Goths under Anaolsus near Arles, then turning to suppress the raiding *Iuthungi* and *Bacaudae* in Raetia and Noricum, notably at Augusta Vindelicorum, where evidence of his campaign may be represented by a Pontic belt buckle.[12] Wijnendaele argues that Aetius' actions were not sanctioned by the Imperial government, and that his campaigning in Gaul and Noricum was a result of an unwillingness of the army or his Huns to partake in an overseas campaign. Instead he suppressed the *Iuthungi* and *Bacaudae* where he could keep a close eye on Ravenna, before moving against the Franks.[13] In 432, after a series of military defeats at the hands of Gaiseric, Bonifatius and his *bucellarii* returned to Italy, and Placidia attempted to oust Aetius, drawing him to Ravenna by appointing him consul. Bonifatius engaged him at the Battle of Ariminium (Rimini). The showdown took place 5 Roman miles outside of Rimini, between the two generals' personal *bucellarii*, probably somewhere between Rimini and Bellaria. Aetius had allegedly used a longer lance and wounded Bonifatius in combat during the battle. Despite Wijnendaele's scepticisim, Marcellinus *comes*' story of Aetius' use of a longer lance may be true, as the Huns probably used longer lances than the Goths. However, Aetius was defeated and forced to retire to his personal estate, while Bonifatius was granted the supreme command. Bonifatius would not hold his position for long, having been wounded in the battle, and he died shortly thereafter. His son, Sebastianus, succeeded him in his position and attempted to have Aetius assassinated.[14] Aetius fled the empire and turned once more to his arm of leverage in the court of Rua, returning with an embassy that threatened war if Sebastianus was not deposed. Sebastianus was evidently unpopular with the Roman Army and court, and so Aetius was quickly reinstated.[15]

Aetius again set to work against the enemies of the empire in 435, and on 5 September that year he was acknowledged as *magnificus vir parens patriusque noster*, putting him in the equivalent position of his predecessors Stilicho and Constantius III as manager over the child-emperor Valentinian III.[16] In 436 the Burgundians and Goths revolted in tandem, and the Armorican *bacaudae* also rose up. Aetius split his forces, putting one army under his general Litorius and commanding another army himself, and moved simultaneously against the Armoricans and Burgundians, putting down the revolts.[17] Litorius then moved south and defeated the Goths outside Narbona (Narbonne), relieving the siege.[18] In 437 the Burgundians rose up once more and Aetius, with Hun *symmachi*, annihilated them, allegedly slaying over 20,000 and their king, Gundicar, with them, immortalizing him in the *Niebelungen* cycle.[19] In 438 he may have campaigned against the Suebi, but he also oversaw the implementation of the *Codex Theodosianus* law code in Rome, before going on to defeat the Goths at the Battle of *Mons Colubrarius*, where he rode down the retreating Goths personally.[20] However, in 439 Litorius, pressing the advantage, was captured and executed after the Goths sallied from Tolosa during his siege. Aetius returned to take control of the situation, ending the war with a successful night attack on the Gothic camp.[21] Upon his return to Italy a statue was erected in his honour and a eulogy issued by his panegyricist Merobaudes.[22]

Events then transpired in Africa that drastically altered his situation. On 19 October 439, Gaiseric entered and sacked Carthage, cutting off the Romans' largest grain supply and tax base, and according to Heather, precipitating the collapse of the West.[23] Furthermore, by 441, the Suebic king Rechila had seized almost all of Spain, which was another vital source of income for the empire.[24] In response, Aetius and Sigisvult were both recalled to Italy, and after relieving the siege of Panormus (Palermo) in Sicily, they prepared to mount a massive expedition to retake Carthage with the eastern Roman navy and field armies.[25] However, this was quickly cut short by the invasion of the eastern empire by the Persians and Attila the Hun, and in 442 a truce was negotiated.[26] Unable to neglect the remaining portions of the empire, Aetius elected to send his forces to Spain under Astyrius and Merobaudes in 441 and 443, and the Alans against the Armoricans in 442.[27] By July 444, however, the empire was bankrupt, and a new sales tax called the *siliquaticum* had to be levied in order to pay the army.[28] Despite this, in northern Gaul Aetius and his new *comes et magister militum per Gallias*, Majorian, campaigned against the Franks of Chlodio, alleviating the siege of Turonum (Tours) in late 444 and then defeating them at *Vicus Helenae*, near modern Arras, in 445.[29] In 446 he mounted a large campaign against the Suebes under his general, Vitus, with Gothic forces supplementing the diminished Roman army. However, the Goths deserted after initial successes and Vitus was subsequently defeated.[30] Shortly after this campaign, the remaining Roman government in Britain sent a missive requesting military aid, but he was unable to assist them.[31] In 448 he again defeated the *bacaudae* of Armorica, at which point their leader, Eudoxius, fled to Attila, while in Spain the *bacaudae* revolted again with Suebic support and defeated the *foederati* pacifying the region, seizing most of Tarraconensis in 449.[32]

Much like his predecessor Stilicho, Aetius' career has been pockmarked with controversy by historians, most recently by Christine Delaplace who puts the loss of Africa squarely on his shoulders.[33] However, most historians do not blame Aetius for Africa's loss, thinking it was outside of his control. Hughes states that no matter who managed the West, they simply could not find all the answers to the myriad of problems they faced. Wijnendaele has recently stated that they all had parts to play, and that Aetius' regionality made him not much different from the barbarian *reges* he fought against.[34] As shown above, it was clearly Felix who instigated the civil war of 427, and even if Prosper's accusation of Vandal invitation is true, only Bonifatius or Felix can be blamed: the fatal blow to the West arguably rests not on the shoulders of Aetius or Bonifatius, but of Theodosius II's appointee, Felix.[35] Aetius has often been held on the moral high ground in comparison to Ricimer, with the well-being of the empire at the forefront of his mind, but his assassination of Felix and possibly unsanctioned campaigning in 430–32 shows a mix of his political savvy and dubious motives. Another point of comparison is against that of Stilicho, in the aspect of their total dominance over their child-emperors. McEvoy points out that unlike Stilicho, Aetius' power remained offset by the authority of Theodosius II until his death in 450.[36] By 450, it had taken all of Aetius' leadership ability to salvage the situation he was in. Most of Gaul was under Roman control, Italy and the Mediterranean were threatened but defended, Spain was in a difficult but rectifiable situation and even a sliver of Britain may still have been connected to the Imperial government. Although his ulterior motives were at times suspect, it ultimately came into his best interests to do everything possible to maintain the empire, and maintaining the Roman Army was an obvious facet of those interests.

Federates, Hospitalitas and Professional Soldiers in 450

Beginning around 325, a number of changes implemented since the reign of Gallienus in the 260s were formalized, which by the end of the fourth century would result in the *Notitia Dignitatum*: a register of units and dignitaries for the eastern and western halves of the empire.[37] Such a register is invaluable to the understanding of Aetius' army, considering its final edit probably occurred between 419 and 428.[38] The *Notitia* makes a distinction between two grades of soldiers: *comitatenses* (or field armies) and *limitanei* (border armies). Although often considered to be neglected units, the *limitanei* were supposed to be of equal quality to the *comitatenses*, but assigned to the role of managing border trade and small raids rather than suppressing usurpers and large Germanic confederations.[39] Amongst the *comitatenses* was another grade of unit: the *auxilia* and *legiones palatinae*, which were likely specialists and elite regiments who eventually seem to have become the core of the field armies. Along with the *limitanei* and *comitatenses* were the quintessential imperial guard: the *scholae palatinae* and *protectores domestici*, units created to replace the old praetorian guard and establish a reliable personal army for the emperor to fight usurpers.[40] However, by 450 the *scholae palatinae* had effectively become a parade unit, while the *protectores domestici* served as a placeholder unit for future politicians.[41] Meanwhile, the division between *comitatenses* and *limitanei* had become blurred by the time of Aetius, with many units having been drawn into the field armies and given the label *pseudocomitatenses*. Furthermore, parts of the former *limes* had by this point been overrun by Germanic groups.[42]

One of the most common misconceptions about the Roman Army, and Aetius' army in particular, was that by the fifth century the Romans had replaced their professional units with barbarian mercenaries.[43] In 1996 Hugh Elton produced a study which argued that approximately three-quarters of the soldiers and officers within Roman units were composed of Roman recruits, a study which Halsall noted as problematic in methodology but sufficient in results.[44] Volunteer soldiers were still common in late antiquity, and the last documented call for conscription of recruits was in 428, while in 444 a call for conscripts in order to collect *aedorationes* (monetary donatives) was issued instead. Elton also argues that until about 455, the West had the income available to maintain the entirety of its army.[45] However, authors like Liebeschuetz continue to argue that the bulk of the field army was no longer composed of 'Roman' troops by the time of Aetius' campaigns, and that any Roman regiments left were irrevocably tied to their billeting posts.[46] He cites Sidonius' description of the Roman Army being comprised of Heruls, Franks, Sarmatians and other Germanics, as well as Aetius' heavy use of Gothic and Hunnish *foederati*.[47] However, this fails to take into account the literary listing tradition, which Sidonius took part in, and his list of Aetius' allies may not reflect the reality of the army's composition.[48] The barbarians settled within the empire also ruled over large numbers of Romans living in their settlement areas, and it must not be forgotten that these Roman men were called upon by their new leaders to serve in military functions. Likewise, professional Roman regiments utilizing interspersed foreign recruits may have also operated similarly, where military culture overrode ethnic disparities; therefore the common distinctions between *foederati* and formal army regiments should be called into question.[49] Although Aetius employed regiments of *foederati* en masse, a complete lack of professional 'Roman' regiments is contrary to the admittedly disparate primary source evidence, for Sidonius Apollinaris also makes several more direct mentions of Aetius' army. In one, he describes the army marching to fight the Battle of the Catalaunian Fields:

> '*Vix liquerat alpes aetius, tenue et rarum sine milite ducens robur in auxiliis, geticum male credulus agmen incassum propriis praesumens adfore castris.*'
> (Sid. Apol. *Carmina*, 7.329)

In another he states that:

> '*Principis interea gladio lacrimabile fatum clauserat aetius; cuius quo tutius ille magna palatinis coniungeret agmina turmis, evocat hunc precibus.*'
> (Sid. Apol. *Carmina*, 5.305)

The first passage describes Aetius crossing the Alps with 'few and sparse Auxiliaries', which could either mean old *limitanei* units or *auxilia palatinae*. In describing that they are 'without professional soldiers', Sidonius states that they were not regular Roman troops: what he seems to imply is that Aetius crossed the Alps with federates in 451, probably his personal *bucellarius*, and we will return to this soon. However, the second passage, referring to events in 454 or 455, has Sidonius use '*palatinis turmis*', which could refer to the *scholae palatinae*, technically still the guard troops of Valentinian III. His use of '*cuius … magna agmina*', which literally means 'great marching columns', could indicate that he was describing how the *scholae* were combined into Aetius' mobile field army in 455. This seems a likely interpretation, as he is poetically contrasting the '*turma*', which usually describes cavalry, with '*agmen*', which not only covers infantry but is used to describe 'field armies' elsewhere in the text.[50] Other accounts of 'Roman' troops at this time include the defenders of Aquileia in 452 and the cavalry Majorian commanded at *Vicus Helenae*.[51] Furthermore, the chronicler Hydatius states that in 446, the general Vitus was sent to reconquer Spain with a significant 'Roman' force supplemented by Gothic *foederati*, while the *vita Orientii* also remarks that Litorius' army at the siege of Tolosa in 439 was 'Roman', and largely spared despite being defeated.[52] The *Liber Legum Novellarum Divi Valentiniani Augustus* for 24 June 440 makes a clear differentiation between *milites* and the *foederati*, as well as stating that Aetius would soon arrive with a 'large band'. It should be noted, however, that it calls the eastern Roman army an *exercitus* and Aetius' army a *manus*.[53] The Alans of Sambida and Goar are settled by Aetius in Valentinois and along the Loire in 440 and 442 as 'military veterans', rather than *foederati*.[54] This is an unusual distinction, pointing out the possibility that Aetius' Alans were serving as Roman soldiers in professional cavalry regiments, and not as 'allied units' like those who served under Stilicho.[55] By the time of the *Notitia*'s last edit, an official regiment of *Comites Alani*, trained and supplied as professional *vexillatio palatina*-grade cavalry, was in service with the Praesental Italian army.[56] The point of the argument here is not to show, however, that the army was 'ethnically' Roman; merely to show that the professional, mobile field army still existed. Its ethnic composition was irrelevant to its operation.

There is also significant archaeological proof of the fifth-century army's existence, primarily consisting of regional styles of belt buckles as well as continued wide-belt finds. The distribution of these fittings shows a new frontier that extended initially along the Meuse but later seems to have moved south towards the Sambre, while Drinkwater shows that the rest of the Gallic *limes* remained on the Middle and Upper Rhine.[57] Aetius' campaigning near Arras and Worms seems to reinforce both these conclusions. Similarly, the distribution of Viminacium-type brooches shows a continued presence on the Upper to Middle Danube as far as Pannonia Prima, and also in Noricum Mediterraneum, near the old *Claustra Alpium Iuliarum* fortifications which themselves yield evidence of both Roman and Germanic presence into the 430s, before much of the line was abandoned in favour of fortified hinterland settlements.[58] However, these fittings and brooches also serve as direct evidence of widespread Germanic imitation and influence in the army during the fifth century, and weapons burials dominating these finds serve as evidence of the heavy use of Germanics as recruits. Some authors have stated that the shutdown of the Trier and Lyon mints are proof of the decline of the professional Roman Army, but that fails to take into context the shutdown of the eastern frontier mints, change in Roman payment methods from bronze to gold coinage, and that the capital of Gaul had moved from these two centres to Arles in the south. The archaeological evidence suggests that the Army was paid in gold coinage in the Theodosian period, which was funded by the mints in Ravenna, Rome and Aquileia, as well as with subsidies from Constantinople and Thessalonica.[59] Furthermore, Keller/Prottel type-6 crossbow brooches and Viminacium-type brooches also provide evidence for an identifiably Roman military and bureaucratic presence into the mid-fifth century.[60] Dolphin buckles are also considered to be a unique Roman style and are found distributed across fifth-century Spain, Gaul, northern Italy and North Africa as well, again suggesting there was still an extensive presence of identifiably 'Roman' soldiers.[61]

Federate forces are a different matter than the Romans. In the fourth century, the majority of raids conducted by cantons numbered fewer than 2,000 men, most in the range of 600–1,000.[62] The leaders of these cantons, *regales* and *optimates*, would have their own personal retinues of armoured, professional warriors, numbering typically less than 200 men.[63] The Romans called these retinues *comitatus*, although in the Germanic dialects they had their own terms like the Frankish *antrustiones*.[64] These military leaders were paid sums of gold coins by the Roman state, which they would then redistribute to their followers as part of the gifting system that was essential to their culture and societal structure.[65] However, this traditional model does not necessarily correlate to the methodology of settlement and military service after entering the Roman sphere. The fifth century saw dramatic changes in societal structure, which was heavily influenced by the incorporation of Roman administrative systems and Roman treaty agreements.

It is necessary to give a brief overview of the nature of fifth-century settlement, a process recorded through primarily later sources and one that evolved over the course of the late empire. A modern reconstruction of this process, and one that forms a basis of most modern theories, was composed by Walter Goffart in 1980. Earlier authors such as Ernst Gaupp, Hans Delbrück and others had proposed that the *foederati* were settled by dividing the estates in designated regions into lots, in which portions of one or two thirds of the land were then allocated to the settler, based on the Roman system of billeting soldiers.[66] However, Goffart instead proposed that this process had nothing to do with landed settlement at all, but rather that *foederati* were instead given a draft on the revenue generated from notional units of tax assessment of land. Walter Goffart's work was inspired by his research into late antique taxation; when he analyzed the *Codex Theodosianus* he noticed that in spite of the work of previous authors there were no distinct statements about land, provisions or fiscal coinage regarding barbarian settlements: only allocation.

Goffart then noted that Roman taxation worked on notional units of assessment and value, and drafts on these units of assessment were used to pay some bureaucratic officials.[67] Furthermore, it is possible that this same method of finance may have been applied to revenues from Roman towns and cities.[68] A similar system for commuting Roman soldiers' payments in-kind to cash had also appeared in the early fourth-century military, although the billeting of soldiers and the *hospitalitas* of Germanic federates was noticeably different.[69] Goffart began his discussion of Germanic settlement with the Ostrogothic settlement, since the sources recording the nuances of said settlement were contemporary to the settlement itself, unlike the *Codex Euricianus* or *Lex Burgundionum*. He found that Cassiodorus' *illatio tertiarum* was not a tax on a third of the revenues of land specifically for the payment of troops, but the allocation of a third of existing tax revenues for the payment of troops.[70] He also identified the *millena* as a unit of both assessment and tax proceeds from agricultural land (also called an *iugum*), and that Gothic troops paid by the *millena* were so-named *millenarii*.[71] Goffart used this construction and then applied it backwards in time to the Visigothic and Burgundian settlements. Goffart determined that in the Visigothic settlement the revenue stream was divided into two-thirds which went to the followers of the Gothic king, with one-third retained for his own treasury.[72] Goffart also built off an earlier premise established by Ferdinand Lot, suggesting that the Burgundians were granted half of the revenue of the land, with half going to the Romans and two-thirds of one half going to the *faramanni*, who were descendants of the Burgundian soldiers.[73]

The most concise summarization of Goffart's thesis can be found in 'The Technique of Barbarian Settlement in the Fifth Century: A Personal, Streamlined Account with Ten Additional Comments'. Goffart's argument cemented itself to this: first, that no conveyance of property was involved in the 'billeting' of a federate, and that it was never a method for dispossessing landowners and redistributing allotments of their estates to barbarian settlers. Second, that *terra* (land) had multiple usages including dwelling, ownership and governmental assessment, and also differed in the rights of the person who occupied it (*possessio* versus *dominium*). Third, that the Visigothic evidence provides a clear example of how the definitions of this *terra* and the division of those definitions operated. Fourth, that the administrative mechanism divided the revenue between a third to the king and two-thirds being hereditary revenue grants (the *sortes*), and that in exchange for the *sors* the hereditary holder of said *sors* owed military service. And finally, that Cassiodorus's *Variae* 2.16.5 is describing the distinction between ownership of the land by Roman landowners and was detached from the property assessment yielding a fiscal revenue.[74] However, Goffart's work was heavily criticized by many prominent English scholars, resulting in his revisiting of the argument to strengthen it several times. In his *Barbarian Tides*, he reinforced his argument by focusing instead on the Visigothic and Burgundian settlements, rather than the Ostrogothic one, where he argued that the laws regarding Gothic and Burgundian settlements fit closely together in their structure and implementation.[75] Goffart also expanded this method of settlement applied to the Goths and other parties to the Frankish settlement, as well as the Vandal settlement in North Africa.[76]

Goffart's most notable supporter is Guy Halsall, who in his 2007 work *Barbarian Migrations and the Roman West*, showed that Goffart posited firstly that his argument revolves around paying accommodated Germanics, not whether they were settled on the land; secondly that the billeting of Roman soldiers never involved actual ownership of the land or tax credits, nor did evidence for the billeting of Germanic troops points towards permanent settlement; thirdly that there were several methods of granting land that could have been implemented but were irrelevant to Goffart's argument; and finally that Goffart's argument was specifically aimed at explaining the curious proportions referred to in the sources and their relationship between different federate settlements.[77] Instead, Halsall argues that the process of *hospitalitas* was different for each specific situation of settlement: for example, the Visigothic and Burgundian settlements occurred when the Roman Empire was on the offensive and had military superiority, while the Ostrogothic settlement occurred in 493 when the Roman aristocracy in Italy had little say in the matter. However, Halsall also makes it clear that these divisions were one type of land and only one method of 'settlement', and that it must be remembered that not all estates were partitioned, nor were all barbarians required to partake in the system according to this method.[78] Examples where barbarians were given land involve primarily the Alans, settled in 440 and 442. In 440, the Alans of Sambida were given *agri deserti*, or unowned lands not producing revenue usually utilized for the settlement of military veterans, while on the Loire in 442, the Alans of Goar (and later Sangiban) were provided the full allotment of revenue from the local landowners, which prompted revolt.[79] As a result the Alans put down the rebellion and took the land by force. *Agri deserti* can also be used to explain the occasional situation where the primary sources do mention settlement or farming.[80] Furthermore, these salaries from the *hospitalitas* system ultimately allowed Germanic soldiers to buy lands for themselves, which constituted another form of landed settlement.[81]

As a result, within the Roman sphere the Germanic federates exhibited traits of Roman organization. For example the Franks, and later the Ostrogoths, possessed professional warriors whom they called *comites* or *domestici*, with followings of warriors-in-training called *pueri* and *iuvenes*, all of whom were paid by these allotted portions of tax revenue under their *foedus*.[82] By the sixth century, there is evidence that the former federates had also organized their militaries in a regimental manner: the Visigoths of Spain had clearly adopted a mix between a decimal and a Roman organization by the sixth century.[83] Haldon and McMahon point out that the establishment of the office of the *comes foederatorum*, first held by Areobindus around AD 420, points towards a formalization and professionalization of *foederati*-designated regiments in the fifth-century east, and therefore the employment of non-Roman *foederati* does not preclude them from being organized like the professional Roman military. The presence of *optiones* in both field army and *foederati* regiments may suggest similar organization, although McMahon points out distinct differences in their structure as well.[84] Simpson suggests that this seems to be how the *Notitia Dignitatum*'s *laeti* of the Sambre-Meuse *limes* and other regions operated, while Reuter shows that the 'ethnic' *numeri* of the *Notitia* were very clearly organized and operated as professional Roman regiments.[85] McMahon concludes that sixth-century *foederati* regiments likely consisted of Roman and foreign soldiers with a shared military culture.[86] As shown above, they were effectively paid in a similar manner to the professional army. Likewise, as a result of their cooperation with the Roman government, they were also likely provided the produce of the Roman military *fabricae*.[87] With the increasing administrative and organizational complexity of the settled peoples on Roman soil, that allied *foederati* operating under their own leaders should still be treated as quintessential militias (like those fielded by the fourth-century trans-Rhenian and trans-Danubian super-confederations) seems to be a false conclusion. It might be more accurate to portray these *foederati* as additional 'client field armies' or even 'client bureaucracies'.

Despite its significant Germano-Alan components, the professional army maintained the advantages the Roman Army had enjoyed for the past four centuries of military conflict, including semi-standardized military equipment, centralized supply and logistics, and superior training.[88] Elton makes particular note of the incredible mobility of Aetius' army, its implied logistical efficiency and ability to replenish manpower and its effectiveness at pacification, although Wijnendaele argues that Aetius' campaigning rapidity was due to the need to provide funding to the army through loot and the slave trade, which doubled as building a power base in Gaul.[89] However, his statement that the Roman Army did not lose a single major military engagement without extenuating circumstances between AD 350 and 500 is undoubtedly false.[90] The eastern Roman army suffered major military catastrophes under Attila at the aforementioned River Utus and the Chersonese in 447, both of which were set-piece battles, and may have resulted in the near destruction of at least three field armies.[91] The same can be said of the African army at the Battle of Lake Fezarra in 430 against Gaiseric, Aspar's forces in a second engagement with Gaiseric in 432, the Gallic army and Litorius at the siege of Tolosa in 439 and finally Vitus' campaign in 446 where a Roman army was defeated by Rechila after the Visigoths deserted.[92] Even so, the western Roman army achieved far more military successes than defeats. This might in part be attributed to superior tactics and generalship, but also to new lance-and-bow cavalry tactics adopted in the late fourth through to the mid-fifth centuries, and more aggressive strategies characterizing the army under Aetius, as well as the overall superior quality of the Roman forces.[93] Indeed, there is no reason to suggest that Aetius' professional forces were any less competent or likely to achieve victory, even when outnumbered, than those of Constantine or Julian II.

The Federated Peoples of Gaul

Aetius' allies would be crucial to securing enough forces for the massive battle at the Catalaunian Fields. Jordanes, who provides our principal account of the battle, says of the allies of Aetius:

> 'Now these allies arrived: *franci, sarmatae, aremoriciani, liticiani, burgun-diones, saxones, ripari, olibrones,* once Roman soldiers, I now consider truly the finest of the allies, and some other Celtic or Germanic peoples.'
> (Jordanes, *De Origine Actibusque Getarum,* 36.191)[94]

This list of allies isn't as clear-cut as it seems. Although some authors have grouped the Alans under *sarmatae* and Romans under *ripari* and *olibrones,* these peoples seem to be an addendum to the three principal allies Jordanes has already covered, a distinction that can easily be made from the account considering that the Goths and Romans have already been mentioned and that the Alans are next to feature in his narrative.[95] The *sarmatae* were likely old *laeti* settled in the late third and early fourth centuries AD.[96] The *ripari* and *olibrones* cannot be the Roman field army since they are listed as additional allies. The complex identities and sociopolitical realities of the peoples in Gaul are worth elaborating on, in order to show that the classic concept of an army consisting primarily of non-professional 'mercenary allies' may not be the best representation of the force Aetius brought to the field.

Addressing Jordanes' list in order, the first people he lists are from the kingdom of Chlodio, one group of Franks on the Upper Rhine commonly referred to as the *Salii.* It has now been established that the misnomer 'Salian Franks' is a result of an error by Julianus in his understanding of the Germanic terminology, and the name actually referred to a legal status in Frankish society, not an ethnonym.[97] Some Franks were incorporated into north-west Roman Gaul in a region called *Toxandria* under Constantius in 342, and had been a nuisance on and off over the course of the century afterwards.[98] The first indication for a unified body of Franks living on the Roman side of the Rhine, north of the Meuse, is evidenced by their king, Chlodio, who is mentioned as living during about 420–50.[99] The areas they controlled had slowly expanded over the course of this time: Chlodio had established his capital possibly in Atuatuca Tungrorum (Tongres) in the 420s and briefly seized Augusta Treverorum (Trier) and Colonia Agrippina (Cologne) in 432, before being driven back by Aetius again, following which they again expanded from 437–44, seizing Cambriacum (Cambrai), Tournacum (Tournai) and Atrebates (Arras). This expansion is archaeologically evidenced by the gradual shift of the Roman *limes* to the Meuse and Sambre rivers.[100] They later advanced south to attack Turonum on the Loire, which was defended by Majorian (who may have been *magister militum per Gallias*).[101] Luckily, this resulted in Sidonius' preservation of the campaign, in which the Franks were defeated at the Battle of *Vicus Helenae* near Arras in 445, in which he provides a description of their dress and warfare:

> 'for this youth likewise subdues monsters, on the crown of whose pates lies the hair that has been drawn towards the front, while the neck, exposed by the loss of the covering, shows bright. Their eyes are faint and pale, with a glimmer of greyish blue. Their faces are shaven all round, and instead of beards they have thin moustaches which they run through with a comb. Close-fitting garments confine the long limbs of the men; they are drawn up high so as to expose the knees, and a broad belt supports their narrow waist. It is their sport to send axes hurtling through the vast void, and know beforehand where the blow will fall, to whirl their shields, to outstrip with leaps and bounds the spears they have hurled and reach the enemy first. Even in boyhood's years the love of fighting is full grown.'
>
> (Sidonius Apollinaris, *Carmina*, 5.237–50)[102]

Despite his poetic comparison with the monsters defeated by the centaurs, most of his description is archaeologically evidenced.[103] Combs are a common find in Frankish interments, and decorative wide belts modelled on the late Roman style were popular in warrior burials. Weapons are often buried with children and adolescents, particularly seaxes (knives) and lances, while *franciscae* (throwing axes) and javelins are often found in warrior burials.[104] The Franks of the era prior to Clovis were disunited, and some have argued that they cannot be archaeologically identified, indistinct from local Roman military forces.[105] Swift argues that militarized Frankish settlements were spread down the Sambre/Meuse defensive *limes* against the Roman defences, and were culturally distinct yet heavily Roman–influenced.[106] These settlements might best be compared to those along the Middle Rhine, which were not evidence of Alamannic rule over the region but Roman continuity. Because of their extensive ties in serving as a part of the Roman defensive system, evidenced via coin hoards on the Rhine and Sambre as well as various individual finds, their obligation to support Aetius was paramount.[107]

The other people in Belgica, and the next on Jordanes' list, were the *Sarmatae*. The term 'Sarmatian' was not necessarily archaic by this time, but was often used generically; however, since Jordanes does not use it to discuss the Alans earlier in the text, it seems likely that he is referring to federates separate from those Alans of Sangiban. In the *Notitia Dignitatum*, compiled in the West from approximately AD 405–428, multiple groups of *laeti* are listed in the region of northern and middle Gaul and northern Italy. It is thought that these were professional regiments of Romano-Sarmatians who had been settled by Constantine in the early fourth century, and now had integrated into both the Roman Empire and its defensive system. Many of these settlements in northern Gaul can be found in the region of the Seine and the Loire, and evidence for a differentiation between semi-professional and non-professional units can be found in the distinguishing between settlements of *gentiles* and *laeti*. These *laeti* may be federates of sorts, but they might best be described as semi-professional soldiers, having integrated into the Roman system in the fourth century, and were not 'soldier-farmers' as the *gentiles* in North Africa were.[108] It is therefore likely that these regiments of *laeti*, stationed in Lugdenensis and Belgica Secunda, are the Sarmatians whom Jordanes calls upon in his description of the Battle of the Catalaunian Fields.

The *armoricani* and *liticiani* are another set of peoples mentioned by Jordanes. Although the Armoricans are certainly the ancestral people of modern-day Brittany, who had revolted on and off throughout the fifth century, the Liticians are a group that is otherwise unknown. Ralf Scharf has suggested that '*Liticiani*' was an error, and *laeti* was meant.[109] However, Fleuriot and Snyder have both suggested that *Liticiani* derives from *Litani*, and that since 'n' and 'u' are often confused in the copying process, then these may be *Litaui* from the area of Wales and Cornwall.[110] If indeed this is true, then this could coincide with his later *Britones*, who had crossed the Channel to *Armorica* from the part of Britain known as *Letavia* or *Litauia*.[111] Furthermore, the support of the British could have come from their continued relationship with the Roman government. After the *comes Britanniarum* command was established and sent to Gaul sometime in the first decade of the fifth century, there were still a large number of Roman units stationed in the province. The visit and alleged 'alleluia victory' by Germanus of Auxerre and the reference to the 'Groans of the Britons' are both signs that there was still a relationship between the imperial and British provincial bureaucracies.[112] There is also clear evidence of cultural continuity between southern Britain and Roman northern Gaul into the 440s, and the presence of type-6 crossbow *fibulae* suggests a continued presence of imperial authority and governance into the mid-fifth century.[113] It is likely that some Britons loyal to the empire would have moved to Armorica, and many would have been willing to support Aetius' forces, but the development of Armorica and the relationship between pro-Roman Britons and the Roman Empire is difficult to establish and trace.[114]

Thanks to the surviving works of Constantius of Lyon, some information survives about the Roman forces in Britain in the middle of the fifth century. In 429 Germanus led a Romano-British force consisting of light infantry in the '*alleluia* victory', also called the Battle of Mold, defeating a force of raiding Picts and Saxons.[115] The fact that they are made to come across as irregular troops, which Germanus had to reform, suggests they were mostly comprised of town *vigiles* and private militias, possibly with some old *limitanei* garrisons. In 435 the forces of the Armoricans were small enough to be defeated by Hunnish *bucellarii* or *foederati* under the command of Litorius.[116] Much later, in approximately 470, Riothamus marched from Armorica into Aquitania with an army of 12,000 men to help the Romans combat Visigothic domination of southern Gaul and Spain.[117] However, the issue arises that this is a rather large number and that Riothamus probably had elements of Frankish or Saxon *foederati* in his forces as well. It is known that the *possessores* of Gaul were no stranger to raising private armies themselves when the need arose, as shown by their quarrelsome conflicts with Aetius and the Alans, but there is no feasibility to this number as an estimate for the forces provided by the Armoricans and Britons alone during the conflict in 451. However, it does provide an accurate representation of the mixed composition of Gallic armies, as it consists of local Romans funded by private warlords, Franks and Saxons.

As longstanding allies of the Romans, and one of the groups that went on to form the Saxon confederation, the *Frisii* make for a likely candidate to be Jordanes' *Saxones*. Part of the Frisian confederation was relocated into the Roman Empire in 297, after which they seemingly disappear from contemporary sources.[118] However, there have been distinct Frisian earthenware finds called *terp tritzum* in the regions of modern-day Kent and Flanders dating to the fourth century.[119] Although Frisian settlers may indeed have accounted for the 'Saxons' at the battle, there is still no evidence that they had any requirement of military service, except for an obscure reference found in the *Notitia Dignitatum*, where there is a listing of the *cohors prima Frixiagorum* stationed at Vindobala on Hadrian's Wall.[120] Scholars have suggested that this was a copyist's error, and that it was actually meant to say '*Frisiavonum*'.[121] Furthermore, there was also an altar found outside Melandra castle dedicated by a member of a *cohors Frixiavonum*.[122] These men need not be *Frisii per se*, but Frisian auxiliaries had been serving in the Roman Army since the first century AD. Finally, evidence for Frisian service may also be evidenced by both independent solidi and a large coin hoard of Valentinian III in the *terp* region of the modern Netherlands.[123] However, due to the multinational composition of Germanic confederations and the ambiguity of Roman terminology, for all intents and purposes it is best to assume that multiple groups like the *Frisii*, *Frisiavones*, *Saxones*, *Suiones*, *Franci* or *Anglii* all fell under Jordanes' *Saxones*.

The presence of *Suiones* in Jordanes' *Saxones* may be supported by various coin hoards found on the island of Oland in modern Sweden which primarily come from the Theodosian period, and particularly consist of issues of Valentinian III; none of these examples date later than the first issues of Marcian in 451–52. These coins were deposited in five-year intervals from 420–22 to 441, coinciding with imperial consular donatives to soldiers, and were probably from payments to professional soldiers in the service of Valentinian III.[124] In his criticism of Hedeager, Nasman concedes that leaders from Oland may have visited the court of the Huns to swear fealty, even though the Huns never actually set foot in Scandinavia.[125] Aetius may have made connections with leaders from the fringes of *barbaricum* during his own time there, allowing him to draw recruits from Oland and Scandinavia when he came to power later.[126] Hunnish treaty terms also forbade the recruitment of peoples within Attila's empire, which could also explain the presence of these coins dating to the 430s through 450s, as the Romans looked outside the boundaries of the Hun Empire for soldiers. Aetius' and Attila's machinations might also explain its later destruction, if the outside invasion hypothesis proves correct, where tensions between peoples who had chosen to support the Huns and soldiers who had served Aetius boiled over.[127] The presence of Scandinavian soldiers at the battle may also explain the presence of the Huns throughout Scandinavian mythology and sagas.[128]

Jordanes and Sidonius both mention Burgundians in the armies of Aetius and Attila, on opposite sides.[129] Originally, the Burgundian groups had all been relatively clustered together in the first quarter of the fifth century, centred in Bourbetomagus near the point where the Main intersects the Rhine, and spread out upstream along the Main.[130] In 430 the Hunnish King Octar attacked and attempted to vassalize some of these Burgundians, who allegedly fled across the Rhine into Gundicar's kingdom. After consulting the local bishop, they returned and ambushed the Huns with a force of 3,000 men in the forests of west Germania, soundly defeating them.[131] Gundicar's Burgundians would not be so lucky: revolting with the Visigoths against the Romans in 436, they were defeated by Aetius and given a new treaty. However, in 437 they rose up again and Aetius led a force of Huns against Borbetomagus, utterly annihilating Gundicar's kingdom, allegedly slaying 20,000 Burgundians and killing Gundicar as well.[132] These Burgundians were resettled in Sapaudia in 443 and would later form the Burgundian kingdom, but would remain adherent to Roman terms until after Aetius' death.[133] Gundicar's Burgundians are rather well attested thanks to the *Lex Burgundionum*, which preserves the terms of their settlement.[134]

Hughes makes a note of the *Alamanni*, who are not present in the Roman sources surrounding the battle. The last record of the *Alamanni* at this point is of one of their groups near Noricum, called the *Iuthungi*, who were defeated by Aetius in 430.[135] Maenchen-Helfen supports the theory that Attila passed north of Alamannic lands and came down the Main.[136] Hughes states that Attila had to pass through Alamannic territory to get to the Rhine River, or otherwise pass north and leave his rear unsecured.[137] Although he suggests they merely bowed to Hunnish pressure and allowed them to pass, it is possible some *Alamanni* may have joined Attila's campaign. However, Drinkwater argues that the *Alamanni* were doing more to defend Rome than to extort it, making note of Germanic archaeological presence in garrison points along the Upper and Middle Rhine in the mid-fifth century. He also suggests that this projection of military presence by the Romans could not have been destroyed in a fortnight, because it had existed for more than a century.[138] The established garrisons still existed, but their manpower was now a mix of Roman and German, and Drinkwater goes on to say that, like the Burgundians and Franks, there were likely *Alamanni* serving on both sides of the armies.[139]

Jordanes, in his description of the Battle of the Catalaunian Fields, makes mention of a group called the *Ripari*. At first what comes to mind is that the *Ripari* are the Ripuarian Franks, a parallel most authors have drawn, but records of these Franks as a differentiated group only come from later sources, some of whom drew on Jordanes regarding this part of fifth-century history.[140] The term

'*Ripuari*' in describing the Rhine Franks first appears in the late sixth and seventh centuries, and was not a fifth-century term.[141] In the eastern half of the empire, the *limitanei* were still maintaining their role as border guards on the Danubian and oriental *limes*, even receiving significant funding in 443 to strengthen the defence against the Huns.[142] A law of 443 increased the punishment for *limitanei* working lands they held, indicating that by the 440s they apparently owned farms in the provinces of their postings.[143] In the west, Severinus of Noricum seems to indicate that until 454, not only were the Upper Rhine and Danubian *limes* intact, but in fairly decent condition.[144] Drinkwater makes note of the large number of Germanic and Roman artifacts in burials at Roman forts along the Upper and Middle Rhine, and he suggests Aetius maintained the *limes* with a mix of local Roman and Germanic recruits, and also supplied his field army with Franks and *Alamanni*.[145] It is possible that the concept of a group of 'Ripuarian Franks' at the time of the battle is mistaken, and that these in fact referred to *limitanei* on the Rhine frontier, called *ripenses* or *riparienses*.[146] These soldiers were drawn from the locals settled around their garrison posts, and large portions of them may have been recruited from the Franks and *Alamanni*.[147] With these forces, Aetius' recapture of Trier and Cologne after the new *foedus* in 445 gave the Romans an arm of military control to use against left-bank and right-bank Germanics.[148] Therefore, Jordanes' *Ripari* might be a corrupted term for grades of Romano-Franco-Alamannic *limitanei* troops drawn from the Rhine frontier to help fight the Huns, who may have later developed into the 'Ripuarian Franks'.

Jordanes lastly mentions troops called *Olibrones*, which could be a corruption but otherwise doesn't translate. They are described as

> 'once Roman soldiers, I now consider truly the finest of the allies'
> (Jordanes, *De Origine Actibusque Getarum*, 36.191).[149]

Hughes suggests that these men were Frankish troops who replaced the *limitanei* on the Middle Rhine, but as already discussed the *Ripari* more likely account for this.[150] Barnish equates them with the *Breones*, who were militia of Theodoric the Great stationed in Raetia mentioned in Cassiodorus' *Variae*.[151] This reading seems likely, as it could be a possible addition to the list for the purpose of Gothic propaganda. However, there is another possibility: as the Roman Army declined and taxes were lost, it's entirely possible that the Roman forces that were cut may have been resigned to city garrisons. The law of 440 describes the assignment of Italian field army troops to cities in Sicily and along the southern coast in response to the Vandal raids.[152] Likewise, this may have also happened in northern Gaul. Before Attila advanced, Aetius may have 'reactivated' these retired veterans who were serving as militias and city garrisons at their billeting posts like Liebeschuetz argues, in order to reinforce the primary field army.[153] This would certainly fit the description of forces who were 'once Roman soldiers'.

However, if these men were so well equipped and were former Roman soldiers, it is possible that this describes Aetius' personal *bucellarius*. *Bucellarii* were usually barbarian troops in service of high-ranking generals, but could consist of Roman forces as well; these private armies were limited in size by the western Roman government after Stilicho had introduced the practice.[154] Still, these forces tended to number in the thousands, with Zeno's Isaurians able to man the walls of Constantinople in 447 and Aspar's being large enough to take on the imperial guard in 471.[155] Aetius' career, along with that of his rival Bonifatius, was dominated by his use of external political forces and large followings of both *bucellarii* and *foederati* to retain and excise power.[156] However, after the change in Hunnish leadership in 439, it seems most of Aetius' Hunnic *foederati* were recalled, as there is no mention of these Huns afterwards.[157] Therefore, Aetius may have only retained his core following of his most loyal *bucellarii*, as evidenced by the two who had assassinated Valentinian III in 455.[158] Either interpretation is suitable for the characterization of the *Olibrones*, and they would likely have been a valuable asset on the field.

Estimating the Size of the Coalition Army

The size of the late Roman Army, and of the late Roman legion itself, is extremely controversial and relies on a few scraps of evidence. Before beginning this attempt at estimating its size, it must be stated that this is based on the fundamental assumption that Roman regiments were standardized at this time. This is an inherently flawed assumption, as the Roman Army was in a constant state of transition from the third to the sixth centuries, and there seems to have been no established set of standards for the size of many regiments until the time of the *Strategikon*. It is clear from the *Notitia Dignitatum*, a variety of literary sources and the Anastasian-era tablets from Perge that the late Roman legion and most other types of regiment varied widely in size. What follows is a list of primary source accounts of unit sizes in the fourth to sixth centuries, with an attempt to reconstruct a theoretical standard, or at least average, size for each regiment type for the purpose of estimating army strengths.

At the turn of the fifth century, Claudian and Orosius mention a force of two legions and five *auxilia palatina* units numbering 5,000 men.[159] Zosimus mentions five Dalmatian *tagmatai* numbering 6,000 and an *Ile* numbering 600 men, as well as Stilicho's thirty Roman legions at Pollentia.[160] Sozomen mentions six *arithmoi* of 4,000 men.[161] John Malalas also mentions two *arithmoi* of the *Mattiarii* and *Lanciarii* totalling 1,500 men, but he also calls them *lochoi*.[162] Ammianus mentions seven *legiones* and *numeri* numbering less than 20,000 at Amida, consistently refers to detachments of units numbering 300 men and two *alae* totalling 700 men, as well as making several references to other detachments.[163] Finally, there are the controversial Panopolis *Papyri*, which make no mention of unit sizes themselves. However, by utilizing sixth-century Roman sources Duncan-Jones extrapolated potential unit sizes, including approximately 1,100 men for the detachments of

Legio II Traiana, 1,078 for *Legio III Diocletiana*, 121 for a unit of *equites sagittarii*, 164 for *Cohors XI Chamavorum*, 118 for one *ala* and 21 for a unit of *dromedarii*.[164] A.H.M. Jones also provides estimates for these same units, giving the figures of 2,751 men for *III Diocletiana*, 2,157 for *II Traiana*, 367 for the *ala* and 215 for the *dromedarii*, 512 men for *XI Chamavorum* and 242 for the *equites sagittarii*. A later papyrus records that the *equites promoti* of *II Traiana* numbered 264 men, and another papyrus from Justinan's time records an *arithmos* of 508 men.[165] The *numerus* of *Legio V Macedonica* at Memphis in 399 records that they consumed 835 rations per day, suggesting that they numbered from 300–400 men. However, the legion had many small detachments in nearby cities, including Antaepolis and Heliopolis, so the force at Memphis was not at its full strength.[166] Similarly, a papyrus of the *Legio XIII Gemina* in Lower Egypt estimates it numbered around 800–900 men based on its 949 *annonae diurnae* in AD 325.[167]

Anything that is seemingly simple about these numbers is not, especially when cross-referenced with the *Notitia*. First to observe are the records of *arithmoi* and *numeri*, which are the same kind of unit.[168] The six *arithmoi* of Sozomen number 666 each, and the *arithmos* of the Papyrus numbers 508, which would show a potential strength of the *numerus* of around 600 men, possibly eight centuries totaling 640.[169] Using this number, it provides some clarity to Claudian's record of the two legions and five *auxilia palatina* units that were led by Mascezel into Africa in 398. If the *palatina* units, which can be equated with the *numeri* of the *Augustei, Sagittarii Nervi*, the *Felices Iuniores* or *Seniores*, the *Invicti Seniores* and the *Leones Iuniores* or *Seniores*, are assigned numbers of 640, then that would leave another 1,800 men for the two legions to fill, making them number about 900 men each.[170] Zosimus' record of the five legions from Dalmatia would suggest five legions of 1,200, but actually the Dalmatian *comitatenses* consists of four legions and one *numerus*, suggesting a *numerus* of 640 and four legions of 1,340.[171] The aforementioned fragments from Perge, dating to the reign of Anastasius in 498, suggest a legion that may have numbered around 1,200 infantry and 300 cavalry, depending on the incomplete number of *munifices*. Elements of its proposed organization express some similarities to the structure of legions and *Banda* mentioned in the works of Aelian, Arrian, Urbicius and the *Strategikon*.[172]

Next are the references to cavalry. Ammianus' mention of 700 men in two *turmae* and Zosimus' *ile* or *ala* of 600 would seem to coincide with possibly both qunigenary- and milliary-strength *alae*.[173] But Julian, in his letter to the Athenians, and Zosimus both say he received a guard of 360 men from Constantius: this nearly matches Ammianus' 350-man *turma*.[174] It may, however, be safest to assume the *ala* continued to be its principate strength of 512 men.[175] The newest cavalry units are called *cunei*, which seems like an adoption of the name for the Alanic or Hunnic cavalry structure. A record by Synesius records *unnigardae* operating in units of forty and 200, all under the same leader, which would suggest a Hunnish *cuneus* could have numbered 240 men; providing the Romans adopted the organization of their *cuneus* from the steppe nomads, this could suggest an organization of the Roman-style *cuneus*.[176] The evidence for this, however, is circumstantial; there could be other reasons why these units were primarily found on the Middle and Lower Danube. It is also possible the Romans adopted this name for the 256-man *tarantiarchia*, which is mentioned by the second-century author Arrian.[177]

Taking numbers and applying them to the *Notitia Dignitatum* is an even bigger challenge. First one must account for variations in unit size, and secondly account for copies, transfers, errors, destroyed units and of course the date chosen. For example, the *comes Illyricum* wasn't created until possibly 402, and the *comes Britanniarum* was created after 395, but prior to 405, and did not arrive in Gaul until 408.[178] Knowing when a command was created also helps to judge where new field army units were drawn from. Luckily, thanks to a law passed on 14 April 400, we know that these upgraded *pseudocomitatenses* units were organized as legions.[179] Secondly, there remains the question of units whose sizes can only be guessed at. In the West, there were fifty-eight *legiones*, eighty-six *numeri*, forty-two *cohortes*, fifty-six *milites*, seven *auxilia*, fifty-six *equites*, nine *alae*, fourteen *cunei*, two *comites* and four unknown classified regiments.[180] Much of the *Notitia Dignitatum*'s accuracy is corroborated by primary sources, such as Zosimus' mention of the thirty regiments Stilicho collected to fight Radagasius, which rather closely matches the thirty-six regiments of the Italic Praesental army in the *Notitia*.[181] Using the numbers presented above, an analysis of the *Notitia Dignitatum* would show the Western Roman Empire fielded about 229,728 men in both the field armies and border garrisons at about AD 419, providing some forces hadn't already been destroyed.[182]

Such a number seems exceptionally large for the time of Aetius, and indeed it is. By 450, the remaining units in Britain, Africa and Spain had all disappeared, which would leave an army of about 136,320 men, of whom 91,360 would have belonged to the field armies and 44,960 to the *limitanei*.[183] The Armoricans, who probably had elements of the *comes Britanniarum*'s army, would cut another 5,312 *comitatenses* from the Gallic field army, provided this army wasn't destroyed under Constantine III's rebellion, leaving the field forces with 86,048 men.[184] According to Heather, the loss of Zeugitana and Byzacena is estimated to have cut an estimated 240,000 *solidi* per annum from the imperial revenue stream, while the tax lost from the provinces of Numidia and the three Mauretanias is recorded amounting to 106,200 *solidi*. These numbers amount to approximately 57,700 infantry or 22,971 cavalry, or roughly 45,335 men if an equal percentage from each were taken, based on Elton's figures of 6 and 10.5 *solidi* per annum for infantry and cavalry respectively.[185] More recent estimates of soldiers' pay by Warren Treadgold indicate that these numbers are probably off, depending on the ratio of *comitatenses* to *limitanei* forces disbanded. There is also the factor of soldiers and officers who received multiple units of pay, the number of which is impossible to calculate as regimental organization from this period remains unknown. Treadgold estimates the pay of a *limitaneus* as 4 *solidi* at one *annona*, and a *comitatensis* at approximately four *annonae* at 16 *solidi* during the

Theodosian dynasty, meaning that only about 21,637 *comitatenses* would need to be cut, or alternatively 86,650 *limitanei*.[186] About 19,392 of these men were probably absorbed by the aforementioned cessation of Pannonia Valeria and Pannonia Secunda to the East, but the rest would have had to come from existing forces. If we take into account the Pannonian garrisons as part of the cut and apply the rest to the field armies, this would leave Aetius with 69,258 *comitatenses* and 25,568 *limitanei*, assuming the remaining retirements applied to field forces.

The Romans tried various methods of recouping these losses: they opened up trade with Greece, enforced tax laws and passed a law specifically for the payment of soldiers called the *Siliquaticum*, but these measures ultimately didn't compare to the North African revenue, and Valentinian III declared bankruptcy in 444.[187] In 446, the army of Vitus suffered a reputedly embarrassing defeat at the hands of the Suebes, on top of the earlier routing of the Gallic army in 439 by the Visigoths, and also the defeats of Roman forces in Spain in 429 and those sent against Boniface in 427, further reducing their numbers. Many forces had also been resigned to the defence of important walled cities in Gaul and Italy.[188] At some point, Marcellinus seems to have become independent, taking with him the army of the *comes Illyricum*, reducing the *comitatenses* to 58,538 men. According to Elton, the Romans also suffered from manpower and conscription issues during the fifth century, although the number of volunteer soldiers remains uncertain.[189] If we assume these losses could not be replenished, we can maybe resign about half of this number due to these externalities alongside foregone and largely unknown logistical costs, bringing the count down to 29,269 men. Coello shows that the few recorded Roman units in the third and early fourth centuries operated from day to day at about 70–80 per cent of their paper strength, meaning that this force more likely numbered 20,488 *comitatenses* and 17,898 *limitanei*.[190] Of course, such precision is impossible, and a safer estimate would be about 20,500 *comitatenses* and 18,000 *limitanei*. These garrisons were probably spread down the *limes* from the Sambre-Meuse line to Mogontiacum, then up the Rhine and down the Danube to Comagenis, and finally to Siscia and into the Julian alps.[191] Even then, these numbers are not definitive due to the serious flaws in such a methodology, such as the generic labelling of units as '*numerus*', indications in the primary sources that legion size varied with some significance and the overall lack of sources. However, this comes within range of the estimates by Herwig Wolfram, who states that with an annual income of 40,000lb of gold in 450, the Western Roman Empire would have to spend over 60 per cent of its income to maintain an army of 30,000 men.[192] By 472, they could barely field 6,000.[193]

The total size of the federate contribution can be estimated using prior authorship and information from primary sources. Delbruck put forth a convincing rejection of the argument that the figures found in primary sources claim that barbarian armies numbered in the tens or hundreds of thousands, and instead shows that most barbarian forces would typically range in the vicinity of 5,000, with exceptions.[194] Heather estimates that at a maximum, the early Visigothic kingdom of Aquitaine could field a theoretical 25,000 men.[195] The Alans had been the backbone of the defence in Roman Gaul for years, and must have been able to match the Hunnish forces if they were placed in the centre of the formation. They therefore probably numbered around 10,000–15,000 men, especially considering there were at least two groups of Alans available to Aetius.[196] The various Franks were split between supporting elder and younger candidates, or being subordinates of Rome or Attila, and assuming they could amass a total force like they invaded Gaul with in the 350s, then Aetius may have had around 5,000–10,000 Franks available to him. If we assume the maximum estimate for a raiding warband – approximately 2,000 men, according to Hugh Elton – and use the four large coin hoards of Valentinian III as evidence for the leaders of these main warbands, using the maximum estimate of a standard warband to account for those unattested by coin hoards, then 8,000 men seems to be a plausible estimate.[197] Socrates' record of a force of 3,000 Burgundians describes those living across the Rhine from Gundicar, but is a realistic figure.[198] The Burgundians of Gundicar could evidently field significant numbers, enough for 20,000 of them to be slaughtered in 436, but this figure likely includes non-combatants.[199] They were significantly diminished, but had plenty of time to recover since the sack of Worms and may have been able to field a comparable number to the Franks, possibly in the vicinity of 5,000–10,000 men. The Armoricans, who are thought to have controlled the local *limitanei* garrisons and possibly some old British forces, could field several thousand men: allegedly 12,000 later under Riothamus.[200] However, this later force included large numbers of Saxons and Franks, but it still serves as a decent estimate for the other assorted federates Jordanes lists: the Sarmatian *laeti* garrisons, the 'Saxons', as well as the Armoricans and *Litaui* themselves.[201]

Using the proposed maxima, this force would be upwards of maybe 70,000 men. However, it often escapes the academic discourse that the Germanics also suffered from attrition, deserters, 'paper soldiers' and the need to leave garrisons behind. Therefore, if we apply the same figure of 70 per cent strength that affected the Roman regiments to that of the *foederati*, then one could envision a force of about 49,000 men. This was then coupled with the 20,500-strong western Roman army and approximately 2,000 *riparienses* withdrawn from the *dux Mogontiacenses* command on the Rhine.[202] Furthermore, Aetius had a personal *bucellarius* of several thousand men, large enough to clash in a full-scale battle outside Ariminium in 432, after which Aetius inherited Bonifatius' retinue. If each of these two forces was as large as a large canton, then Aetius' *bucellarii*, consisting of Pelagia's Goths and Aetius' Huns, as well as some Romans, Alans and others, may have numbered 4,000 men or more. For comparison, Aspar's numbered around 5,000, while Belisarius had 7,000, the largest recorded.[203] Combined with Aetius' personal Gothic and Hunnic *bucellarii*, then the total force could number a theoretical 75,500 men. Of course, one must remember that these estimates are not absolute, just plausible figures.

Chapter 3

The Hun Confederation

There have been a couple of commonly cited reasons for why the Huns conquered Europe: namely the 'Hunnish' bow and stirrups.[1] Neither of these assumptions are in any way supported by the archaeological record, with the earliest iron stirrups in the Carpathians dating from the 570s to the 610s and probably attributable to an introduction around the time of the Avar migration. An example from the Middle Volga dates from the late fifth to early sixth century, suggesting at earliest a Sabir (Xianbei) introduction, since they emigrated to that region. Stirrups probably originated in the Ordos loop around AD 300 and weren't transmitted to the Huns prior to their migration.[2] Furthermore, Hunnic bows and trilobate arrowheads were already present in Europe as far west as Britain, and in widespread use by Roman infantry and cavalry archers.[3] Hunnish warriors were likely no more capable or well-equipped than the Alans who fought similarly to them, and instead conquered Europe due to their superior upper-level organization. The misguided concept that the Huns were a loose confederation of horseback-dwelling wanderers that poured into Europe has for some time been debunked. The Hunnish lifestyle is usually described as nomadic, but more accurately portrayed as semi-sedentary, with families guiding their flocks in a cycle between two specific summer and winter pastures and setting up semi-permanent camps at each location.[4] The narrative of Ammianus, on which some authors still base their view of the Huns, is now rather widely discredited. His description of Hunnic government, lifestyle and warfare is considered generic, biased and misinformed.[5] It is also believed to be a form of *topos*, paralleling Herodotus' description of the Scythians like Jordanes' allusion to Marathon.[6] In reality, Hun society is only vaguely reflected by the Roman authors, but much of what is known can be correlated to the *Xiongnū* model.[7] Arguments about steppe state formation based on reliance on raiding sedentary agricultural societies have been called into question, and a more commercial motive combined with partial sedentary influence for sophisticated organization is now generally accepted.[8]

The Hunnish Empire was a quasi-feudal dualist state structure divided into primary kingdoms of left and right, each of which had a lesser kingdom of its own. That this internal ranking system of kings existed among the Huns is indirectly acknowledged by Olympiodorus during his visit to the court of Charaton in 412.[9]

Maenchen-Helfen shows how the primary sources reflect that there was a division in rule between west and east between Attila and Bleda, although he does not believe the institution was permanent.[10] The emperor of the Huns ruled from the kingdom of the left (east) and may have preserved the title of *chanyu*. The last known *chanyu* is attested in AD 91, so the title may have carried on by continuity of the ruling dynasty. However, it was probably a Yeniseian loanword, while the title *aniliki* is used by the Danubian Volga Bulgars and is an Oghuric word. *Shah* and *yabgu* are also attested among contemporary Iranic-speaking steppe nomads, so it remains uncertain. The term *qagan* (also of Yeniseian origin) doesn't appear to come into use until after 400, and reaches Europe with the Eurasian Avars.[11] The left also had a king, who was typically the emperor's appointed heir, and seem to have practised succession based on a form of agnatic seniority. His title may have been *ilik*, as attested by Attila's son 'Ellak', pointing towards *aniliki* and *alik* or *ilik* as the titles of these rulers.[12] Underneath the kings of left and right were kings of south and north, respectively. These four Hunnish kings would sit alongside the Hun emperor, along with other important officials and figures of power. Originally, in the *Xiongnu* empire, there were many bureaucrats called *gu-tu* marquises, a stratified council of twenty-four lesser kings who commanded up to 10,000 men, who were prominent within the Hunnish state.[13] These institutions probably survived into Roman times, unidentified due to sparsity of source material, or under different names. Alongside them, the emperor had a 'council of six horns', or *ulticur*, which seems to have survived into Roman times, mistaken as a separate tribe by both Jordanes and Agathias, and later appearing in early Bulgaria.[14] The Huns also inherited an organized military with a regimental decimal system, an organization which not only persisted into near-modern times, but was also adopted by migration-era Germanics within both the Hunnic and Roman spheres.[15]

Several Hunnish tribes are recorded in the primary sources, including the *Alcildzur* or *Amilzur* (*Alpidzur*), *Tongur*, *Ultzinzur*, *Bittugur*, *Bardor* and *Akatir* Huns, as well as the later *Saragur*, *Onogur*, *Ogur*, *Kutrigur* and *Utigur* Huns after the AD 480s.[16] There were also several other groups that might be Hunnish, such as the *angisciri* and the *sadages* in the Balkans, and the *Barsil* (*Barselts*), *Xailandur*, *Bnjr* (*Brjân*) and *Mask'ut'* in the Caucasus.[17] The dilemma comes from the fact that there are more 'Hunnish' peoples than there are allowable elements of their organization, but some could be ruled out as part of the central Hunnish state structure. The *Alpidzur* and *Tongur* Huns were likely Oghur-speakers living on the Volga before the Hun invasion, and not part of their empire. It is thought that these groups may have been the 'Huns' fighting alongside the Goths and with the Romans in the late fourth century and the 'deserters' demanded to be handed over in the 420s.[18] These people, who spoke a dialect that either was Hunnish or very close to it, took up the ethnonym 'Hun' as a fear tactic. This also shows the complex reality of the Eurasian steppes, where identity and ethnicity cannot be assumed to be synonymous. Likewise the *angisciri* and *sadages* are never explicitly stated to be Hunnish, having other plausible etymologies, but are still mentioned in relation to the Huns. The Caucasian peoples, some of whom may have been Hun, others Iranic, can also be effectively ruled outside the European Hunnish sphere.[19] There are, however, four groups explicitly called or easily determined to be Huns: foremost among them the *Akatir* Huns, positioned just north of the Crimea, who seem to have been the dominant confederation of the eastern 'kingdom of the left' where the emperor and his heir typically sat.[20] Along with the *Akatir* Huns, another people named as the *Ultzinzur* Huns are listed first in the peoples following Attila's son, Dengzich; their name also bears similarity to the Turkic rendition of Uldin (*Ultzin*).[21] It is entirely possible that this was the dominant confederation of the western 'kingdom of the right' that settled on the Middle Danube. The power of these two groups and their choice of settlement locations was likely economic: alongside the fur trade and proximity to the Black Sea ports or the Roman *limes*, both of their settlement locations were the ends of the axes of the Amber Route.[22] The Amber Routes doubled as the primary routes of communication through *barbaricum*, which would allow the Huns to control their vassal peoples effectively. Beyond this, it is difficult to find a plausible explanation as to why anyone would want to settle in the malaria-infested plains and swamps of the Middle Danubian valley. This would of course make the remaining two groups, the *Bittugur* and *Bardor* Huns, the major confederations of the lesser two kingdoms of 'north' and 'south'. However, which of these two peoples belonged to which division cannot be ascertained from the source material, nor their settlement locations, although they may have been positioned in the Wallachian plain and Dniester regions.

The Hunnish military was organized into a decimal system, like their predecessors and antecessors. Under the kings were the commanders of 10,000, named *intimates* and *logades* by Priscus but probably called *ämäcur* in the Hunnish tongue, and under each *ämäcur* were regimental commanders of 1,000, 100 and ten.[23] These units were clan-based, and the numbers they commanded probably reflected total population, not exclusively soldiers. The clan-based nature likely accounts for the description of irregularly sized divisions in their lines, as stated in the *Strategikon*.[24] There is a certain logic to this, as clan units in the steppes make the best economic sense when numbering between about 500 and 1,000 members.[25] Rank was also hereditary in these societies, and they were ordered according to cosmology, geographic directions, colours and number.[26] We also know that the Huns had a royal guard, who may have borne the same name as the Gok-Turkic *böri* (wolves) after Iranic steppe origin myths, or *ṭarḫâns*, possibly a *Xiongnū* word. They likely numbered around 1,000 men and had members who rotated in and out of the unit over time.[27] Personal retainers also appeared in the decimal divisions, as each division was a mix of troop types including professional soldiers, noblemen's *comitatus* and of course levied men.[28]

The Huns also seem to have had some organized logistics, suggested by the use of boats for transport across rivers and the replenishment of carts and wagons, as well as horses and fodder. The extensive use of two-wheeled wagons, pulled behind their mounts, gave the Huns the advantage of being strategically mobile. The Huns also had four-wheeled wagons in the style of those found in the form of Sarmatian-era toys in the Crimea.[29] However, they did not live in these wagons, but had both temporary and semi-permanent tents like those depicted in the first-century AD rock art at Minusinsk, for use when they travelled between summer and winter grazing grounds.[30] According to Theophylact Simocatta, the later Turks also had a private preserve for the *qagan* which served both as his hunting grounds and a stockpile for weapons.[31] Campaigns were planned thoroughly in advance, with different groups being assigned military targets.[32] Their method of life made them mobile in war, at least when utilizing purely mounted steppe armies, able to cover allegedly 200km in a day.[33] Of course, operating alongside sedentary vassals drastically reduced their mobility.

Alongside organized logistics, the Huns utilized technicians and engineers to build and maintain siege equipment. Heather suggests that the Huns had learned this from a mix of experiences, including employment under Aetius and the need to pressure the wealthy Silk Road fortresses in Bactria and Sogdiana, but that captured Romans probably provided the number of specialists needed to produce such equipment on this scale.[34] It has even been suggested that their own engineers had carried over knowledge of the traction trebuchet into Europe, although this is probably an Avar introduction.[35] Hun engineers also had the capability to build sophisticated structures like bridges and military fortifications, such as the fourth- to fifth-century fortress at Igdui-Kala in Kazakhstan.[36] As a whole, the Huns were more sophisticated in logistics and warfare than is typically thought by modern authors. However, Fyfe points out that there were still severe limitations on the logistical capabilities of the Hun military machine, and that despite the fact they were probably more sophisticated than often assumed, they were still not able to compete with the ability of the Roman Empire to supply and maintain armies in the field.[37]

Hun Tactics

In part thanks to Hollywood, modern artists, and their popular association with the later Mongols, the Hun warrior is usually misrepresented and poorly understood. Thompson was the first to note that the Huns could not have conquered Europe without iron armour and weapons.[38] Contrary to the popular belief that hordes of lasso-armed warriors clad in leather and furs overwhelmed Roman armies and swept across Europe, the Hun warrior was comparatively brightly dressed and well-armed. The average Hun probably wore one or two linen tunics under a heavy wool kaftan, which would have provided decent protection from arrows at a long range.

Over this would have been worn the *sagion voulgarikon*, which may mean 'Bulgar cloak'. He also would have had a Pannonian cap or Phrygian-style cap adorning his head.[39] Wealthier Huns would have worn tunics and kaftans decorated with silk, adorned with decorations in the central Asian styles and sometimes lined with fine furs. The Huns wore Persian-style trousers, a Pontic-style belt with a kidney-shaped or rectangular buckle and flat stiffeners with large domed rivets, and a pair of riding boots, often secured with a shoe-buckle. Wealthier Huns would have had Pontic-Danubian cloisonné fittings for their belts and horse tack.[40] The Hun was armed with a 120–150cm long asymmetric Qum-Darya type composite recurve bow, with about thirty or forty arrows that used steel trilobate arrowheads, capable of splitting shields not properly faced with cow leather or gut. These arrows and bow would be carried in a C-shaped bowcase or a *gorytos* with cylindrical quivers.[41] Alongside that, he would have carried a 3–4m lance called a *kontos*, used either two-handed or couched in the armpit and slung across the back when partaking in mounted archery, and adorned with decorative pennons (which the Romans called *flammulae*) on the end.[42] Lassos were useful and were probably used to a small degree in close-combat, but primarily for capturing or controlling horses. Wealthier Huns could afford a narrow *langseax*, or even a *spatha* of the Asiatic-type, while the wealthiest could afford metal armour and helmets.[43] These were usually constructed as bandhelmets, spangenhelmets, segment helmets or lamellar helmets, and armour could either be maille, scale or hanging lamellar.[44] The steppe nomads were specifically famed for their ability to produce lamellar, called *ferreis lamminis* by Rufus, and as it spread to the east maille armour also became popular.[45] Finds near Badabag, Romania, in a Roman context may suggest a Hunnish or Alan introduction of hanging lamellar to Europe, although it had existed since much earlier times in central Asia. However, Menander made note that iron was sparse in the steppes and quilted garments were far more common due to the availability of wool and flax.[46] The Hun warrior probably required about two or three horses for campaign, equipped with tack and high-backed steppe saddles, and wealthier Huns protected their mounts with quilted wool barding or even metal armour.[47]

In steppe society all members were warriors, with both pre-modern Turkic and Mongol languages indifferent in their terminology distinguishing 'man' from 'warrior'. There was probably a formal rite of initiation as well, in which they acquired a warrior-name.[48] Some Hun warriors may have been female, as Iranic-speaking societies utilized female commanders and combatants, but there is as yet no objective proof from Hunnish burials.[49] Procopius, who claims some females were found amongst the Sabir Xianbei, parallels a passage found in Odenathos, preserved and reiterated in many Roman sources, and therefore cannot be used as direct evidence.[50] However, the possibility cannot be entirely dismissed, as women could hold power in Hun society: John Malalas records that at one point the Sabirs were ruled by a queen named Boa/Boarez/Boareks, while Menander later notes that an Utigur woman named Akkagas ruled over territories in the Gok-Turkic

Qaganate.[51] In Attila's era there is the case of Bleda's former wife, who ruled a fiefdom within Attila's empire and whom Priscus calls a 'sovereign'.[52] Priscus' tale of the Greek merchant at Attila's court confirms that the Huns had slave soldiers as well.[53] Although they do not appear to have been present in exceptional numbers, Priscus' account suggests that they did have a significant presence. Slave soldiers in the Hun army likely filled a similar role as they had throughout history: serving both in battle and in the maintainence of their employers' equipment, horses and other furnishings. They also probably had logistical functions. Hun warriors themselves trained from childhood, particularly through hunting, the 'Scythian' method of which is noted by the *Strategikon* to have been exceptionally dangerous. The *Strategikon* places much emphasis on hunting as a form of training, and even states that the Scythian drill derives from their hunting methods.[54] Hunting of course taught the basic usage of weapons, horsemanship and coordination as a group.

The Romans adopted Hunnish and Alan warfare due to its effectiveness, which is now typically called 'lance-and-bow' warfare. This name is taken from the ability of Alan and Hunnish warriors to fight effectively with both the lance and the bow, switching back and forth between them in combat, while before this adoption the Roman cavalry typically separated lance-armed and bow-armed soldiers. The *Strategikon* records many advanced cavalry warfare tactics based on steppe warfare, which were probably adaptations of Alan and Hun tactics. Some drills, such as the so-called 'Scythian' and 'Alan' drills, may have been directly adopted from these peoples, as indicated by the names.[55] These include dividing cavalry regiments into designated *koursorses* and *defensorses*, and utilizing drilled formation wheels, feints and flanking manoeuvres, as well as other tactics.[56] Although the *Strategikon*'s manoeuvres were likely more advanced and more reliant on a professional, regimental army, there is no reason to see why the Huns, with their decimally organized army, could not have either used or developed precursor manoeuvres from which these strategies draw. Ignoring their large employment of Germanic infantry, and focusing on their cavalry tactics, the Huns probably fought similarly to most steppe nomads, including the Scythians, Parthians, Avars and of course the Mongols.[57] They did not make as extensive use of heavy shock lancers as the Alans and Sarmatians, but use of the lance played an important role in their tactics.[58] The Caucasian Huns are later attested as having cataphracts among their number.[59]

The Huns resorted to harassment of infantry and cavalry with their bows, which used trilobate diamond-shaped arrowheads.[60] These heads were capable of splintering shields of planked construction in about three shots, and as a result most shields in the late Roman era were faced with cow leather or gut, rather than linen as in earlier times.[61] The third cutting surface on these arrowheads would have also made them more effective against quilted linen and wool armour, which dominated the Eurasian steppes. However, considering that their opponents also used the same technology, and that shields had already been adapted to defend against these arrowheads, this likely did not give the Huns a significant advantage during set-piece battles. They would, however, have been very effective in small-scale raiding and ambushes. Emphasis on Hunnish archers and their skill is horrendously overstated, especially in popular culture. The abilities of modern Mongol competition archers do not make for a truly accurate comparison to the standard Hun warrior, or his ability to shoot in formation in the chaos of a battle. Man makes this comparison and emphasizes it heavily, but the Hun advantage was in organization; they were no better archers than their Sarmatian forebears.[62] Certainly the Hun horse-archer was well trained, as the *Strategikon* shows, but they were no superior in skill than those who came before or after them, and most would not have been much better than the average Roman horse-archer.

Against cavalry the Huns had an initial advantage until the adoption of lance-and-bow warfare by the Roman Empire. Although the Alans fought similarly, it is now accepted that they were defeated over the course of many engagements over a long period of time, and outcompeted by superior Hunnish organization, not defeated due to some new revolutionary military innovation. The Germanic and Roman cavalry were another matter. Eastern Germanic peoples like the *Greuthungi* are known to have employed some steppe cavalry, but they served more as support for infantry and as a screening force than a real cavalry arm.[63] The Romans had dedicated units of specific kinds of cavalry, but had yet to adopt lance-and-bow warfare until their widespread employment of Alans in the early fifth century, limiting the effectiveness of their dedicated cavalry arm.[64] Superior numbers of cavalry on the steppes, as well as superior tactics, meant that the Romans and Germanics could be outmanoeuvred.

However, set-piece battles were uncommon, and the Huns preferred not to engage in them unless they had a major advantage. The majority of Hunnish military operations are somewhat reflected in Aetius' and Litorius' campaigns, which involved aggressive attacks against enemy forces, usually before they could form a battle line.[65] In situations that could result in a set-piece battle, where two large armies were both present, the Huns would typically attack before the enemy, like Aetius and Litorius, could properly draw up their battle line.[66] This may not seem exceptional, but without a proper battle line, infantry could not form an effective shield wall against the Huns, which would make their horse-archery tactics more effective as there would be exploitable gaps. This would also create openings for lancers to exploit. However, the Huns preferred to lure enemy armies into unfavourable terrain and use ambush tactics, as reflected in the campaign of Peroz against the Hepthaltites.[67] They also employed such tactics later against the Umayyad Caliphate, hiding in the thick brush of the Caucasus and shooting at the Arabs. By similar means the Avars almost abducted the emperor Heraclius himself in 619.[68]

When in battle, they preferred to deploy in units of irregular width, joined into the appearance of a single line, with an even and dense front.[69] However, they often deployed in two or three lines, usually in deep columns.[70] The number of divisions in the army depended on terrain: Theophylact Simocatta shows the Avars dividing into twelve and fifteen divisions in two different engagements, and in one they were mistaken as a single line, as in the *Strategikon*.[71] In battle they would divide up and scatter into loose units, forming wedge formations as well as coherent battle lines.[72] This was likely an observation of cavalry tactics similar to those the Romans of the *Strategikon* later used themselves, which is simply poorly represented in Roman sources and thus poorly interpreted by modern authors. The Huns had complex tactics for battle, although preferred to achieve victory in a set-piece battle by methods such as encirclement or feigned retreat.[73] The Alan drill practised this oft-recorded mid-battle feigned retreat and counterattack, and based on contemporary descriptions it was their standard assault tactic against the front of an enemy line. If possible, they would surround the army and employ the Scythian drill.[74] Upon victory, the Huns would pursue their enemies relentlessly, cutting them down in the pursuit, and then proceed to harass and besiege the enemy camp until they gave in to Hunnish demands.[75] This is what set them apart, and why Hunnish victories were so devastating.

The Huns were also superb at siege warfare, and contrary to statements that they did not possess infantry or were encumbered when on foot from a life of riding, they proved themselves more than capable as foot soldiers, especially during sieges.[76] Priscus recounts a tale of the siege of Naissus, which records the Huns attacking the city with covered battering rams, ladders and using siege towers as a firing platform for their men.[77] Despite its parallels with Thucydides, his description holds up when compared to other sources. Procopius describes a siege by the Romans and the Sabir (Xianbei) Huns in the Lazic wars:

'Now when these *Sabeiroi* saw that the Romans were in despair and at a loss how to handle the situation, they devised a contrivance such as had never been conceived by anyone of the Romans or the Persians since men have existed, although there have always been and still are great numbers of engineers in both states. Although both sides have often been in need of this device throughout their history, in storming the walls of forts situated on rough and difficult ground, not one of them has had the idea that now occurred to these barbarians ... These *Sabeiroi* improvised a ram, not in the customary form, but using a new method of their own innovation. They did not put beams into this engine, either upright or transverse, but they bound together some thick rods and fitted them in place everywhere instead of the beams; then they covered the entire engine with hides and so kept the shape of a ram, and hung a single beam by loose chains, as is customary, in the centre of the engine. Its head was made sharp and covered over with iron like the barb of a missile, as it was intended to deal repeated blows to the circuit wall. They made the engine so light that it no longer had to be dragged or pushed along by the men inside, but forty men, who were also going to draw back the beam and thrust it forward against the wall, being inside the engine and concealed by hides, could carry the ram upon their shoulders with no difficulty.'

(Procopius, *The Wars of Justinian*, 8.11.27–31)[78]

The engine Procopius describes is a battering ram made of wicker covered in hide, rather than timbers in a framework. This account is quite similar to Priscus' description of the siege towers used at Naissus, as well as his description of the battering rams.[79] Gregory of Tours, via Sidonius, also confirms the Hun usage of battering rams.[80] In those cases, the rams and towers were also constructed of wicker with a cover of hides, with a pointed iron-tipped beam on a chain suspended from the middle.[81] This contrasts with what was evidently the typical fashion, which had four upright beams connected with eight horizontal beams, then covered with hide.[82] Procopius also notes that men with hooked pikes stood on either side of the engine to drag the rubble out of the way, and were also used to remove missiles, debris and liquid fire thrown by the Persians from the engine.[83] The Persians, having bought the services of the *Sabir* Huns, would rely on their ability to build such devices during the siege of Arkhaioupolis. It is in this passage that Procopius records that while the light infantry brought up the rams, the Huns would ride around the parapets and pin down the defenders with dense missile fire.[84] Rams would have been the primary tool of the Hunnish assaults, since late antique walls were constructed using a stone brick facing and a rubble core. When this outer facing was sufficiently worn down, the wall section would collapse, allowing the Huns to breach the walls. Roman authors noted that clay brick absorbed the impact of rams much better than stone, which may explain the decorative lines of clay bricks integrated into late Roman buildings, probably for earthquake resistance just as much as for battering rams in fortifications.[85] The siege towers of Priscus, which give added elevation, would have helped enhance this strategy of cover for the rams. It seems likely that some such towers were pulled by oxen, much like those employed in the siege of Rome by Vitiges in 537, although Priscus states they were pushed by men.[86] Ladders were also used to assault walls, although they seem to have had less emphasis placed on them than rams by Roman authors, likely for literary reasons. The Huns themselves, being mostly cavalry, would not typically have manned the siege equipment – in Procopius' accounts the engines themselves are manned by Romans and Persians, and supported by light infantry like the *Heruli* or *Daylami*. Similarly, the Huns used Germanic vassals in this role, and the Germanic majority in their population made for a predominately mixed army.

The Hunnish Vassal States

The trans-Rhenian and trans-Danubian peoples are relatively poorly attested in the written sources during this period, and it is difficult to treat them with the depth given to some of the federated militaries of Gaul and Spain. As a result, this section cannot be as comprehensive as that given to the Roman allies, and much of it therefore relies on sources from after the collapse of Attila's empire or on archaeological evidence. However, many of Attila's vassals who participated in the battle can be identified thanks to both Sidonius Apollinaris and Jordanes, who list the participants.[87] These lists need to be scrutinized, as the Romans had a tradition of simplifying, generalizing or using specific names in emulation of Herodotus. Sidonius, for example, uses Herodotus' *Geloni* quite often.[88] Luckily, in Sidonius' case his choice of latinized ethnonyms is carefully selected, from both contemporary and ancient *gentes*, in order to incorporate them into the meter. Sidonius states:

> 'After the warlike Rugian follows the fierce Gepid, with the Gelonian accompanying; the Burgundian compels the Scirian; forward rush the Hun, Bellonotian, Neurian, Bastarnian, Thuringian, Bructerian, or the Frank, he who[se land] is brushed by the water of the Neckar.'
> (Sidonius Apollinaris, *Carmina*, 7.321–25)[89]

Once more, much of this cannot be taken literally: as E.A. Thompson noted, the *Bellonoti* are a corruption of Valerius Flaccus' *Balloniti*, while the *Neuri, Bastarni, Bructeri* and *Geloni* had all disappeared centuries ago.[90] These peoples were merely a part of the Roman literary listing tradition, but Sidonius does adequately incorporate real peoples into the meter, including the *Gepidae, Burgundi, Sciri, Toringi* and *Franci*, as well as the Huns themselves.[91] Jordanes adds the Goths of Valamir, Vidimer and Thiudimer to that list, collectively known as the *Amali* Goths.[92] However, it should be noted that the trans-Danubian Goths were far more complex, as will be discussed shortly. Not listed but probably present were the *Heruli, Suebes* and the *Sadages*, possibly the *Sclaveni* and *Antes*, as well as some Sarmatians and Alans. Although often called 'German' or 'Germanic' barbarians, this modern invention has little to do with the peoples who invaded the Roman world in the fifth century. These peoples were bound more by familial ties than the literary tropes of Tacitus or an overarching language family of which these individual groups had absolutely no knowledge.[93] As a result, familial ties to the Hun ruling class would have played an important role in the relationship between these peoples in the Hun Empire, and to their prominence under Attila.

The first people mentioned in both Sidonius' and Jordanes' lists are the *Gepidae*, or the Gepids. The *Suda* also names Attila of 'the race of the Gepid Huns' in its garbled abridgment of Priscus.[94] The Gepids were a Germanic people whose burials dominate the D3 archaeological period after the Hun collapse in the Middle Danubian region.[95] In the fourth century they are believed to have lived in the Upper Carpathians on the Upper Tisza and the Kris/Coros rivers, north of the *Tervingi* culture. Rapid changes in material culture make it possible to monitor the rise of their identity and locate them in Upper Transylvania in the early fifth century, when they began to come under Hun domination and expanded into the former territories of the *Tervingi*.[96] Etymology has attempted to associate the Gepids to the *Tervingi* and other Gothic groups as Gothic offshoots, but Goffart shows there is little if any evidence to support a connection.[97] Although Jordanes' political propaganda places the Gepids of Ardaric and Valamir's Goths as virtual equals of Attila, and Christiansen convincingly expresses his doubts on whether Ardaric even existed, scattered evidence suggests the Gepids did play a very prominent role.[98] Their association with Attila's Huns has even led Kim to suggest that Ardaric was himself a Hun, along with much of the ruling class, although he has received criticism for these claims.[99] Ardaric was praised by Attila 'above all the other chieftains', except for Valamir of course, although this is likely just pro-Gothic propaganda on Jordanes' part.[100] However, Huns did play prominent roles in the Gepid power structure, including Attila's son, Giesmos, who was married to Ardaric's daughter.[101] Princely burials among the Gepids of the first half of the fifth century can be identified by the significant quantities of gold and silver artifacts, as well as the presence of composite bows which denoted middle and upper-class warrior burials. The presence of diadems and bronze cauldrons were also prominent in high-status burials, showing the considerable Hun influence in their society.[102] Mingarelli argues that Hun influence may have led to the development of a dualist kingship structure within the Gepid state based on the Hunnish model, after the Battle of Nedao. He also notes that there are plenty of examples where this did not occur, however, and Gepid state structure and stratification remains conjectural.[103]

The other primary group associated with Attila, or at least considered such due to the emphasis placed upon them by Jordanes, were the *Amali* Goths. Generally speaking, the Gothic groups present at the Battle of the Catalaunian Fields or under Hun domination are often just lumped together as 'Ostrogoths', but this does not accurately reflect the reality of the Goths under the Hun Empire. Heather notes that there were at least six groups outside of the Roman Empire in the Hunnic sphere, including the *Amali* of Valamir, the Goths of Bigelis, the Goths following Dengzich, the Goths of Triarius settled in Thrace in 470 (who may have been the same as those settled in 421–27) and two groups in the Crimea.[104] The *Sadages* may have been related to or were the same as the *Sadagarii* settled with Candac's Alans, and based on Jordanes' claims of ancestry, may have been a seventh and eighth groups of Goths.[105] There is some debate about whether the generically labelled 'Goths' were all separate groups, as for example Kim thinks that the *Amali* were the Goths following Dengzich, although Kim's interpretation of ethnically Hunnic-led and Hunnic-loyal Germanics is problematic.[106] However, Hunnic representatives within these societies are evidenced by nomad princely graves within the clusters of fifth-century Chernjacov burials.[107] Not all of them were under Hun dominion either, as Heather thinks the Crimean groups (the *Tetraxitae* and the Goths of Dory) were independent and the Thracian Goths were Roman *foederati*.[108] In all of this, the *Amali* seem to have been a relatively insignificant group of Gothic aristocrats who killed and overthrew Vintharius around 450. According to Heather's interpretation,

Valamir, who is equated with Balamber, married Vintharius's daughter, ousted his son, Beremud, and reconciled with Gesemund, consolidating several Gothic groups.[109] After his success, the Amali gained significant power, although whether they were as dominant as Jordanes suggests is open to question, especially considering he thought of both the Gepids and *Amali* as Goths and therefore both had to be right-hand men of Attila.[110] This of course excludes competing dynasties, such as the two later mentioned groups of Bigelis and those under Dengzich. Goths were populous in the Carpathian and Danubian regions, and there must have been prominent groups other than the *Amali* during Attila's time. Heather thinks that Valamir came to power in the region after the Battle of Nedao, and was simply one of many sub-units of Goths following Attila before his death.[111] Jordanes also abbreviates the circumstances of their settlement, stating that they received lands in Pannonia under Marcian after Nedao, but that may have been the mere legitimization of their settlement.[112] The area around their capital Bassianae (Donji Petrovci) had been evacuated after Sirmium's destruction and cessation in 441–43, and Attila seems to have set them up in the buffer region after the acquisition.[113] Goths were also present on the banks of the Dniepr near the forest zone, archaeologically evidenced by burials of the elite classes, which Kazanski suggests could be equated with Vintharius' kingdom. Other concentrations of late Chernjacov burials are found in Volhynia and near Olbia, suggesting Gothic groups settled in those areas as well.[114]

Next on Sidonius' list, brushing aside the extinct *Geloni* and the already mentioned Burgundians, are the *Sciri*. The status of the *Sciri* in the Hunnish Empire is seemingly well recorded: Edekon/Edeko or Edica, possibly an ethnic Hun and the ambassador to Attila's court, was king of the *Sciri* at the time, which suggests that the *Sciri* had resisted Hun invasion and thus had their aristocracy replaced.[115] Considering the actions of the *Sciri* under Uldin in the Balkans, it very well could have been a punishment for one or more attempted revolts as a vassal state.[116] There were at least three groups that can be bunched together under the name of *Sciri*: the *Sciri* themselves, the *Angisciri* of Jordanes and the *Torcilingi*. Wolfram proposes that the *Torcilingi* were the ruling class of the *Sciri*, like the *Iuthungi* and the *Alamanni*, a conclusion which is now widely accepted.[117] The *Angisciri* were a group mentioned under Dengzich in the 460s, tied to his Huns and who participated in their war against the Goths in support of the *Sadages*.[118] They are said to have lived along the Lower Danube, and may have been separate from the *Sciri* of Edeco and Odoacer, as both Kim and Maenchen-Helfen believe.[119] Jordanes groups the *Sciri* of Odoacer with the *Heruli* and the *Rugi*, suggesting they were positioned probably somewhere above Pannonia on the Middle Danube, but they were not present among the revolting vassals Jordanes lists at Nedao.[120] Both groups of *Sciri* appear to have remained initially loyal to the Huns, and the *Angisciri* seem to have been a splinter of the main body that retreated with the Huns to the Lower Danube after the Battle of Nedao.[121] The main body of the *Sciri* took their place in the middle Alföld region between the Danube and the Tisza, and they may have been settled there prior to the Battle of Nedao.[122] The *Sciri* would play a prominent role later in the century under Edeco and Odoacer, fighting the Goths of Valamir and eventually deposing the last western Roman emperor.

The *Heruli* have also been another conundrum in the sources, as there appear to have been two groups: Hydatius mentions some crossed into Gaul in 406 with the Vandals, Alans and Suebes. Steinacher rejects the conclusion of a separate western Herul group, but it is reasonable to suspect Hydatius' information is accurate as *Heruli* were settled close to the Pannonian region at the time, from whence these other groups came.[123] Halsall proposes these *Heruli* later joined with *Heruli* that had migrated with the Goths of Alaric when they entered Gaul, and integrated into their kingdom in Aquitaine.[124] These may be the *Heruli* who attacked northern Spain in the later fifth century, as there was no separate group living near the North Sea, although they may have also been attached to Majorian's army as well.[125] However, the rest of the *Heruli*, situated on the Middle Danube, found themselves under Hun dominion. They appear to have been closely linked to the *Sciri* and *Rugi*, as well as the Suebes of Hunimund, and so must have been situated just west of the Danube bend, established in the eastern *Wienviertel* and southern Moravia, extending east to the north of the Hun-dominated Hungarian steppes to border the Gepids at the little Carpathians.[126] The *Heruli* are described by Jordanes as fighting as 'light armed warriors', which when taken in the context of the passage, could suggest they were operating not as light infantry but light cavalry, as they are listed just after the 'heavy armed' Alans. Procopius mentions Herul cavalry served at Daras.[127] Traditional Germanic cavalry consisted of usually javelin-armed skirmishers and lancers, although with Hun influence may very well have included horse archers too.[128] However, Hydatius and Procopius describe them as able light infantry too, who protected themselves only with a shield and either a quilted gambeson or heavy kaftan.[129] The Heruls in past scholarship have been treated not as a *gens*, but a military brotherhood, inviting comparison with the Vikings, but this outdated scholarship has since been rejected.[130] They had a significant kingdom on the Middle Danube that was closely intertwined with those around it via Odoacer, king of the *Sciri*, and other familial ties.

The other people with whom the *Sciri* of Odoacer were associated were the *Rugi*, whom Wolfram believes to have entered the stage by establishing federate status with Aetius or Valentinian III around 454–55, just after Nedao.[131] Their position on the frontier was tenuous: Goffart argues that the Middle Danubian region was dominated by too many armed groups for stability and not enough production to maintain those positioned there after Attila's collapse.[132] During Attila's empire, the Rugians had found stability through vassalage and marriage alliance. Heather argues that the *Rugi* and other groups under Hun occupation had developed a strong sense of identity which allowed them to persist through their constant incorporation into other kingdoms, which Goffart reflects in stating their hostility towards other groups after the break-up of Attila's empire.[133] The *Rugi* are attested to have grown in power under their King Flaccitheus, but these events are of unsure date and the formation of a kingdom of the *Rugi* does not appear to have occurred until the 460s. Eugippius' statement regarding the hostility of the Goths of Lower Pannonia towards him suggests this occurred around the same time as the war with the neighbouring *Sciri*, *Heruli* and other peoples in the mid-460s.[134] It is entirely possible that like the Goths, there were several separate groups of *Rugi* under the Hun Empire. Priscus tells of a group of *Roubous* under a certain Valips who attack the town of Noviodunum at the mouth of the Danube, but they likely cannot be equated with the *Rugi* of Noricum as some authors have.[135] Gordon dates these events to 435 or 441, being part of a group trying to flee Hun domination or part of Attila's war in 441, but this seems unlikely and it would be more in character with Priscus' description of turmoil on the Danube in the 460s.[136] They could very well be a separate group, if they are *Rugi* at all. Some *Rugi* are attested by Jordanes to have settled near Bizye in the 460s, although these may also be confused with Priscus' *Roubous*.[137]

The *Thoringi*, or Thuringians, are first attested alongside the *Rugi* by Vegetius in the late fourth century AD, being famed for the quality of their horses. The culture commonly associated with the Thuringians can be identified by brooch finds ranging from the *Thuringer Walde* to the Elbe, from Hanover to Leipzig, with outliers towards Berlin and another concentration in Bohemia, the distribution of which can arguably identify the core region of Thuringian settlement. It has been argued that brooch finds in the Middle Rhine region represent encroachment and contestation in the region in the mid-fifth to late fifth centuries.[138] They also evidently exerted influence as far south as the Danube.[139] These Franks who contested the region are likely the same ones recorded by Sidonius, his *Bructeri* and the Franks of the Neckar. Allegedly, in 450 the king of the Thuringians was Bisinus, who gave Childeric eight years of refuge in his kingdom during his exile. Bisinus was allegedly married to a Lombard wife named Menia, suggesting close connections between the *Thoringi* and the *Langobardi*. Indeed, the concentration of Thuringian-associated brooches and other artefacts in the region of Bohemia may be representative of a trade relationship with the region, one in which the Lombards were located.[140] The Huns allegedly subjected the Lombards according to the Lombard origin myths, deposing their leader Agelmund and replacing him with Laimichio.[141] It was probably around the same time that they subjected the Thuringians, likely under the campaigns of Rua and Octar, that this occurred. If the theory of Childeric's relationship as the older brother of Chlodio's offspring is to be believed, then the Thuringians and the peoples around them – namely the Neckar and *Bructeri* Franks – were all at the forefront of the political debate on the Rhine that led to the invasion. Goffart argues that the ability of the Thuringian families to form these long-distance political connections through marriage was the most noteworthy development of these peoples.[142]

The Size of the Invasion Army

It should first be noted that an attempt in determining the size of the Hunnish invasion force carries with it several problems. The army of the Huns was certainly significant in size, with ancient authors claiming as many as 500,000 and scholars suggesting as little as 30,000.[143] The only source that provides a somewhat realistic figure is the *Suda*, which in its garbled abridgement of Priscus states that it numbered 'tens of thousands'.[144] These exaggerated numbers can be explained by the observations of the author of the *Strategikon*, who states that large numbers of remounts, as well as the arrangement of an army, can make the reporting of accurate numbers difficult.[145] Roman accounts of the sizes of their armies from around the period must be utilized and combined, along with modern research, to attempt to provide an accurate estimate of Attila's forces.

It is commonly accepted that Huns relied heavily on cavalry warfare, although this has been challenged by scholars such as Lindner. Despite this, the evidence continues to point towards a predominantly cavalry-centred Hunnish force, with both Lindner's arguments for an infantry-centred army and counter-arguments against a cavalry army for the 'ethnic Huns' themselves remaining largely unaccepted.[146] However, Lindner's scepticism of the size of a cavalry force the Huns could field is rightfully founded, as the ancient Hungarian plains were not the sprawling grasslands encountered today, but more a smattering of pasture intermixed with swamps. Grassland was vital for the Hun army, as emphasized by the *Strategikon* of Maurice, which advises attacks in February or March against the Huns when their mounts are weak, or summer campaigns of burning the grassland to starve their flocks and mounts.[147] Lindner places a maximum estimate of 15,000 cavalry for Attila's Huns based on the size of the ancient Hungarian plain and assuming a value of ten horses per family, although it seems Marco Polo's eighteen horses per family may be more accurate.[148] Therefore, the Huns under Attila could likely field a fighting force of approximately 8,000–15,000 steppe cavalry. However, this is only half of the Hunnish Empire, which controlled lands extending to the Don-Kuban region, with the *Akatir* Huns being centred north of the Crimea. Agathias records a force of 7,000 *Kutrigur* Huns from the Pontic region ravaging Thrace in 558, while Procopius states 12,000 *Kutrigur* Huns were sent to aid the Gepids against the Lombards.[149] The *Kutrigur* Huns were half of the continuation of Attila's empire, and ruled over the *Akatir* Huns who had lost their status in the late fifth to mid-sixth century. Both peoples were settled west of the Sea of Azov.[150] Although much later, this estimate of 7,000–12,000 men may still be useful for an estimate of the relative military capacity of the nomads in the region. When the eastern Huns of the Dniester and Don are combined with the western Huns of modern Hungary, Dacia and Wallachia, then the total Hunnish military capacity could be estimated at 15,000–27,000 men. This estimate is somewhat supported by the contemporary account of Socrates, who states that Octar led a force greater than

10,000 men.[151] However, this was the Hunnish core of Attila's army, and Lindner is indeed correct in assuming that the rest of it was overwhelmingly dominated by Germanic infantry.

Although some of the peoples Attila ruled were larger, organized states, according to Delbruck the majority of the barbarian groupings in Europe likely could not field armies larger than the thousands range.[152] It is known the Goths fielded a significant portion of the army; Heather suggests a possible fighting force of 10,000–15,000 troops for the *Amali* Goths in 454, when they fought off Hunnish attempts to reassert their domination.[153] This may be a bit large, as Theodoric is recorded as having only 6,000 men in 479/480, but it will work for the combined forces of all the Gothic groups under Attila.[154] It is therefore likely the Gepids made up another bulky portion of Attila's army, possibly also around 15,000 men. Considering the other tribes, Socrates writes that in AD 430, 3,000 right-bank Burgundians resisted the Hunnish King Octar; for once a reasonable army size is given, and this could be in the range of the number of forces contributed for the campaign of 451.[155] Procopius records a force of 3,000 and 1,500 *Heruli* fighting on either side of the Lombard-Gepid conflict in 549, and Heather believes the Heruls may have been able to field 5,000–10,000 men before the first split in 511.[156] The *Rugi*, *Sciri* and *Heruli*, along with presumably Italic forces, were able to field a significant number of men against Theodoric in 489, probably somewhere around 15,000–20,000.[157] Just using Heather's rough estimate for the *Heruli*, it seems likely that they may have each supplied around 5,000 men to Attila's army, although the *Sciri* might have been towards the upper, 10,000-strong end of this range due to the fact that enough were present to be able to split off a smaller force. A number of Franks also supported Attila, although fewer within the empire supported the elder brother, but Atilla did have groups to draw on outside the empire; we will ascribe this combination of Franks, the Neckar Franks and *Bructeri* a figure of 5,000. The Thuringians and Lombards must have been able to field a similar amount, again possibly 5,000 each. Like the Romans, the Huns themselves seem to have provided the central bulk of the army at around 27,000 men.[158]

Adding this up would put Attila's army at a staggering, theoretical 100,000 men. Mobilization in Hun society was all-inclusive due to the high mobility of horse-dwelling nomads, meaning the Huns likely fielded near the theoretical maximum of their forces.[159] However, much like the Romans and their allies, it often escapes mention that the Huns and their vassals also suffered from deserters, attrition and the other issues that plague armies. Desertion in particular was a big issue in enforcing strict discipline within the Hun armies, and based on the terms found within Hunnish treaties as well as for the later Avars, large numbers of fugitives were a serious problem.[160] Likewise, the Huns could not have taken all of their settled forces into Gaul, lest all of *barbaricum* remain empty. Therefore, we will apply the approximate 70 per cent figure used in the prior chapter to Attila's vassals, bringing it down to a still exceptional 71,100 men.[161] Attila's combined forces must have numbered in this range to have matched the combined Roman armies at the Utus mentioned in Chapter 1, which totalled a similar size. An army this large would have been exceedingly difficult to organize and coordinate: the baggage train alone would have stretched for kilometres, not to mention reserve horses, camp followers and other facets of barbarian logistics. Malchus records a wagon train of 2,000 wagons for a large army of possibly as many as 25,000 Goths, and Attila's must have been almost three times larger.[162] It is therefore no wonder the primary sources thought Attila's army was so massive, and could easily have been perceived as much larger than it actually was. Fyfe shows that this would have significantly hampered Attila's movement in his campaigning, which explains why Hunnic psychological warfare tactics had to be implemented, otherwise an entire campaigning season would conclude before any significant impact could be achieved.[163]

Chapter 4

The Campaign of 451

A ccording to the traditional chronology, Attila began his campaigning season. in February or March 451, in time to arrive at and sack Divodurum Mediomatricum (Metz) on 7 April.[1] There is some issue with starting the invasion at this date, as the detail comes to us via Hydatius, who probably received his information by word of mouth. Hydatius' work isn't entirely contemporary either, his chronicle being completed about 469 but having been started at an unknown date.[2] However, in support of Hydatius' claim, Gregory of Tours also retells this date, saying Attila reached Divodurum on Easter eve and sacked it on Easter itself.[3] In order to arrive at Divodurum on 6 April, Attila likely would have had to launch his campaign in February and breach the Rhine in March. Late February was the time at which the Hunnish cattle and horses were at their weakest, and it therefore seems very unlikely Attila would have mobilized in the late winter.[4] The Huns had to wait for their livestock to recover and collect their eastern vassals before they could proceed west. Therefore, Attila likely did not begin his campaign until the end of March at the earliest, and probably set out in April. That he allegedly sacked Divodurum on 7 April can probably be explained away by the two Christian scholars trying to emphasize his barbarity in his ignorance of the Christian holy day.[5] However, it cannot entirely be ruled out that Divodurum was indeed sacked on 7 April. If it occurred on Easter, this would have allowed word of the event to be easily transmitted with a semblance of accuracy, as those who reported it would have seen it as more notable and therefore easier to remember. April, however, was about the date at which Attila's forces set out from central Europe.

Rather than in March as usually presumed, by late April and having acquired his western vassals en route, Attila had reached the Rhine. Sidonius claims that Attila crossed by felling the forests on the shores and ferrying his army over to the left bank with boats, but this seems unlikely.[6] If anything like this occurred, it is possible that Attila could have constructed pontoon bridges for his army and baggage train to cross, which may be supported by both Priscus' account of the siege of Naissus and Vegetius' advice on crossing rivers.[7] An enticing thought is that it may even be possible that Attila had one or more traditional wooden bridges constructed specifically for the purpose of his invasion, an engineering feat matching that performed by Caesar centuries before.[8] However, it is more likely that both Priscus' and Sidonius' accounts could be a reference to the

Persian crossing of the Hellespont in 481 BC.[9] Attila had large numbers of cavalry and a significant wagon train accompanying his army, meaning he would have been forced to capture at least one of the Roman bridges which were typically guarded by fortresses on both banks of the Rhine, or construct pontoon bridges to circumvent these fortresses. Furthermore, like in 447, Attila wanted to cripple Roman military capacity and their sway over the local Germanics, meaning he would have to quickly overpower the *limitanei* fortresses and city garrisons. He also needed a clear exit across the Rhine when his campaign was finished. With these logistical and strategic concerns, Attila would have had to pick a fortress and crossing that was placed along one of the major Roman highways in order that he might travel down river along the Rhine, eliminating the garrisons before proceeding further into Gaul. The Roman Rhine presented Attila with plenty of options in this regard.

The first seriously fortified cities Attila came upon were Mogontiacum, Borbetomagus and Argentoratum, now known as Mainz, Worms and Strasburg, all of which are alleged to have been devastated by the Huns.[10] Argentoratum had the most up-to-date fortifications, having been converted from a legionary fortress under Julian, while Mogontiacum and Borbetomagus seem to have had far fewer projecting towers and larger circuits, making them more difficult to defend.[11] These cities were under nominal Roman control, and the *limitanei* in this region were mostly a mix of Romans and local Germanics, so the cities likely had some sort of a garrison.[12] The Roman highway system along the Rhine runs north from Vindonissa (Windisch) and Augusta Raurica (Augst) to Argentoratum, Borbetomagus and Mogontiacum. Eventually it reaches Colonia (Cologne) and then Tricesima (Xanten), the former of which Attila is also alleged to have sacked.[13] Attila could have crossed at a number of points, but he needed his rear open for his eventual retreat at the end of the campaigning season. Man thinks he crossed at both Argentoratum and Confluentes (Koblenz), with his forces meeting at Augusta Treverorum (Trier).[14] However, this is unlikely as it would have been most logical for him to cross at Argentoratum, sacking that city, and then march up the Rhine eliminating local forces as he went. A burial dating to the later D2 period, or about AD 420–50, is known from Mundolsheim just north of Strasburg, that according to Kazanski likely belonged to a nomadic aristocrat.[15] It is possible that this may support Attila's crossing at Argentoratum, with the individual having died during the siege and being quickly interred outside the city.[16] Alternatively, Attila could have also crossed at several points, linking up with his forces as he advanced downstream along the Rhine. This would have cut down on siege time, as his army was large enough that he could have attacked and quickly taken several cities at once, even if divided into two or more columns. Alongside Argentoratum, Attila sacked Borbetomagus and Mogontiacum, but had he proceeded further north to Colonia that would have been counterproductive, since it would only lead him to the long route down the northern coast of France and not to the major Roman military and administrative centres in the heart of Gaul. Therefore, he must have turned west at Mogontiacum into Gaul, on the road through Augusta Treverorum and Divodurum to Durocortorum (Rheims).[17]

The hagiographies of the local saints, summarized mainly by Thomas Hodgkin, confuse the events of the invasion of Gaul.[18] Hodgkin notes many of the cities listed were compiled in Hainault in the fourteenth century, while most of the hagiographies are not contemporary, and the ones that are contemporary rearrange the lives and death dates of the saintly figures so they might coincide with Attila's onslaught to perform their divine deeds. If these sources were accepted purely at face value, then Attila would have sacked virtually every city and town in northern Gaul barring only a small handful, including some as impossibly far south as Narbona (Narbonne). Yet in the timeline of his invasion he certainly could not have done so, despite the remarkable speed of his advance. This is why authors such as Man and Hughes propose that Attila split off a small force to harass northern Gaul and bring the Franks to submission, while his main army proceeded towards the Alans of Aurelianum.[19] This would solve the issue of interpreting these hagiographies, in that the tales preserve some historical truth, while corroborating the archaeological destruction layers from this time period which clarify what cities were attacked.[20] Kim, whose interpretation will be discussed later, suggests that Attila left Odoacer behind after his invasion to manage his new vassals and harass the remaining Romans and Alans. His interpretation, based on the premise of Roman defeat, doesn't seem likely, but it is entirely possible that this force Attila sent to harass the Franks and northern Gaul may have been led by Odoacer and composed of *Sciri*, who are present in Sidonius' list of participants.[21] These forces were sent north to Colonia, taking the road west to Atuatuca Tungrorum (Tongres), allowing for Gregory's confusion with the account of St Servatius of Tongeren.[22] They eventually went through the region of Turnacum (Tournai), Cambriacum (Cambrai) and Samarobriva (Amiens) before reaching Caesaromagus (Beauvais), ravaging the countryside as they went but avoiding the cities themselves.[23] When Attila engaged Aetius and eventually retreated from Gaul, these forces were cut off, and Odoacer and the *Sciri* would play an important role in the events of Gaul during the late fifth century. However, it should be noted that Goffart thinks Odoacer's presence in Gaul is contestable at best.[24]

By the end of May, Attila had advanced rapidly across Gaul, his massive army overpowering local garrisons and plundering surrendered towns. Like in the Balkans, Attila probably practised a policy of raze and receive, where by annihilating one city other cities would open themselves to his forces for a comparatively 'light' sacking. During this process the citizens would be taken out onto the plains while the town was plundered, which would also explain Priscus' tale of the piles of bones outside Naissus.[25] Man thinks Augusta Treverorum was bypassed, but it seems more likely the city opened its gates without a fight.[26] Its dated, second-century walls were also too long to adequately defend without a large garrison, much like those of

Divodurum.[27] Most of the cities Attila came across seem to have surrendered, until he came to Divodurum, with its 60-hectare circuit walls: the largest in late Roman Gaul. Their significant length may have been counterproductive to the city's defence, which would have had a limited garrison.[28] There was a single regiment dedicated to its defence, a Roman *pseudocomitatenses* legion called the *Prima Flavia Metis*, which would have been no match for an army of 70,000. According to Gregory:

> 'The Huns migrated from Pannonia and laid waste the countryside as they advanced. They came to the town of Metz, so people say, on Easter eve (6 April). They burned the town to the ground, slaughtered the populace with the sharp edge of their swords and killed the priests of the lord in front of their holy altars. No building in the town remained unburnt except the oratory of Saint Stephen, Levite and first martyr.'
> (Gregory of Tours, *Decem Libri Historiarum*, 2.6)[29]

Divodurum was annihilated but for Saint Stephen's oratory, so it would seem Attila razed this city in the hopes of the next few opening their gates to him.[30] This prevented Attila from being bogged down in long sieges and kept his forces mobile, reducing attrition. The former capital of Augusta Treverorum, Divodurum and the military centre at Durocortorum were all sacked, while Attila seems to have bypassed the fortified town of Senones (Sens).[31] Nicasius is said to have been struck down by Attila himself. Hodgkin justifies the account, reasoning that the fact bishops had become local administrators and collected significant wealth made them prime targets.[32] From Durocortorum, Attila likely marched south-east through Durocatalaunum (Chalons-en-Champagne), then Iatinon (Meaux) and Metlosedum (Melun), before taking the road on to Aurelianum (Orleans).[33] This would appear to approach but then bypass Paris, concurring with the tale of Saint Genevieve who allegedly saved Paris with the help of St Germanus of Auxerre, the city's inhabitants saving themselves through prayer and turning Attila instead towards Orleans.[34]

The Siege of Orleans

Before early June, Attila approached the city of Aurelianum, which had been bequeathed to the Loire Alans in 442 under Goar.[35] There are several accounts of Attila's siege of Aurelianum: the primary two accounts are by Jordanes and in the *Vita Aniani*, who give two different tales, while Gregory also briefly mentions it.[36] Of these, the *Vita Aniani* is more or less corroborated by Gregory, and is believed to be based on the incomplete history of Sidonius Apollinaris.[37] According to Jordanes, Attila never even attacked the city, Aetius and Theodoric having arrived first due to their suspicion of Sangiban, whose realm included Aurelianum, throwing up earthen fortifications.[38] The *Vita Aniani* recounts that with Bishop Anianus having returned to the city, Attila laid siege and prepared a final assault, which was withheld for three days due to torrential rain. At some point during the siege, the *Vita Aniani* claims a captured bishop was shot down by one of the defenders on the walls. On the fourth day, 14 June, Attila was about to breach the walls with rams when Aetius and his army alleviated the besiegers.[39] Gregory states that the city was attacked with battering rams and corroborates the *Vita Aniani*, claiming that Anianus prayed and then told the people to pray and look for aid three times, on the last of which they saw the arrival of Aetius just as the walls were about to be breached.[40] As usual, Jordanes is the one who is suspect: comparing the Catalaunian Fields to Marathon, he portrayed Aurelianum in the same light as Athens, where neither the Persians nor the Huns reached the city.

The Alan defence of Aurelianum may have been quite a spectacle. The Alans were heavy cavalrymen and sieges were not part of their usual repertoire, although since many had served as Roman soldiers they would likely have been familiar with the tactics and able to capably defend the city. As mounted steppe warriors, however, the Alans may have a historical parallel in the Athenian cavalry and Scythian archers recruited to defend the north wall of Athens, albeit they are recorded serving as a police force.[41] The city was well fortified, having a 22-hectare perimeter with projecting towers, last updated in the late fourth century AD. The walls were similar in appearance to others in the region, including surviving examples that can be found at nearby Sens and Le Mans. A small portion of the wall survives in the foundations of the city cathedral, showing the late fourth-century construction.[42] Although the city's main structures were certainly protected by its fortifications, many of the city's inhabitants likely lived in housing and other structures outside the walls – the so called *suburbanus*.[43] Furthermore, the local Alans were quite spread out, their presence in the region attested by the D2 Pontic plate brooches ranging across large swathes of the Loire and Saone valleys.[44] Residing in villages in the fields along the Loire and Saone, they may have retreated towards the city's protective escarpments or other fortified centres. As a result, there was likely more population than could be contained within the city circuit. Jordanes' claim regarding the erection of defensive earthworks is likely true, as like most Roman fortifications the city's walls had trenches and traps surrounding them which could be hastily repaired in the event of an invasion.[45] Furthermore, it is entirely possible that an earth and timber palisade may have been constructed around the extramural city to both contain the Alan livestock and delay Attila's attack. A few cities were also known to have defensive forewalls: most notably Constantinople, but those from Massilia (Marseilles), Aquileia and Thessalonica also date to the late fourth and fifth centuries, with that of Aquileia being made of turf like Aurelianum's.[46] Alternatively, the earthen wall may not have been outside the city, but instead composed a rampart against the interior of the circuit wall, in order to make it resistant to battering rams as Vitruvius states. Although a possibility, this was exceedingly rare in late antiquity due to the interior space requirements.[47] If the city had an outer earthwork and timber palisade that had been erected to protect the extramural districts, then mounted cavalry would have been an effective harassing force that could rapidly respond to breaches or other trouble spots during the siege. However, a wood and earth palisade would have easily been surmounted by Attila's forces, and the majority of the city's defence must have focused on the Roman walls. If the city had a Roman garrison, which seems likely, the protruding towers may have had defensive artillery including *ballistae*, like the one found at Orsova, and the stone-throwing *onager*.[48] The walls would have made for a formidable defence, bristling with both soldiers and artillery, but Attila had overcome these obstacles before at Viminacium, Singidunum, Naissus and other major fortified cities in the East.

It seems likely that Attila did besiege the city, and Sidonius records that he breached the walls themselves, but the city inside was left untouched.[49] Stone and brick-faced rubble core walls of several metres in thickness would have been relatively impervious to contemporary torsion artillery, provided Attila had any, although they were useful against battlements, the upper sections of towers and the defenders. The focus of the attack, however, would have been on the susceptible but heavily defended gatehouses, primarily utilizing rams.[50] Attila had at his disposal ladders, covered siege towers and covered battering rams, which could be transported past the earthen defences that surrounded the city.[51] The problem lies with the *Vita Aniani*'s dating: the siege of Aurelianum would not have been a simple affair, and it likely would have taken some time just to prepare a strong assault. If Attila's final assault was supposed to occur on 10 June, it seems likely that he had arrived at Aurelianum at least a week before, if not longer, for him to have had the time needed to construct the large numbers of siege machines Priscus recounts in his comparable tale of the siege of Naissus. Rain from 10–13 June would have hampered Attila's assault for another few days, since his equipment would be saturated, so the claim that he was actively besieging the city on 14 June doesn't seem likely if this account is correct.[52] Sidonius claims the city walls were breached, but it is uncertain whether this was in the final assault or before: the *Vita Aniani* is supposed to have been based on his lost panegyric on Anianus, which was based on his lost history of the war. Anianus' involvement is somewhat overstated, although like the later Sidonius at Clermont, he probably played an important role in the defence.[53] It seems the tales of divine intervention preserved in the *Vita Aniani* confuse the whole account. However, it would make far more sense to claim that Attila gave up and the city was saved by Anianus via prayer, than if the city was rescued by Aetius, although the portrayal of Anianus as an envoy might have necessitated Aetius' involvement. Where Gregory claims it was saved by Anianus' prayer alone, the *Vita Aniani* states instead that Aetius and Thorismund attacked Attila's army as it was beginning to enter the city.[54] It was certainly in the profile of Aetius' style of command to ambush a besieging army, so it is impossible to say

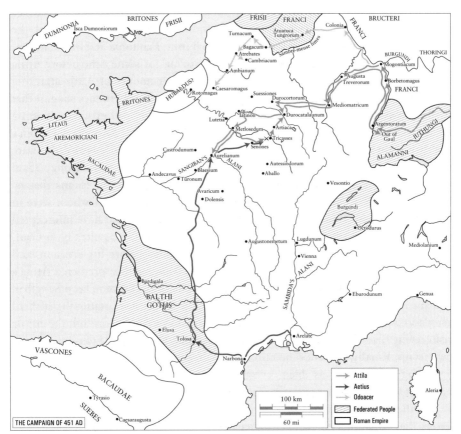

Map 5. The Campaign of 451.

whether Attila withdrew on his own accord or not with any surety.[55] It can only be said that at some point on 14 June, Attila and his forces withdrew from the city, and Aetius' army arrived.

The Roman Counteroffensive

At some point in 451, Aetius received word that Attila was collecting and mobilizing his armies for a new invasion. This may have come from internal spies at Attila's court such as the secretaries Constantius and Orestes, other members of the Roman embassy or even as rumour spread down from Pannonia and into Italy, but it is fairly clear that the Romans had been preparing for some time before Attila attacked, as Gregory makes it clear that there were rumours of Attila attacking Gaul well before the invasion began.[56] Maenchen-Helfen and Hughes suggest that Attila's crossing of the Rhine took the Romans by surprise, as they were expecting an invasion of Italy, but this seems somewhat unlikely.[57] Maenchen-Helfen's interpretation of the letters of Pope Leo puts forward that Leo was already aware of the invasion, and predicted Attila would rapidly tear his way through Gaul and come down into Italy through the Western Alps. His letter claims that he would be unable to provide his most important bishops, many of whom were in Gaul. Leo thought that only Sicily itself was safe.[58] Attila could have intercepted and destroyed coalition armies before they assembled if he was already in Gaul, meaning Aetius must have assembled most of his allies before his invasion, and Sangiban's presence in Aurelianum may indicate Aetius either predicted Attila's movements or at the least knew he could delay Attila. The choice to keep Sangiban and the Alans in Aurelianum is likely comparable to his later stationing of field army forces in Aquileia the next year, which would force Attila to assault the city or risk leaving himself exposed throughout the campaign and unable to retreat on his own terms. Finally, Jordanes' mention of the presence of *ripari* and *olibrones* at the battle suggests Aetius was able to evacuate at least some of the Roman garrisons of northern Gaul to join his army in front of Attila's advance.[59]

Furthermore Sidonius, an eyewitness to the invasion, states clearly in his letters that Tonantius Ferreolus had been preparing for an invasion for some time, stockpiling supplies and presumably military equipment as well.[60] Ferreolus' preparations would have to be quite massive: later sources recount that the army of Illyricum required 520 wagons to supply 15,000 men, while the two armies of the Anastasian war with Persia, numbering 12,000 and 40,000 men respectively, required 630,000 *modii* of wheat for their campaign in 503.[61] Based on these figures, in order to supply the army at the Catalaunian Fields, assuming it numbered roughly 75,500 men at approximately 12.1 *modii* per man (105.6 litres of dry measure), would have required approximately 2,617 wagons and 913,550 *modii* of wheat. The Romans and the *bucellarii* alone would have required 919 wagons and 320,650 *modii* of wheat. Fortunately, some of the burden on Ferreolus may have been reduced by the fact most of this coalition was composed of *foederati*, as the federates would have carried a few weeks' worth of campaigning supplies with them, provided from their own stocks.[62] Likewise, the supply of weapons, armour and missiles would also have been a taxing endeavour, but military cuts over the last decade may have also resulted in a surplus of this equipment. Bearing in mind the necessity of multiple, massive baggage trains and the taxing requirements of food and fodder, it makes sense that Aetius took as long as he did to move against Attila, even if he was thoroughly prepared.

The year of 451 would have therefore opened with rounds of diplomacy from the Huns and the Romans to the various federates on the Rhine and Danube, particularly with the Franks, who were divided during the conflict. Jordanes' emphasis on Attila's attempts to persuade the Alans to betray Aetius are likely unfounded, and if Aurelianum is a parallel with Athens, they are likely based on the Persian demands for the city to surrender in Herodotus.[63] On the other hand, it does seems likely that the Goths were reluctant to involve themselves in the conflict, even if not by the persuasion of Attila's diplomats, and that it did take significant effort on Aetius' and Avitus' part to convince them to abide by their treaty.[64] It is likely that there was a convening of the Council of the Seven Gauls, who appointed Avitus as the chief negotiator with Theodoric, as he had been the negotiator of the last treaty with the Goths in 439.[65] Prosper suggests that the arrival of news of the sack of Divodurum ultimately persuaded Theodoric.[66] However, Sidonius' claims here may also play on Herodotus, casting the Goths stoically awaiting the Huns much in the same light as the Athenians who resolutely awaited the Persians.[67] Regardless, it is still widely and rightfully seen as a testament to Aetius' diplomatic and administrative ability that he was able to construct treaties that made provision for him to assemble these federates in a combined force to face Attila.[68] By the time Attila crossed the Rhine in late April, Aetius was in Italy, his army in Arelate (Arles) and various *foederati* were already mobilizing to meet him somewhere in southern Gaul, possibly at Arelate or the Gothic capital of Tolosa (Toulouse). Aetius, accompanied by an escort, then proceeded from presumably Ravenna to Arelate, arriving there in early May, and his forces must have set out for Aurelianum before the end of May.[69]

At this point Attila made the difficult decision to end his campaign. It is unknown how long he had been besieging Aurelianum, but if the story of the *Vita Aniani* is accurate, his assault on the city had been delayed for too long. Aetius neared the city with his forces on 14 June, as Attila was packing up his camp and preparing to escape Gaul with his plunder. It was at this point that Aetius made what was probably the biggest strategic blunder of his entire career, choosing to pursue Attila's retreating column and engage him in a set-piece battle. As much as Aetius is praised for his command ability and his 'rearguard action' in the fall of the West, it is interesting to note that in his lifetime, he is only ever recorded as having fought two set-piece battles, at Ariminium and the Catalaunian Fields, and won neither.[70] The Roman army also suffered whenever it engaged in set-piece battles during his tenure, notably under Litorius in 439 and Vitus in 446.[71] Despite Aetius' remarkable successes elsewhere, his command talents were clearly based on the Hunnish method: Aetius' recorded military victories in which any detail survives, including *Mons Colubrarius* and *Vicus Helenae*, were aggressive attacks on a forming enemy line or ambushes.[72] Aetius was a trickster and an ambush commander, one who used every tactical advantage possible before his last resort: the set-piece battle. It is completely unknown why Aetius made the decision to pursue, but it seems likely that he had promised to his federates either battle against Attila, or possibly a share of the looted goods Attila had acquired, and may have been forced to do so merely to appease the men now attached to his army. On a political level, it may have been due to his need to ensure stability on the Rhine by enforcing Romano–Frankish authority, as that was one of his prime recruiting grounds.[73] Whatever the reason, Aetius set up camp outside the city on 14 June, collecting his forces together and joining his Alans into the army under the leadership of Sangiban, before beginning the pursuit of Attila on 15 June.[74]

Chapter 5

The Battle of the Catalaunian Fields

Attila retreated from Aurelianum to the 'Catalaunian Fields, which are also called the Mauriac Plains, extending in length one hundred *lueva* [150,000 paces], as the Gauls express it, and seventy in width', and both armies arrived at the battlefield by 19 June.[1] Similarly, Prosper places the battle on the Catalaunian Fields, while the associated *additamenta altera* places it near Troyes. The *Gallic Chronicle* of 511 also places it near Troyes.[2] Hydatius states it was on the Catalaunian Fields, but near Metz.[3] Gregory of Tours and the Lex Burgundionum, though, state it was on the Mauriacian Fields.[4] The *Chronicon Paschale* erroneously places it on the River Danube, while Theophanes states it was on the Loire.[5] The town once known as Catalaunum is now known as Chalons-en-Champagne, on the River Marne, but whether the battle took place here is entirely unknown. Jordanes states that the battle was fought on a steep ridge, with a brook flowing along the plain.[6] But there is one problem: the Catalaunian Fields have only gradual variance in elevation, and there are no steep ridges. Many authors have nevertheless attempted to pin down the site of the battle: Thomas Hodgkin thought it was at Mery-Sur-Seine, while Maenchen-Helfen believed it was at Beauvoir 25 miles east of Troyes. More recently, Richardot proposed a location of La Cheppe just north of Chalons-en-Champagne, although the so-called 'Attila's Camp' is well known to be an iron-age hillfort, unrelated to the battle.[7] John Man thinks they skirmished at Châtres and fought at Mery-sur-Seine.[8] However, these theories offer no etymological basis between '*mauriacus*' and 'Moirey' or 'Mery', and are at best unsound.

Archaeological finds dating to the nineteenth century include the fabled 'Treasure of Pouan', once thought to be from the grave of the Gothic King Theodoric I, who died and was buried on the battlefield.[9] The *spatha* from the burial belongs to the Osterburken-Kemathen family of blades and Behmer type-3 handles, with sliders of the Flonheim-Planig-type Variant A, mouthband of the Beauvais-Planig type and U-form scabbard chape. Its guard and pommel probably belonged to the Behmer Type-I, such as those preserved at Nydam or Samson, although it classifies as a Behmer Type-III hilt. Pouan dates to the third quarter of the fifth century, and is notable because it is believed to be the first example of a Germanic gold-hilt *spatha*, similar to later Merovingian patterns like the Blucina or Childeric burials.[10] This is important because it is sometimes assumed to have been under the reign of Childeric when *cloisonné* was introduced to the Franks from the Huns, suggesting that the Pouan blade may have belonged to a Germanic warrior serving under the Huns. Furthermore, the ring found in the burial is engraved with the name 'Heva', which is either Gothic or Burgundian, contingents of whom had fought on both sides, meaning the buried man may have been a participant in the battle.[11] However, the topography of the Pouan-les-Valles area is not varied enough in elevation to support the theory of a steep ridge (although there are several low hills in that area), and Pouan is now believed to date to after the battle, so this largely rules it out as a location for the battlefield. Another local find consisting of a possible fragment of a Bieberweir-type imitation ridge helmet, a fragment of maille and an Illerup-Whyl type-C blade was unearthed by the River Marne in 1916 at Sarry, just outside Chalons-en-Champagne. It is broadly dated to the D1 period (being the late fourth century), but the blade typology can be found from the C2–D3 periods (early fourth to late fifth centuries).[12] This burial may be related to Attila's path of retreat, as a Hunnic cauldron was also found nearby on the bank of the River Marne; however, this relationship between the burial and Attila's presence cannot be proven.[13] Likewise the Pouan burial could still be related, also being buried near Attila's path of retreat after the battle, but the refined datation makes this rather unlikely.

It is possible Attila decided to retreat from Orleans along the route he came in on: which points towards Attila heading along the road north to Iatinon (Meaux), and then east again towards Bibe (Pierre-Morains) and the Catalaunian Fields. It would also allow Attila to meet up with any forces that split off from the main army to ravage Frankish lands, had he done so. There is one likely location about 30km west of Chalons-en-Champagne, where an approximately 9km-long ridge runs between the towns of Avize and Vertus.[14] This ridge is just opposite a steep hill called Le Mont Aime and runs north to south, as Hughes suggests it would because Attila was retreating to the east. It is also extremely steep on the east face, which Attila would have had to climb to attack the Romans on top.[15] Nearby there also used to be a small stream on the south side, which ran alongside an old Roman road leading to Bibe, which then proceeded east towards Durocatalaunum.[16] This road runs right past Avize and Vertus, and it is therefore logical to assume this ridge is a possible location for the site of the battle, based on the topography of the area, its correspondence to features described in the sources and the proximity to Chalons-en-Champagne. However, there is a third, and probably correct, identification of the battlefield.

The final, and maybe the most likely possibility, is a ridge known as Montgueux about 6km south-west of Troyes, a location proposed by Girard in 1885 and recently reassessed by Simon MacDowall in his 2015 Osprey publication on the battle.[17] This was also identified by Lebedensky in 2011, who also noticed a correlation with the legend of Saint Mesmin, but placed the battle a bit south of Girard and MacDowall near Tourvelliers.[18] The argument for its location here stems mostly from the second *Additamenta Altera* to Prosper's *Epitoma Chronicon*, which states that:

> 'The battle raged five miles down from *Tecis* on the field called *Maurica* in *Campania*.'
>
> (*Additamenta ad Chronicon Prosperi Hauniensis*, s.a. 451)[19]

This text places the site of the battlefield 5 Roman miles away from *Tecis*, possibly Troyes, which corresponds nicely to the ridge of Montgueux. Girard states that the slopes around Montgueux were known as '*les Maures*' in 1885. Several other features have names that correspond to the site being formerly named *Maurica*: a former road called the '*Voie des Maures*', and the plains outside the city near Montgueux are still called '*les Maurattes*' by the locals and on official maps. In fact, the foot of the ridge is known as '*l'Enfer*' or 'hell' and the stream just south of it is known as '*La Riviere de Corps*' or 'the river of the bodies'.[20] Prosper is not the only contemporary source that places the battle here: the *Gallic Chronicle* of 511 states it was near Tricasses, the *Lex Burgundionum* calls it the '*pugna Mauriacensis*', Jordanes gives it as an alternate name for the location and Gregory of Tours, who could have been writing from Renatus Frigeridus' account, also states the battle took place at Maurica.[21] Therefore Girard and MacDowall present quite a compelling and substantiated argument, which purports this location to be the site of the battlefield. If so, that creates quite a different scenario for Attila's retreat from Orleans, one that involves several possible routes, rugged terrain and the well-fortified town of Troyes.

The Retreat to the Catalaunian Fields

Attila's retreat from Aurelianum began on 14 June, and both armies arrived at the battlefield by 19 June, according to Bury. Bury conjectures that the battle took place on 20 June, based on the date of 14 June in the *Vita Aniani*, meaning both armies must have been present by 19 June. It should be noted that there are alternative dates: Hodgkin places it in early July, while Clinton has it after 27 September. Bury based this off the traditional date of the relief of Orleans and the rough estimate of an army marching 20 miles per day to Mery-sur-Seine, but even when the battlefield location is reconsidered, his traditional datation remains plausible.[22] Nevertheless, the best guess that can be provided is late June or July, as the chronology of Hydatius' events puts it roughly in this timeframe.[23] Attila departed north along the Roman road to Metlosedum, as his baggage train was likely unable to cross the fields and take the direct path to Senones, while he spread out the rest of his massive army as much as he could.[24] He then turned south and bypassed Senones, avoiding the fortified city, and took the road east towards Troyes. Attila probably camped for the night at Fontvannes on 18 June, then having marched to the bank of the Seine set up his camp just in front of the Roman bridge at Saint-Lye.[25] The open Maurattes would have provided Attila's massive train of horses plenty of grazing room as he set up camp on 19 June, which would be rounded up and stabled together the night before the battle.[26] Aetius was too close for him to attempt a crossing of the Seine, which would have rendered him vulnerable to attack, and he now had no other choice than to engage Aetius in a set-piece battle.[27]

It was probably at this time that Jordanes' account of Attila consulting his soothsayers took place. At first it seems unlikely that such a tale, written with the obvious purpose of contrasting pagan and Christian moralisms and emphasizing Attila's barbarity to his audience, would be true, but that doesn't take into consideration the context of the battle. When Attila arrived at Fontvannes on 18 June, early the following morning before dawn on 19 June was the first appearance of Halley's Comet, an event recorded in both Chinese chroniclers and Hydatius which helps date the battle. The comet appeared in China on 9–10 June, while Hydatius states it appeared on the fourteenth *Kalend* of July (fourteen days before 2 July), and could be seen until early August. Thorismund officially succeeded Theodoric after its appearance, according to Hydatius.[28] Comets were portents in ancient times and it seems reasonable to conclude that if Attila consulted soothsayers, it would have been under its sky. Of course, this also would have terrified the Christian Romans and their allies, who were just as superstitious as the Hunnic army. John Man remarks that it is interesting that Jordanes makes no note of this; but it may have been irrelevant to Jordanes' narrative, as it would not enhance Attila's barbarity for his readers.[29] It is amusing to note that the Battle of Hastings and the Battle of the Catalaunian Fields, both considered 'major turning points' in western history, are associated with this astronomical phenomenon. The fact the battle was fought directly under its gaze allows the timeframe of its occurrence to be secured between 18 June and the first half of August.

By the time Attila had reached Metlosedum, Aetius was already beginning his pursuit. Having arrived with his main army at Aurelianum, Aetius must have delayed for a day or two to retrieve the Alans and Romans who had been defending the city.[30] Foregoing his reserve horses and baggage train, with them secure at Aurelianum or possibly Senones, Aetius cut across the fields from Aurelianum to Senones to catch Attila. He would have resupplied at Ad Fines, Aquae Segestae and Senones before arriving at Fontvannes on 19 June. His soldiers would have been carrying provisions for only a few days as they set out from each location, using light individual tents made from cloaks and poles, but they were in friendly territory with resupply points and could pull supplies from the baggage train nearby when needed.[31] With the threat of Hun harassment or a major ambush, they would have fortified their camp each night. Arriving at Fontvannes along the Vanne on 19 June, Aetius and his allies trapped Attila between the Seine, the fortified city of Tricasses and their own forces.[32] Tricasses, fearing the outcome, allegedly sent a group of churchmen to Attila under the orders of the bishop. The *Passio Memorii* claims they were promptly martyred, but that seems unlikely if this preserved a real tradition, and they may have instead negotiated with Attila, but were ultimately rejected.[33] Aetius, meanwhile, would have taken what time he had to personally survey the battlefield situation on the evening of 19 June.[34]

Allegedly, the battle began on the evening prior to the main engagement, with the Franks and Gepids having skirmished and killed 15,000 of each other, the Franks emerging victorious.[35] Simon MacDowall suggests that based on the terrain of the narrow path leading from Sens to the Maurattes and Troyes, Attila must have set up a tactical delay here with his Germanic Gepids in a shield wall, probably supported by archers.[36] Although a feasible proposal, there is an interesting alternative: a small engagement prior to the main battle is part of a strategy recommended by both the *Strategikon* and Vegetius for engaging a powerful and unknown enemy.[37] Although the Huns were certainly not unknown, the western Romans hadn't fought against them in twenty-four years, and the concept of going up against Attila, who had defeated three large Roman armies in the 440s, would have been inherently demoralizing for Aetius' coalition.[38] Aetius, therefore, may have sent out a detachment of Franks to fight and defeat one of Attila's detachments or foraging parties, bringing back this news and raising the morale of the army. However, both possibilities could easily be reconciled, with Aetius sending Frankish forces against an intentional delay set up by Attila along the route to the Catalaunian Fields. It is also possible that the Romans may have caught the rear of Attila's column as they approached the vicinity of Fontvannes, ambushing the last of the forces departing Attila's camp.[39] Regardless, encouraged with news of a small victory, the Romans and their federates prepared for battle.

The Opening and Order of Battle

The *les Maures* ridge at Montgueux is positioned about 8km from Fontvannes and 7km from Saint-Lye. The ridge itself is not exceptionally long, only a few kilometres at most, and now covered by patches of forest, farmland and vineyards.[40] Marching out from their camp, the soldiers of either side probably would have carried a day's provision of rations and extra water for the summer heat.[41] Although Attila had a direct line of advance across the Maurattes to the hills of Montgueux, Aetius would have had three routes available to him: the path through the hills to modern Grange-l'Eveque, a second path that led up to the ridge just north of the Montgueux ridge or the modern D660 running south of Montgueux just south of Troyes.[42] The south face of Montgueux is steeper than the north and east face of the *les Maures* ridge, but due to the sheer size of his army, Aetius probably had no other option than to send the Gothic main line down the D660 to ascend the Montgueux ridge from the south face, while the Romans could travel the path to Grange-l'Eveque and the Alans the centre path to the middle of the *les Maures* ridge.[43] It has been suggested that Attila lured the

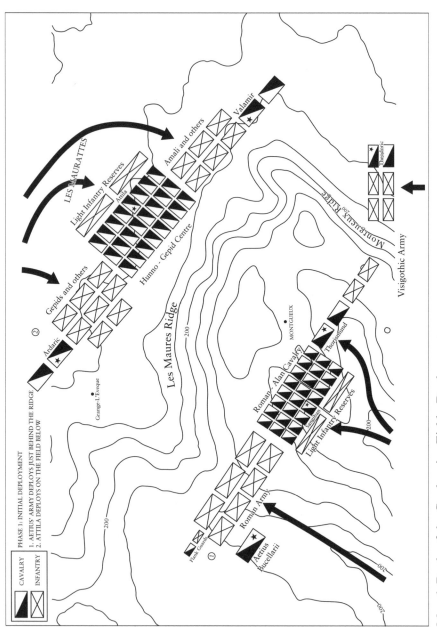

Map 6. Battle of the Catalaunian Fields, Deployment.

coalition forces to the Catalaunian Fields, hoping to fight Aetius on even ground, but this seems unlikely: Attila knew Aetius would not give up his advantageous position, and the *Strategikon* also mentions it is best to fight the steppe peoples on elevated, unbroken ground.[44]

The *Strategikon* states that when facing a large opposing force, the men should be drawn up not on top of the hill, but slightly behind it; when the enemy approaches to about the distance of a mile, only then should the men begin to advance up the slope, in order that they do not see the enemy's true size and are not disheartened.[45] Rance shows that both the *Strategikon* and Vegetius are largely based on both Aelian and Arrian, who Aetius certainly would have been familiar with. He also points out that some of the *Strategikon*'s description of cavalry tactics are the same as in Vegetius and maybe even Ammianus. As a result, it is rather sufficient to assume Aetius may have deployed his forces according to its advice.[46] If the battle took place at Montgueux, then Aetius would have ascended the ridge from the path around it on the north face, which was comparatively shallow and would have been ideal for his ascent, and also obscured Attila's army from view until they marched down onto the slope.[47] Furthermore, Jordanes states that the battle was begun at the ninth hour of the day, to which Hughes suggests both sides had spent the majority of the day carefully drawing up their armies, while Macdowall proposes that it was spent marching to the site of the battlefield and lining up in formation.[48] This is supported by the *Strategikon*, which describes the transitions needed to be made from marching to formation.[49] On the summer solstice, the next day, the ninth hour takes place at approximately 2.31 pm.[50] If the Roman forces were facing north-east, as Hughes suggests, this would put the sun in the eyes of the Hunnish forces. This may have influenced the outcome of the battle, as it would likely inhibit their ability to aim as well as blind their troops attacking uphill.[51]

The exact position of the armies and the formations deployed within this general order of battle are much more difficult to ascertain. As Kim points out, the language barriers between troops dictated that the initial deployment would be key to the course of the battle, as neither Aetius nor Attila could possibly know what occurred on all fronts, and throughout the course of the battle victory or defeat would remain uncertain.[52] According to Jordanes, the Gepids and several other subject nations were facing the Romans, while the Huns faced the Alans under Sangiban in the centre.[53] Thorismund, as Hughes suggests, is on the left flank of the Goths with the Alan cavalry to his left.[54] To the right of the Alans and Thorismund are the Visigoths, facing the Amali Goths and other Gothic groups, respectively under Theodoric and Valamir. Hughes theorizes that this formation made the Huns face a cavalry centre, while Attila was probably expecting a Roman infantry centre. However, it should be noted that because Jordanes may be paralleling the Battle of Marathon, this cavalry-centred deployment may not reflect the reality of the battlefield deployment, and the Alans and Huns were positioned in the centre purely as part of the *topos*.[55]

It is known that steppe armies typically preferred to deploy in three lines; a fact supported by the *Strategikon*, which suggests the adoption of deep formations for Roman lance-and-bow cavalry. Attila's Huns and the opposing Alans both probably deployed in the centres of their formations in a series of three lines with the individual regiments in deep columns.[56] An important part of this formation, and something Aetius would have known, is that dense formations of melee cavalry or lancers supported by horse archers were an effective way of dealing with the Huns; the Alans were therefore perfectly suited to this task. The Alans of this time are recorded as having been heavily armoured cataphract lancers, and Hughes notes that decades of fighting alongside Aetius would have made them able to effectively coordinate with the Romans.[57] It's possible the Romanized Alans would have formed lines ten deep in an open formation, as they were a large cavalry force.[58] Both the Hunnish and Alanic lines were probably supported with infantry, like how Stilicho rallied the Alans at Pollentia.[59]

However, the wings of this formation were in large part dominated by Germanics. Under Hunnish guidance, the *Strategikon*'s description of the 'Scythian' peoples forming up battle lines in units of irregular width, rather than in three defined parts like the Romans and Persians, is probably what one could largely expect for Attila's army.[60] Within these main divisions, the Germanics themselves would have formed up into their warbands according to their leader, canton or kinship. The concept of irregular masses of barbarians is largely mistaken. These Germanics, particularly the Aquitanian Goths, partially adopted the Roman or Hunnish organization, often grouped into units of 50, 100, 500 and 1,000, at least by the sixth century. However, their regimental organization was probably still tied to individual *pagi* or cantons.[61] The Roman *foederati*, meanwhile, were probably deployed somewhat similarly to *foederati* in the sixth century, at around seven files deep with *iuvenes* in the back for missile support, somewhat emulating Roman deployment.[62] Although the *Strategikon* describes the front of Germanic formations typically dense and even, they may have also formed up in *cunei*. The *cuneus* was essentially a trapezoidal column that jutted out in the centre of the line, with the leaders and best warriors positioned at the front, using the mass and momentum of the tactic to break an enemy line, and at the same time retaining control of the army through essentially a 'follow the leader' system of operation.[63] Contrary to popular expectation, the Romans were facing a very well-organized Germanic opponent, something to which they had been forced to adapt around two centuries prior to the battle.

Thanks once more to the *Strategikon*, and to authors like Arrian, much is known about Roman combined arms deployments. According to the *Strategikon*, any army numbering over 15,000 men should deploy in two lines, and any army fewer than 24,000 men should deploy in three main divisions in the first line and four divisions in the second, so this probably indicates how Aetius' Roman army was deployed. The lines would probably have been eight or sixteen men deep. At this size, about a third to half of his army would have been dedicated to missile support.[64] With such a large force, the infantry would have probably been deployed laterally, and in two lines, with archers at the rear of the infantry files or among the files and on the flanks, and with infantry armed with javelins and *plumbatae* in the files behind the main combat infantry. On either side of the overall battle line, on both the Roman far left and Gothic far right, would probably have been more skirmishers and flank guards of cavalry and heavy infantry.[65] These cavalry and flank guards would have been posted behind the infantry, with additional *defensorses* ready in the reserves, as well as a few extra reserve regiments on the left side of Aetius' line for flanking manoeuvres.[66] However, it is impossible to effectively determine the deployment of the army since the *Strategikon* presents no situation in which a cavalry centre is used in deployment. The later battles of Daras and Callinicum also possessed cavalry centres, but the circumstances of these battles are too different to make an effective comparison.[67]

The Battle of Montgueux

Due to the distances involved between the camps and the *les Maures* ridge, both armies were probably deployed rather close to the ridge itself before beginning their advance to meet on the slope. Scouts and cavalry patrols stationed at regular intervals along the Roman line would have immediately relayed news of the Hunnish advance, and likewise Hunnish scouts would have relayed news of the Roman mobilization.[68] Jordanes describes the rush to attain and hold the crest of the ridge running down the centre of the battlefield:

> 'The factions met, as we have said, on the Catalaunian Fields. The battlefield was a sloping plain rising sharply on one side to a hill. And which both armies were wanting to obtain, because the opportunity of position confers no small benefit; the Huns with their forces occupied the right half, the Romans and Visigoths with their allies the left, and so began the contest about the unoccupied crest.'
> (Jordanes, *De Origine Actibusque Getarum*, 38.197)[69]

MacDowall presents the interpretation that the Goths under Thorismund and Huns fought over the Montgueux ridge, while the rest of the armies fought on the plain below the extended *les Maures* ridge that stretched to the north.[70] He suggests that Aetius needed a decisive battle, and that Attila would not venture forth if he remained on the ridge. However, any attempt to retreat over the Seine was not only blocked by the fortified town of Troyes, but also would have been disastrous if Aetius attacked during the process. Attila had probably intended to lure Aetius into battle on the plains outside Troyes, but accidentally trapped himself against the Seine: he was likely therefore forced to give into Aetius' choice of battlefield, lest Aetius starve him out. In many prior analyses, it has been interpreted that there was a hill on the battlefield while most of the battle took place on the plain.[71] Hughes correctly shows that this interpretation is contrary to what is directly stated by Jordanes, and that the battle took place entirely on the ridge.[72] Therefore, due to the tactical necessity of acquiring a position on the ridge, Attila likely advanced first. Hughes suggests both sides advanced up the ridge as quickly as possible, with the Romans, Alans and Thorismund attaining the crest before the Huns and advancing down the other side, while the *Amali* Goths seem to have attained it from the Visigothic far right.[73] This resulted in the Hunnish alliance being forced into an uphill battle at the base of the ridge, barring the Visigoths who had failed to overtake the crest. This scenario can be explained by the paths leading up to the *les Maures* ridge, as detailed before. The Goths were forced to climb the south face, which was the steepest, meaning their ability to obtain sufficient mass to hold the ridge would have been hampered.[74] Meanwhile the Romans, Alans and presumably Thorismund with the Gothic cavalry, Huns, Gepids and *Amali* Goths all had roughly even terms on which to advance up the slope. Aetius and his coalition forces, already having the high ground, would have advanced a short distance down-slope to engage, while the Gothic flank struggled over the Montgueux ridge itself.

The battle probably began with the order to move to engage, which likely resulted in a cavalry charge on the flanks and in the centre. The Romans, Alans, Huns, Goths and other cavalry units would have taken down the decorative pennons on their lances and leaned into their mounts, covering their horses' front and neck with their shields and couched their lances under the armpit. The cavalry would not have engaged at a gallop, but at a trot, holding formation as they moved to engagement range.[75] Likewise, the infantry would have advanced at a jog, keeping pace with the cavalry, initially in open order. At three bowshots they would move to close order, at less than two bowshots the order to form *fulcum* was given, then at one bowshot the light infantry began to engage.[76] When the Roman left and the *Amali* Gothic right attained the crest, the infantry would have braced themselves behind their shields while the rear ranks pushed from behind, adding mass to the formation and bracing it against oncoming infantry.[77] The race to attain the hill likely resulted in both sides clashing immediately, issuing the *barritus* and other war cries, while loosing javelins and missile volleys throughout their rapid advance.[78] At first glance, it wouldn't have been much different from prior Roman battles with trans-Danubians, like Strasburg, Adrianople or the Utus.

Jordanes then mentions a lull in the battle just after this initial contact, in which Attila allegedly gives a speech.[79] There are different interpretations of why the battle in Jordanes is divided into two parts. Tackholm suggests that the rush to attain the hill was not a central part of the battle itself, although Hughes thoroughly disagrees with that sentiment, and if the battle took place in the vicinity of Avize/Vertus or on the *les Maures* ridge, then the advantage of holding the ridge was undoubtedly

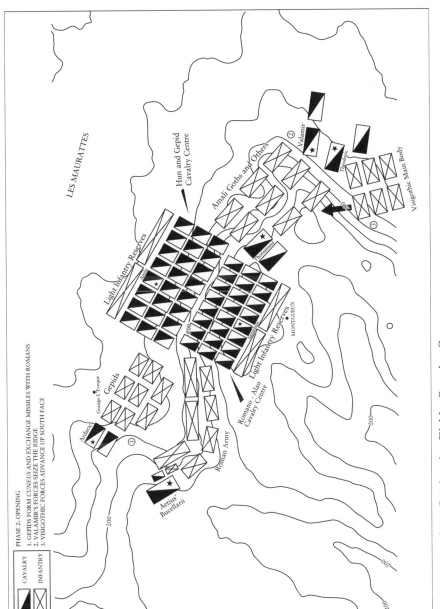

CAVALRY

INFANTRY

PHASE 2: OPENING

1. GEPIDS FORM CUNEUS AND EXCHANGE MISSILES WITH ROMANS
2. VALAMIR'S FORCES SEIZE THE RIDGE
3. VISIGOTHIC FORCES ADVANCE UP SOUTH FACE

LES MAURATTES

Hun and Gepid
Cavalry Centre

Light Infantry Reserves

Amali Goths and Others

Valamir

Theodoric

Visigothic Main Body

Attila

Andames

Gepids

Grange-L'Eveque

Ardaric

Roman Army

Romano - Alan
Cavalry Centre

Light Infantry Reserves

Sangiban

MONTGUEUX

Aetius'
Bucellarii

Map 7. Battle of the Catalaunian Fields, Opening Stage.

the focal point of the battle.[80] Tackholm states that Attila's speech is not something Jordanes fabricated, as he draws it from Cassiodorus, but was unable to make it properly fit in the centre of the battle narrative.[81] Instead, the speech was originally created by Cassiodorus to be placed at the beginning of his narrative, and moved to the centre for some sort of literary effect.[82] Kim argues that Jordanes casts Attila as a hubristic Xerxes with a suicidal obsession over defeating the Goths, something that would not be found in Priscus' cautious and hesitant characterization of the man and his actions.[83] Despite this, during Attila's heroic and classicized speech, Cassiodorus/Jordanes reports on the Roman, and not the Gothic, actions during the battle:

> 'You all know how slight a matter are the arms of the Romans: I say not even by the first wound, but they are hampered by the dust itself, while they arrange in order and connect their formations and shieldwall.'
>
> (Jordanes, *De Origine Actibusque Getarum*, 39.204)[84]

Brodka believes that this passage does not stem from Jordanes but from Priscus, as a criticism on the low quality of the late Roman Army.[85] However, it was not in Priscan character to write such speeches, a facet which belongs to Cassiodorus/Jordanes.[86] Whately suggests this section of the *Getica* is a political statement on the Romans of his day: he may be criticizing the defensive tactics of the late Roman military, using such wording to make this strategy seem disgraceful.[87] Jordanes, according to Whately, seems to show his support for Belisarius' choice of aggressively engaging in set-piece battles in the first Gothic war, and therefore this whole passage could be interpreted as showing a Roman reluctance to engage.[88] The next point to observe about this passage is that Cassiodorus/Jordanes specifically uses the word '*testudineque*' in the speech, possibly indicating the use of the *fulcum* formation. A common tactic of the Roman military, the 'marching testudo' or '*fulcum*' was a highly protective but fairly mobile infantry shieldwall. It was also recommended for engaging steppe nomads.[89] Jordanes, allegedly comparing the Romans to the Plateans, gives no detail otherwise on this side of the battlefield, leaving the events of the engagement to anyone's guess.[90] However, this speech serves a literary purpose in that it detracts from the value of Roman contribution to the battle and emphasizes the Goths, which is likely the central purpose of this selection.[91]

Meanwhile the real action, and the pivotal point in the battle, was in the centre and the right half of the field. According to Jordanes, the battle devolved into a confused and disorganized melee between both sides.[92] Obviously it was not a random melee reminiscent of Hollywood portrayals of ancient warfare, but it is easy to envision that both sides lost their overall cohesion in attempting to coordinate the massive armies, resulting in some confusion. This is what Jordanes seems to record as happening as the Visigoths, Alans, the Huns and their Gothic allies all competed for the centre and right side of the battlefield. The problem lay in that the Visigothic wing had not attained the crest of the ridge with the rest of the allied forces, except for Thorismund.[93] The situation was about to go sour for the Goths: Theodoric attempted to rally his men in order to pull up the right side of the Gothic position, and was slain either by a fall from his horse or the 'spear of Andag' on the side of the Huns.[94] The Goths began a full retreat, but Thorismund is claimed to have rallied the Gothic cavalry long enough to make a devastating strike at the Hunnish centre, cutting through the Huns and allegedly nearly slaying Attila.[95] Again, as Kim suggests, this envisages the Battle of Marathon, where Thorismund and the Visigoths are portrayed as the Athenian regulars and are the heroes of the battle.[96]

An Alan and Gothic retreat would certainly have cost Aetius the battle, but the text of Jordanes indicates otherwise:

> 'Then the Visigoths, separating from the Alani, fell upon the horde of the Huns and they would nearly slay Attila. Except he had prudently first taken flight and immediately enclosed himself and his followers within the camp, which he had fortified with wagons. A frail defence indeed; yet there they sought refuge for their lives, whom but a little while before no walls of earth could withstand.'
>
> (Jordanes, *De Origine Actibusque Getarum*, 40.210)[97]

Jordanes uses the word '*dividentes*' in his description of these events, indicating that there was a major gap forming in the coalition battle line. He also states that Attila had taken flight shortly before the Goths attacked, indicated by '*prius*', which may suggest that the Hunnish centre was already collapsing at the time, and Attila had personally already begun to retreat to his camp. Jordanes attributes this gap in the allied formation to an Alan retreat. However, it is extraordinarily unlikely that the Alans would have broken and routed: the Alans were placed in the centre of the formation because they were the most loyal and fought in a similar manner to the Huns, which Aetius clearly took advantage of in his initial deployment.[98] Jordanes is merely covering for the Goths, who broke and routed when their leader perished, and pinning the blame on his usual scapegoat instead.[99]

This positioning shows that the situation in the centre of the field would have been confusing, as it consisted of two highly mobile and predominately cavalry forces in competition on the main slope. The Huns and Alans both had little room to manoeuvre to either side, due to the Roman and Gothic infantry blocs, which at first seems to be an illogical deployment. Both Ammianus Marcellinus and Pseudo-Maurikios note the Huns used the traditional steppe tactics of erratic formations and heavy use of light missile cavalry: these were horsemen the Alans could bludgeon in close-order combat, let alone in a surprise attack, and the *Strategikon* specifically advises the use of cataphract cavalry against the Huns.[100] Armed with both lances and bows, and probably with Roman armour, the Alans of Sangiban and Sambida would have been more than a match for the Huns. On the other hand,

Arrian records that the Alans had a tendency to break if under heavy missile fire, although he writes three centuries before the battle.[101] However, if this presumption of Alanic military behaviour held true into the fifth century, the Huns may have thought that the Alans would break when put up against their missile superiority, and risked the engagement anyway.[102]

In prior battles, the Huns had room to manoeuvre when engaging, because they were typically pitted against an infantry bloc in the centre of the enemy army, such as the battles of the River Utus and the Chersonese.[103] In a situation where the Huns were directly deployed against an infantry centre, any gaps in the line created by Hunnish manoeuvres would not be easily exploitable and would render manoeuvring infantry units vulnerable to the Huns when the regiments separated. Their method of breaking up infantry walls was employed through the *Strategikon*'s Alan drill, where the assault troops would lure the regiments out to exploit the gaps created by their breaks of engagement.[104] This would allow the Huns to pick away and break up an otherwise impenetrable shieldwall by firing into the sides of the regiments, like the primary sources indicate they were able to do.[105] This may have been the key to Hunnish success in Europe, since they primarily faced infantry armies with cavalry on the flanks. However, against a cavalry centre this picture suddenly changes. The Alans were able to keep pace with the Huns, so whenever the Huns cycled their attacks, it would give ground for the Alan cavalry to exploit, whilst the Alan manoeuvres would also allow the Huns small gaps to exploit. Trapped between two infantry blocks on the flanks, the Huns were not able to beat the Alans by outmanoeuvring them to the sides or engaging them at a range. Instead, it appears the Huns and Alans were both forced into a close-combat situation: if they disengaged to use their typical lance-and-bow tactics, the Alans would exploit the brief gaps and over time push the Huns back, eventually splitting the Hunnish line in half and allowing them to overrun the flanks. Therefore, Attila must have been forced to fight the Alans on their terms, where superior armour and mass gave them the inevitable advantage in a series of prolonged melees. By the time Theodoric was slain, the Hunnish centre had been worn down enough by attrition that it was breaking. Although logical, this picture of the battle relies on a spectacular performance by the Alans, whom sadly no primary source accredits. Jordanes does inadvertently praise the Alans with a second victory over the Huns a year after the battle, and although a separate and probably fabricated engagement, it does provide a testament to the importance of the Alans.[106]

Jordanes' own portrayal of the battle at this point is blurred: the Gothic right is breaking, but at the same time the Hunnish centre has given way under Alan pressure, while the Romans and Gepids remain stationary. The oddball factor still remained for Jordanes to utilize: Thorismund, who Jordanes states attacked the Hunnish centre and nearly slew Attila.[107] Hughes' positioning of Thorismund and the Gothic cavalry supporting the Alans logically makes sense in this situation.[108]

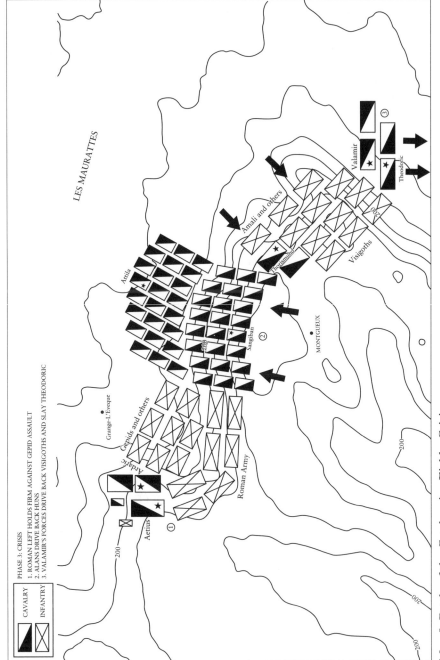

CAVALRY

INFANTRY

PHASE 3: CRISIS

1. ROMAN LEFT HOLDS FIRM AGAINST GEPID ASSAULT
2. ALANS DRIVE BACK HUNS
3. VALAMIR'S FORCES DRIVE BACK VISIGOTHS AND SLAY THEODORIC

LES MAURATTES

Attila

Ardaric

Gepids and others

Grange-L'Eveque

Roman Army

Aetius

Sangiban

MONTGUEUX

Amali and others

Thorismund

Visigoths

Valamir

Theodoric

200

200

200

Map 8. Battle of the Catalaunian Fields, Crisis.

The best reconstruction is that the Alans split the Hunnish line and, along with some of the cavalry under Thorismund, pursued Attila back to his camp. The collapse of the centre prompted the retreat of the Gepids, upon whom Aetius ordered an aggressive pursuit. At Mons Colubrarius in 438, Aetius is stated to have personally ridden down the retreating Goths, indicating he likely did the same with the Gepids and Attila. Aetius would have led the Roman cavalry on the left flank in riding them down, much in the Hun and Alan practice, while the infantry, reserve cavalry and the flank guards followed in an orderly fashion at a significant distance to guard against feigned retreat. The Huns were well known for fighting fiercely even during a retreat, and the pursuit across the *Maurattes* to Attila's camp must have been a slow and contentious series of skirmishes.[109] Meanwhile, on the right side, Valamir and the *Amali* pursued the Goths to the south, off the Montgueux ridge and down the route of the D660 back to their camp. This placed them out of sight of the centre and left of the battle line, and back towards the allied camps at Fontvannes.

The Outcome and Aftermath

According to Jordanes, the fighting lasted into the night, as both armies slowly made their way back to their camps. The Visigoths had been utterly devastated after their line broke, while the Hunnish centre also suffered from the coalition pursuit. Fighting at Attila's camp would have been fierce, as the Huns employed a tactic used by both the Pechengs and Khazars where they formed a makeshift palisade out of their wagons and using stakes and shields, with gaps for sallies, like fighting against a walled fortress.[110] According to Jordanes, Thorismund had been separated from his Gothic troops and ended up in the Hunnish camp, but after a skirmish was rescued by his personal retainer and they retreated back to their own camp.[111] Aetius, meanwhile, had been leading the pursuit and also become separated from his Roman army, and made his way back to the Gothic camp, fearing total disaster.[112] At the same time, the *Amali* Goths under Valamir would have been marching back towards the Hunnish encampment as well, presenting an obstacle the allied forces would have had to manoeuvre around as they returned to Fontvannes. This confusion at the end of the battle certainly would have made it impossible to determine any immediate victor.

Man believes that the morning of 21 June was a dry, cloudy one. The Romans ventured out onto the battlefield, littered high with corpses interspersed by the occasional grazing horse, and saw no sign of the Huns drawing up a battle line to renew the engagement.[113] But Jordanes records Attila continued to menace the coalition:

> 'Yet he did nothing cowardly, like one that is overcome, but with clash of
> arms sounded the trumpets and threatened an attack. He was like a lion

CAVALRY

INFANTRY

1. ALANS AND THORISMUND BREAK THE HUNS, SPLITTING THE LINE.
2. VISIGOTHS RETREAT LEARNING OF THEODORIC'S DEATH.
3. ROMANS PURSUE THE GEPIDS.

LES MAURATTES

Thorismund

Ardaric

Aetius

Georges l'Esperie

MONTGUEUX

Sangiban

Valamir

200

Map 9. Battle of the Catalaunian Fields, Retreat.

pierced by hunting spears, who paces to and fro before the mouth of his den and dares not spring, but ceases not to terrify the neighbourhood by his roaring.'

(Jordanes, *De Origine Actibusque Getarum*, 40.212)[114]

This, as Whately suggests, is an allusion to the *Aeneid*, where Turnus is described the same way and in the same position.[115] Attila's willingness to fight would have been affected by a variety of factors, but with the Huns having taken the brunt of the fighting, Attila chose not to continue the battle. Allegedly the Huns were impeded by Roman archers placed within the confines of the Roman camp.[116] However, neither were the Romans and their allies willing to engage. It may be possible that, contrary to Man's view, the morning of 21 June saw signs of a storm, and thus battle was not joined due to the possibility of rain.

Hyun Jin Kim uses these passages to suggest that the Romans had been defeated. Kim believes that the entire allied battle line collapsed, separating Aetius and Thorismund from their forces, with the Hunnish army chasing the Roman coalition back to their camps. Thorismund and Aetius were then trapped and forced to fight their way back to their own camps, with Aetius knowing that he had lost. However, the Huns were unable to besiege the allies because of Roman missile superiority from their position at Fontvannes.[117] There are notable flaws with his theory. First, this would leave Thorismund and Aetius on the ridge during the retreat, nowhere near Attila's camp 8km to the north-east. Secondly, Aetius may have feared defeat due to the rout inflicted upon the Visigoths, the results of which would have been apparent throughout their camp. His explanation for the inability of the Huns to approach the allied encampments could readily be countermanded with the suggestion that Aetius and the federates moved their camps onto the Maurattes in order to properly besiege Attila, as Jordanes states.[118] This would have been risky, but the mobile Alans would have served as a deterrent for any attempt at harassment during the process, and it would have enabled an effective siege of Attila by starving his horses, while the Romans could keep supplying their forces thanks to the foresight of Ferreolus.[119] Alternatively, this passage could be referencing the pursuit to the Gothic camp after the collapse of the Gothic line.

The simple answer to who was the victor is recorded in the primary sources: Prosper Tiro, often a critic of Aetius, probably preserves the real answer as he likely wrote what he could discern about the battle within the following year. He says that:

'In this conflict although inestimable casualties were inflicted, because neither side yielded, it is accepted that the Huns were defeated, because those who survived returned to their own lands having lost the will to fight.'

(Prosper Tiro, *Epitoma Chronicon*, s.a. 451)[120]

Hydatius, also a contemporary to the battle, claims only that the casualties were extreme.[121] The contemporary *Gallic Chronicle* of 452 says Attila inflicted and received a grave setback, and returned to his own lands, while the *Gallic Chronicle* of 511 makes no indication of whom the victor was. Instead, it merely notes the deaths of Theodoric and Laudaricus and claims that one participant of the battle remarked '*cadavera vero innumera*', or 'truly countless bodies'.[122] Tackholm shows that after the fifth century, the result of the battle becomes progressively biased in favour of the Goths and against Aetius.[123] Tackholm notes that beginning with Cassiodorus, authors have no reservation in stating that the Goths achieved victory over Attila in the battle. He states this propaganda is far more conspicuous in Jordanes.[124] Brodka and Kim show the battle is a classic case of Herodotean format, where Attila's *hubris* is struck down by *nemesis*.[125] This ultimately serves as part of Jordanes' message of Gothic superiority, probably in relation to the later Battle of Vouille.

The Battle of the Catalaunian Fields is quickly remembered as being one of the bloodiest in Roman history: Hydatius lists the count at an exceedingly high 300,000 men and Jordanes' figure of 165,000 is also impossible, while Fredegar is more specific in stating that 200,000 Goths and 150,000 Huns were slain.[126] If one takes a zero off the end of each figure, 30,000, 16,500, 20,000 or 15,000 men wounded or dead seem to be plausible figures, while the *Lex Burgundionum*'s creation of a deliminating year for 451 indicates that the casualties were indeed quite extreme.[127] It also seems that if the Romans were the ones who stayed in a virtual stalemate for the entirety of the battle, then they may have taken the fewest number of casualties on the allied side. It would furthermore have been beneficial to Aetius if his temporary allies took the brunt of the losses, weakening their position to threaten Gaul, but also detrimental in that they would not be able to fight Attila as effectively again. For the Huns, the casualties must have been equally as devastating as those inflicted upon the Aquitanian Goths. Although Attila and Aetius both seemed to threaten renewing the engagement, neither side had the wherewithal to draw up a battle line and risk a continuation.[128] Thus, both sides began looting the battlefield and disposing of the dead, while Attila entered into negotiations to ensure a safe retreat from Gaul. According to Fredegar, the battle lasted three days. Assuming there is some truth in his chronicle, then it is possible the 'siege' lasted from 21–22 June, after which Attila began negotiations on 23 June.[129]

The garbled account of the chronicle of Fredegar, a piece that has been assessed several times already, has this to say about Aetius after the Battle of the Catalaunian Fields:

'Agecius [Aetius], who was very quick at devising a plan, came to Attila at night and said to him, "It has been my desire to deliver this region from the faithless Goths by your strength, but it cannot at all be done. Up to now you have been engaging the least of their fighters, but this night Theodoric [II], the brother of Thorismund, comes with a host beyond measure and the boldest fighters of the Goths. You cannot withstand them; I do hope at least you can escape."

'It was then that Attila gave Agecius [Aetius] 10,000 solidi so that he could retreat to Pannonia without interference.'

(Fredegar, *Chronica Epitomata*, 2.53)[130]

Fredegar's account of a particularly avaricious Aetius is not to be trusted, but he does preserve a concept mentioned by quite a few other authors: that Aetius clearly had some intention for the Huns to survive the battle.[131] This is a notion that Cassiodorus and Jordanes, and the later authors who used their works as a basis, probably drew from Sidonius Apollinaris, where he states:

'That the Huns, whose flight aforetime shook us, shall by a second defeat be made to do me service.'

(Sidonius Apollinaris, *Carmina*, 7.344–46)[132]

Tackholm, Hughes and several other authors all agree that Aetius clearly wanted a return to the status quo prior to AD 439, when the Huns regularly supplied him with *foederati*.[133] But there may be further information preserved here: at the end of his campaign in 452, Attila met with Trygetius, Pope Leo and other diplomats in order to establish a treaty before he retreated from Italy.[134] O'Flynn suggests Fredegar may preserve a similar notion, that Aetius and Attila actually did meet after the battle.[135] Like his later campaign, Attila probably received an embassy from Aetius and his allies on the day after the battle. Contrary to Fredegar, the Goths and particularly the Franks would certainly have wanted to be involved in any treaty's establishment. Interestingly, the *Vita Lupi* may preserve Attila's presence at the negotiation, as Saint Lupus is said to have met with Attila: however, the events described cannot be necessarily attributed to Lupus (who may have died before the battle), nor can they be definitively considered as accurate.[136]

Still in a fairly strong position, it is possible that Attila made his usual demands of tribute and ransom of hostages, as well as Silvanius' stolen dinnerwear, but both he and Aetius probably focused on settling the Frankish succession, which was the primary cause of the war to begin with.[137] Fredegar's two figures of 10,000 *solidi* for Aetius' deception of the Goths and Huns may preserve that part of their treaty called for an immediate tribute to be paid at the time, although the number itself is probably fabricated.[138] The situation with Eudoxius, the Armorican doctor who fled to Attila's court, may have also been settled at this time.[139] If Lupus or his successor was present, his role was likely to ransom hostages, as is seen with the Bishop of Sirmium and Pope Leo's envoy to Attila. In turn, his presence at the envoy gave the bishop increased political clout.[140] Finally, it is possible that in addition to the prior suggestions of Odoacer leading a secondary army to Attila's either during or after the campaign, he may have instead been designated an advisor to the Franks in this treaty. If a treaty was brokered in the aftermath of the battle, it was evidently not written with the same degree of permanence in which the treaty of 452 was constructed. Rather, Attila was nominally confident that the Romans would not pursue him and decided he was able to begin his withdrawal from Gaul. Evidence of the route of his withdrawal can be found at the city of Durocatalaunum (Chalons-en-Champagne), where a burial consisting of an Illerup-Whyl type blade, a fragment of maille, the ridge of a Bieberwier-type imitation ridge helmet (misidentified as a saddle) and a separate deposition of a Hun cauldron near the Marne bank suggests he may have passed through the region.[141] The burial at Pouan may still also be related, as the road ran near Pouan through Artiaca (Arcis-sur-Aube).[142] His retreat through the town of Catalaunum would have assuredly left an impression on the people, and hence may be the reason many authors refer to it as the Battle of the *Campus Catalauniensis* rather than the *Campus Mauriacus*.

A few days after the battle, as Attila retreated out of Gaul, both Thorismund and the Frankish king consulted Aetius as to how to proceed; Jordanes and Gregory of Tours both state he told them to head home and secure their thrones, a theory which Hughes takes at face value.[143] Considering the comparison between securing the Gothic throne and sedition in Athens after the Battle of Marathon, Kim suggests this is another one of Jordanes' allusions, and states the Goths simply retreated because they had taken heavy losses, which is a viable proposition.[144] Tackholm, on the other hand, states it simply makes no logical sense for him to let his largest army go in the face of a still threatening Hunnish enemy, but theorizes Thorismund calculated that if Attila was not outright defeated, continued prohibition of Hunnish service for the Romans would be best for the Goths.[145] Thorismund was no fool, having grown up among the Gothic aristocracy, and knew what the political circumstances of the death of Theodoric would entail. He would also express a notoriously anti-Imperial agenda through his brief reign. Therefore, with the Hunnish retreat assured he made the most pragmatic decision for his people, returning with his battered army to Tolosa in order to administer to the Aquitanian court. Thus, acting out of his own interestis, Thorismund left Aetius with no hope of a total victory and no fresh supply of Hunnish mercenaries, and the other commanders still staring down Attila.[146] Unlike the Goths, where the succession was probably rather secure, the dynastic situation with the sons of Chlodio was of legitimate concern to them. Now that a third of the coalition army had departed, it was probably at this point that the Franks, too, up and left the field.[147] Although Jordanes shows his clear bias against Sangiban elsewhere, he makes no mention of disloyalty here. The Burgundians, who were likely under Aetius' *comes foederatorum* Ricimer, may have also stayed, along with the *Litaui* and Armoricans. I would suggest that due to the proximity of their territories to the Franks, some of the Saxons/*Frisii* also returned home. With almost half of the coalition returning home, and the Huns unable or unwilling to fight, leaving Gaul laden with valuables, the Romans and the Alans decided they had 'won' the battle of the Catalaunian Fields.

Chapter 6

The Effects of the Battle

N ews of the battle spread to northern Aquitaine before the end of the year, where Prosper wrote down his version of the engagement in the *Epitoma Chronicon*. By 452, it had spread across the Empire, which had major repercussions for Attila. Although the upper echelons of the western Roman and barbarian courts knew it had actually been a disastrous affair, Prosper, also the nearly contemporary *Gallic Chronicle* and Hydatius indicate that for the majority of the population, it did not appear as anything less than a bloody victory, or at the least did not matter to them otherwise. To the citizens of the Empire, and certainly for the sake of Roman propaganda, it had finally been a victory over Attila, but for northern Gaul the invasion had not yet ended, as Odoacer may have remained at large in the region.[1] Jordanes makes note of a second battle in the same area, but whether this is fictional or a preservation of a real fact remains unknown. Goffart thinks this tale in Jordanes preserves an elsewhere recorded battle between the Gepids and Burgundians in 455. However, it is one of the few passages in his book where the Alans are given due credit.[2] The Alans may have been ordered against Odoacer by Aetius later that year, and reducing his potential to threaten northern Gaul would have been vital to restoring Roman authority in the region. However, it is also possible that Odoacer may have remained behind of his own volition, or due to a term set in the presumed treaty after the battle, where he may have been agreed on as an attaché to the Frankish court. This latter case would be more logical as there is little word of his actions until the mid-460s, and any force continuing to campaign in northern Gaul over the course of the 450s would have been noticed, even in the scant accounts of chroniclers or hagiographers.[3]

On a strategic level, the campaign against Attila had yielded mixed results for Aetius: his major recruiting grounds on the Rhine and in northern Gaul were devastated, the *limes* were broken, his own veteran army damaged and the Romans had also lost a great deal of taxable wealth in the region. Tonantius Ferreolus had requested immediate aid for the region after the conflict, while Avitus and other Gallic elites used their own wealth to alleviate the situation.[4] On the other hand, central Gaul had been successfully defended and the major cause for conflict, the Frankish succession, had been decided in the Romans' favour. Likewise, the Roman army had gone through the battle comparatively unscathed, with the majority of the losses having been absorbed by the Alans, Goths and their allies. However, the satisfaction of the barbarian federates Aetius had called upon to achieve this result remains in question, and as will be shown, some were not overtly sated by the concessions they may have been promised or given for their participation. Attila was in a similar situation, as his prior campaigns had been vastly more successful than his pillaging of Gaul. Although major Roman cities such as the former capital of Augusta Treverorum would have yielded significant plunder, and he likely received some immediate gold payments from a treaty just after the battle, he had neither achieved nor completed most of his objectives. Although he had destroyed the *limes*, the Rhine was still under marginal Roman control, as the younger son (possibly Merovech) and not the elder (possibly Childeric) was king of the Franks, while the Romano-federate armies hadn't been soundly annihilated as he had hoped. The Eastern Roman Empire was still neglecting to pay him the tribute he demanded, and Marcian seemed keen (if unable) to mobilize against him.[5] For these reasons, Attila decided he needed a decisive victory against the Western Roman Empire.

The Invasion of Italy

Attila had taken heavy losses at the Catalaunian Fields, and his vassals must have had to press for new young men to raise forces for his invasion of Italy.[6] However, Attila did not need as large an army as he had in 451, as he likely knew the allies of the Romans would not join Aetius in Italy, nor were the most significant of them – the Goths – capable of fighting after their rout by the *Amali*. In April 452, Attila assembled his vassals and marched through Noricum Mediterraneum to the passes of the Julian Alps, the easiest and least defensible entry into Italy. Both Maenchen-Helfen and Hughes point out that Aetius' retreat to defend Aquileia was probably a far better defence than the Alpine *limes* would have offered.[7] Primary sources and some modern authors criticize Aetius for not blockading the Alps, but in reality the mid-fourth-century *tractus Italiae circa alpes* had been largely abandoned in the first three decades of the fifth century in favour of the fortified hinterland settlements, and since the late fourth century hostile forces crossing the Alpine passes had all gone unopposed.[8] Attila was able to cross the passes, but was forced to besiege these fortified settlements en route.[9]

Again, like in 451, Aetius had prepared for this eventuality: having recognized the failure of the Danubian *limes* against Attila's army, and seen the successful defence of Aurelianum, he recognized that attempting to defend the Alpine passes was infeasible. Instead, according to Jordanes, Aquileia was staffed by the 'bravest soldiers of the Romans' with a significant amount of supplies and other provisions to endure a prolonged siege.[10] A lesson he had learned from the inhabitants of Asemus, Attila knew he could not leave his rear undefended, and was therefore forced to lay siege to the major military centre.[11] Similarly to Aurelianum, Aquileia's walls were renovated in the third century AD, and possessed an earthen forewall.[12]

The city of Aquileia was fiercely defended for three months before Attila considered withdrawing. However, he allegedly saw a portent of a stork leaving a tower, a version of a story found in central Asia in the *Chin Shu*, and instead ordered an immediate assault: it fell to Attila, who had utilized various siege machines in the attack. From a lost fragment of Priscus, Maenchen-Helfen believes the portent is a *topos* as the movements of birds were considered ominous in classical religion, but that this particular way of telling the story has central Asian influence.[13] After razing the city to the ground, an event which would become the legend for the founding of Venice, Attila proceeded south along the Roman road, sacking Concordia, Altinum and then Patavium. Like in the Balkans campaigns and the war in Gaul, these cities likely offered no resistance after seeing what had happened to Aquileia.[14] Attila then proceeded to ravage northern Italy along the Po River valley, skipping the cities of Vicentia (Vicenza), Verona, Brixia and Pergamon (Bergamo) before sacking Mediolanum (Milan) and then moving south to Ticinum (Pavia).[15] This was likely due to a combination of lost time from the siege of Aquileia forcing him to ignore these cities, and the need to make a statement by sacking one of Rome's former capitals. Allegedly, Priscus states that upon sacking Mediolanum, Attila ordered a painting of 'Scythians' kneeling before a Roman emperor reversed to that of emperors pouring gold at his feet, a story which may actually be true, and the emperors pouring gold were probably intended to be Valentinian III and Theodosius II.[16] The sermon given shortly after the sacking describes that the majority of the citizens were spared, able to flee while the Huns plundered the city.[17]

Aetius may have also chosen to fortify these bypassed cities with the rest of his army in order to slow Attila down, as many of them were standard billeting posts for some of the Italic army regiments. Many also had large circuit walls, some dating as far back as Augustus or earlier, which were upgraded in the third century.[18] However, Maenchen-Helfen thinks that like in Gaul, they were sacrificed to slow Attila down.[19] There is no account of Aetius offering any further resistance after the fall of Aquileia; however, unlike the Catalaunian Fields, Aquileia was not a strategic blunder on the part of Aetius or his federates' poor judgement, but simply a brute-force overcoming of Aetius' military intuition. Aetius may have mobilized light forces such as lance-and-bow cavalry and infantry skirmishers to harass stragglers and foraging parties after the Roman army was defeated at Aquileia, but it is doubtful he could have done more to defend Italy. His remaining field army troops were likely tied up preparing to depart Italy at Ravenna, billeted in the Po cities or at the major pass at Bononia which would serve as a launching point to outmanoeuvre and trap Attila if he decided to attack Ravenna or Rome.[20]

Attila's invasion of Italy went on for at least another month before his army began to succumb to the local famine and some form of sickness of the bowels, likely dysentery. Confusingly, Marcian sent Aetius, a man who had been the prefect of Constantinople and later of the East, to assist in a campaign against Attila, but whatever forces he could offer likely were few as the East had been

Map 10. The Campaign of 452.

repeatedly devastated by the invasions of the 440s.[21] As a result an embassy was put together consisting of Pope Leo I, Trygetius (who had negotiated the Vandal treaties) and Italian aristocrat and ex-consul Gennadius Avienus.[22] The selection of representatives may have been a diplomatic platitude considering Attila's demands to Theodosius in 449, where he would only speak with men of consular rank.[23] They met with Attila in northern Italy, and although ecclesiastical sources like to overstate that Pope Leo persuaded him to return home, it is likely that he was employed to ransom hostages as this was a role of bishops in envoys in the era. In return, his role garnered him prestigious political clout, and of course led to the later hagiographical praise.[24] The terms of this treaty remain unknown, but it undoubtedly imposed more severe conditions than the compact that may have been put together after the Catalaunian Fields. It likely included the standard terms of an increased tribute and the return of Hunnish fugitives.[25] It is known that Leo had brought with him a large sum of gold to purchase back captured Romans, probably at the same rate demanded of the East at 12 *solidi* per man, and he was able to obtain the release of the majority of the captives.[26] The fate of the Frankish Kingdom may have also been decided at this point: Childeric would eventually become king of the Salian Franks in 457, which means that presumably the younger brother of Chlodio had died by that time. In this case, it is possible that Attila may have agreed to allow the younger brother, assuming he was Merovech, to remain on the throne on the condition that the older brother, assuming he was Childeric, be his designated successor. It may have also provisioned Odoacer, still in the region, as a permanent attaché to the Frankish leadership. Finally, an exchange of new hostages was probably agreed on to cement the terms, and Attila finally retreated from Italy.

The invasion of Italy would have disastrous consequences for the Western Roman Empire, and for Aetius himself; it is alleged that Aetius even advised the court at Ravenna to flee from Italy, to probably either Arelate or Constantinople, after Attila had sacked Aquileia.[27] The sacking of Aquileia also weakened the Roman ability to defend the eastern route into Italy as much as Aetius' apparent failure weakened his position. This came on top of earlier political moves by Aetius to further his authority as manager of the West: in 450 or 451, he had removed Majorian from command and replaced him with Agrippinus.[28] This move was the result of either Aetius or his wife, Pelagia, betrothing his son, Gaudentius, to Valentinian III's daughter, like Stilicho had done just before his own demise.[29] Yet, for the time being, Aetius still had full control of the administration and army, and would continue to exert his authority in Roman Gaul and Spain, which had devolved into a tricky mess since the battle.

The Fall of Aetius

In 452, Thorismund was evidently displeased with the lack of payment or concessions after having served at the Catalaunian Fields, and he chose to revolt against the Romans. It is also likely that since Theodoric was dead, the Goths considered their prior treaty from 439 invalid, and demanded a new, more favourable treaty. Indeed, the deliminating year of 451 in the *Lex Burgundionum* could be an indication that Aetius had rewritten some of the barbarian's *foedera* as a reward for their service.[30] Thorismund's first move is recorded by Prosper, who states that the Goths advanced north and defeated the Alans of Sangiban, an event which is likely garbled by Jordanes in recording a second invasion of Gaul in which the Goths and Alans fought off Attila alone.[31] However, Jordanes' account could still refer to the Alans fighting Odoacer.[32] Regardless, the defeat of the Alans was a major blow to Roman hegemony in Gaul, as the Alans provided much of Aetius' manpower for his professional cavalry and were a containing military backbone for the whole region. This reduced Roman control north of the Seine to a tenuous position: after 454, strongholds at Andecavus (Angers), Suessiones (Soissones) and Augusta Treverorum became the new bastions of authority in the region, and other warlords appear in the 460s–470s as well, usually in or near the arms manufacturing centres of the *Notitia*.[33]

Having effectively crippled Aetius' most loyal military arm, on top of heavy losses from the sack of Aquileia, the professional Roman army was weak and unable to call upon additional reinforcements. Thorismund now had the opening to besiege the Gallic capital of Arelate (Arles) and demand new terms.[34] Present in the city was the *praefectus praetoriano per Gallias* who had prepared Gaul for the Hun invasion, Tonantius Ferreolus, and when the city was put to siege he invited Thorismund into Arelate for a banquet, persuading him to lift the siege and agree to a treaty.[35] Whether Aetius and his forces had a role in the alleviation of the siege is uncertain, as Ferreolus' role as envoy in Sidonius was intended to contrast with military impotence; so it is possible that although Aetius was unable to engage Thorismund directly, he still may have been able to starve him out, and Thorismund relented in a game of attrition.[36] It seems that as part of this treaty, Thorismund's brother, Frederic, may have been appointed honorary *magister militum*.[37] However, unfortunately for Thorismund, his younger brothers Theodoric II and Frederic had pro-Roman opinions, and may have been disappointed by indecisiveness in the siege of Arelate. As a result, he was assassinated and Theodoric II installed, who immediately lent aid to Aetius by having Frederic campaign against the *bacaudae* of Roman *Tarraconensis*, presumably alongside Aetius or Agrippinus with Roman forces.[38] In 453, a treaty was concluded with the Suebes, returning Carthaginiensis to Roman control.[39] Considering the Goths were enticed into a pro-Roman alliance with Aetius, and the nature of the Spanish campaign immediately afterwards, it seems that in 453, Aetius was setting a plan in motion that ultimately would be carried out under Avitus and Majorian: to cross the straits of Gibraltar and retake Africa.

Unfortunately for the empire, Aetius would not live to complete his objective and restore the Western Roman Empire's primary tax base. After denying Valentinian

III a campaign to unite the empire upon Theodosius II's death, deposing Majorian and putting his son in line for the throne, blundering at the Catalaunian Fields and failing to defend northern Italy, and losing his military backbone at Aquileia, Emperor Valentinian III was allegedly persuaded by his eunuch Heraclianus to assassinate his manager.[40] The importance of the Huns, the Catalaunian Fields and the invasion of Italy in Aetius' downfall is somewhat disputed, but McEvoy believes that their role was pivotal to Aetius, who was the first fifth-century general to draw on an external force for the source of his power.[41] Whether his successor, Petronius Maximus, was actually involved or was only attributed involvement due to the unpopularity of his short reign is uncertain, but McEvoy argues that Valentinian III had no support outside of his own household in Aetius' assassination. On 21 September, AD 454, Aetius was delivering a financial account when Valentinian III and Heraclianus drew their weapons and struck him over the head, murdering him. Allegedly the rest of the Senate followed suit.[42] Aetius' ally in the court, Boethius, was also hung and paraded through the city alongside him.[43] Valentinian III quickly tried to take control and win the loyalty of the army by appointing Majorianus, who had served as *comes et magister militum per Gallias* under Aetius in the 440s, as *comes domesticorum* and ordered him to combine the army into Valentinian's own *schola palatina*.[44] He did not appoint a new *comes et magister utriusque militiae* and *patricius*, which upset Petronius Maximus, who had hoped to replace Aetius.[45] McEvoy suggests that, coupled with his practice on the *campus Martius*, Valentinian was seeking to become an active emperor himself.[46]

As for the new active emperor Valentinian III, his disruption of the child-emperor system stirred unrest within the Roman bureaucracy, and we will never know if he would have ever made a capable military ruler, as Petronius Maximus bribed Aetius' former *bucellarii* to murder him. Two Goths or Huns named Optila and Thraustila would carry out this deed. The Roman army allegedly so despised Valentinian for Aetius' murder that none of them even attempted to stop the assassination.[47] Aetius' unfortunate assassination seems to have triggered the final stages of the collapse of the West. Marcellinus, the *comes Illyricum*, revolted against Valentinian III upon Aetius' death, and evidently was able to amass a force large enough that not even the East would dare to challenge him. Priscus states that his army consisted of 'Scythians', probably Goths and Huns, while the *Suda* claims it was composed of well-equipped soldiers, suggesting that at least part of Aetius' army and his Hunno-Gothic retainer defected to Marcellinus.[48] Still in power and loyal to his father-in-law, thanks to the Battle of the Catalaunian Fields, the son of Chlodio immediately revolted in northern Gaul, while the *Alamanni* expanded across the Rhine and the Saxons raided down the coast.[49] The territory recovered in Spain was immediately retaken by the Suebes, and, most consequentially, the treaty with Gaiseric was now void, as both Roman leaders were dead.[50] Petronius Maximus declared himself emperor and forced Valentinian III's wife, Eudoxia, to marry him, but he was not to last as he was stoned outside the city of Rome fleeing the Vandal army marching up the coast of a now defenceless Italy, culminating in the sack of the city itself.[51]

The Collapse of Attila's Empire

The last two years of Aetius' reign also saw major events transpire in the Hun realm. According to both Jordanes and Priscus, Attila was planning a campaign against Marcian and the Balkans when, in 453, he took a new bride by the name of Ildico, drowning in his own blood during his sleep on his wedding night, likely due to cirrhosis. Rumours circulated that he had been poisoned by his new wife, or that Aetius had bribed someone to poison him, but these were probably just court gossip.[52] Because Attila had usurped the traditional system of the East's dominance over the West in the *Xiongnū* organization, there was some dispute over who the emperor would be, and one of Attila's princes, Ardaric, seems to have taken this opportunity to attempt to seize part of the empire for himself.[53] Kim suggests Ardaric was a Hun, but this view is considered problematic and not widely accepted.[54] However, Kim may be correct in his theory that Ardaric sought to propose his son as a candidate for Attila's posting of king of the west.[55] The breakup of Attila's empire is described as '*magna... certamina*' by Jordanes, and Mingarelli notes that this description may be a literary parallel of the breakup of Alexander's empire. He notes the use of '*sua discessione*' to describe Ardaric's withdrawal by Jordanes, and instead of a metaphorical withdrawal, Mingarelli argues Jordanes is describing the withdrawal of various barbarian leaders from the negotiation table concerning the division of Attila's empire between his sons. With a crisis in the negotiations, Ardaric and others found an opportunity for revolt, and in late 453 open war broke out within the Hunnic Empire.[56]

Although some authors have inferred that the sons of Attila were fighting each other, the '*contentio*' used to describe their situation suggests instead they were again at the negotiating table.[57] The sons of Attila quickly put aside their differences to quell this abrupt revolt, which culminated in the Battle of the River Nedao, which most likely took place somewhere in modern Hungary or Serbia.[58] According to Jordanes, the Goths, Gepids, *Rugi*, Suebes, Alans and *Heruli* all fought at the battle.[59] It is very likely that the majority of these nations fought on both sides, and allegedly Ardaric's victory was unexpected. Of Ellak's forces, 30,000 are said to have been slain, along with Ellak himself.[60] The Battle of Nedao may well have stemmed from a passage from Priscus, possibly nearly as extensive as Priscus' probable account of the Catalaunian Fields. Mingarelli suggests that much like the death of Theodoric, there was a section on the death of Ellak that featured in Priscus' account and was cut from Jordanes. He also notes that it was likely the literary sister to the Catalaunian Fields in Jordanes, being the description of Jordanes' desired outcome of that battle, and therefore falling into Cassiodorus-Jordanes' portrayal of a gradual progression of the Goths between Ermanaric and

Theodoric's kingdoms.[61] Like the sack of Worms in 436, some elements of the breakup of Attila's empire may have been preserved in the *Hervararsaga*, albeit Mingarelli argues that it is an entirely fictional, unreliable source, with the primary objective of fabricating a line of succession.[62]

After Ardaric's success, Heather suggests Valamir and the *Amali* Goths revolted separately, possibly as late as 459–61 when they established a relationship with the imperial administration.[63] Jordanes describes the retreat of many of the Hun vassals, including Alans, Sarmatians, *Sciri*, *Sadages/Sadagarii*, *Rugi* and the Huns of Emnetzur and Ultzindur, who resettled along the Lower Danube.[64] The Gepids also took to asserting their authority, as they are said to have attacked the Burgundians in 455, who were likely those on the Main, not those in Sapaudia. Goffart, believing this to relate to the 'second battle of the Catalaunian Fields', sees a precedent for this in Socrates where the Burgundians defeat Octar's Huns, and this is reflected by Jordanes' and Fredegar's accounts of two battles.[65] Still, it seems that at this point widespread civil war had broken out between the brothers and the vassals, and some Huns appear to have also split away from Attila's empire. Some of these Huns were settled under Emnetzur and Ultzindur in Dacia Ripensis in 457 or 458.[66] However, the breakaway of these various ethnic groups, Germanic or otherwise, was not a permanent dissociation, and they would often switch allegiances over the course of the Hun retreat from the Carpathian region. As a result, the chronology of Hunno-Germanic interactions during the 460s is difficult to reconstruct.

After Nedao, Attila's son Ernak had replaced Ellak as king of the *Akatir* Huns, who were once again the dominant branch of the empire, while Dengzich (*Däŋiziq*) seems to have ruled the western half. In about 461–63, the leader of the *Amali* Goths, Valamir, had attacked the western Balkans and been granted concessions from the Romans. He then turned north and attacked the *Sadages*, who in turn asked Dengzich and the Huns for help.[67] However, Dengzich's involvement in the west was not met with approval by Ernak, who was busy with wars in his own lands.[68] In 463, Priscus states that the Avars, a people who would emigrate into Europe in 558, attacked the *Sabeiroi*, the ancient Hun rivals of the Xianbei, who in turn attacked the *Onogouroi*, *Ourogoi* and *Saragouroi*, the latter of whom defeated the *Akatir* Huns of Ernak and became dominant in the Pontic region.[69] These latter peoples likely had formed the *Tieh'le* confederation, which had been destroyed by the Rouran in 391–402, and pushed into the central Asian steppes, before emigrating again over the Volga and putting pressure on the Huns' eastern border.[70] Their movement in the 460s was likely spurred by the height of the second megadrought cycle, which intensified the military pressure on their eastern border.[71] Without his brother's support, Dengzich set out against Valamir with an army including the lesser *Bittugur* and *Bardor* Huns, as well as the *Angisciri*. He laid siege to Bassianae in 463, resulting in Valamir calling off his campaign against the *Sadages*.[72] The *Sciri* of Edeco and the Suebes under Hunimund also became involved against the Goths, due to an entanglement between Hunimund and Thiudimer.[73] The

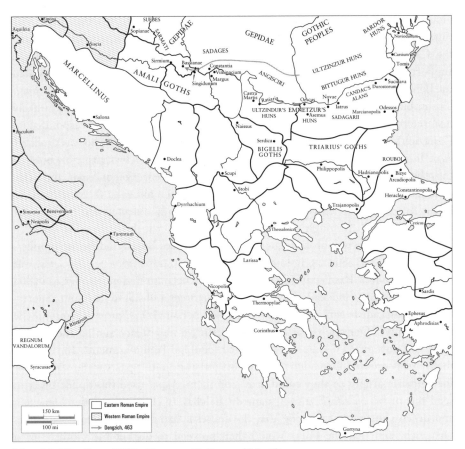

Map 11. The Late Fifth-Century Balkans, 454–69.

Romans chose to back the *Sciri* as well, against Aspar's judgement, sending forces from Illyricum.[74] Dengzich, the Romans and the *Sciri* were allegedly all defeated by Valamir in separate engagements, but he was killed in battle against the *Sciri* in about 466.[75] At about this same time or shortly afterwards, Goths under Bigelis attempted to establish themselves in the Roman Balkans as well, while Huns under Hormidac attacked Serdica.[76]

With their power beyond the Dniester slipping, Dengzich and Ernak petitioned the Romans for a new treaty and a trade marketplace on the Danube, as was tradition. However, the Romans rejected their proposition. Furthermore, it seems that at this time, Ernak was again at war with the *Saragur* Huns, who also attempted to breach the Caspian Gates and successfully raided Lazica and Armenia.[77] Without the support of Ernak, who did not want another war on two fronts, Dengzich invaded the Balkans in 467, supported by a force of Goths. Kim thinks these were the *Amali* Goths, but Heather suggests they were various small groups, with the term likely just referring to Danubian barbarians in general.[78] The Romans responded to Dengzich's invasion with emissaries and a force led by Anagastes, who was probably *dux Moesiae secundae* or *dux Scythiae*, as well as one under Ostrys, probably holding the other of those two posts. Both men were Goths of the faction of Aspar, and likely commanded armies of primarily *foederati*. Without the forces to face the Huns in battle, Anagastes sent emissaries to Dengzich, whom he rejected and in turn sent his own to Leo.[79] Although they had come to an accord, the brief truce between Leo and Dengzich was broken when Dengzich's forces began raiding for supplies, and in response Basiliscus, holding the post of *magister militum per Thracias*, was sent against him.[80] Basiliscus' forces seem to have been limited in number, as in 468 they were forced to blockade Dengzich and his forces and starve them out. Shortly after the blockade began, Aspar arrived with his personal *bucellarius* to reinforce the Roman army.[81] Dengzich sent envoys requesting a new treaty, stating they would agree to Leo's terms if they were provided food and land allotments. In response the Romans ordered Dengzich to divide his forces into four parts while waiting for the emperor's reply, so they could provision them. Aspar used this opportunity to send one of his *bucellarii*, a Hun named Chelchal, to the Goths under Dengzich and deceive them into thinking that the emperor had formed a treaty with only Dengzich, and that the Huns would then proceed to exploit the Goths.[82] As a result, the Huns were attacked by the Goths, and the Romans became aware of this disturbance and ordered their men to kill any of the barbarians who came against their forces. Dengzich and the Goths quickly realized their deception and banded together against the Romans, but as Aspar's *bucellarii* had already destroyed the forces they had been assigned to provision, they outflanked Dengzich's army and forced the Huns to break through the battle line of the other Roman generals and escape. Anagastes pursued Dengzich's army after this battle and defeated him in 469. Dengzich was decapitated and his head paraded through Constantinople, before it was symbolically mounted on the restored *Xylokerkos* Gate, rebuilt after the earthquake in 447. Modern authors remark it fitting that the son of Arnegisclus, slain at the Utus in 447, should slay the son of Attila in the same theatre two decades after.[83]

The withdrawal of the Hun polity from the Carpathian region had major repercussions for the Roman Empire. The rise of Valamir's *Amali* Goths led to the defeat of the *Sciri*, *Heruli* and *Rugi* in the Middle Danubian region at the Battle of the River Bolia, after which Odoacer led his federates into service with the West.[84] This ultimately paved the way for the deposition of Romulus Augustulus, the last western emperor. Odoacer's involvement indirectly relates these events back to the Catalaunian Fields, to which it can be argued that a mix of the collapse of Hun power and the rise of Odoacer shows that the battle to a limited degree contributed to the deposition of the last ruler in the West.

This was the end for Attila's empire, according to some authors.[85] However, Kim and many others suggest that the Huns of Ernak, who had been defeated by the *Saragur* Huns, merged with them to form the *Utigur* Bulgars, while the remainder of Dengzich's Huns became the *Kutrigur* Bulgars.[86] Steppe identity was highly fluid, and the Huns remain prominent players, identified not by a generic usage of the term but their own ethnonym, into the sixth century. But they were also concurrently called Bulgars, such as in the recruitment of some such forces by Zeno in 479, showing that after the 470s these terms likely became synonymous.[87] The suggestion of a Hunnish polity as a continuation of Attila's empire north of the Black Sea into the sixth century is still considered conjectural, but it is plausible that his sons continued the Hun government and royal line until their conquest by the Avars. The term Hun therefore became an appellation of *Xiongnū* imperial dynastic status among steppe nomads, in a similar manner to the term Roman.[88] This Hunno–Bulgar empire would continue to be a nuisance in the Balkans into the 550s, inflicting military defeats on the Romans in 493 and 499.[89]

The Rise of Frankish and Burgundian Gaul

The total collapse of Roman Gaul ultimately began with Attila's invasion itself, but was ensured by the destruction of the Alans, the elimination of the Rhine *limes* and the collapse of Aetius' army. Marcellinus had revolted in 454, and Aegidius possibly at the same time. Ricimer and Majorian seem to have had some professional army regiments as well, while Agrippinus, Aetius' *magister militum per Gallias*, does not seem to have ever been popular enough to win the backing of the field army.[90] Without an emperor on the throne or an army to oppose them, the Goths of Aquitaine would be the first barbarian power to enthrone an emperor, promoting their own hero of the Hun invasion and Aetius' former *praefectus praetoriano per Gallias*, Eparchius Avitus, to the throne.[91] However, the collapse of Roman Gaul was precipitated by another factor: a divide between the Italic and Gallic aristocracies, which was managed by Aetius but grew under Avitus. MacGeorge argues that

Ricimer's motivation to depose Avitus was due to this animosity between the Italic and Gallic families.[92] Avitus had come into power with the aid of Gothic *foederati*, which upset the Italic aristocracy so much that he was forced to order them to disband, leaving him exposed to his *comes domesticorum*, Majorian.[93] With the aid of the Roman army under Ricimer, who had recently defeated the Vandals near Agrigentum (Agrigento), Majorian defeated Avitus and his Romano–Gothic army under the *comes et magister utriusque militiae* Missianus in a battle near Placentia (Piacenza).[94] Majorian then had to put down a failed uprising by Marcellus, also likely inflicting losses on the Roman army.[95] The eastern emperor Leo I, an appointee of the Alan *magister militum* Aspar, rewarded both Majorian and Ricimer with the titles of *magister militum* and *patricius*, and after Majorian's *comes* Bruco defeated a band of 900 *Alamanni* raiding northern Italy, the people and Senate acclaimed him emperor, which was begrudgingly accepted by Leo.[96]

It should be noted that Majorian's reign saw a series of successes comparable to those of Aetius, but achieved with completely different forces: he is never mentioned as having explicitly Roman troops, although Romans were certainly a part of his army. Instead, his armies were comprised of *foederati* and *symmachi*: the semi-professional mixed regiments of the people settled within the empire, and mercenaries hired from outside the empire through treaty.[97] That 900 *Alamanni* constituted a serious threat shows how ineffective or dispersed the Roman Army was at the time. Unlike under Aetius, the Roman Army at this stage no longer had the logistics or manpower to maintain itself even at the level it did after the fall of Carthage, and Majorian was likely the first emperor to truly recruit barbarians *en masse* to replace the professional forces. Some of these were Huns under a certain Tuldila, who had served in the Italian campaign at Aquileia and were probably drawn from a group settled on the Danube during the collapse of Attila's empire.[98] Others may have been *Rugi*, Gepids, *Heruli* and Goths from Noricum and Pannonia, and it is likely that Majorian agreed to formally recognize the territory and revenue they controlled in exchange for their military services. He may have also withdrawn some of the remaining Pannonian *limitanei* as well.[99] These forces were poorly disciplined; the Huns began looting the countryside, nor were the barbarians willing to recognize Majorian's authority in pardoning them.[100] However, one army he did have access to was part of Aetius' forces under the control of Aegidius, whom Majorian had appointed *comes et magister militum per Gallias*, replacing Agrippinus.[101] Agrippinus had been at odds with Aegidius for some time, and based on Mathisen's suggestion that he hailed from eastern Lugdunensis, may have been in the same pro-Burgundian political camp as Ricimer. He evidently fell out of favour during Majorian's reign and was sentenced to execution, but seems to have been pardoned by Ricimer after Majorian's assassination.[102] Allied to Aegidius was first the younger son of Chlodio until 457, and then his successor, Childeric, who complemented Aegidius' local Roman and Alan forces with Frankish *foederati*.[103] Able to entrust Aegidius to handle both the

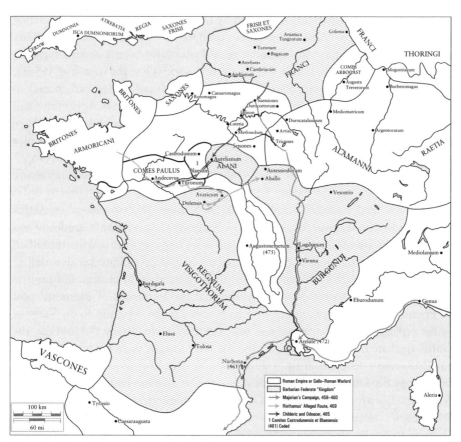

Map 12. The Collapse of Gaul, 452–70.

defence of northern Gaul and the mischief of the demoted Agrippinus, Majorian rebuilt the decrepit *classis Misenensis* and *classis Ravennensis* fleets to defend against the raiding Vandals, and personally defeated them near Sinuessa.[104] With his new federate forces having arrived to supplement his Roman troops, he marched into Gaul to reverse the losses in the region.

Possibly the most important player in the collapse of Roman Gaul during Majorian's reign was the Burgundian kingdom. Wolfram argues that after the Catalaunian Fields, many Burgundians from the Main began merging with those in Sapaudia, which is partially evidenced by the use of the battle as a deliminating year in their law code.[105] Over the course of the 450s they had increased significantly in influence: Agrippinus' appointment in 452 may have been a reward for their service at the Catalaunian Fields, like Frederic's in 453. Over the course of 455–57, they had agreed with the citizens of Lugdunum (Lyon) and the local aristocracy to take control of the city, possibly as part of an agreement with both Agrippinus and Avitus.[106] Much to Sidonius' dismay, the citizens of Lugdunum did not recognize Majorian as emperor: as a result, Sidonius' fifth panegyric was as much a plea to Majorian to spare the city, as it was to the city to support the new emperor.[107] Majorian then marched into the Rhone valley and defeated the Burgundians before laying siege to and quickly taking Lugdunum, a circumstance which greatly upset Ricimer, who had probably begun his service as *comes foederatorum* when Aetius settled the Burgundians in Sapaudia in 443. Ricimer was an uncle of Gundobad and the brother-in-law of Gundioc, and was born of a Gothic mother and Suebic father, and Majorian's inhibition of the Burgundians would precipitate his downfall.[108] But Majorian, with the assistance of Aegidius, pressed on to besiege and capture Arelate.[109] After this siege Majorian confirmed the legitimacy of Paeonius' post as Praetorian Prefect, providing he accepted a certain Magnus from Narbona as his replacement, in order to win over the Gallic aristocracy.[110] However, the Goths retaliated, laying siege to Arles, but were caught unaware by Nepotianus and Majorian's federate army.[111] Incorporating the Visigothic and Burgundian forces into his army, he ordered his new *comes et magister militum per Hispenias*, Nepotianus, with a large force of Goths under Suniericus, into Spain to defeat the Suebes.[112] Securing Spain, Majorian prepared 300 ships for a campaign against Gaiseric to retake Africa, while Marcellinus was sent by the East to campaign in Sicily.[113] However, Gaiseric bribed the citizens of Portus Illicitanus (Elche) to set fire to the fleet, prematurely ending Majorian's campaign and resulting in the ultimate failure of Aetius' strategy to recover the West.[114]

This would precipitate Majorian's downfall, as he returned to having earned the ire of both the Italic aristocracy and Ricimer, his Burgundian *comes et magister utriusque militiae*, with Burgundian interests. Because Majorian had reined in Burgundian power and reduced them back to the territory they controlled under Aetius, Ricimer met Majorian with his own Roman forces and had him arrested and deposed, before executing him.[115] Having been alienated by the Italic government and some of Majorian's policies, much of the Gallic aristocracy was willing to align itself with the local federate warlords instead of the government.[116] As a result, Lugdunum and most of the Rhone valley fell back into Burgundian hands, greatly increasing their power in southern Gaul.[117] Like with the death of Aetius, the empire's generals and armies all fragmented, with neither Nepotianus, Aegidius or Marcellinus willing to recognize Libius Severus, let alone Leo. Ricimer immediately had Nepotianus replaced by Arborius in Spain.[118] Aegidius threatened to invade Italy, but his campaign was interrupted by the Goths, while Marcellinus was probably bogged down dealing with the aforementioned raid by Hunimund around this time.[119] As a result, Ricimer reinstated Agrippinus as *comes et magister militum per Gallias* and sent him against Aegidius. Agrippinus handed over Narbona, which Aetius had tirelessly defended, to the Goths to gain their support against Aegidius, all the while weakening the empire further.[120] The Burgundians gained even more clout in the ailing empire when Gundioc was appointed in 463 as a replacement for Agrippinus, highlighting both the level of assimilation they had achieved as well as the Roman inability to influence Gaul directly.[121]

Childeric, meanwhile, would soon gain the upper hand in northern Gaul. The events of Attila's campaign and the death of Aetius quickly created a power vacuum in north-east Gaul, which drew Frankish and Alamannic expansion as the frontier kings were 'sucked' into the gap. Frankish expansion seems to have come as far as just before Augusta Suessionem (Soissons), while the *Alamanni* exerted influence up to Tricasses (Troyes).[122] Childeric was at some point possibly granted the command of *dux Belgicae secundae*, but there is debate about the nature of the letter of Remigus. He was buried with a Keller/Prottel type-7 crossbow *fibula*, which was a clear marker of a late fifth-century high-ranking bureaucrat or commander. His appointment may have come alongside Aegidius' promotion to *comes et magister militum per Gallias*.[123] Soon, Roman control in middle Gaul would fall apart as well. Early in his career, Childeric had helped Aegidius and the Alans defeat the Visigoths at the Battle of Aurelianum (Orleans) in 463, where Theodoric II's brother, Frederic, was slain. This conflict may have been part of the rivalry between Aegidius and Agrippinus, Ricimer's replacement for him.[124] Around this time he also repulsed the Goths again near Cainonense (Chinon).[125] Aegidius had then sent ambassadors to the Vandals in 464 or 465, seeking assistance against the Goths, but fell ill and died probably in 464 or 465, leaving another warlord, the *comes tractus Aremoriciani* Paul, as the only significant Roman force in the region.[126] Meanwhile, the last of the Alans were defeated by Ricimer in 464.[127] The Goths, seizing the opportunity, again attacked north over the Loire in 465, but were defeated by Childeric, Paul and Odoacer. Childeric and Odoacer then defeated Paul and drove him back to Andecavus (Angers), laying siege to and taking the city, before proceeding to execute him. At this time Childeric obtained possession of the Roman provinces in the Seine-Loire region, and made Syagrius his vassal, incorporating him into his court. However, Odoacer then turned on Childeric, but Childeric defeated him and drove him back to the Danube, where he returned to rule the *Sciri*, now an independent group in Pannonia.[128]

These events show how the Battle of the Catalaunian Fields, coupled with additional costly defeats at Piacenza and Arelate, had weakened the Visigoths enough that armies which they once vastly outnumbered they could likely now only match on the field: Majorian's Romans and *foederati* had probably barely numbered over 10,000 men at Arelate, and Aegidius and Childeric combined likely couldn't field many more. The 12,000 Armoricans (along with presumably Saxons and Franks) of Riothamus had to be defeated by ambush in 469–70.[129] Although they continued to field large armies, particularly in Spain, in Gaul their military failure was apparent.[130] Combined with the collapse of Roman hegemony, the Franks were now in a prime position to expand south, and after 465 everything north of the Loire was effectively ruled by Childeric. Many have considered Syagrius to have remained a significant power in the region, but James argues that his authority was piecemeal, as evidenced by the plethora of other independent rulers holding Roman titles in the region, as listed briefly by MacGeorge.[131] The Goths would not attempt to expand north again after this, barring possibly their involvement in the support of Syagrius' revolt in 486–87, but when Clovis demanded the Goths hand over Syagrius after he had fled to Tolosa, they immediately conceded.[132] Frankish hegemony in southern Gaul would be permanently established by the Battle of *Campus Vogladensis* (Vouille) in 507, in which the Battle of Catalaunian Fields may have inadvertently played an indirect but politically significant part. Cassiodorus' letters just before the battle encourage the Visigoths by recounting their tale of the defeat of Attila, and how Aetius and Theodoric exacted revenge for the destruction of the kingdom of Ermanaric. However, these two heroes were flawed as the disunion of the Roman-Goth coalition spoiled a supreme victory. Barnish shows how Cassiodorus had cast Clovis as the new Attila and Theodoric the Great as the new Aetius. Jordanes portrays Theodoric as an improvement on his fifth-century heroes, and his rhetoric serves as a rallying of Gothic morale.[133] It would forever remain a point of pride and propaganda in Gothic history.

Conclusion

It can be certain that the Battle of the Catalaunian Fields was not the decisive victory that saved western civilization, or saw the triumph of Christianity over the pagans, as Creasy portrays it.[1] More accurately, it has been cast as a testament to Roman diplomatic and administrative efficacy by authors such as Arther Ferrill, Meghan McEvoy and Williams and Friell.[2] Geoffrey Parker called it a 'triumph of Roman defensive strategy'.[3] It is also called a battle of coalitions, the first since the forgotten Battle of Qarqar. Although the nature of many of these federates serving the Romans may have been more akin to that of professional Roman soldiers than allied contingents of *symmachi*, it cannot be forgotten that it was still a battle of nations. The campaign was a massive military undertaking which probably stretched the resources of the embattled Western Roman Empire to its limit. It has been called the last great infantry battle of the Roman Empire, where afterwards cavalry would always play the decisive role. In fact, one could consider it quite the opposite, where the Battle of the Catalaunian Fields became the first great cavalry battle of the Roman Empire. The battle was ultimately decided by cavalry – it was an Amal noble, probably riding mounted, who struck down the also mounted Theodoric which resulted in the collapse of the Gothic line, while the entire centre of the battlefield was dominated by the mounted Alans and Huns, along with Thorisumund and his Gothic cavalry. Simultaneously, it was likely the one of the greatest military undertakings by the combined forces of Germanic Europe, at least prior to the Middle Ages. Christopher Kelly asserts that the battle represented the limits of the power of the Hunnish state, although his statement that the Huns never decisively defeated the Romans in a pitched battle is completely contrary to the major military disasters in the Balkans in 441–47.[4]

The Battle of the Catalaunian Fields itself, however, is not the most important battle of the fifth century, as is often implied, nor is it one of those engagements that saved western civilization, as held by Creasy. Rather, it is heavily overshadowed by the Battle of the River Utus, as well as its smaller but significant counterpart in the Battle of the Chersonese. These two engagements resulted in the destruction of four Roman field armies, totaling 93,376 men, while Attila's campaigns resulted in the severe depopulation and deurbanization of the Balkans north of the Haemus Mountains, as well as the destruction of the Danubian defensive system from Pannonia Valeria up to Novae: approximately 46,400 men.[5] These are paper strength numbers, but this single event resulted in the loss of approximately

139,776 men inside of a single year – a devastating 44 per cent of the eastern Roman army.[6] Of course, that assumes every man in each regiment was killed, which is impossible, but the Huns and their ilk were known to be particularly ruthless in their pursuit of defeated armies, and casualty rates were notoriously and exorbitantly high.[7] It forced a change in policy in the Eastern court, which now relied on paying off the Germanic groups roaming in the northern Balkans rather than attempting to subdue them militarily. The empire also began to rely more on internal defence in the Balkans, constructing the long walls near Arcadiopolis and moving the administration of Illyricum to Thessalonica.[8] The Danube itself would not serve as a proper buffer for the rest of the fifth century, or arguably ever again.[9] Without this buffer, and with a rural, depopulated region that was difficult to defend, the Battle of the River Utus thus indirectly provided an opening for the Slavic migration: a movement of peoples which would permanently transform the Balkans. Already in the 460s, the Goths were filling the vacuum in Thrace, where Aspar allowed the Goths of Triarius to fan out across the region.[10] It also resulted in the loss of one of the Eastern Roman Empire's largest recruiting grounds in Thrace, and prevented them from restoring the army to a condition where they were able to assist the West for two decades, when they finally launched a campaign under Basiliscus in 468.[11] Their inability to assist Aetius and the West in 441, and then from 447–68, could be argued to have been a major factor in the collapse of the Western Roman Empire, and it could be said that the Battle of the River Utus was more instrumental than the Battle of the Catalaunian Fields in this regard. Finally, the Utus and the Hun invasions resulted in the beginning of a shift in Roman foreign policy, where negotiating with and buying off potential threats was seen as a more successful endeavour than risking costly military engagement. This trend is reflected in the writing of the fifth century and later, as shown by Blockley, where the discernible disinterest in military events is a reflection of the changing nature of Roman foreign policy.[12]

The Battle of the Catalaunian Fields has been considered the decisive battle of the fifth century, and one of the great decisive battles of the world. Bachrach, utilizing Clauzewitz's methodology, argues that this cannot be said with certainty.[13] The engagement itself was strategically unnecessary and tactically indecisive, with the majority of authors in agreement that the war had already been decided at Orleans.[14] It did not prevent a second invasion in 452, nor did it in any way lead to Attila's downfall. As Bury points out, the decisive battle that led to the collapse of the Hun Empire was on the River Nedao in 454.[15] In comparison to the possibly continent-spanning repercussions of the Balkans invasions, the Battle of the Catalaunian Fields' impact lies in the region of Gaul and the long-term development of migration-era Gaul. It paved the way for the Frankish and Burgundian kingdoms to entrench themselves and flourish by weakening the Goths of Aquitaine for over a decade. It also ultimately contributed to the final collapse of the western Roman army, although the siege of Aquileia and the attack on the Alans of Valentinois and

Orleans by Thorismund may have been more detrimental to that effect. In fact, it could be argued that the Catalaunian Fields had a certain counter-decisiveness in its results.

Nevertheless, the Battle of the Catalaunian Fields was important to ethnogenesis in migration-era Gaul, becoming a source of pride and propaganda for both the Ostrogoths and Visigoths in their wars against the Franks.[16] Just as Theodoric was cast as the new Aetius, Pippin would later fulfill that role for the Franks.[17] It also became a political tool of the Romans, who cast Avitus as a new Cincinnatus in the fifth century, idealized Aetius as a model Roman in the sixth century and held it as a prime allegory for political criticism of Justinian's military policy.[18] Barnish also states that it became an important moment in Frankish and Burgundian history, as they faced their own nomadic ally in the Avars. He sees the battle as part of a recreation of the identity of Gaul, where kings, bishops and nobles are related to each other and the ties between the Gallic priesthood and aristocracy are cemented by the Attila crisis.[19] The Battle of the Catalaunian Fields could be considered the highlight of Alan history, since it was the Alans who fought off the besiegers and formed the centre of Aetius' line, bludgeoning and cutting down the Huns in the middle of the battlefield, before eventually breaking them. It may also be considered one of the most embarrassing moments of Gothic history, where despite the pride and propaganda they placed around it, the Goths had almost cost Aetius the battle. Furthermore, their actions following the battle under Thorismund were less than amicable, especially compared to the relationship between Theodoric and the Romans that Cassiodorus liked to portray. Jordanes considered it a case of parricide in his portrayal due to the casting of the *Amali* against the *Balthi*. In fact, Jordanes states that Theodoric was allegedly born on the day of a great Gothic victory over the Huns, but Wolfram thinks that Jordanes moved it to a later date based on his age when he was a hostage at Constantinople, and he was actually born around the time of the Catalaunian Fields. Jordanes changed it because the Catalaunian Fields wasn't the great Amal victory he hoped for in his message.[20] The battle also became a facet of other cultures, and is a possible source for the widespread inclusion of Huns in Scandinavian culture.[21] Evidence of the Hun invasion of Gaul may also have lingered in British culture. Gildas' description of the Saxons sweeping across Britain, breaching its cities with battering rams, burning them to the ground and slaughtering their bishops hardly represents the transformation of late antique Britain, but are a rather characteristic attribute of Attila's campaign, and may have been applied to the Saxons for literary and/or political effect.[22]

Finally, the potential location of the Battle of the Catalaunian Fields at Montgueux certainly deserves some attention. I would argue that at the least, an archaeological survey for possible excavation sites should be performed on the ridges around Montgueux, as well as the nearby plain below and to the south, in order to ascertain the battlefield's precise location. Satellite LIDAR imaging of the region around Saint Lye and Fontvannes, if possible, may reveal the presence of any former camps, as such massive armies surely would have left a significant impression on the landscape. It may also be worth watching development at Chalons-en-Champagne and Sarry, considering the archaeological finds along the Marne, as there may be further burials which construction projects could reveal. Finds related to the battle could answer many questions about the Roman military, the Hun military and of course reveal more about the battle itself.

The Catalaunian Fields is a battle that remains constructed on circumstantial evidence, and with no surviving copies of Frigeridus, Priscus, Sidonius or Cassiodorus having been found, it will remain so, lest one of these works should reveal itself on the recycled pages of some medieval manuscript. Despite this inconvenience, the battle does make for an excellent case study in many ways: in the world of historiography it is a prime example of the expression of classical literary authorship, with the battle being organized in a standard literary format by which all accounts of Roman battles should probably be assessed. In ethnography it shows the complexity of fifth-century identity, military service and the changing face of the European sociopolitical landscape. Finally, it also serves as a prime example of the usefulness of Roman military manuals in reconstructing the strategy and tactics of both the Romans and their adversaries, although such reconstructions must be acknowledged as conjecture. The Catalaunian Fields may not be the most important or decisive battle of the fifth century, but it may be the most important representation of our modern understanding of the fifth century.

Appendix A

Chronology

284	Diocletian becomes emperor, beginning of the Dominate. The Roman administration is partitioned into the Tetrarchy.
300	By this time the northern *Xiongnū* had become the Huns, conquering much of modern Kazakhstan. The *Alpidzur*, *Tongur*, *Itimari* and *Boisci* confederation settles on the Volga around this time.
311	Southern *Xiongnū* sack Luoyang. Records of this event form the linguistic basis of the Hun-*Xiongnū* connection.
313	Battle of the Milvian Bridge.
324	Constantine unifies the Roman Empire and moves the capital to Constantinople.
325	First ecumenical Council of Nicaea.
329	Southern *Xiongnū* are conquered by the state of Jie.
350	Chionite Huns occupy Sogdia.
350–58	War between the Chionite Huns and Sassanid Persians.
357	Battle of Strasburg.
359–60	Kidara and the Chionite Huns conquer the Kushan Empire, establishing the Kidarite Huns.
360	A megadrought caused by the El Niño Southern Oscillation peaks in this year, spurring migration on the central Asian steppes.
360–70	Huns drive various Oghur-speakers and Alanic peoples west, establishing themselves in the Don-Volga region.
370–75	Huns and Alans drive the *Greuthungi* west into the *Tervingi*.
376	The *Tervingi* and *Greuthungi* appear on the Danube asking for sanctuary. First reports of the Hun arrival in Europe reach Ammianus Marcellinus.
377	Gothic revolt, *Greuthungi* cross the Danube and join the *Tervingi*.
378	Battle of Adrianople, the Roman army is defeated and Emperor Valens is killed.

383	*Terminus post quem* for Vegetius' *Epitoma Rei Militaris*.
391	Aetius is born.
394	Battle of the Frigidus. Alaric comes to power amongst the Goths.
395	Theodosius dies, the empire is inherited by his sons Honorius and Arcadius. Stilicho becomes manager of the West. The Huns under Kursik and Basik launch a massive invasion down through Armenia into Syria and Mesopotamia, but are defeated by the Sassanids.
397	The Huns launch a second raid into Anatolia but are defeated by Eutropius.
398	Gildo revolts in Africa but is suppressed by Stilicho. *Terminus post quem* for Attila's birth, assuming an average lifespan of 55 years. The *Notitia Dignitatum* is first compiled.
399	Gaudentius Aetius is made *comes Africae*. Flavius Aetius is enrolled in the *protectores domestici*.
400	Revolt of Gainas. Uldin is a king of the Huns by this point.
401	The *Tieh'le* confederation is broken up by the Rouran and begins to migrate west.
402	Theodosius II becomes co-emperor with Arcadius. Alaric is defeated at Pollentia.
403	Stilicho defeats Alaric near Verona.
404–05	Uldin raids Thrace and campaigns in Germania, triggering the invasion of Radagasius. Aetius is sent to the court of Alaric until 408. The *Notitia Dignitatum* is passed to the Western Roman Empire.
406	Alans, Vandals and Suebes cross the Rhine in the winter. Constantine III revolts in Gaul. Stilicho, Sarus and Uldin break the siege of Ticinum and defeat Radagasius at the Battle of Faesulae.
408	Stilicho is assassinated. Alaric lays siege to Rome. Aetius is sent to the court of Uldin. Arcadius dies and Theodosius II becomes sole emperor.
409	Second siege of Rome by Alaric. Alaric defeats a detachment of the Dalmatian army under Valens sent to reinforce the city. Gerontius promotes Maximus as emperor in Spain. Honorius requests a force of Huns to stop Alaric.
410	Alaric sacks Rome.
411	Uldin dies, Charaton becomes emperor of the Huns. Constantius III becomes *magister utriusque militiae* and lays siege to Gerontius and Constantine III at Arles. Gerontius flees to Spain and Constantine III surrenders. Jovinus usurps in northern Gaul with the help of Goar's

Alans, and settles the Burgundians of Gundicar around Borbetomagus in exchange for their support. Edobichus is defeated.

412   Olympiodorus' embassy is sent to the court of Charaton. Donatus is executed by this time.

413   Athaulf defeats Jovinus. The Alans of Goar either join the Goths or defect to the Romans.

414   The Alans, possibly those of Goar or Sambida, defect to the Romans at the siege of Bazas, forcing the Goths to abandon the siege. Constantius III campaigns against the Goths, pushing them into Hispania.

418   The Visigoths are established in Aquitania along the Garonne. Theodoric becomes king after Wallia dies. Charaton dies somewhere around this time.

420   *Terminus ante quem* for Attila's birth, assuming a minimum age of succession at 18 years.

421   Theodosius II goes to war with Persia. Constantius III is appointed co-emperor and dies. Castinus becomes *magister utriusque militiae*.

422   Rua and Octar invade Thrace, targeting the *Alpidzur, Tongur, Itimari* and *Boisci* confederation. Castinus is defeated by the Vandals in Spain.

423   Honorius dies and no successor is nominated. With the support of Castinus, Theodosius II is briefly sole ruler of the Roman Empire.

424   Castinus promotes Ioannes to the throne and usurps. Aetius is sent to the court of Rua to retrieve Hun reinforcements.

425   Gaudentius Aetius is made *magister militum per Gallias* but is killed in a revolt against Ioannes. Theodosius II launches a campaign under the command of Aspar and Ardaburius to put Valentinian III on the throne. Ioannes and Castinus are executed. Aetius returns with a Hun army and uses it as leverage to have himself appointed *magister militum per Gallias*.

426   Aetius defeats the Goths outside Arelate.

427   Flavius Constantius Felix brands the *comes Africae*, Bonifatius, a traitor and begins a civil war. Two expeditionary forces are sent against Bonifatius.

428   Aetius defeats the Franks. *Terminus ante quem* for edits to the *Notitia Dignitatum*.

429   The Vandals cross the Straits of Gibraltar and invade Africa. Bonifatius is restored to Placidia's favour.

430   Octar dies while attempting to subjugate the Burgundians, and the Huns are defeated. Felix is hanged by the army at Aetius' instigation, and Aetius is made *magister utriusque militiae*. Bonifatius engages Gaiseric near Lake Fezzara and is defeated. Gaiseric lays siege to Hippo Regius.

431   Aetius defeats the Goths of Anaolsus, and then campaigns against the *Iuthungi* and *Bacaudae* in Noricum. Hippo Regius is sacked, and Bonifatius with reinforcements under Aspar are defeated in a field battle by Gaiseric.

432   Bonifatius is appointed *magister utriusque militiae* and recalled to depose Aetius. Aetius is defeated at the Battle of Ariminium, but Bonifatius dies from his wounds. Sebastianus becomes *magister utriusque militiae* and Aetius flees the empire.

433   Aetius returns with an embassy from Rua, threatening war if he is not reinstated. Sebastianus is exiled.

434   Honoria becomes pregnant after an affair with her aide Eugenius.

435   Aspar, Valentinian III and Trygetius agree to a treaty with Gaiseric. Aetius is made *patricius*, cementing his control of the West. Litorius is sent against the *Bacaudae* of Armorica.

436   Goths and Burgundians simultaneously revolt, laying siege to Narbona. Aetius defeats the Burgundians, Litorius defeats the *Bacaudae*.

437   Siege of Narbona is alleviated. Aetius and the Huns massacre the Burgundians.

438   Rua dies, Attila and Bleda succeed as kings of the Huns. The Huns establish the treaty of Margus with the Eastern Roman Empire. Aetius defeats the Visigoths at the Battle of *Mons Colubrarius* and campaigns against the Suebi. The Theodosian Code is adopted. Priscus' history begins here.

439   Litorius and the Huns are defeated outside Tolosa by the Visigoths. Aetius defeats the Goths in a night attack on their camp. Carthage is sacked by Gaiseric.

440   Bleda and Attila defeat the *Sorosgi* by this time. Theodosius II, with Aetius and Sigisvultus, launch a massive expedition to retake Carthage. The Alans of Goar are settled at Aurelianum.

441   Exploiting the lack of forces in the Balkans, Attila invades Moesia and sacks Viminacium, Margus, Singidunum and Sirmium. Rechila takes most of Spain. Astyrius is sent to Spain in response and defeats the *Bacaudae*.

442   The Vandal campaign is called off and a treaty is signed with Gaiseric, due to the Hun threat. The East enters into a temporary truce with Attila waiting for its forces to be recalled. The Alans of Goar are sent against the Armorican *Baucaudae*. The Alans of Sambida are settled in modern Valentinois.

443   Attila again attacks, sacking Ratiaria and Naissus. The East enters into a new treaty with the Huns, raising the tribute. Merobaudes defeats the *Bacaudae* in Spain. The Burgundians are resettled in Sapaudia.

444   Theodosius II refortifies the Danube. The Franks of Chlodio take Arras and besiege Turonum.

445   Attila assassinates his brother Bleda and becomes emperor of the Huns. The siege of Turonum is lifted by Aetius' arrival, and Aetius and Majorian defeat Chlodio at *Vicus Helenae*.

446   Vitus is sent against the *Suebes* with the Roman army and the Visigoths, but the Goths desert and he is defeated. The 'Groans of the Britons' letter is sent. Aetius is granted a third consulship and a triumph in Rome. *Terminus ante quem* for Vegetius' *Epitoma Rei Militaris*.

447   An earthquake strikes Constantinople and opens up the Theodosian walls. Attila uses this opening to invade, destroying the Roman army at the River Utus, but the walls are repaired before he reaches Constantinople. He defeats the Romans again on the Thracian Chersonese and then ravages the Balkans. A new treaty, increasing the tribute and forcing the evacuation of the Danube, is established at the end of the year.

448   Aetius and Goar defeat the Armorican *Bacaudae* once more.

449   The king of the Franks, Chlodio, dies, causing a succession dispute. Priscus' embassy is sent to the court of Attila, with the ultimate goal of assassinating him, which fails. The *Bacaudae* revolt in Tarraconensis and with Suebic support seize most of Spain by the end of the year. Honoria sends her missive to Attila.

450   Theodosius II is killed by a fall from his horse, and Marcian ascends to the throne.

451   Attila invades Gaul. Argentoratum, Borbetomagus, Augusta Treverorum, Divodurum Mediomatricum and Durocortorum are all sacked. Aurelianum is besieged. Aetius mobilizes a coalition to meet the invasion and Attila retreats in the face of its advance. Aetius' forces meet Attila on the Catalaunian Fields, where Theodoric is killed, but the battle is inconclusive. Attila retreats from Gaul.

452   Attila invades Italy, sacking Aquileia and penetrating as far as Milan. An embassy led by Pope Leo, Trygetius and Gennadius Avienus

negotiate a treaty and Attila withdraws. Marcian sends another general named Aetius to harass the Huns along the Danube.

453   Attila the Hun dies of a burst blood vessel, likely due to cirrhosis of the liver. The Visigoths under Thorismund besiege Arelate but are persuaded to abandon the siege by Tonantius Ferreolus. Dissatisfied with his policy, Thorismund's brothers have him assassinated. Aetius and the Visigoths under Frederic campaign in Spain, retaking the provinces of Tarraconensis and Carthaginiensis.

454   The Gepids under Ardaric lead a revolt against Attila's sons, defeating them at the Battle of Nedao in Pannonia. Valamir and the *Amali* Goths revolt separately. Flavius Aetius is assassinated by Valentinian III while discussing finances before the court.

455   Valentinian III is assassinated by Aetius' *bucellarii* at the instigation of Petronius Maximus. Maximus is stoned to death fleeing Rome in an extremely short, unpopular reign. With the treaty void, the Vandals sack Rome. The Gepids attack the Burgundians on the Main. Avitus is promoted to emperor by the Visigoths.

456   Ricimer defeats the Vandals near Agrigentum. Majorian and Ricimer depose and execute Avitus. Prosper completes and publishes his *Epitoma Chronicon*.

457   The *Alamanni* invade Italy but are defeated by Bruco. The victory is attributed to Majorian, who is promoted to emperor. Emnetzur and Ultzindur are settled in Dacia Ripensis. Valamir and the *Amali* raid Illyricum. Childeric succeeds to the Frankish throne. Marcian dies and Leo becomes emperor.

458   Majorian defeats the Vandals at Sinuessa. He then proceeds into Gaul, retakes Lugdunum from the Burgundians and breaks the Visigothic siege of Arelate.

459   Nepotianus and Sunericus campaign against the *Suebes* and reconquer Spain.

460   Majorian and his army prepare a fleet to cross to Mauretania at Portus Illicitanus, but Gaiseric persuades the citizens to burn the fleet.

461   Majorian returns to Italy where he is intercepted by Ricimer, deposed and executed. Ricimer appoints Libius Severus as emperor. Agrippinus cedes Narbona to the Goths in exchange for support against Aegidius. Valamir attacks the *Sadages* and Dengzich campaigns against Valamir.

463   Aegidius defeats the Goths at the Battle of Aurelianum with the help of Childeric, and Frederic is slain in the fighting. Aegidius repulses

the Goths again at Cainonense. Gundioc is appointed *magister militum per Gallias* by Ricimer, replacing Agrippinus. The *Saragur* Huns, driven west by the *Onogurs*, *Oghurs*, *Sabir* Xianbei and the Eurasian Avars, attack the Huns of Ernak. Dengzich lays siege to Bassianae, and Valamir breaks off his campaign to allieviate the siege. The Romans back the *Sciri*, who declare war on Valamir alongside the *Suebes* of Hunimund on the Danube.

464   A group of Alans invades Italy from Gaul but are defeated by Ricimer. Aegidius sends an embassy to the Vandals.

465   Aegidius dies of disease. Childeric, a Roman *comes* named Odoacer and Paul repulse the Goths again at Aurelianum, but Childeric and Odoacer turn on Paul and take Andecavus, before Childeric turns on Odoacer. Childeric gains control of northern Gaul as far as the Loire. Odoacer returns to the *Sciri* on the Danube.

466   By this point Valamir has defeated the *Suebes*, *Sciri* and Dengzich, but is killed in battle against the *Sciri*. The Goths of Bigelis settle in Thrace. Huns under Hormidac sack Serdica.

467   Dengzich and Ernak petition the Romans for a new treaty and a border market, but are declined. Dengzich invades the Balkans but is blockaded by Anagastes.

468   Aspar defeats Dengzich through deception. Anthemius, the eastern Roman army and the eastern Roman navy attempt to retake Carthage with the help of Marcellinus. Marcellinus defeats the Vandals in Sicily. They are defeated in the Battle of Cape Bon by Gaiseric. Ricimer assassinates Marcellinus.

469   Dengzich is defeated and executed by Anagastes and paraded through Constantinople. Riothamus leads the Armoricans against the Visigoths in support of Anthemius and captures Avaricum. The *Amali* Goths defeat a coalition of *Sciri*, *Suebes*, *Rugii* and *Heruli* at the Battle of the River Bolia.

470   Riothamus and his army are defeated at Dolensis. Odoacer becomes part of the *protectores domestici*.

471   Aspar is executed at the instigation of Zeno. Anthemiolus and a Roman force are sent to alleviate the siege of Arelate, but are defeated by Euric.

472   Gundobad is made *magister utriusque militiae*. Anthemius is executed by Ricimer and his forces sack Rome. Olybrius is appointed emperor, but Ricimer dies of natural causes shortly afterwards, followed by Olybrius as well.

473	Gundobad promotes Glycerius to emperor. Arelate and Massilia are conquered by the Visigoths.
474	Leo dies and Zeno becomes emperor. Julius Nepos deposes Glycerius. Priscus publishes all eight volumes of his *Historia Byzantiae*.
475	Gundioc dies and Gundobad leaves the court to become king of the Burgundians. Julius Nepos appoints Orestes *magister utriusque militiae*, who appoints Odoacer *comes foederatorum*. Augustonemetum is ceded to Euric. Nepos is deposed by Orestes and Romulus Augustulus appointed.
476	Odoacer revolts against Orestes, and Romulus Augustulus is deposed by Odoacer. End of the western Roman administration.
477–78	Sidonius begins, but does not complete, his history of the Hun invasion and his life of Anianus.
479	First mention of the reformed Hunnic state as the *Kutrigur* and *Utigur* Bulgars.
486	Syagrius, Aegidius' son, revolts against Clovis, but is promptly defeated and flees to the Visigoths.
487	Syagrius is relinquished by the Visigoths and executed by Clovis.
507	The Franks defeat the Visigoths at the Battle of Vouille, conquering Aquitania.
526–33	Cassiodorus completes and publishes his Gothic history.
534	Cassiodorus publishes his letters.
551	Jordanes publishes his *De Origine Actibusque Getarum*.
553	Procopius completes his *Hyper ton Polemon Logoi*.
558	The Hunno-Bulgar *Kutrigurs* and *Utigurs*, after fighting a civil war instigated by Justinian, are overrun by the Eurasian Avars.
566	Victor Tonnenesis publishes his *Chronicon*.
582	*Terminus post quem* for the commissioning of the *Strategikon*.
594	Gregory of Tours' *Decem Libri Historiarum* is published.
602	*Terminus ante quem* for the publishing of the *Strategikon*.
624	Isidore completes his *Historia de regibus Gothorum, Vandalorum et Suevorum*.
658	*Terminus post quem* for the publication of the Chronicle of Fredegar
733	The *Gallic Chronicle* of 511 is compiled.

Appendix B

A Force Estimate of the *Notitia Dignitatum*

Tabulation of Forces in the *Notitia Dignitatum: In Partibus Orientis*

Command	Grade	Infantry Strength	Cavalry Strength	Combined
Eastern Roman Empire[1]				
Magister Militum Praesentalis I	Comitatenses	17,280	6,144	23,424
Magister Militum Praesentalis II	Comitatenses	16,000	6,144	22,144
Magister Militum per Orientem	Comitatenses	19,520	5,376	24,896
Comes Limitis Aegypti	Limitanei	8,160	6,656	14,816
Comes per Isauriam	Limitanei	1,920	0	1,920
Dux Thebaidos	Limitanei	13,120	10,752	23,872
Dux Palaestinae	Limitanei	6,240	9,216	15,456
Dux Arabiae	Limitanei	4,320	7,168	11,488
Dux Foenicis	Limitanei	4,320	9,728	14,048
Dux Syriae et Eufratensis Syriae	Limitanei	3,840	6,144	9,984
Dux Osrhoenae	Limitanei	1,920	7,680	9,600
Dux Mesopotamiae	Limitanei	2,880	6,656	9,536
Dux Armeniae	Limitanei	7,680	6,144	13,824
Magister Militum per Thracias	Comitatenses	20,160	3,584	23,744
Dux Scythiae	Limitanei	11,840	1,792	13,632
Dux Moesiae Secundae	Limitanei	14,240	1,792	16,032
Magister Militum per Illyricum	Comitatenses	23,040	1,024	24,064
Dux Moesiae Primae	Limitanei	10,880	2,048	12,928
Dux Daciae Ripensis	Limitanei	14,080	0	14,080
	Total	201,440	98,048	299,488
			Comitatenses	118,272
			Limitanei	181,216

Magister Militum Praesentalis I

Infantry

Unit	Grade	Organization	Paper Strength
Lanciarii Seniores	Legio Palatina	Legion	960
Iovani Iuniores	Legio Palatina	Legion	960
Herculani Iuniores	Legio Palatina	Legion	960
Fortenses	Legio Palatina	Legion	960
Nervii	Legio Palatina	Legion	960
Mattiarii Iuniores	Legio Palatina	Legion	960
Batavi Seniores	Auxilia Palatina	Numerus	640
Brachiati Seniores	Auxilia Palatina	Numerus	640
Salii	Auxilia Palatina	Numerus	640
Constantiniani	Auxilia Palatina	Numerus	640
Mattiaci Seniores	Auxilia Palatina	Numerus	640
Sagitarii Seniores Gallicani	Auxilia Palatina	Numerus	640
Sagitarii Iuniores Gallicani	Auxilia Palatina	Numerus	640
Tertii Sagitarii Valentis	Auxilia Palatina	Numerus	640
Defensores	Auxilia Palatina	Numerus	640
Raetobarii	Auxilia Palatina	Numerus	640
Anglevarii	Auxilia Palatina	Numerus	640
Hiberi	Auxilia Palatina	Numerus	640
Visi	Auxilia Palatina	Numerus	640
Felices Honoriani Iuniores	Auxilia Palatina	Numerus	640
Victores	Auxilia Palatina	Numerus	640
Primi Theodosiani	Auxilia Palatina	Numerus	640
Tertii Theodosiani	Auxilia Palatina	Numerus	640
Felices Theodosiani Isaurii	Auxilia Palatina	Numerus	640
		Infantry	17,280

Magister Militum Praesentalis I

Cavalry

Unit	Grade	Organization	Paper Strength
Equites Promoti Seniores	Vexillatio Palatina	Ala	512
Comites Clibanarii	Vexillatio Palatina	Ala	512
Comites Sagittarii Iuniores	Vexillatio Palatina	Ala	512
Comites Taifali	Vexillatio Palatina	Ala	512
Equites Arcades	Vexillatio Palatina	Ala	512
Equites Catafractarii Biturigenses	Vexillatio Comitatenses	Ala	512
Equites Armigeri Seniores Gallicani	Vexillatio Comitatenses	Ala	512
Equites Quinto Dalmatae	Vexillatio Comitatenses	Ala	512
Equites Nono Dalmatae	Vexillatio Comitatenses	Ala	512
Equites Primi Scutarii	Vexillatio Comitatenses	Ala	512
Equites Promoti Iuniores	Vexillatio Comitatenses	Ala	512
Equites Primi Clibanarii Parthi	Vexillatio Comitatenses	Ala	512
		Cavalry	6,144
		Total	23,424

Magister Militum Praesentalis II

Infantry

Unit	Grade	Organization	Paper Strength
Matiarii Seniores	Legio Palatina	Legion	960
Daci	Legio Palatina	Legion	960
Scythae	Legio Palatina	Legion	960
Primani	Legio Palatina	Legion	960
Undecimani	Legio Palatina	Legion	960
Lanciarii Iuniores	Legio Palatina	Legion	960
Regii	Auxilia Palatina	Numerus	640
Cornuti	Auxilia Palatina	Numerus	640
Tubantes	Auxilia Palatina	Numerus	640
Constantimiani	Auxilia Palatina	Numerus	640
Mattiaci Iuniores	Auxilia Palatina	Numerus	640
Sagittarii Seniores Orientales	Auxilia Palatina	Numerus	640
Sagittarii Iuniores Orientales	Auxilia Palatina	Numerus	640
Sagittarii Dominici	Auxilia Palatina	Numerus	640
Vindices	Auxilia Palatina	Numerus	640
Bucinobantes	Auxilia Palatina	Numerus	640
Falchovarii	Auxilia Palatina	Numerus	640
Thraces	Auxilia Palatina	Numerus	640
Tervingi	Auxilia Palatina	Numerus	640
Felices Theodosiani	Auxilia Palatina	Numerus	640
Felices Arcadiani Iuniores	Auxilia Palatina	Numerus	640
Felices Theodosiani[2]	Auxilia Palatina	Numerus	640
Felices Arcadiani Iuniores[3]	Auxilia Palatina	Numerus	640
Secundi Theodosiani	Auxilia Palatina	Numerus	640
		Infantry	16,000

Magister Militum Praesentalis II

Unit		Cavalry	
	Grade	Organization	Paper Strength
Comites Seniores	Vexillatio Palatina	Ala	512
Equites Brachiati Iuniores	Vexillatio Palatina	Ala	512
Equites Batavi Iuniores	Vexillatio Palatina	Ala	512
Comites Sagittarii Armeni	Vexillatio Palatina	Ala	512
Equites Persae Clibanarii	Vexillatio Palatina	Ala	512
Equites Theodosiaci Seniores	Vexillatio Palatina	Ala	512
Equites Catafractarii	Vexillatio Comitatenses	Ala	512
Equites Catafractarii Ambianenses	Vexillatio Comitatenses	Ala	512
Equites Sexto Dalmatae	Vexillatio Comitatenses	Ala	512
Equites Secundi Scutarii	Vexillatio Comitatenses	Ala	512
Equites Scutarii	Vexillatio Comitatenses	Ala	512
Equites Secundi Clibanarii Parthi	Vexillatio Comitatenses	Ala	512
		Cavalry	6,144
		Total	22,144

Magister Militum per Orientem

Infantry

Unit	Grade	Organization	Paper Strength
Felices Arcadiani Seniores	Auxilia Palatina	Numerus	640
Felices Honoriani Seniores	Auxilia Palatina	Numerus	640
Quinta Macedonica	Comitatenses	Legion	960
Martenses Seniores	Comitatenses	Legion	960
Septima Gemina	Comitatenses	Legion	960
Decima Gemina	Comitatenses	Legion	960
Balistarii Seniores	Comitatenses	Legion	960
Prima Flavia Constantia	Comitatenses	Legion	960
Secunda Flavia Constantia Thebaeorum	Comitatenses	Legion	960
Secunda Felix Valentis Thebaeorum	Comitatenses	Legion	960
Prima Flavia Theodosiana	Comitatenses	Legion	960
Prima Armeniaca	Pseudocomitatenses	Legion	960
Secunda Armeniaca	Pseudocomitatenses	Legion	960
Fortenses Auxiliarii	Pseudocomitatenses	Legion	960
Funditores	Pseudocomitatenses	Legion	960
Prima Italica	Pseudocomitatenses	Legion	960
Quarta Italica	Pseudocomitatenses	Legion	960
Sexta Parthica	Pseudocomitatenses	Legion	960
Prima Isaura Sagittaria	Pseudocomitatenses	Legion	960
Balistarii Theodosiaci	Pseudocomitatenses	Legion	960
Transtigritani	Pseudocomitatenses	Legion	960
		Infantry	19,520

Magister Militum per Orientem

Cavalry

Unit	Grade	Organization	Paper Strength
Comites Catafractarii	Vexillatio Comitatenses	Ala	512
Bucellarii Iuniores	Vexillatio Comitatenses	Ala	512
Equites Armigeri Seniores Orientales	Vexillatio Comitatenses	Ala	512
Equites Tertio Dalmatae	Vexillatio Comitatenses	Ala	512
Equites Primi Scutarii Orientales	Vexillatio Comitatenses	Ala	512
Equites Secundi Stablesiani	Vexillatio Comitatenses	Ala	512
Equites Tertii Stablesiani	Vexillatio Comitatenses	Ala	512
Equites Promoti Clibanarii	Vexillatio Comitatenses	Ala	512
Equites Quarti Clibanarii Parthi	Vexillatio Comitatenses	Ala	512
Equites Primi Sagitarii	Vexillatio Comitatenses	Ala	512
Cuneus Equitum Secundorum Clibanariorum Palmirenorum	Vexillatio Comitatenses	Cuneus	256
		Cavalry	5,376
		Total	24,896

Comes Limitis Aegypti

Infantry

Unit	Grade	Organization	Paper Strength
Legio Quinta Macedonica	Limitanei	Legion	960
Legio Tertiadecima Gemina	Limitanei	Legion	960
Legio Tertia Diocletiana Thebaidos	Limitanei	Legion	960
Legio Secunda Traiana	Limitanei	Legion	960
Cohors Tertio Galatarum	Limitanei	Cohort	480
Cohors Secunda Astarum	Limitanei	Cohort	480
Cohors Prima Sagittariorum	Limitanei	Cohort	480
Cohors Prima Augusta Pannoniorum	Limitanei	Cohort	480
Cohors Prima Epireorum	Limitanei	Cohort	480
Cohors Quarta Iuthungorum	Limitanei	Cohort	480
Cohors Secunda Ituraeorum	Limitanei	Cohort	480
Cohors Secunda Thracum	Limitanei	Cohort	480
Cohors Quarta Numidiarum	Limitanei	Cohort	480
		Infantry	8,160

Comes Limitis Aegypti

Cavalry

Unit	Grade	Organization	Paper Strength
Ala Tertia Arabum	Limitanei	Ala	512
Ala Octava Vandilorum	Limitanei	Ala	512
Ala Septima Sarmatarum	Limitanei	Ala	512
Ala Prima Aegyptiorum	Limitanei	Ala	512
Ala Veterana Gallorum	Limitanei	Ala	512
Ala Prima Herculia	Limitanei	Ala	512
Ala Quinta Raetorum	Limitanei	Ala	512
Ala Prima Tingitania	Limitanei	Ala	512
Ala Apriana	Limitanei	Ala	512
Ala Secunda Assyriorum	Limitanei	Ala	512
Ala Quinta Praelectorum	Limitanei	Ala	512
Ala Secunda Ulpia Afrorum	Limitanei	Ala	512
Ala Secunda Aegyptiorum	Limitanei	Ala	512
		Cavalry	6,656
		Total	14,816

Comes per Isauriam

Infantry

Unit	Grade	Organization	Paper Strength
Legio Secundae Isaura	Limitanei	Legion	960
Legio Tertia Isaura	Limitanei	Legion	960
		Infantry	1,920
		Total	1,920

Dux Thebaidos

Infantry

Unit	Grade	Organization	Paper Strength
Legio Tertia Diocletiana	Limitanei	Legion	960
Legio Secunda Flavia Constantia Thebaeorum	Limitanei	Legion	960
Legio Tertia Diocletiana	Limitanei	Legion	960
Legio Secunda Traiana	Limitanei	Legion	960
Legio Prima Valentiniana	Limitanei	Legion	960
Legio Prima Maximiana	Limitanei	Legion	960
Legio Tertia Diocletiana	Limitanei	Legion	960
Legio Secunda Valentiniana	Limitanei	Legion	960
Milites Miliarenses	Limitanei	Numerus	640
Cohors Prima Lysitanorum	Limitanei	Cohors	480
Cohors Scutata Civum Romanorum	Limitanei	Cohors	480
Cohors Prima Apameanorum	Limitanei	Cohors	480
Cohors Undecima Chamavorum	Limitanei	Cohors	480
Cohors Nona Tzanorum	Limitanei	Cohors	480
Cohors Nona Alamannorum	Limitanei	Cohors	480
Cohors Prima Felix Theodosiana	Limitanei	Cohors	480
Cohors Quinta Suentium	Limitanei	Cohors	480
Cohors Sexta Saginarum	Limitanei	Cohors	480
Cohors Septima Francorum	Limitanei	Cohors	480
		Infantry	13,120

Unit	Grade	Organization	Paper Strength
		Dux Thebaidos	
	Cavalry		
Cuneus Equitum Maurorum Scutariorum	Limitanei	Cuneus	256
Cuneus Equitum Scutariorum	Limitanei	Cuneus	256
Equites Sagittarii Indigenae	Limitanei	Ala	512
Equites Sagittarii Indigenae	Limitanei	Ala	512
Equites Sagittarii Indigenae	Limitanei	Ala	512
Equites Sagittarii Indigenae	Limitanei	Ala	512
Equites Sagittarii Indigenae	Limitanei	Ala	512
Equites Promoti Indigenae	Limitanei	Ala	512
Equites Felices Honoriani	Limitanei	Ala	512
Ala Prima Abasgorum	Limitanei	Ala	512
Ala Secunda Hispanorum	Limitanei	Ala	512
Ala Germanorum	Limitanei	Ala	512
Ala Quarta Britonum	Limitanei	Ala	512
Ala Prima Hiberorum	Limitanei	Ala	512
Ala Neptunia	Limitanei	Ala	512
Ala Tertia Dromedariorum	Limitanei	Ala	512
Ala Octava Palmyrenorum	Limitanei	Ala	512
Ala Septima Herculia Voluntaria	Limitanei	Ala	512
Ala Prima Francorum	Limitanei	Ala	512
Ala Prima Iovia Catafractan	Limitanei	Ala	512
Ala Octavo Abydum	Limitanei	Ala	512
Ala Secunda Herculia Dromedariorum	Limitanei	Ala	512
		Cavalry	10,752
		Total	23,872

Dux Palaestinae

Infantry

Unit	Grade	Organization	Paper Strength
Legio Decima Fretensis	Limitanei	Legion	960
Cohors Duodecima Valeria	Limitanei	Cohors	480
Cohors Decima Carthaginiensis	Limitanei	Cohors	480
Cohors Prima Argentaria	Limitanei	Cohors	480
Cohors Quarta Frygum	Limitanei	Cohors	480
Cohors Secunda Gratiana	Limitanei	Cohors	480
Cohors Prima Equitata	Limitanei	Cohors	480
Cohors Secunda Galatharum	Limitanei	Cohors	480
Cohors Prima Flavia	Limitanei	Cohors	480
Cohors III Palaestinorum	Limitanei	Cohors	480
Cohors Secunda Cretensis	Limitanei	Cohors	480
Cohors Prima Salutaria	Limitanei	Cohors	480
		Infantry	6,240

Dux Palaestinae

Cavalry

Unit	Grade	Organization	Paper Strength
Equites Dalmatae Illyricani	Limitanei	Ala	512
Equites Promoti Illyricani	Limitanei	Ala	512
Equites Scutarii Illyricani	Limitanei	Ala	512
Equites Mauri Illyricani	Limitanei	Ala	512
Equites Thamudeni Illyricani	Limitanei	Ala	512
Equites Promoti Indigenae	Limitanei	Ala	512
Equites Promoti Indigenae	Limitanei	Ala	512
Equites Sagittarii Indigenae	Limitanei	Ala	512
Equites Sagittarii Indigenae	Limitanei	Ala	512
Equites Sagittarii Indigenae	Limitanei	Ala	512
Equites Primi Felices Sagittarii Indigenae Palaestini	Limitanei	Ala	512
Equites Sagittarii Indigenae	Limitanei	Ala	512
Ala Prima Miliaria Sebastena	Limitanei	Ala	512
Ala Antana Dromedariorum	Limitanei	Ala	512
Ala Constantiana	Limitanei	Ala	512
Ala Secunda Felix Valentiana	Limitanei	Ala	512
Ala Prima Miliara	Limitanei	Ala	512
Ala Idiota Constitua	Limitanei	Ala	512
		Cavalry	9,216
		Total	15,456

Dux Arabiae

Infantry

Unit	Grade	Organization	Paper Strength
Legio Tertia Cyrenaica	Limitanei	Legion	960
Legio Quarta Martia	Limitanei	Legion	960
Cohors Prima Miliaria Thracum	Limitanei	Cohors	480
Cohors Prima Thracorum	Limitanei	Cohors	480
Cohors Octava Voluntaria	Limitanei	Cohors	480
Cohors Tertia Felix Arabum	Limitanei	Cohors	480
Cohors Tertia Alpinorum	Limitanei	Cohors	480
		Infantry	4,320

Above left: Author Evan Schultheis portraying a mid-fifth century *auxilia palatina* officer of the *Placidi Valentiniani Felices* based on the mosaics of the *Basilica di Santa Maria Maggiore*.

Above right: Re-enactor Benjamin Franckaert of *Letavia* portraying a mid-fifth century infantryman in northern Gaul. (© Asier Cruz)

Below: The equipment of a Spanish Roman soldier, first half of the fifth century AD. (Courtesy of *Septimani Seniores* reenactment group)

Above left: Re-enactor Denis Neumann portraying a North Sea warrior in Roman service during the first half of the fifth century AD. (© Denis Neumann)

Above right: Re-enactor Seb Herzynia portraying a mid-fifth century eastern Germanic warrior. (Courtesy of Seb Herzynia)

Below: Hunnic Asiatic-type *spatha* and narrow-bladed *langseax*. (Courtesy of Seb Herzynia)

Above: A late Roman *fulcum*, or shieldwall. (© *Horizonphotos* Bruno Hanniquet)

Below left: A late Roman field tent, made from a pair of short poles and a spear, with wool canvas, tent pegs and rope. Tents like this would have been used by the armies of both sides when marching away from the baggage train. (Photo by Francis Hagan of the *Barcarii*)

Below right: Copy of the *spatha* from Pouan-Sur-Valles, Champagne, at the *Römisch-Germanischen Zentralmuseums Mainz*. (Courtesy of Matthew Bunker)

Above left: Fragment of a Bieberweir-type imitation ridge helmet from Sarry, now housed in the *musée d'Archéologie nationale*. (Courtesy of Gwendal St Hubbins)

Above Right: Reconstruction of the Bieberweir-type imitation ridge helmet from Fernpass, Austria, by Patryk Nieczarowski for the re-enactment group *Foederati*. (Courtesy of *Foederati*)

Above left: Saddle and belt fittings from the burial at Mundolsheim, near Strausburg, in the *Musée archéologique*. (Courtesy of Benjamin Franckaert)

Above right: Reconstruction of a mid-fourth century Alan *lamellenhelm* from Kispek, Dagestan, by Patryk Nieczarowski for the re-enactment group *Foederati*. (Courtesy of *Foederati*)

Above: Restored section of the Theodosian Walls. (© *Wikimedia Commons*)

Below: Remains of the walls of Orleans. (Photo courtesy of the *Archives municipales d'Orléans*)

Above: The remains of the walls of Le Mans, incorporated into later structures. The walls of Orleans would have looked very similar, possibly also decorated with elaborate brickwork. (Photo courtesy of Guillaume Marty)

Left: Remains of the walls of Sens, incorporated into later structures. (Photo courtesy of Simon MacDowall)

The River Vanne at Fontvannes, where Aetius and his federates would have camped. (Photo courtesy of Simon MacDowall)

Above: The Montgueux ridge, as seen from the south face. The Visigoths had to advance up this ridge during the deployment phase. Cavalry skirmishing likely occurred along the base of this ridge. (Photo courtesy of Simon MacDowall)

Below: The Montgueux ridge, as seen from the north. This side is much shallower than the south face. (Photo courtesy of Simon MacDowall)

The *les Maures* ridge, where the centre-right of the formation would have been stationed. The Goths, Thorismund and Alans could all be found here. (Photo courtesy of Simon MacDowall)

Further along the *les Maures* ridge, where the centre of the formation was positioned. The Alans of Sangiban could be found here. (Photo courtesy of Simon MacDowall)

The centre-left of the *les Maures* ridge, where the Alan left and Roman right flanks could be found. (Photo courtesy of Simon MacDowall)

Dux Arabiae

Cavalry

Unit	Grade	Organization	Paper Strength
Equites Scutari Illyrici	Limitanei	Ala	512
Equites Promoti Illyricani	Limitanei	Ala	512
Equites Dalmati Illyricani	Limitanei	Ala	512
Equites Mauri Illyricani	Limitanei	Ala	512
Equites Promoti Indigenae	Limitanei	Ala	512
Equites Promoti Indigenae	Limitanei	Ala	512
Equites Sagittarii Indigenae	Limitanei	Ala	512
Equites Sagittarii Indigenae	Limitanei	Ala	512
Ala Nona Miliaria	Limitanei	Ala	512
Ala Sexta Hispanorum	Limitanei	Ala	512
Ala Secunda Constantiana	Limitanei	Ala	512
Ala Secunda Miliarensis	Limitanei	Ala	512
Ala Prima Valentiana	Limitanei	Ala	512
Ala Secunda Felix Valentiana	Limitanei	Ala	512
		Cavalry	7,168
		Total	11,488

Dux Foenicis

Infantry

Unit	Grade	Organization	Paper Strength
Legio Prima Illyricium	Limitanei	Legion	960
Legio Tertia Gallica	Limitanei	Legion	960
Cohors Tertia Herculia	Limitanei	Cohors	480
Cohors Quinta Pacta Alamannorum	Limitanei	Cohors	480
Cohors Prima Iulia Lectorum	Limitanei	Cohors	480
Cohors Secunda Aegyptorum	Limitanei	Cohors	480
Cohors Prima Orientalis	Limitanei	Cohors	480
		Infantry	4,320

Dux Foenicis

Cavalry

Unit	Grade	Organization	Paper Strength
Equites Mauri Illyricani	Limitanei	Ala	512
Equites Scutari Illyricani	Limitanei	Ala	512
Equites Promoti Indigenae	Limitanei	Ala	512
Equites Dalmati Illyricani	Limitanei	Ala	512
Equites Promoti Indigenae	Limitanei	Ala	512
Equites Promoti Indigenae	Limitanei	Ala	512
Equites Sagittarii Indigenae	Limitanei	Ala	512
Equites Sagittarii Indigenae	Limitanei	Ala	512
Equites Sagittarii Indigenae	Limitanei	Ala	512
Equites Saraceni Indigenae	Limitanei	Ala	512
Equites Saraceni	Limitanei	Ala	512
Equites Sagittarii Indigenae	Limitanei	Ala	512
Ala Prima Damascena	Limitanei	Ala	512
Ala Nova Diocletiana	Limitanei	Ala	512
Ala Prima Francorum	Limitanei	Ala	512
Ala Prima Alamannorum	Limitanei	Ala	512
Ala Prima Saxonum	Limitanei	Ala	512
Ala Prima Foenicum	Limitanei	Ala	512
Ala Secunda Salutis	Limitanei	Ala	512
		Cavalry	9,728
		Total	14048

Dux Syriae et Eufratensis Syriae

Infantry

Unit	Grade	Organization	Paper Strength
Legio Quarta Scythica	Limitanei	Legion	960
Legio Sextadecima Flavia Firma	Limitanei	Legion	960
Cohors Prima Gotthorum	Limitanei	Cohors	480
Cohors Prima Ulpia Dacorum	Limitanei	Cohors	480
Cohors Tertia Valeria	Limitanei	Cohors	480
Cohors Prima Victorum	Limitanei	Cohors	480
		Infantry	3,840

Dux Syriae et Eufratensis Syriae

Cavalry

Unit	Grade	Organization	Paper Strength
Equites Scutarii Illyricani	Limitanei	Ala	512
Equites Promoti Illyricani	Limitanei	Ala	512
Equites Sagittarii Indigenae	Limitanei	Ala	512
Equites Promoti Indigenae	Limitanei	Ala	512
Equites Sagittarii Indigenae	Limitanei	Ala	512
Equites Sagittarii	Limitanei	Ala	512
Equites Sagittarii	Limitanei	Ala	512
Equites Dalmatae Illyricani	Limitanei	Ala	512
Equites Mauri Illyricani	Limitanei	Ala	512
Equites Promoti Indigenae	Limitanei	Ala	512
Ala Prima Nova Herculia	Limitanei	Ala	512
Ala Prima Iuthungorum	Limitanei	Ala	512
		Cavalry	6,144
		Total	9,984

Dux Osrhoenae

Infantry

Unit	Grade	Organization	Paper Strength
Legio Quarta Parthica	Limitanei	Legion	960
Cohors Prima Gaetulorum	Limitanei	Cohors	480
Cohors Prima Eufratensis	Limitanei	Cohors	480
		Infantry	1,920

Dux Osrhoenae

Cavalry

Unit	Grade	Organization	Paper Strength
Equites Dalmati Illyricani	Limitanei	Ala	512
Equites Promoti Illyricani	Limitanei	Ala	512
Equites Mauri Illyricani	Limitanei	Ala	512
Equites Promoti Indigenae	Limitanei	Ala	512
Equites Promoti Indigenae	Limitanei	Ala	512
Equites Sagittarii Indigenae	Limitanei	Ala	512
Equites Sagittarii Indigenae	Limitanei	Ala	512
Equites Sagittarii Indigenae Medianenses	Limitanei	Ala	512
Equites Sagittarii Indigenae Primi Osrhoeni	Limitanei	Ala	512
Ala Septima Valeria Praelectorum	Limitanei	Ala	512
Ala Prima Victoria Iovia	Limitanei	Ala	512
Ala Secunda Paflagonum	Limitanei	Ala	512
Ala Prima Parthorum	Limitanei	Ala	512
Ala Prima Nova Diocletiana	Limitanei	Ala	512
Ala Prima Salutaria	Limitanei	Ala	512
		Cavalry	7,680
		Total	9,600

Dux Mesopotamiae

Infantry

Unit	Grade	Organization	Paper Strength
Legio Prima Parthica Nisibena[4]	Limitanei	Legion	960
Legio Secunda Parthica[5]	Limitanei	Legion	960
Cohors Quinquagenaria Arabum	Limitanei	Cohors	480
Cohors Quartodecima Valeria Zabdenorum	Limitanei	Cohors	480
	Infantry		2,880

Dux Mesopotamiae

Cavalry

Unit	Grade	Organization	Paper Strength
Equites Scutarii Illyricani	Limitanei	Ala	512
Equites Promoti Illyricani	Limitanei	Ala	512
Equites Ducatores Illyricani Primi Ducatores	Limitanei	Ala	512
Equites Felices Honoriani Illyricani	Limitanei	Ala	512
Equites Promoti Indigenae	Limitanei	Ala	512
Equites Promoti Indigenae	Limitanei	Ala	512
Equites Sagittarii Indigenae Arabanenses	Limitanei	Ala	512
Equites Scutarii Indigenae Pafenses	Limitanei	Ala	512
Equites Sagittarii Indigenae Thibithenses	Limitanei	Ala	512
Equites Sagittarii Indigenae	Limitanei	Ala	512
Ala Secunda Nova Aegyptiorum	Limitanei	Ala	512
Ala Octava Flava Francorum	Limitanei	Ala	512
Ala Quintadecima Flavia Carduenorum	Limitanei	Ala	512
		Cavalry	6,656
		Total	9,536

Dux Armeniae

Infantry

Unit	Grade	Organization	Paper Strength
Legio Quintadecima Apollinaris	Limitanei	Legion	960
Legio Duodecima Fulminata	Limitanei	Legion	960
Legio Prima Pontica	Limitanei	Legion	960
Cohors Tertia Ulpia Miliaria Petraeorum	Limitanei	Cohors	480
Cohors Quarta Raetorum	Limitanei	Cohors	480
Cohors Miliaria Bosporiana	Limitanei	Cohors	480
Cohors Miliaria Germanorum	Limitanei	Cohors	480
Cohors Prima Theodosiana	Limitanei	Cohors	480
Cohors Apuleia Civum Romanorum	Limitanei	Cohors	480
Cohors Prima Lepidiana	Limitanei	Cohors	480
Cohors Prima Claudia Equitata	Limitanei	Cohors	480
Cohors Secunda Valentiana	Limitanei	Cohors	480
Cohors Mochora	Limitanei	Cohors	480
		Infantry	7,680

Dux Armeniae

Cavalry

Unit	Grade	Organization	Paper Strength
Equites Sagittarii	Limitanei	Ala	512
Equites Sagittarii	Limitanei	Ala	512
Ala Rizena	Limitanei	Ala	512
Ala Dale Arizae	Limitanei	Ala	512
Ala Theodosiana	Limitanei	Ala	512
Ala Felix Theodosiana	Limitanei	Ala	512
Ala Prima Augusta Colonorum	Limitanei	Ala	512
Ala Auriana	Limitanei	Ala	512
Ala Prima Ulpia Dacorum	Limitanei	Ala	512
Ala Secunda Gallorum	Limitanei	Ala	512
Ala Castello Tablariensi Constituta	Limitanei	Ala	512
Ala Prima Pretorica Nuper Constituta	Limitanei	Ala	512
		Cavalry	6,144
		Total	13,824

| Magister Militum per Thracias | | | |
| Infantry | | | |
Unit	Grade	Organization	Paper Strength
Solenses Seniores	Comitatenses	Legion	960
Menapii	Comitatenses	Legion	960
Prima Maximiana Thebaeorum	Comitatenses	Legion	960
Tertia Diocletiana Thebaeorum	Comitatenses	Legion	960
Tertiodecimani	Comitatenses	Legion	960
Quartodecimani	Comitatenses	Legion	960
Prima Flavia Gemina	Comitatenses	Legion	960
Secunda Flavia Gemina	Comitatenses	Legion	960
Constantini Seniores	Comitatenses	Legion	960
Divitensis Gallicani	Comitatenses	Legion	960
Lanciarii Stobenses	Comitatenses	Legion	960
Constantini Dafnenses	Comitatenses	Legion	960
Balistarii Dafnenses	Comitatenses	Legion	960
Balistarii Iumiores	Comitatenses	Legion	960
Pannoniciani Iuniores	Comitatenses	Legion	960
Tzanni	Comitatenses	Legion	960
Solenses Gallicani	Comitatenses	Legion	960
Iulia Alexandria	Comitatenses	Legion	960
Augustenses	Comitatenses	Legion	960
Valentinianenses	Comitatenses	Legion	960
Gratianenses	Comitatenses	Legion	960
		Infantry	20,160

Magister Militum per Thracias

Unit	Grade	Organization	Paper Strength
	Cavalry		
Comites Arcadiaci	Vexillatio Palatina	Ala	512
Comites Honoriaci	Vexillatio Palatina	Ala	512
Equites Theodosiaci Iuniores	Vexillatio Palatina	Ala	512
Equites Catafractarii Albigenses	Vexillatio Comitatenses	Ala	512
Equites Sagittarii Seniores	Vexillatio Comitatenses	Ala	512
Equites Sagittarii Iuniores	Vexillatio Comitatenses	Ala	512
Equites Primi Theodosiani	Vexillatio Comitatenses	Ala	512
		Cavalry	3,584
		Total	23,744

Dux Scythiae

Infantry

Unit	Grade	Organization	Paper Strength
Legio Secunda Herculia	Limitanei	Legion	960
Legio Secunda Herculia Cohors Quinta Pedatura Inferior	Limitanei	Legion	960
Legio Secunda Herculia Cohors Quinta Pedatura Inferior	Limitanei	Legion	960
Legio Prima Iovia	Limitanei	Legion	960
Legio Prima Iovia Cohors Quinta Pedatura Inferior	Limitanei	Legion	960
Legio Prima Iovia Cohors Quinta Pedatura Inferior	Limitanei	Legion	960
Legio Prima Iovia Cohors et Legio Secunda Herculia Musculorum Scythicorum et Classis	Limitanei	Legion	960
Milites Navclarii	Limitanei	Numerus	640
Milites Superventores	Limitanei	Numerus	640
Milites Scythici	Limitanei	Numerus	640
Milites Secundi Constantini	Limitanei	Numerus	640
Milites Scythici	Limitanei	Numerus	640
Milites Primi Constantini	Limitanei	Numerus	640
Milities Quinti Constantini	Limitanei	Numerus	640
Milites Prima Gratianenses	Limitanei	Numerus	640
		Infantry	11,840

Dux Scythiae

Cavalry

Unit	Grade	Organization	Paper Strength
Cuneus Equitum Scutariorum	Limitanei	Cuneus	256
Cuneus Equitum Solentium	Limitanei	Cuneus	256
Cuneus Equitum Stablesianorum	Limitanei	Cuneus	256
Cuneus Equitum Stablesianorum	Limitanei	Cuneus	256
Cuneus Equitum Catafractariorum	Limitanei	Cuneus	256
Cuneus Equitum Arimgerorum	Limitanei	Cuneus	256
Cuneus Equitum Arcadum	Limitanei	Cuneus	256
	Cavalry		1,792
	Total		13,632

Dux Moesiae Secundae

Infantry

Unit	Grade	Organization	Paper Strength
Legio Prima Italica	Limitanei	Legion	960
Legio Prima Italica Cohors Quinta Peditura Inferior	Limitanei	Legion	960
Legio Prima Italica Cohors Quinta Peditura Inferior	Limitanei	Legion	960
Legio Undecima Claudia	Limitanei	Legion	960
Legio Undecima Claudia Cohors Quinta Peditura Inferior	Limitanei	Legion	960
Legio Undecima Claudia Cohors Quinta Peditura Inferior	Limitanei	Legion	960
Naves Amnicari et Milites	Limitanei	Numerus	640
Milites Praeventores	Limitanei	Numerus	640
Milites Constantini	Limitanei	Numerus	640
Milites Dacisci	Limitanei	Numerus	640
Milites Tertii Navclarii	Limitanei	Numerus	640
Milites Novenses	Limitanei	Numerus	640
Milites Primi Moesiaci	Limitanei	Numerus	640
Milites Moesiaci	Limitanei	Numerus	640
Milites Quarti Constantiani	Limitanei	Numerus	640
Milites Cimbriani	Limitanei	Numerus	640
Milites Navclarii Altinenses	Limitanei	Numerus	640
Cohors Quarta Gallorum	Limitanei	Cohort	480
Cohors Prima Aureliana	Limitanei	Cohort	480
Cohors Tertia Valeria Bacarum	Limitanei	Cohort	480
	Infantry		14,240

Dux Moesiae Secundae

Unit	Cavalry		
	Grade	Organization	Paper Strength
Cuneus Equitum Scutariorum	Limitanei	Cuneus	256
Cuneus Equitum Solentium	Limitanei	Cuneus	256
Cuneus Equitum Scutariorum	Limitanei	Cuneus	256
Cuneus Equitum Armigerorum	Limitanei	Cuneus	256
Cuneus Equitum Secundorum Armigerorum	Limitanei	Cuneus	256
Cuneus Equitum Scutariorum	Limitanei	Cuneus	256
Cuneus Equitum Stablesianorum	Limitanei	Cuneus	256
		Cavalry	1,792
		Total	16,032

Magister Militum per Illyricum

Infantry

Unit	Grade	Organization	Paper Strength
Britones Seniores	Legio Palatina	Legion	960
Auxilia Palatina	Legio Palatina	Legion	960
Ascarii Seniores	Legio Palatina	Legion	960
Ascarii Iuniores	Legio Palatina	Legion	960
Petulantes Iuniores	Legio Palatina	Legion	960
Sagittarii Lecti	Legio Palatina	Legion	960
Invicti Iuniores	Legio Palatina	Legion	960
Atecotti	Legio Palatina	Legion	960
Matiarii Constantes	Comitatenses	Legion	960
Martii	Comitatenses	Legion	960
Dianenses	Comitatenses	Legion	960
Germaniciani Seniores	Comitatenses	Legion	960
Secundani	Comitatenses	Legion	960
Lanciarii Augustenses	Comitatenses	Legion	960
Minervii	Comitatenses	Legion	960
Lanciarii Iuniores	Comitatenses	Legion	960
Timacenses Auxiliarii	Pseudocomitatenses	Legion	960
Felices Theodosiani Iuniores	Pseudocomitatenses	Legion	960
Burgaracenses	Pseudocomitatenses	Legion	960
Scupenses	Pseudocomitatenses	Legion	960
Ulpianenses	Pseudocomitatenses	Legion	960
Merenses	Pseudocomitatenses	Legion	960
Secundi Theodosiani	Pseudocomitatenses	Legion	960
Balistarii Theodosiani Iuniores	Pseudocomitatenses	Legion	960
		Infantry	23,040

Magister Militum per Illyricum

Cavalry

Unit	Grade	Organization	Paper Strength
Equites Sagittarii Seniores	Vexillatio Comitatenses	Ala	512
Equites Germaniciani Seniores	Vexillatio Comitatenses	Ala	512
		Cavalry	1,024
		Total	24,064

Dux Moesiae Primae

Infantry

Unit	Grade	Organization	Paper Strength
Legio Quarta Flavia	Limitanei	Legion	960
Legio Septima Claudia	Limitanei	Legion	960
Legio Septima Claudia	Limitanei	Legion	960
Auxiliares Reginenses	Limitanei	Cohort	480
Auxiliares Tricorniensis	Limitanei	Cohort	480
Auxiliares Novenses	Limitanei	Cohort	480
Auxilium Margense	Limitanei	Cohort	480
Auxilium Cuppense	Limitanei	Cohort	480
Auxilium Gratianense	Limitanei	Cohort	480
Auxilium Taliatense	Limitanei	Cohort	480
Auxilium Aureomontanum	Limitanei	Cohort	480
Milites Contra Margum in Castris Augusto Flavianensibus	Limitanei	Numerus	640
Milites Exploratores	Limitanei	Numerus	640
Milites Exploratores	Limitanei	Numerus	640
Milites Vicentienses	Limitanei	Numerus	640
Milites Exploratores	Limitanei	Numerus	640
Praefectus Classis Histricae	Limitanei	Cohort	480
Praefectus Classis Stradensis et Germensis	Limitanei	Cohort	480
		Infantry	10,880

Dux Moesiae Primae

Cavalry

Unit	Grade	Organization	Paper Strength
Cuneus Equitum Constantiacorum	Limitanei	Cuneus	256
Cuneus Equitum Promotorum	Limitanei	Cuneus	256
Cuneus Equitum Sagittariorum	Limitanei	Cuneus	256
Cuneus Equitum Dalmatarum	Limitanei	Cuneus	256
Cuneus Equitum Promotorum	Limitanei	Cuneus	256
Cuneus Equitum Sagittariorum	Limitanei	Cuneus	256
Cuneus Equitum Dalmatarum	Limitanei	Cuneus	256
Cuneus Equitum Dalmatarum	Limitanei	Cuneus	256
		Cavalry	2,048
		Total	12,928

Dux Daciae Ripensis

Infantry

Unit	Grade	Organization	Paper Strength
Legio Quinta Macedonica	Limitanei	Legion	960
Legio Quinta Macedonica	Limitanei	Legion	960
Legio Quinta Macedonica	Limitanei	Legion	960
Legio Tertiadecima Gemina	Limitanei	Legion	960
Legio Tertiadecima Gemina	Limitanei	Legion	960
Legio Tertiadecima Gemina	Limitanei	Legion	960
Legio Tertiadecima Gemina	Limitanei	Legion	960
Legio Tertiadecima Gemina	Limitanei	Legion	960
Legio Quinta Macedonici	Limitanei	Legion	960
Auxilium Miliarentium	Limitanei	Cohort	480
Auxilium Primorum Daciscorum	Limitanei	Cohort	480
Auxilium Crispitienses	Limitanei	Cohort	480
Auxilium Mariensium	Limitanei	Cohort	480
Auxilium Claustrinorum	Limitanei	Cohort	480
Auxilium Secundorum Daciscorum	Limitanei	Cohort	480
Milites Exploratores	Limitanei	Numerus	640
Cohors Secundi Reduci Sosta	Limitanei	Cohort	480
Cohors Nove	Limitanei	Cohort	480
Praefectus Classis Histricae	Limitanei	Cohort	480
Praefectus Classis Ratianensis	Limitanei	Cohort	480
		Infantry	14,080
		Total	14,080

Tabulation of Forces in the *Notitia Dignitatum: In Partibus Occidentis*

Command	Grade	Western Roman Empire		
		Infantry Strength	Cavalry Strength	Combined
Magister Peditum	Comitatenses	28,480	3,584	32,064
Magister Peditum	Limitanei	4,800	0	4,800
Magister Equitum	Comitatenses	37,120	6,144	43,264
Dux Sequanica	Limitanei	960	0	960
Dux Tractis Armoriciani et Nervicani	Limitanei	3,360	0	3,360
Dux Belgicae Secundae	Limitanei	1,600	0	1,600
Dux Mogontiacenses	Limitanei	2,880	0	2,880
Comes Britanniarum	Comitatenses	2,240	3,072	5,312
Dux Britanniarum	Limitanei	13,280	3,840	17,120
Comes Litoris Saxonici	Limitanei	1,600	512	2,112
Comes Hispenias	Comitatenses	10,560	0	10,560
Comes Hispenias	Limitanei	2,880	0	2,880
Comes Tingitaniae	Comitatenses	2,240	1,536	3,776
Comes Tingitaniae	Limitanei	2,880	512	3,392
Comes Africae	Comitatenses	11,200	9,728	20,928
Comes Africae	Limitanei	15,360	0	15,360
Dux Mauritaniae	Limitanei	5,760	0	5,760
Dux Tripolitaniae	Limitanei	11,520	0	11,520
Comes Illyricum	Comitatenses	10,720	0	10,720
Dux Pannoniae Secundae	Limitanei	9,120	3,584	12,704
Dux Pannoniae Valeriae	Limitanei	3,360	3,328	6,688
Dux Pannonia Primae et Norici Ripenses	Limitanei	4,960	2,560	7,520
Dux Raetiae	Limitanei	2,400	2,048	4,448
Total		189,280	40,448	229,728
			Comitatenses	126,624
			Limitanei	103,104

Magister Peditum's Italian Command

Infantry

Unit	Grade	Organization	Paper Strength
Iovani Seniores	Legio Palatina	Legion	960
Herculani Seniores	Legio Palatina	Legion	960
Divitenses Seniores	Legio Palatina	Legion	960
Tongrecani Seniores	Legio Palatina	Legion	960
Pannoniciani Seniores	Legio Palatina	Legion	960
Moesiaci Seniores	Legio Palatina	Legion	960
Cornuti Seniores	Auxilia Palatina	Numerus	640
Brachiati Seniores	Auxilia Palatina	Numerus	640
Petulantes Seniores	Auxilia Palatina	Numerus	640
Celtae Seniores	Auxilia Palatina	Numerus	640
Heruli Seniores	Auxilia Palatina	Numerus	640
Batavi Seniores	Auxilia Palatina	Numerus	640
Mattiaci Seniores	Auxilia Palatina	Numerus	640
Iovii Seniores	Auxilia Palatina	Numerus	640
Victores Seniores	Auxilia Palatina	Numerus	640
Cornuti Iuniores	Auxilia Palatina	Numerus	640
Leones Iuniores	Auxilia Palatina	Numerus	640
Exculcatores Seniores	Auxilia Palatina	Numerus	640
Grati	Auxilia Palatina	Numerus	640
Sabini	Auxilia Palatina	Numerus	640

Felices Iuniores	Numerus	Auxilia Palatina	640
Honoriani Atecotti Iuniores	Numerus	Auxilia Palatina	640
Brisigavi Iuniores	Numerus	Auxilia Palatina	640
Honoriani Mauri Iuniores	Numerus	Auxilia Palatina	640
Galli Victores	Numerus	Auxilia Palatina	640
Placidi Valentiniani Felices	Numerus	Auxilia Palatina	640
Gratianenses Iuniores	Numerus	Auxilia Palatina	640
Octaviani	Legion	Comitatenses	960
Thebaei	Legion	Comitatenses	960
Mattiarii Iuniores	Legion	Comitatenses	960
Septimani Iuniores	Legion	Comitatenses	960
Regii	Legion	Comitatenses	960
Germaniciani Iuniores	Legion	Comitatenses	960
Prima Iulia Alpina	Legion	Pseudocomitatenses	960
Tertia Iulia Alpina	Legion	Pseudocomitatenses	960
Honoriani Marcomanni	Numerus	Pseudocomitatenses	640
Milites Pontinenses	Legion	Pseudocomitatenses	960
Veneti	Legion	Limitanei	960
Milites Iuniores Italicorum	Legion	Limitanei	960
Ravennatia cum Ciuris Eiusdem Civitatis	Legion	Limitanei	960
Comensis cum Ciuris Eiusdem Civitatis	Legion	Limitanei	960
Misenates	Legion	Limitanei	960
		Infantry	33,280

Magister Peditum's Italian Command

Unit	Grade	Organization	Paper Strength
Cavalry			
Comites Seniores	Vexillatio Palatina	Ala	512
Equites Promoti Seniores	Vexillatio Palatina	Ala	512
Equites Brachiati Seniores	Vexillatio Palatina	Ala	512
Equites Cornuti Seniores	Vexillatio Palatina	Ala	512
Comites Alani	Vexillatio Palatina	Ala	512
Equites Mauri Feroci	Vexillatio Comitatenses	Ala	512
Equites Constantes Valentinianenses Seniores	Vexillatio Palatina	Ala	512
		Cavalry	3,584
		Field Army	32,064
		Limitanei	4,800
		Total	36,864

Magister Equitum's Gallic Command

Infantry

Unit	Grade	Organization	Paper Strength
Lanciarii Sabarienses	Legio Palatina	Legion	960
Leones Seniores	Auxilia Palatina	Numerus	640
Brachiati Iuniores	Auxilia Palatina	Numerus	640
Salii Seniores	Auxilia Palatina	Numerus	640
Gratianenses	Auxilia Palatina	Numerus	640
Bructeri	Auxilia Palatina	Numerus	640
Ampsivarii	Auxilia Palatina	Numerus	640
Valentinianenses Iuniores	Auxilia Palatina	Numerus	640
Batavi Iuniores	Auxilia Palatina	Numerus	640
Britones	Auxilia Palatina	Numerus	640
Honoriani Atecotti Seniores	Auxilia Palatina	Numerus	640
Sagittarii Nervii Gallicani	Auxilia Palatina	Numerus	640
Iovi Iuniores Gallicani	Auxilia Palatina	Numerus	640
Mattiaci Iuniores Gallicani	Auxilia Palatina	Numerus	640
Atecotti Iuniores Gallicani	Auxilia Palatina	Numerus	640
Ascarii Seniores	Auxilia Palatina	Numerus	640
Armigeri Defensorses Seniores	Comitatenses	Legion	960
Lanciarii Gallicani	Comitatenses	Legion	960
Menapii Seniores	Comitatenses	Legion	960
Secunda Britannica	Comitatenses	Legion	960

(Continued)

Magister Equitum's Gallic Command

Infantry

Unit	Grade	Organization	Paper Strength
Ursarienses	Comitatenses	Legion	960
Praesidenses	Comitatenses	Legion	960
Geminiacenses	Comitatenses	Legion	960
Cortoriacenses	Comitatenses	Legion	960
Honoriani Felices Gallicani	Comitatenses	Legion	960
Milites Prima Flavia Gallicana Constantia	Pseudocomitatenses	Legion	960
Milites Martenses	Pseudocomitatenses	Legion	960
Milites Abrincateni	Pseudocomitatenses	Legion	960
Defensorses Seniores	Pseudocomitatenses	Numerus	640
Milites Mauri Osismiaci	Pseudocomitatenses	Legion	960
Prima Flavia Metis	Pseudocomitatenses	Legion	960
Milites Superventores Iuniores	Pseudocomitatenses	Legion	960
Ballistarii	Pseudocomitatenses	Legion	960
Milites Defensorses Iuniores	Pseudocomitatenses	Legion	960
Milites Garronenses	Pseudocomitatenses	Legion	960
Milites Anderetiani	Pseudocomitatenses	Legion	960
Milites Acincenses	Pseudocomitatenses	Legion	960
Corniacenses	Pseudocomitatenses	Legion	960
Septimani Iuniores	Pseudocomitatenses	Legion	960
Cursarienses Iuniores	Pseudocomitatenses	Legion	960
Musmagenses	Pseudocomitatenses	Legion	960

Romanenses	Pseudocomitatenses	Cohort	480
Auxilia Insidatores	Pseudocomitatenses	Cohort	480
Turnacensimani	Pseudocomitatenses	Numerus	640
Abulci	Pseudocomitatenses	Numerus	640
Exploratores	Pseudocomitatenses	Numerus	640
		Infantry	37,120

Magister Equitum's Gallic Command

Cavalry

Unit	Grade	Organization	Paper Strength
Equites Batavi Seniores	Vexillatio Palatina	Ala	512
Equites Cornuti Iuniores	Vexillatio Palatina	Ala	512
Equites Batavi Iuniores	Vexillatio Palatina	Ala	512
Equites Brachiati Iuniores	Vexillatio Palatina	Ala	512
Equites Honoriani Seniores	Vexillatio Comitatenses	Ala	512
Equites Honoriani Taifali Iuniores	Vexillatio Comitatenses	Ala	512
Equites Armigeri Seniores	Vexillatio Comitatenses	Ala	512
Equites Octavo Dalmatae	Vexillatio Comitatenses	Ala	512
Equites Dalmatae Passerentiaci	Vexillatio Comitatenses	Ala	512
Equites Primi Gallicani	Vexillatio Comitatenses	Ala	512
Equites Mauri Altes	Vexillatio Comitatenses	Ala	512
Equites Constanti Feroces	Vexillatio Comitatenses	Ala	512
		Cavalry	6,144
		Total	43,264

Dux Sequanica

Infantry

Unit	Grade	Organization	Paper Strength
Milites Lataviensis	Limitanei	Legion	960
		Infantry	960
		Total	960

Dux Tractis Armoriciani et Nervicani

Infantry

Unit	Grade	Organization	Paper Strength
Cohortis Prima Nova Armoricana	Limitanei	Cohors	480
Milites Carronenses	Limitanei	Legion	960
Miletes Mauri Benetori	Limitanei	Legion	960
Milites Mauri Osimaci[1]	Limitanei	Legion	960
Milites Superventores[2]	Limitanei	Legion	960
Milites Martenses[3]	Limitanei	Legion	960
Milites Prima Flavia[4]	Limitanei	Legion	960
Milites Ursarienses[5]	Limitanei	Legion	960
Milites Dalmatii	Limitanei	Legion	960
Milites Grannonenses[6]	Limitanei	Legion	960
		Infantry	3,360
		Total	3,360

Dux Belgicae Secundae

Infantry

Unit	Grade	Organization	Paper Strength
Sambricae	Limitanei	Unknown	640
Milites Nervii	Limitanei	Legion	960
		Infantry	1,600

Dux Belgicae Secundae

Cavalry

Unit	Grade	Organization	Paper Strength
Equites Dalmatae	Limitanei	Ala	512
		Cavalry	512
		Total	2,112

Dux Mogontiacenses

Infantry

Unit	Grade	Organization	Paper Strength
Milites Pacenses[7]	Limitanei	Legion	960
Milites Menapi[8]	Limitanei	Legion	960
Milites Anderitiani[9]	Limitanei	Legion	960
Milites Vindici	Limitanei	Legion	960
Milites Martenses[10]	Limitanei	Legion	960
Milites Secunda Flavia	Limitanei	Legion	960
Milites Armigeri[11]	Limitanei	Legion	960
Milites Bingenses	Limitanei	Legion	960
Milites Defensorses[12]	Limitanei	Legion	960
Milites Balistarii[13]	Limitanei	Legion	960
Milites Acinenses[14]	Limitanei	Legion	960
		Infantry	2,880
		Total	2,880

Dux Britanniarum

Infantry

Unit	Grade	Organization	Paper Strength
Legio Sexta	Limitanei	Legion	960
Numerus Barcarii Tigrisienses	Limitanei	Numerus	640
Numerus Nervii Dictenses	Limitanei	Numerus	640
Numerus Vigilium	Limitanei	Numerus	640
Numerus Exploratores[15]	Limitanei	Numerus	640
Numerus Directorum	Limitanei	Numerus	640
Numerus Defensorum[16]	Limitanei	Numerus	640
Numerus Solenses	Limitanei	Numerus	640
Numerus Pacenses	Limitanei	Numerus	640
Numerus Longovicianorum	Limitanei	Numerus	640
Numerus Supervenientium Petueriensium	Limitanei	Numerus	640
Cohortis Quarta Lingona	Limitanei	Cohors	480
Cohortis Prima Cornovii	Limitanei	Cohors	480
Cohortis Prima Frixiagorum (Prima Frisiavonum)	Limitanei	Cohors	480
Cohortis Prima Batavorum	Limitanei	Cohors	480
Cohortis Primae Tungrorum[17]	Limitanei	Cohors	480
Cohortis Quarta Gallorum	Limitanei	Cohors	480
Cohortis Prima Asturum	Limitanei	Cohors	480
Cohortus Secunda Dalmatarum	Limitanei	Cohors	480
Cohortis Prima Aeliae Dacorum	Limitanei	Cohors	480
Cohortis Secunda Lingonum	Limitanei	Cohors	480
Cohortis Prima Hispanorum	Limitanei	Cohors	480
Cohortis Secunda Thracum	Limitanei	Cohors	480
Cohortis Prima Aeliae Classicae	Limitanei	Cohors	480
Cohortis Prima Morinorum	Limitanei	Cohors	480
Cohortis Tertia Nerviorum	Limitanei	Cohors	480
Cohortis Sexta Nerviorum	Limitanei	Cohors	480
		Infantry	13,280

Dux Britanniarum

Cavalry

Unit	Grade	Organization	Paper Strength
Equites Dalmatarum	Limitanei	Ala	512
Equites Crispianorum	Limitanei	Ala	512
Equites Catafractorum[18]	Limitanei	Ala	512
Alae Primae Asturum	Limitanei	Ala	512
Alae Sabinianae	Limitanei	Ala	512
Alae Secundae Asturum	Limitanei	Ala	512
Alae Petrianae	Limitanei	Ala	512
Numerus Maurorum Aurelianorum[19]	Limitanei	Numerus	640
Cuneus Sarmatarum	Limitanei	Cuneus	256
Alae Primae Herculeae	Limitanei	Ala	512
		Cavalry	3,840
		Total	17,120

Comes Britanniarum

Infantry

Unit	Grade	Organization	Paper Strength
Exculcatores Victores Iuniores Britanniciani	Pseudocomitatenses	Numerus	640
Primani Iuniores	Pseudocomitatenses	Numerus	640
Secundani Iuniores Britannici	Pseudocomitatenses	Legion	960
		Infantry	2,240

Comes Britanniarum

Cavalry

Unit	Grade	Organization	Paper Strength
Equites Catafractarii Iuniores	Pseudocomitatenses	Ala	512
Equites Scutarii Aureliaci	Pseudocomitatenses	Ala	512
Equites Honoriani Seniores	Pseudocomitatenses	Ala	512
Equites Stablesiani	Pseudocomitatenses	Ala	512
Equites Syri	Pseudocomitatenses	Ala	512
Equites Honoriani Taifali	Pseudocomitatenses	Ala	512
		Cavalry	3,072
		Total	5,312

Comes Litoris Saxonici

Infantry

Unit	Grade	Organization	Paper Strength
Numerus Fortensium	Limitanei	Numerus	640
Milites Tungrecanorum[20]	Limitanei	Legion	960
Numerus Turnacensium[21]	Limitanei	Numerus	640
Cohortis Primae Baetasiorum	Limitanei	Cohors	480
Legionis Secundae Augustae[22]	Limitanei	Legion	960
Numerus Albucorum[23]	Limitanei	Numerus	480
Numerus Exploratorum[24]	Limitanei	Numerus	480
		Infantry	1,600

Comes Litoris Saxonici

Cavalry

Unit	Grade	Organization	Paper Strength
Equites Dalmatarum Brandodunensium	Limitanei	Ala	512
Equites Stablesianorum Gariannonensium[25]	Limitanei	Ala	512
		Cavalry	512
		Total	2,112

Comes Hispenias

Infantry

Unit	Grade	Organization	Paper Strength
Ascarii Seniores[26]	Auxilia Palatina	Numerus	640
Ascarii Iumiores	Auxilia Palatina	Numerus	640
Sagittarii Nervii[27]	Auxilia Palatina	Numerus	640
Exculcatores Iuniores	Auxilia Palatina	Numerus	640
Tubantes	Auxilia Palatina	Numerus	640
Felices Seniores	Auxilia Palatina	Numerus	640
Invicti Seniores	Auxilia Palatina	Numerus	640

Victores Iuniores	Auxilia Palatina	Numerus	640
Invicti Iuniores Britanniciani	Auxilia Palatina	Numerus	640
Brisigavi Seniores	Auxilia Palatina	Numerus	640
Salii Iuniores Gallicani	Auxilia Palatina	Numerus	640
Fortenses	Comitatenses	Legion	960
Propugnatores Seniores	Comitatenses	Legion	960
Septimani Seniores	Comitatenses	Legion	960
Vesontes	Comitatenses	Legion	960
Undecimani	Comitatenses	Legion	960
Legionis Septima Gemina	Limitanei	Legion	960
Cohortis Secunda Flavia Pacatiana[28]	Limitanei	Legion	960
Cohortis Secunda Gallica	Limitanei	Cohors	480
Cohortis Lucensis	Limitanei	Cohors	480
Cohortis Celtiberae	Limitanei	Cohors	480
Cohortis Prima Gallica	Limitanei	Cohors	480
		Infantry	13,440
		Field Army	10,560
		Limitanei	2,880
		Total	13,440

Comes Tingitaniae

Infantry

Unit	Grade	Organization	Paper Strength
Mauri Tonantes Seniores	Auxilia Palatina	Numerus	640
Mauri Tonantes Iuniores	Auxilia Palatina	Numerus	640
Constantiniani	Comitatenses	Legion	960
Septimani Iuniores[29]	Comitatenses	Legion	960
Cohortis Secunda Hispania	Limitanei	Cohors	480
Cohortis Prima Herculea	Limitanei	Cohors	480
Cohortis Prima Ityrea	Limitanei	Cohors	480
Cohortis (Unknown)	Limitanei	Cohors	480
Cohortis Pacatiana[30]	Limitanei	Cohors	480
Cohortis Tertia Asturia	Limitanei	Cohors	480
Cohortis Friglensa	Limitanei	Cohors	480
		Infantry	5,120

Comes Tingitaniae

Cavalry

Unit	Grade	Organization	Paper Strength
Equites Scutarii Seniores	Comitatenses	Ala	512
Equites Sagittarii Seniores	Comitatenses	Ala	512
Equites Sagittarii Cordueni	Comitatenses	Ala	512
Ala Herculea	Limitanei	Ala	512
		Cavalry	2,048
		Field Army	3,776
		Limitanei	3,392
		Total	7,168

| | Comes Africae | | |
| | Infantry | | |
Unit	Grade	Organization	Paper Strength
Celtae Iuniores	Auxilia Palatina	Numerus	640
Armigeri Propugnatores Seniores	Legio Palatina	Legion	960
Armigeri Propugnatores Iuniores	Legio Palatina	Legion	960
Cimbriani	Legio Palatina	Legion	960
Secundani Italicani	Comitatenses	Legion	960
Primani (Legio Prima Flavia Pacis)	Comitatenses	Legion	960
Secundani (Legio Secunda Flavia Virtutis)	Comitatenses	Legion	960
Tertiani (Legio Tertia Flavia Salutis)	Comitatenses	Legion	960
Constantiniani (Legio Secunda Flavia Constantiniana)	Comitatenses	Legion	960
Tertio Augustani	Comitatenses	Legion	960
Fortenses	Comitatenses	Legion	960
Constantiaci	Pseudocomitatenses	Legion	960
Sixteen Unnamed Limitanei Units (Milites?)	Limitanei	Legion	15,360
		Infantry	26,560

Comes Africae

Cavalry

Unit	Grade	Organization	Paper Strength
Equites Stablesiani Italiciani	Equites	Ala	512
Equites Scutarii Seniores	Equites	Ala	512
Equites Stablesiani Africani Iuniores	Equites	Ala	512
Equites Marcomanni	Equites	Ala	512
Equites Armigeri Seniores	Equites	Ala	512
Equites Sagittarii Clibanarii	Equites	Ala	512
Equites Sagittarii Parthii Seniores	Equites	Ala	512
Equites Cetrati Seniores	Equites	Ala	512
Equites Primo Sagittarii	Equites	Ala	512
Equites Secundo Sagittarii	Equites	Ala	512
Equites Tertio Sagittarii	Equites	Ala	512
Equites Quarto Sagittarii	Equites	Ala	512
Equites Sagittarii Parthii Iuniores	Equites	Ala	512
Equites Cetrati Iuniores	Equites	Ala	512
Equites Promoti Iuniores	Equites	Ala	512
Equites Sagittarii Iuniores	Equites	Ala	512
Equites Honoriani Iuniores	Equites	Ala	512
Equites Scutarii Iuniores Scholae Secundae	Equites	Ala	512
Equites Armigeri Iuniores	Equites	Ala	512
		Cavalry	9,728
		Field Army	20,928
		Limitanei	15,360
		Total	36,288

Dux Mauritaniae

Infantry

Unit	Grade	Organization	Paper Strength
Fortenses[31]	Limitanei	Legion	960
Augustenses[32]	Limitanei	Legion	960
6 Unidentified Limitanei (Milites?)	Limitanei	Legion	5,760
		Infantry	5,760
		Total	5,760

Dux Tripolitaniae

Infantry

Unit	Grade	Organization	Paper Strength
Fortenses[33]	Limitanei	Legion	960
Munifices[34]	Limitanei	Legion	960
12 Unidentified Limitanei (Milites?)	Limitanei	Legion	11,520
		Infantry	11,520
		Total	11,520

Comes Illyricum

Infantry

Unit	Grade	Organization	Paper Strength
Sagittarii Tungri	Auxilia Palatina	Numerus	640
Iovii Iuniores	Auxilia Palatina	Numerus	640
Sequani	Auxilia Palatina	Numerus	640
Cohortis Raeti	Auxilia Palatina	Cohors	480
Sagittarii Venatores	Auxilia Palatina	Numerus	640
Cohortis Latini	Auxilia Palatina	Cohors	480
Valentinianenses Felices	Auxilia Palatina	Numerus	640
Honoriani Victores	Auxilia Palatina	Numerus	640
Seguntienses	Auxilia Palatina	Numerus	640
Tungri	Auxilia Palatina	Numerus	640
Honoriani Mauri Seniores	Auxilia Palatina	Numerus	640
Honirani Mattiarii Gallicani	Auxilia Palatina	Numerus	640
Tertiani (Legio Tertia Italica)	Comitatenses	Legion	960
Legio Tertia Herculea	Comitatenses	Legion	960
Pacatianenses	Comitatenses	Legion	960
Mauri Cetrati	Comitatenses	Legion	960
Propugnatores Iuniores[35]	Comitatenses	Numerus	640
Lanciarii Lauriacenses	Pseudocomitatenses	Legion	960
Lanciarii Comaginenses	Pseudocomitatenses	Legion	960
Secunda Iulia Alpina	Pseudocomitatenses	Legion	960
Cohortis Catarensis	Pseudocomitatenses	Cohors	480
		Infantry	10,720
		Total	10,720

Dux Pannoniae Secundae

Infantry

Unit	Grade	Organization	Paper Strength
Auxilia Herculensia	Limitanei	Cohors	480
Auxilia Novensia	Limitanei	Cohors	480
Auxilia Augustensia[36]	Limitanei	Cohors	480
Auxilia Praesidentia	Limitanei	Cohors	480
Auxilia Ascarii[37]	Limitanei	Cohors	480
Legionis Sexta Herculea	Limitanei	Legion	960
Legionis Quinta Iovia	Limitanei	Legion	960
Milites Calicarienses	Limitanei	Legion	960
Milites Prima Flavia Augusta	Limitanei	Legion	960
Milites Secunda Flavia	Limitanei	Legion	960
Cohortis Histricae	Limitanei	Cohors	480
Cohortis Tertia Alpina Dardanorum	Limitanei	Cohors	480
Cohortis Prima Pannonica	Limitanei	Cohors	480
Cohortis Aegetensium Suie Secunda Pannonica	Limitanei	Cohors	480
Cohortis Tertia Alpina	Limitanei	Cohors	480
Cohortis Prima Iovia	Limitanei	Cohors	480
Cohortis Prima Thraci Cives Romanorum[38]	Limitanei	Cohors	480
		Infantry	9,120

| Dux Pannoniae Secundae | | | |
| Cavalry | | | |
Unit	Grade	Organization	Paper Strength
Cuneus Equitum Scutariorum	Limitanei	Cuneus	256
Cuneus Equitum Dalmatarum	Limitanei	Cuneus	256
Cuneus Equitum Constantianorum	Limitanei	Cuneus	256
Cuneus Equitum Promotorum	Limitanei	Cuneus	256
Cuneus Equitum Constantium	Limitanei	Cuneus	256
Cuneus Equitum Italicanorum	Limitanei	Cuneus	256
Equites Dalmatae	Limitanei	Ala	512
Equites Promoti	Limitanei	Ala	512
Equites Sagittarii	Limitanei	Ala	512
Ala Sirmienses	Limitanei	Ala	512
		Cavalry	3,584
		Total	12,704

| | Dux Pannoniae Valeriae | | |
| | Infantry | | |
Unit	Grade	Organization	Paper Strength
Auxilia Herculensia	Limitanei	Cohors	480
Auxilia Ursariensia[39]	Limitanei	Cohors	480
Auxilia Vigilium	Limitanei	Cohors	480
Auxilia Fortensia	Limitanei	Cohors	480
Auxilia Insidiatorum[40]	Limitanei	Cohors	480
Legionis Prima Adiutricis[41]	Limitanei	Legion	960
Legionis Secunda Adiutricis[42]	Limitanei	Legion	960
Cohortis Histricae	Limitanei	Cohors	480
Legionis (Unnamed)	Limitanei	Legion	960
Cohortis (Unnamed)	Limitanei	Cohors	480
		Infantry	3,360

Dux Pannoniae Valeriae

Cavalry

Unit	Grade	Organization	Paper Strength
Cuneus Equitum Scutarorum	Limitanei	Cuneus	256
Cuneus Equitum Dalmatarum	Limitanei	Cuneus	256
Cuneus Equitum Constantianorum	Limitanei	Cuneus	256
Cuneus Equitum Stablesianorum	Limitanei	Cuneus	256
Cuneus Equitum Fortensium	Limitanei	Cuneus	256
Equites Dalmatae	Limitanei	Ala	512
Equites Promoti	Limitanei	Ala	512
Equites Mauri	Limitanei	Ala	512
Equites Sagittarii	Limitanei	Ala	512
		Cavalry	3,328
		Total	6,688

Dux Pannonia Primae et Norici Ripenses

Infantry

Unit	Grade	Organization	Paper Strength
Legionis Decima Gemina	Limitanei	Legion	960
Legionis Quartadecima Gemina Milites Liburnariorum	Limitanei	Legion	960
Histricae	Limitanei	Numerus	640
Cohortis (Unknown)	Limitanei	Cohors	480
Legionis Secunda Italica	Limitanei	Legion	960
Legionis Prima Noricorum	Limitanei	Legion	960
		Infantry	4,960

Dux Pannonia Primae et Norici Ripenses

Cavalry

Unit	Grade	Organization	Paper Strength
Cuneus Equitum Dalmatarum	Limitanei	Cuneus	256
Cuneus Equitum Stablesianorum	Limitanei	Cuneus	256
Equites Promoti	Limitanei	Ala	512
Equites Sagittarii	Limitanei	Ala	512
Equites Dalmatae	Limitanei	Ala	512
Equites Mauri	Limitanei	Ala	512
		Cavalry	2,560
		Total	7,520

Dux Raetiae

Infantry

Unit	Grade	Organization	Paper Strength
Legionis Tertia Italica[43]	Limitanei	Legion	960
Milites Ursarienses[44]	Limitanei	Legion	960
Cohortis Nova Batavorum	Limitanei	Cohors	480
Cohortis Tertia Brittorum	Limitanei	Cohors	480
Cohortis Sexta Valeria Raetorum[45]	Limitanei	Cohors	480
Cohortis Prima Herculea Raetorum[46]	Limitanei	Cohors	480
Cohortis Quinta Valeria Frygum	Limitanei	Cohors	480
Cohortis Tertia Herculea Pannoniorum	Limitanei	Cohors	480
Cohortis Herculea Pannoniorum	Limitanei	Cohors	480
		Infantry	2,400

Dux Raetiae

Cavalry

Unit	Grade	Organization	Paper Strength
Equites Stablesiani Seniores	Limitanei	Ala	512
Equites Stablesiani Iuniores	Limitanei	Ala	512
Ala Prima Flavia Raetorum	Limitanei	Ala	512
Ala Secunda Valeria Sequanorum	Limitanei	Ala	512
		Cavalry	2,048
		Total	4,448

Notes

Introduction

1. '*subito cum rupta tumultu barbares totas in te transfuderat arctos Gallia.*' Sidonius Apollinaris, *Carmina*, 7.319.
2. For the sake of simplicity, 'Catalaunian Fields' has been chosen for this work.
3. A.H.M Jones, *The Later Roman Empire: A.D. 284–602*, Vol.1 (Norman: University of Oklahoma Press, 1964), 194; Guy Halsall, *Barbarian Migrations and the Roman West* (Cambridge: Cambridge University Press, 2007), 252–53; Peter Heather, *The Fall of the Roman Empire: A New History of Rome and the Barbarians* (Oxford: Oxford University Press, 2006), 338–39; Jones' massive two-volume work barely ascribes half a page, Halsall's ethnographic study roughly a page and Heather roughly a page and a half.
4. Edward Gibbon, *The History of the Decline and Fall of the Roman Empire*, Vol.2 (New York: Modern Library, 2003), 1,089.
5. Edward Shepherd Creasy, *Fifteen Decisive Battles of the World: From Marathon to Waterloo* (Oxford: Oxford University Press, 1915), 158–74.
6. Arther Ferrill, *The Fall of the Roman Empire: The Military Explanation* (London: Thames and Hudson, 1986), 150; John Julius Norwich, *A Short History of Byzantium* (New York: Vintage Books, 1999), 49.
7. Samuel Barnish, 'The Battle of Vouille and the Decisive Battle Phenomenon in Late Antique Gaul', in *The Battle of Vouille, 507: Where France Began* (Boston: Walter de Gruyter, 2012), 11–42.
8. John Bagnell Bury, *History of the Later Roman Empire* (New York: Dover Publications, 1958), 291–94.
9. Ulf Tackholm, 'Aetius and the Battle on the Catalaunian Fields', *Opuscula Romana* 7, no.15 (1969), 259–76.
10. Samuel Barnish, 'Old Kaspars: Attila's Invasion of Gaul in the Literary Sources', in *Fifth Century Gaul: A Crisis of Identity?* (Cambridge: Cambridge University Press, 1992), 38–47.
11. Arne Søby Christiansen, *Cassiodorus, Jordanes and the History of the Goths: Studies in a Migration Myth* (Copenhagen: Museum Tusculanum Press, 2002), 323–41.
12. Conor Whately, 'Jordanes, the Battle of the Catalaunian Fields and Constantinople', *Dialogues d'historie ancienne* 8 (2012), 57–70.

13.   Hyun Jin Kim, *The Huns, Rome and the Birth of Europe* (Cambridge: Cambridge University Press, 2013), 69–85.

14.   Heinrich Harke, review of *The Huns, Rome and the Birth of Europe*, by Hyun Jin Kim, *The Classical Review* 64, no.1 (2014), 260–62.

15.   Hyun Jin Kim, 'Herodotean Allusions in Late Antiquity: Priscus, Jordanes and the Huns', *Byzantion* 85 (2015), 127–42.

16.   Arther Ferrill, *The Fall of the Roman Empire: The Military Explanation*, 147–50.

17.   Phillipe Richardot, *La Fin de l'Armee Romaine* (Paris: Economica Press, 2005), 351–77.

18.   Iaroslav Lebedensky, *La campagne d'Attila en Gaule 451 apr. J.-C.* (Clermont-Ferrand: Lemme Edit, 2011).

19.   Ian Hughes, *Aetius: Attila's Nemesis* (Barnsley: Pen & Sword Books Ltd, 2012), 163–75.

20.   Simon MacDowall, *Catalaunian Fields AD 451: Rome's Last Great Battle* (Oxford: Osprey Publishing, 2015).

21.   Christopher Kelly, *The End of Empire: Attila the Hun and the Fall of Rome* (New York: W.W. Norton & Company, 2006), 231–52; John Man, *Attila: The Barbarian King who Challenged Rome* (New York: Thomas Dunne Books, 2005), 213–44.

22.   Istvan Bona, *Das Hunnenreich* (Budapest: Theiss, 1991); Istvan Bona, *Les Huns: Le Grande Empire Barbare d'Europe (IVe–Ve Siecles)* (Paris: Errance, 2002).

23.   The standard translation is that by Charles C. Mierow.

24.   Christiansen, *Cassiodorus, Jordanes, and the History of the Goths*, 324–25.

25.   Walter Goffart, *TheNarrators of Barbarian History (A.D. 550–800): Jordanes, Gregory of Tours, Bede and Paul the Deacon* (Princeton: Princeton University Press, 1988), 42–43; Christiansen, *Cassiodorus, Jordanes and the History of the Goths*, 88–92, 106; Barnish, 'Old Kaspars', 42–43; Jordanes, *De Origine Actibusque Getarum*, 50.266.

26.   Walter Goffart, *Narrators of Barbarian History*, 62–68.

27.   Barnish, 'Old Kaspars', 40.

28.   Bury, *History of the Later Roman Empire*, 293.

29.   Tackholm, 'Aetius and the Battle on the Catalaunian Fields', 273.

30.   Barnish, 'Old Kaspars', 40.

31.   Christiansen, *Cassiodorus, Jordanes and the History of the Goths*, 339–41.

32.   John Given, *The Fragmentary History of Priscus: Attila, the Huns and the Roman Empire, AD 430–476* (Merchantville: Evolution Publishing, 2014), 4.

33.   Christiensen, *Cassiodorus, Jordanes and the History of the Goths*, 334.

34.   Goffart, *Narrators of Barbarian History*, 14; Barnish, 'Old Kaspars', 38; Sidonius Apollinaris, *Epistulae*, 8.15.

35.   Kim, 'Herodotean Allusions in Late Antiquity', 137.

36. Franz Altheim, *Geschichte der Hunnen*, Vol.4 (Berlin: Walter de Gruyter & Co., 1959), 324–29.
37. John Michael Wallace-Hadrill, *The Long Haired Kings: And Other Studies in Frankish History* (London: Methuen & Company, 1962), 60–63.
38. Kim, *The Huns, Rome and the Birth of Europe*, 77–78.
39. Kim, 'Herodotean Allusions in Late Antiquity', 127–42.
40. Barnish, 'Old Kaspars', 40.
41. Christiansen, *Cassiodorus, Jordanes and the History of the Goths*, 330–31.
42. Barnish, 'Old Kaspars', 41–42.
43. Whately, 'Jordanes, the Battle of the Catalaunian Fields and Constantinople', 64.
44. Whately, 'Jordanes, the Battle of the Catalaunian Fields and Constantinople', 65–66.
45. Bernard S. Bachrach, *A History of the Alans in the West: From their First Appearance in the Sources of Classical Antiquity to the Early Middle Ages* (Minneapolis: University of Minnesota Press, 1973), 28; Kim, *The Huns, Rome and the Birth of Europe*, 77–78.
46. Kim, 'Herodotean Allusions in Late Antiquity', 142.
47. Roger Blockley, 'The Development of Greek Historiography: Priscus, Malchus, Candidus', in *Greek & Roman Historiogrpahy in Late Antiquity: Fourth to Sixth Century AD* (Leiden: Brill Academic Publishing, 2003), 289–315; Barry Baldwin, 'Priscus of Panium', *Byzantion* 50 (1980), 18–61; Kim, 'Herodotean Allusions in Late Antiquity', 127–42.
48. Blockley, 'The Development of Greek Historiography', 302–12.
49. Kim, 'Herodotean Allusions in Late Antiquity', 133.
50. Blockley, 'The Development of Greek Historiography', 302; Marjeta Sasel Kos, 'The Embassy of Romulus to Attila: One of the Last Citations of Poetovio in Classical Literature', *Tyche* 9 (1994), 103.
51. Roger Blockley, *The Fragmentary Classicizing Historians of the Later Roman Empire*, Vol.1 (Liverpool: Francis Cairns, 1981), 52.
52. Blockley, *The Fragmentary Classicizing Historians*, Vol.1, 49–51.
53. Blockley, *The Fragmentary Classicizing Historians*, Vol.1, 51.
54. Blockley, 'The Development of Greek Historiography', 300.
55. Blockley, *The Fragmentary Classicizing Historians*, Vol.1, 67–70; Given, *The Fragmentary History of Priscus*, 125–27 fr. 69; John of Antioch, fr. 293.1.
56. Tackholm, 'Aetius and the Battle on the Catalaunian Fields', 273.
57. Blockley, *The Fragmentary Classicizing Historians*, Vol.1, 61.
58. Blockley, 'The Development of Greek Historiography', 305; Hrvoje Gracanin, 'The Western Roman Embassy to the Court of Attila in A.D. 449', *Byzantinoslavica* 6 (2003), 53–74.
59. Kim, 'Herodotean Allusions in Late Antiquity', 140.
60. Blockley, *The Fragmentary Classicizing Historians*, Vol.1, 52.

61. Blockley, 'The Development of Greek Historiography', 303.

62. Kim, 'Herodotean Allusions in Late Antiquity', 134.

63. Dariusz Brodka, 'Attila, Tyche und die Schlacht auf den Katalaunischen Feldern: Eine Untersuchung zum Geschichtsdenken des Priskos von Panion', *Hermes* 136, no.2 (2008), 227–45; Kim, 'Herodotean Allusions in Late Antiquity', 128.

64. Kim, 'Herodotean Allusions in Late Antiquity', 129–33; Blockley, *The Fragmentary Classicizing Historians*, Vol.1, 54–55.

65. Blockley, *The Fragmentary Classicizing Historians*, Vol.1, 62–63.

66. Blockley, *The Fragmentary Classicizing Historians*, Vol.1, 67–70; Given, *The Fragmentary History of Priscus*, 125–27 fr. 69; John of Antioch, fr. 293.1.

67. Blockley, *The Fragmentary Classicizing Historians*, Vol.1, 65–66; Hydatius, *Continuatio Chronicorum*, 154.

68. Sidonius Apollinaris, *Carmina*, 5.210–24, 274–308; for his career, retirement and reinstatement.

69. Sidonius Apollinaris, *Carmina*, 5.274–308; Hydatius, *Continuatio Chronicorum*, 151.

70. Andrew Gillett, 'The Hero as Envoy: Sidonius Apollinaris' Panegyric on Avitus', in *Envoys and Political Communication in the Late Antique West, 411–533* (Cambridge: Cambridge University Press, 2003), 97–103; Sidonius Apollinaris, *Carmina*, 7.336–56.

71. Gillett, 'The Hero as Envoy', 91–92.

72. Jill Harries, *Sidonius Apollinaris and the Fall of Rome* (Oxford: Oxford University Press, 1994), 75.

73. David Jimenez, 'Sidonius Apollinaris and the Fourth Punic War', in *New Perspectives on Late Antiquity* (Newcastle: Cambridge Scholars Publishing, 2011), 158–72.

74. Gillett, 'The Hero as Envoy', 108–12.

75. Sidonius Apollinaris, *Carmina*, 7.319–28.

76. Sidonius Apollinaris, *Carmina*, 7.328–54.

77. Livy, *Ab Urbe Condita*, 3.26.

78. '*fac, optime, Chunos quorum forte prior fuga nos concusserat olim, bis victos prodesse mihi.*' Sidonius Apollinaris, *Carmina*, 7.344–46.

79. Jordanes, *De Origine Actibusque Getarum*, 41.216–17; Fredegar, *Chronica Epitomata*, 2.53.

80. Barnish, 'Old Kaspars', 38; Sidonius Apollinaris, *Epistulae*, 8.15.

81. Ralph Mathisen, 'Sidonius on the Reign of Avitus: A Study in Political Prudence', *Transactions of the American Philological Association* 109 (1979), 169–70; Harries, *Sidonius Apollinaris and the Fall of Rome*, 31–32; on his connection to Avitus.

82. Harries, *Sidonius Apollinaris and the Fall of Rome*, 27, 47.

83. Harries, *Sidonius Apollinaris and the Fall of Rome*, 73–74; Mathisen, 'Sidonius on the Reign of Avitus', 168; Sidonius Apollinaris, *Epistulae*, 7.12.3; although

specifically discussing Avitus, he notes that Sidonius was prudent in his commentary regarding major political figures.

84. Harries, *Sidonius Apollinaris and the Fall of Rome*, 31–32.
85. Sidonius Apollinaris, *Carmina*, 7.345–46.
86. Christiensen, *Cassiodorus, Jordanes and the History of the Goths*, 334.
87. Gregory of Tours, *Decem Libri Historiarum*, 2.7.
88. Andrew Gillett, 'The Provincial View of Hydatius', in *Envoys and Political Communication in the Late Antique West, 411–533* (Cambridge: Cambridge University Press, 2003), 39; Tackholm, 'Aetius and the Battle on the Catalaunian Fields', 259.
89. Tackholm, 'Aetius and the Battle on the Catalaunian Fields', 260–61.
90. '*Attila post necem fratris auctus opibus interempti multa vicinarum sibi gentium milia cogit in bellum, quod gothis tantum se inferre tamquam custos romanae amicitiae denuntiabat. Sed cum transito Rheno saevissimos eius impetus multae gallicanae urbes experirentur, cito et nostris et Gothis placuit, ut furori superborum hostium consociatis exercitibus repugnaretur, tantaque patricii aetii providentia fuit, ut raptim congregatis undique bellatoribus viris adversae multitudini non impar occurreret. Quo in conflictu quamvis neutris credentibus inaestimabilis strages commorentium factae sint, Chunos tamen eo constat victos fuisse, quod amissa proeliandi fiducia qui superfuerant ad propria reverterunt.*' Prosper, *Epitoma Chronicon*, s.a. 451. Trans. in part by Dr Joseph Tipton.
91. Tackholm, 'Aetius and the Battle on the Catalaunian Fields', 260–61.
92. Tackholm, 'Aetius and the Battle on the Catalaunian Fields', 273; Bernardo Mingarelli, *Collapse of the Hunnic Empire: Jordanes, Ardaric, and the Battle of Nedao* (PhD Thesis, University of Ottowa, 2018), 55–56.
93. Gillett, 'The Provincial View of Hydatius', 47–49.
94. Hydatius, *Continuatio Chronicorum*, 150.
95. Gillett, 'The Provincial View of Hydatius', 54.
96. R.W. Burgess, 'A New Reading for the Hydatius Chronicle 177 and the Defeat of the Huns in Italy', *Phoenix* 42 (1988), 360–62; Hydatius, *Continuatio Chronicorum*, 154.
97. Burgess, 'A New Reading for the Hydatius Chronicle', 358, 360, 362.
98. Burgess, 'A New Reading for the Hydatius Chronicle', 362.
99. Richard Burgess, 'The Gallic Chronicle of 452: A New Critical Edition with a Brief Introduction', in *Society and Culture in Late Antique Gaul: Revisiting the Sources* (Aldershot: Ashgate Publishing, 2001), 52–53.
100. Richard Burgess, 'The Gallic Chronicle of 511: A New Critical Edition', 86–87.
101. '*Acttila Gallias ingressus quasi iure debitam poscit uxorem, ubi gravi clade inflicta et accepta ad propria concedit.*' *Chronica Gallica Anno 452*, s.a. 451.
102. '*Aezius patricius cum Theodorico rege Gothorum contra Attilam regem Ugnorum Tricasis pugnat loco Mauriaco, ubi Theudericus a quo occisus incertum est et*

*Laudaricus cognatus Attilae. Cadavera vero innumera.'*Chronica Gallica Anno *511*, s.a. 451.

103. Tackholm, 'Aetius and the Battle on the Catalaunian Fields', 262–63.
104. Tackholm, 'Aetius and the Battle on the Catalaunian Fields', 263.
105. Cassiodorus, *Variae*, 3.1.1, 1.4.11.
106. Cassiodorus, *Variae*, 3.1.1.
107. Isidore of Seville, *Historia de Regibus Gothorum, Vandalorum, et Suevorum*, 25; Kenneth Wolf, *Conquerors and Chroniclers of Early Medieval Spain*, 2nd ed. (Liverpool: Liverpool University Press, 2011), 76; Tackholm, 'Aetius and the Battle on the Catalaunian Fields', 275.
108. Barnish, 'Old Kaspars', 39.
109. Gregory of Tours, *Decem Libri Historiarum*, 2.7–8.
110. Michel Banniard, 'L'aménagement de l'histoire chez Grégoire de Tours: à propos de l'invasion de 451', *Romanobarbarica* 3 (1978), 23–26; Walter Goffart, *Narrators of Barbarian History*, 14.
111. Barnish, 'Old Kaspars', 39; Gregory of Tours, *Decem Libri Historiarum*, 2.6.
112. Barnish, 'Old Kaspars', 40; Blockley, *The Fragmentary Classicizing Historians*, Vol.1, 67–70; Given, *The Fragmentary History of Priscus*, 125–27 fr. 69; John of Antioch, fr. 293.1.
113. Gregory of Tours, *Decem Libri Historiarum*, 2.5–2.7.
114. Barnish, 'Old Kaspars', 43.
115. Fredegar, *Chronica Epitomata*, 2.53; Barnish, 'Old Kaspars', 44.
116. Barnish, 'Old Kaspars', 44–45.
117. Andrew Gillett, 'The Saint as Envoy: Fifth- and Sixth-Century Latin Bishops' Lives', in *Envoys and Political Communication in the Late Antique West, 411–533* (Cambridge: Cambridge University Press, 2003), 113–71; for a comprehensive discussion on the topic.
118. Barnish, 'Old Kaspars', 45.
119. Barnish, 'Old Kaspars', 45–46.
120. Barnish, 'Old Kaspars', 46–47.
121. Laura Fyfe, *Hunnic Warfare in the Fourth and Fifth Centuries C.E.: Archery and the Collapse of the Western Roman Empire* (Master's Thesis, Trent University, 2016), 113–25.
122. George T. Dennis, *Maurice's Strategikon: Handbook of Byzantine Military Strategy* (Philadelphia: University of Pennsylvania Press, 1984), xvi–xvii.
123. Phillip Rance, 'Maurice's *Strategicon* and "the Ancients": the Late Antique Reception of Aelian and Arrian', in *Greek Taktika: Ancient Military Writing and its Heritage* (Gdańsk: University of Gdańsk, 2017), 218–19.
124. Peter Golden, 'War and Warfare in the Pre-Chingissid Western Steppes of Eurasia', in *Studies on the Peoples and Cultures of the Eurasian Steppes* (Bucharest: Editura Academiei Române, 2011), 84–89; for a comprehensive

discussion of early Byzantine tropes in depicting steppe nomads, including the *Strategikon*.

125. Rance, 'Maurice's *Strategicon* and "the Ancients"', 223–51.
126. Dennis, *Maurice's Strategikon*, xviii.
127. Philip Rance, 'The *Etymologicum Magnum* and the Fragment of Urbicius', *Greek, Roman and Byzantine Studies* 47 (2007), 195–99.
128. Rance, 'The Fragment of Urbicius', 219–24.
129. Rance, 'The Fragment of Urbicius', 196.
130. N.P. Milner, *Vegetius: Epitome of Military Science*, 2nd ed. (Liverpool: Liverpool University Press, 1993), xxxi–xxxiv; Philip Rance, 'Drungus, Δρούγγος and Δρουγγιστί: a Gallicism and Continuity in Roman Cavalry Tactics', *Phoenix* 58 (2004), 103–04.
131. Milner, *Vegetius*, xxxvii–xli.
132. Milner, *Vegetius*, xl.
133. Milner, *Vegetius*, 3.26; Given, *The Fragmentary History of Priscus*, 128–29 fr. 71.
134. Milner, *Vegetius*, xxxv–xxxvi.
135. Milner, *Vegetius*, xvi.
136. Milner, *Vegetius*, xvii–xxv.
137. Milner, *Vegetius*, xxvi–xxvii.
138. Rance, 'Drungus, Δρουγγος and Δρουγγιστί', 106–08.

Chapter 1

1. Etienne de la Vassiere, 'Huns et Xiongnu', *Central Asiatic Journal* 49 (2005), 3–26; Christopher P. Atwood, 'Huns and Xiongnu – New Thoughts on an Old Problem', in *Dubitando: Studies in History and Culture in Honor of David Ostrowski* (Bloomington: Slavica Publishers, 2012), 27–52, esp. 44–45, 48–49.
2. Christopher Atwood, 'The Qai, the Khongai and the Names of the Xiōngnú', in *International Journal of Eurasian Studies*, Vol.2 (Beijing: The Commercial Press, 2015), 43–47.
3. Kim, *The Huns, Rome and the Birth of Europe*, 59, 208; Peter Golden, 'Nomads of the Western Eurasian Steppes: Oyurs, Onoyurs and Khazars', in *Studies on the Peoples and Cultures of the Eurasian Steppes* (Bucharest: Editura Academiei Române, 2011), 144; Christopher Atwood, 'The Qai, the Khongai and the Names of the Xiōngnú', 38–39.
4. Toshio Hayashi, 'Huns were Xiongnu or not? From the Viewpoint of Archaeological Material', in *Altay Communities: Migrations and Emergence of Nations* (Istanbul: Istanbul Esnaf ve Sanatkarlar Odalari Birligi, 2014), 13–26; Omeljan Pritsak, 'The Hunnic Language of the Attila Clan', *Harvard Ukranian Studies* 4 (1982), 428–76; Otto Maenchen-Helfen, *On the World of the Huns: Studies in their History and Culture* (Berkeley: University of California Press, 1973), 403, 441; Kim, *The Huns, Rome and the Birth of Europe*, 29;

Alexander Vovin, 'Did the Xiong-nu Speak a Yeniseian Language?', *Central Asiatic Journal* 44 (2000), 87–104.

5.   Maenchen-Helfen, 'Huns and Hsiung-nu', *Byzantion* 17 (1945), 222–43; Kelly, *The End of Empire*, 43–45.

6.   Kim, *The Huns, Rome and the Birth of Europe*, 29–30.

7.   Procopius, *The Wars of Justinian*, 1.3.2.

8.   Etienne de la Vassiere, 'The Steppe World and the Rise of the Huns', in *The Cambridge Companion to the Age of Attila* (Cambridge: Cambridge University Press, 2015), 185–88.

9.   De la Vassiere, 'The Steppe World and the Rise of the Huns', 182–84; Kim, *The Huns, Rome and the Birth of Europe*, 32–35.

10.   Kim, *The Huns, Rome and the Birth of Europe*, 33–35, 175; Atwood, 'Huns and Xiongnu', 47–48.

11.   Atwood, 'Huns and Xiongnu', 47–48.

12.   Jordanes, *De Origine Actibusque Getarum*, 24.126; Maenchen-Helfen, *On the World of the Huns*, 22–23.

13.   Given, *The Fragmentary History of Priscus*, 5.

14.   Ammianus, *Res Gestae*, 31.2.1.

15.   Jordanes, *De Origine Actibusque Getarum*, 24.121–26

16.   De la Vassiere, 'The Steppe World and the Rise of the Huns', 177; Peter Heather, 'The Huns and the End of the Roman Empire in Western Europe', *English Historical Review* 110, no.435 (1995), 6.

17.   De la Vassiere, 'The Steppe World and the Rise of the Huns', 188–90; Edward R. Cook, 'Megadroughts, ENSO and the Invasion of Late-Roman Europe by the Huns and Avars', in *The Ancient Mediterranean Environment: Between Science and History* (Leiden: Brill, 2013), 91, 100.

18.   Heather, 'The Huns and the End of the Roman Empire', 5–11.

19.   G. Greatrex and M. Greatrex, 'The Hunnic Invasion of the East in 395 and the Fortress of Ziatha', *Byzantion* 54 (1999), 66, 69.

20.   Given, The Fragmentary History of Priscus, 68–69 fr. 8; Heather, *The Fall of the Roman Empire*, 356–57; Blockley, *The Fragmentary Classicizing Historians*, 279, 386; barring Jordanes' 'Balamber' who is probably only a mythical character or an analogue of Valamir used to establish Amal legitimacy.

21.   Jerome, *Epistulae*, 60.16, 77.8.

22.   Greatrex and Greatrex, 'The Hunnic Invasion of the East in 395', 67–71.

23.   Greatrex and Greatrex, 'The Hunnic Invasion of the East in 395', 72.

24.   Maenchen-Helfen, *On the World of the Huns*, 56–57; Claudian, *In Eutropium*, 1.252–54, 2.55–56.

25.   Maenchen-Helfen, *On the World of the Huns*, 59; Zozimus, *Nova Historia*, 5.22.1–3.

26.   Ian Hughes, *Stilicho: The Vandal Who Saved Rome* (Barnsley: Pen & Sword Military, 2010), 165; Maenchen-Helfen, *On the World of the Huns*, 60–62.

27.   Maenchen-Helfen, *On the World of the Huns*, 63–66.

28. Zozimus, *Nova Historia*, 5.46.6, 5.50.1; the number of 10,000 seems realistic in this instance.

29. Olympiodorus, fr. 18.

30. Olympiodorus, fr. 19.

31. Theodoret, 5.37.4–10.

32. Given, *The Fragmentary History of Priscus*, 8.

33. Socrates, *Historia Ecclesiastica*, 7.30.

34. Jeroen P. Wijnendaele, *The Last of the Romans: Bonifatius – Warlord and Comes Africae* (New York: Bloomsbury Academic, 2016), 105–06; Ian Hughes, *Aetius: Attila's Nemesis* (Barnsley: Pen & Sword Miliary, 2012), 86–87.

35. Maenchen-Helfen, *On the World of the Huns*, 386–87; Pritsak, *The Hunnic Language of the Attila Clan*, 444.

36. Jordanes, *De Origine Actibusque Getarum*, 35.180.

37. Given, *The Fragmentary History of Priscus*, 41 fr. 61.

38. Given, *The Fragmentary History of Priscus*, 8 fr. 1.

39. Maenchen-Helfen, *On the World of the Huns*, 92–93.

40. Given, *The Fragmentary History of Priscus*, 11 fr. 1.1; Maenchen-Helfen, *On the World of the Huns*, 93–94.

41. Given, *The Fragmentary History of Priscus*, 11 fr. 1.1.

42. Given, *The Fragmentary History of Priscus*, 11 fr. 1.1; Maenchen-Helfen, *On the World of the Huns*, 91.

43. Given, *The Fragmentary History of Priscus*, 11 fr. 1.1.

44. Cook, 'Megadroughts, ENSO and the Invasion of Late-Roman Europe by the Huns and Avars', 91, 100; Blockley, *The Fragmentary Classicizing Historians*, 227, 380; rendered as Σορόσγους, Blockley notes the Greek indicates they were a people outside Attila's empire.

45. Jordanes, *Vel Summa Temporum Vel Origine Actibusque Gentis Romanorum*, 331.

46. Given, *The Fragmentary History of Pricsus*, 13 fr. 2.

47. Maenchen-Helfen, *On the World of the Huns*, 110; *Liber Legum Novellarum Divi Valentiniani Augustus*, 23.1.

48. Maenchen-Helfen, *On the World of the Huns*, 89; Given, *The Fragmentary History of Priscus*, 44 fr. 7.

49. Kos, 'The Embassy of Romulus to Attila', 105–06; Bona, *Les Huns*, 89.

50. Penny MacGeorge, *Late Roman Warlords* (Oxford: Oxford University Press, 2002), 32–39; Hervoje Gracanin, 'The Western Embassy to the Court of Attila in A.D. 449', *Byzantinoslavica* 61 (2003), 68–70; Given, *The Fragmentary History of Priscus*, 58 fr. 8.

51. Heather, *The Fall of the Roman Empire*, 300–04.

52. Williams and Friell, *The Rome that did not Fall*, 65–66; Heather, *The Fall of the Roman Empire*, 290; Theophanes, 5941; much like the later Battle of Cape Bon with its 1,100 ships, this figure could be an allusion back to Salamis.

53. Williams and Friell, *The Rome that did not Fall*, 66; Given, *The Fragmentary History of Priscus*, 13 fr. 2.

54. David Nicolle, *The Mongol Warlords: Ghenghis Khan, Kublai Khan, Hulegu, Tamerlane* (New York: Firebird Books, 1990), 21; Erik Hildinger, *Warriors of the Steppe: A Military History of Central Asia 500 B.C. to 1700 A.D.* (Cambridge: Da Capo Press, 2001), 127–29.

55. Given, *The Fragmentary History of Priscus*, 13–14 fr. 2.

56. Williams and Friell, *The Rome that did not Fall*, 67.

57. Hugh Elton, 'Military Developments in the Fifth Century', in *The Cambridge Companion to the Age of Attila* (Cambridge: Cambridge University Press, 2014), 128; Candidus, fr. 2.

58. Williams and Friell, *The Rome that did not Fall*, 67.

59. Williams and Friell, *The Rome that did not Fall*, 69–70.

60. Williams and Friell, *The Rome that did not Fall*, 70; Given, *The Fragmentary History of Priscus*, 36 fr. 3.

61. Given, *The Fragmentary History of Priscus*, 14–15 fr. 1B.

62. Given, *The Fragmentary History of Priscus*, 15 fr. 1B.

63. Roger Blockley, 'Dexippus and Priscus and the Thucydidean Account of the Siege of Platea', *Phoenix* 26 (1972), 22–26; Blockley, *The Development of Greek Historiography*, 303.

64. Williams and Friell, *The Rome that did not Fall*, 115.

65. Williams and Friell, *The Rome that did not Fall*, 70; Kelly, *The End of Empire*, 128.

66. Maenchen-Helfen, *On the World of the Huns*, 117.

67. For numbers see Appendix B.

68. Kim, *The Huns, Rome and the Birth of Europe*, 71; Jones, *The Later Roman Empire*, Vol.2, 1,030–031.

69. Williams and Friell, *The Rome that did not Fall*, 74, 252; *Liber Legum Novellarum Divi Theodosii Augustus*, 24.1; Ventzislav Dinchev, 'The Fortresses of Thrace and Dacia in the Early Byzantine Period', in *The Transition to Late Antiquity: On the Danube and Beyond* (Oxford: Oxford University Press, 2007), 479–546; for a comprehensive overview of the late Roman Danubian defensive fortresses.

70. Maenchen-Helfen, *On the World of the Huns*, 85, 105, 118.

71. Williams and Friell, *The Rome that did not Fall*, 78–79; Given, *The Fragmentary History of Priscus*, 78 fr. 8; Blockley, *The Fragmentary Classicizing Historians*, Vol.1, 53; Blockley points out how Priscus' use of phrases such as 'the man in charge of the Romans in the East' makes ranks difficult to pinpoint.

72. Williams and Friell, *The Rome that did not Fall*, 79–80; Blockley, *The Fragmentary Classicizing Historians*, Vol.1, 53; Appendix B; Blockley identifies Arnegisclus as *magister militum per Thracias*.

73. Williams and Friell, *The Rome that did not Fall*, 79; Given, *The Fragmentary History of Priscus*, 41 fr. 61; Elton, 'Military Developments in the Fifth

Century', 129; Malchus, fr. 18.2; 10,000 infantry and 2,000 cavalry. He also states the army in Constantinople numbered 20,000 infantry and 6,000 cavalry. This second number may have been both Praesental armies, each at half-strength. Malchus might also be copying Vegetius 3.1. Interestingly, Vegetius' numbers also coincide with the *Notitia Dignitatum*, as four of the five field armies number 20,000 infantry and 4,000 cavalry.

74. Kelly, *The End of Empire*, 136–39; Kelly thinks that these events happened in the opposite direction, during Attila's retreat out of Gaul. The second battle at the Thracian Chersonese suggests this was not the case.

75. Given, *The Fragmentary History of Priscus*, 36 fr. 4.

76. Williams and Friell, *The Rome that did not Fall*, 79–80.

77. Given, *The Fragmentary History of Priscus*, 37 fr. 5; Kim, *The Huns, Rome and the Birth of Europe*, 71; Williams and Friell, *The Rome that did not Fall*, 112; Appendix B; Williams and Friell think this battle took place in 441–43, which cannot have happened as Attila was nowhere near the Thracian Chersonese in 441–43.

78. Williams and Friell, *The Rome that did not Fall*, 80, 112; Vujadin Ivanisevic, 'The Danubian *Limes* of the Diocese of Dacia in the Fifth Century', in *Romania Gothica II* (Budapest: Eotvos Lorand University, 2015), 653–65; *Chronica Gallica anno 452*, s.a. 447; Theophanes, 5,942; Callinicus, *De Vita Hypatii*, 139.21; Appendix B.

79. Alexander Stanev, 'Elements of the Germanic Fibula Costume South of the Danube River', in *Archaeological Data from the Balkan Provinces of the Eastern Roman Empire V–VI Century* (Ruse: Avangard Print, 2012), 24; Heather, *The Fall of the Roman Empire*, 311.

80. Ivo Topalilov, 'The Barbarians and the City: A Comparative Study of the Impact of the Barbarian Invasions in 376–378 and 442–447 on the Urbanization of Philipopolis, Thrace', in *Byzantium, its Neighbours and its Cultures* (Virginia: Brisbane, 2014), 231–35; Michael Whitby, 'The Balkans and Greece, 420–602', in *The Cambridge Ancient History*, Vol.14 (Cambridge: Cambridge University Press, 2008), 713.

81. Kim, *The Huns, Rome and the Birth of Europe*, 84–88; Williams and Friell, *The Rome that did not Fall*, 173–99.

82. Michael Whitby, 'The Late Roman Army and the Defence of the Balkans', in *The Transition to Late Antiquity on the Danube and Beyond* (Oxford: Oxford University Press, 2007), 137–38.

83. *Vita Hypatii*, 104.

84. Williams and Friell, *The Rome that did not Fall*, 112, 256.

85. Williams and Friell, *The Rome that did not Fall*, 80; Given, *The Fragmentary History of Priscus*, 37–38 fr. 5, 44 fr. 7; Bona, *Les Huns*, 89; MacGeorge, *Late Roman Warlords*, 32–39.

86. Given, *The Fragmentary History of Priscus*, 37–39 fr. 5, 45 fr 7.

87.   Maenchen-Helfen, *On the World of the Huns*, 64; Ying-Shih Yu, *Trade and Expansion in Han China: A Study in the Structure of Sino-Barbarian Economic Relation* (Berkeley: University of California Press, 1967), 41–51, 99–105.

88.   Given, *The Fragmentary History of Priscus*, 39 fr. 5.

89.   Given, *The Fragmentary History of Priscus*, 37–38 fr. 5.

90.   Kelly, *The End of Empire*, 142–43; Kim, *The Huns, Rome and the Birth of Europe*, 71–73.

91.   Williams and Friell, *The Rome that did not Fall*, 80–81.

92.   Altheim, *Geschichte der Hunnen*, Vol.4, 294; Hrvoje Gracanin, 'The Western Roman Embassy to the Court of Attila', 53; Given, *The Fragmentary History of Priscus*, 44 fr. 7; Wolfram, *The Roman Empire and its Germanic Peoples*, 184–85.

93.   Given, *The Fragmentary History of Priscus*, 45–46 fr. 7.

94.   Gracanin, 'The Western Roman Embassy to the Court of Attila', 55.

95.   Given, *The Fragmentary History of Priscus*, 47–50 fr. 8.

96.   Blockley, 'The Development of Greek Historiography', 304–05; Robert Browning, 'Where was Attila's Camp?', *The Journal of Hellenic Studies* 73 (1953), 143–45.

97.   Given, *The Fragmentary History of Priscus*, 58 fr. 8; Blockley, *The Fragmentary Classicizing Historians*, Vol.2, 262–63 fr. 11.2; Gracanin, 'The Western Roman Embassy to the Court of Attila', 68; Priscus calls Promotus *tes Norikon archon choras* and Romanus *stratiotikou tagmatos hegemon*.

98.   Given, *The Fragmentary History of Priscus*, 58 fr. 8; Gracanin, 'The Western Roman Embassy to the Court of Attila', 68.

99.   Peter Kos, 'Barriers in the Julian Alps and the *Notitia Dignitatum*', *Arheoloski Vestnik* 65 (2014), 409–22.

100.   Kos, 'Barriers in the Julian Alps', 413–16.

101.   Gracanin, 'The Western Roman Embassy to the Court of Attila', 69.

102.   Gracanin, 'The Western Roman Embassy to the Court of Attila', 70.

103.   Given, *The Fragmentary History of Priscus*, 58 fr. 8; Cassiodorus, *Variae*, 1.4.11.

104.   Given, *The Fragmentary History of Priscus*, 59 fr. 8.

105.   Given, *The Fragmentary History of Priscus*, 59 fr. 8.

106.   Given, *The Fragmentary History of Priscus*, 68–70 fr. 8; also present was Rusticius, a translator.

107.   Gracanin, 'The Western Roman Embassy to the Court of Attila', 61.

108.   Cassiodorus, *Variae*, 1.4.11; Given, *The Fragmentary History of Priscus*, 54, 69–70 fr. 8.

109.   Gracanin, 'The Western Roman Embassy to the Court of Attila', 63.

110.   Heather, *The Fall of the Roman Empire*, 292.

111.   Gracanin, 'The Western Roman Embassy to the Court of Attila', 63.

112. Bury, *History of the Later Roman Empire*, 224.

113. Marcellinus Comes, *Chronicon*, s.a. 434; Given, *The Fragmentary History of Priscus*, 93 fr. 62.

114. John Bagnall Bury, 'Iusta Grata Honoria', *Journal of Roman Studies* 9 (1919), 89.

115. Gracanin, 'The Western Roman Embassy to the Court of Attila', 64.

116. Hughes, *Aetius: Attila's Nemesis*, 148; Kos, 'The Embassy of Romulus to Attila', 106.

117. Bury, 'Iusta Grata Honoria', 910; Given, *The Fragmentary History of Priscus*, 92–93 fr. 62.

118. Bury, 'Iusta Grata Honoria', 10; Given, *The Fragmentary History of Priscus*, 93 fr. 62.

119. Gracanin, 'The Western Roman Embassy to the Court of Attila', 67.

120. Wolfram, *The Roman Empire and its Germanic Peoples*, 137.

121. Maenchen-Helfen, *On the World of the Huns*, 130; Bona, *Les Huns*, 67.

122. Christiansen, *Cassiodorus, Jordanes and the History of the Goths*, 327–29.

123. Given, *The Fragmentary History of Priscus*, 99–100 fr. 16.

124. Thomas Hodgkin, *Italy and her Invaders* (Oxford: Clarendon Press, 1880), 102–03; Bona, *Das Hunnenreich*, 127; Kim, *The Huns, Rome and the Birth of Europe*, 81–82, 221; Gregory of Tours, *Decem Libri Historiarum*, 2.9, 2.12; Fredegar, *Chronica Epitomata*, 3.11; Kim gives an in-depth overview of the literature on the topic.

125. Given, *The Fragmentary History of Priscus*, fr. 15, fr.16.

126. Gregory of Tours, *Decem Libri Historiarum*, 2.12; Fredegar, *Chronica Epitomata*, 3.11.

127. MacGeorge, *Late Roman Warlords*, 76–77.

128. Given, *The Fragmentary History of Priscus*, 93–94 fr. 62.

129. Brodka, 'Attila, Tyche und der Schlacht auf der Katalaunischen Feldern', 238; Kim, 'Herodotean Allusions in Late Antiquity', 137–38.

130. Gregory of Tours, *Decem Libri Historiarum*, 2.7.

131. Kim, *The Huns, Rome and the Birth of Europe*, 78–79.

132. Kim, 'Herodotean Allusions in Late Antiquity', 138.

133. Jordanes, *De Origine Actibusque Getarum*, 36.185–90.

134. Christiensen, *Cassiodorus, Jordanes and the History of the Goths*, 329–30.

135. Barnish, 'Old Kaspars', 41.

136. Prosper, *Epitoma Chronicon*, s.a. 448.

137. Ferrill, *The Fall of the Roman Empire: The Military Explanation*, 147; Harries, *Sidonius Apollinaris and the Fall of Rome*, 207–09; Meghan McEvoy, *Child Emperor Rule in the Late Roman West* (Oxford: Oxford University Press, 2013), 294–95. Harries explains this system in some detail, in regard to Sidonius' life and connections.

Chapter 2

1. Hughes, *Aetius: Attila's Nemesis*, 4; this description follows the chronology set forth by Ian Hughes.
2. Jeroen P. Wijnendaele, 'The Early Career of Aetius and the Murder of Felix (c. 425–430 CE)', *Historia* 66, no.4 (2017), 469.
3. Hughes, *Aetius: Attila's Nemesis*, 4.
4. Hughes, *Aetius: Attila's Nemesis*, 11, 14, 22.
5. Wijnendaele, 'The Early Career of Aetius', 470–71.
6. Hughes, *Aetius: Attila's Nemesis*, 29–32; McEvoy, *Child Emperor Rule in the Late Roman West*, 245.
7. Hughes, *Aetius: Attila's Nemesis*, 65–66, 68–69.
8. Constantius of Lyon, *Vita Germani*, 12.5; Gildas, *De Excidio Conquestu Britanniae*, 21; Andrew Gillett, 'The Saint as Envoy: Bishops' Lives', 121.
9. Jeroen P. Wijnendaele, 'Warlordism and the Disintegration of the Western Roman Army', in *Circum Mare: Themes in Ancient Warfare* (Leiden: Brill, 2016), 197–200; Wijnendaele, *The Last of the Romans*, 69–86; Hughes, *Aetius: Attila's Nemesis*, 66–68, 75.
10. Hughes, *Aetius: Attila's Nemesis*, 71–73, 79–82.
11. McEvoy, *Child Emperor Rule in the Late Roman West*, 247; Hughes, *Aetius: Attila's Nemesis*, 78–79; Wijnendaele, 'The Early Career of Aetius', 475–77.
12. Hughes, *Aetius: Attila's Nemesis*, 76, 78; Michel Kazanski and Iliya Akhmedov, 'La Tombe de Mundolsheim (Bas-Rhin): Un chef militaire Nomade au service de Rome', *SPISY ARCHEOLOGICKEHO USTAVU AV CR BRNO* 26 (2007), 249–61.
13. Wijnendaele, 'The Early Career of Aetius', 479–80.
14. Wijnendaele, *The Last of the Romans*, 89–106.
15. Hughes, *Aetius: Attila's Nemesis*, 86–87; there is no evidence Aetius actually brought an army of Huns.
16. Hughes, *Aetius: Attila's Nemesis*, 93–94; McEvoy, *Child Emperor Rule in the Late Roman West*, 249.
17. Hughes, *Aetius: Attila's Nemesis*, 95–96; Prosper, *Epitoma Chronicon*, s.a. 436.
18. Prosper, *Epitoma Chronicon*, s.a. 437.
19. Hughes, *Aetius: Attila's Nemesis*, 97; Hydatius, *Continuatio Chronicorum*, 110.
20. McEvoy, *Child Emperor Rule in the Late Roman West*, 256–61; Hughes, *Aetius: Attila's Nemesis*, 99–100; Frank M. Clover, 'Flavius Merobaudes: A Translation and Historical Commentary', *Transactions of the American Philosophical Society* 61, no.1 (1971), 13, Panegyric I, fr. 2B; Hydatius, *Continuatio Chronicorum*, 112.
21. Hughes, *Aetius: Attila's Nemesis*, 102–03; Gillett, 'The Saint as Envoy: Bishops' Lives', 139–40; Hydatius, *Continuatio Chronicorum*, 116; Prosper,

Epitoma Chronicon, s.a. 439; the *Vita Orientii*, 3, claims that Aetius was also captured, but this is impossible as Aetius was in Italy at the time. Orientius, Avitus, Aetius and many others were all part of the negotiations after the truce.

22. Hughes, *Aetius: Attila's Nemesis*, 101–02.
23. Heather, *The Fall of the Roman Empire*, 288–99.
24. Hydatius, *Continuatio Chronicorum*, 119, 121, 123.
25. *Liber Legum Novellarum Divi Valentiniani Augustus*, 9.1.
26. Hughes, *Aetius: Attila's Nemesis*, 120–21; Williams and Friell, *The Rome that did not Fall*, 68–70.
27. Hydatius, *Continuatio Chronicorum*, 125, 128; *Chronica Gallica Anno* 452, s.a. 442; Constantius of Lyon, *Vita Germani*, 28.
28. *Liber Legum Novellarum Divi Valentiniani Augustus*, 6.3.1, 15.1.
29. Hughes, *Aetius: Attila's Nemesis*, 135–36; Sidonius Apollinaris, *Carmina*, 5.210–54.
30. Hydatius, *Continuatio Chronicorum*, 134.
31. Gildas, *De Excidio et Conquestu Britanniae*, 20.
32. Hughes, Hydatius, *Continuatio Chronicorum*, 141–42.
33. J.R. Moss, 'The Effects of the Policies of Aetius on the History of the Western Empire', *Historia* 22 (1973), 711–33; Christine Delaplace, *La fin de l'Empire romain d'Occident: Rome et les Wisigoths de 382–551* (Rennes: University Press of Rennes, 2015), 196–201.
34. McEvoy, *Child Emperor Rule in the Late Roman West*, 247, 263; Wijnendaele, *The Last of the Romans*, 118–19; Wijnendaele, 'The Early Career of Aetius', 482; Hughes, *Aetius: Attila's Nemesis*, 201.
35. Prosper, *Epitoma Chronicon*, s.a. 427; McEvoy, *Child Emperor Rule in the Late Roman West*, 247; Hughes, *Aetius: Attila's Nemesis*, 72.
36. McEvoy, *Child Emperor Rule in the Late Roman West*, 254–56, 259–61.
37. Terence Coello, 'Unit Sizes in the Late Roman Army', (PhD Diss., The Open University, 1995), 31–38.
38. Coello, 'Unit Sizes in the Late Roman Army', 103; A.H.M. Jones, *The Later Roman Empire, 284–602*, Vol.2, (Baltimore: Johns Hopkins University Press, 1986), Appendix II, 1,423.
39. Halsall, *Barbarian Migrations and the Roman West*, 102.
40. Halsall, *Barbarian Migrations and the Roman West*, 102; Jones, *The Later Roman Empire*, Vol.1, 644–45.
41. Hughes, *Aetius: Attila's Nemesis*, 4, 36.
42. Hughes, *Aetius: Attila's Nemesis*, 35–36.
43. Elton, *Warfare in Roman Europe*, 136–37
44. Elton, *Warfare in Roman Europe*, 145–52; Hugh Elton, *Frontiers of the Roman Empire* (London: Routledge, 2012), 151–52; Halsall, *Barbarian Migrations and the Roman West*, 105.

45. Elton, *Warfare in Roman Europe*, 129.

46. Wolfgang Liebeschuetz, 'The End of the Roman Army in the Western Empire', in *War and Society in the Roman World* (London: Routledge, 1993), 273; Bachrach, *Merovingian Military Organization 481–751*, 33–34.

47. Liebeschuetz, 'The End of the Roman Army', 272; Sidonius Apollinaris, *Carmina*, 7.235–37.

48. Sidonius Apollinaris, *Carmina*, 7.235–37; Ralph Mathisen, 'Catalogues of Barbarians in Late Antiquity', in *Romans, Barbarians and the Transformation of the Roman World* (Burlington: Ashgate Publishing, 2011), 17–32.

49. Lucas McMahon, 'The Foederati, The Phoideratoi and the Symmachoi of the Late Antique East (c.a. AD 400–650)', (Master's Thesis, University of Ottowa, 2014), 37; Fatih Onur, 'The Anastasian Military Decree from Perge in Pamphylia: Revised 2nd Edition', *GEPHYRA* 14 (2016), 159.

50. Sidonius Apollinaris *Carmina*, 5.472, 5.486, 7.247, 7.330 are all similar in usage.

51. Sidonius Apollinaris, *Carmina*, 5.217–18; Jordanes, *De Origine Actibusque Getarum*, 42.221.

52. Hydatius, *Continuatio Chronicorum*, 134; *Vita Orientii* 3; Gillett, 'The Saint as Envoy: Bishops' Lives', 139–40.

53. '*Et quamavis clementiae nostrae sollicitudo per diversa loca praesidia disponat atque invictissimi principis Theodosii patris nostri iam propinquet exercitus et excellentissimum virum patricium nostrum Aetium cum magna manu adfore mox credamus cumque vir inlustrissimus magister militum Sigisvuldus tam militum atque foederatorum tuitionem urbibus ac litoribus non desinat ordinare.*' Liber Legum Novellarum Divi Valentiniani Augustus, 9.1.

54. *Chronica Gallica 452*, 124, 126, '*Deserta Valentinae urbis rura alanis, quibus Sambida praeerat, partienda traduntur*' and '*Alanis quibus terrae Galliae ulterioris cum incolis dividenae a patricio Aetio traditae fuerant, resistentes armis subigunt et expulsis dominis terrae possessionem vi adipiscuntur.*' It should be noted that this theory relies upon the term '*praeerat*', which is rather distinct from other terminology used to describe barbarian leadership by the chronicle.

55. Orosius, *Historiae Adversum Paganos*, 7.37; Claudius Claudianus, *De Bello Gothico*, 26.618–37.

56. *Notitia Dignitatum Pars Occidentis*, 6.50, 7.163; Bachrach, *A History of the Alans in the West*, 36.

57. Ellen Swift, *The End of the Western Roman Empire: An Archaeological Investigation* (Stroud: The History Press, 2010), 113–17; Drinkwater, *The Alamanni and Rome*, 327–29.

58. Tina Milavec, 'Crossbow fibulae of the 5th and 6th centuries in the south-eastern Alps', *Arheoloski Vestnik* 60 (2009), 224–25; Slavko Ciglenecki, '*Claustra Alpium Iuliarum, tractus Italiae circa Alpes* and the Defence of Italy

in the Final Part of the Late Roman Period', *Arheoloski Vestnik* 67 (2016), 412–13.

59.   Svante Fischer and Fernando Lopez Sanchez, 'Subsidies for the Roman West? The Flow of Constantinopolitan Solidi to the Western Empire and Barbaricum', *Opuscula* 9 (2016), 158–77; David Wigg-Wolf, 'Supplying a Dying Empire? The Mint of Trier in the Late 4th Century AD', *RGZM – Tagungen* 29 (2016), 217–33; for an in-depth discussion on the end of the mints and military payment.

60.   Swift, *The End of the Western Roman Empire*, 108–13; Tina Milavec, 'Crossbow fibulae of the 5th and 6th centuries in the southeastern Alps', *Arheoloski Vestnik* 60 (2009), 224–26; Robert Collins, 'Brooch use in the 4th- to 5th-century frontier', in *Finds from the Frontier: Material Culture in the 4th–5th Centuries* (London: Council for British Archaeology, 2010), 67.

61.   Joaquin Fernandez, 'Late Roman Belts in Hispania', *Journal of Roman Military Equipment Studies* 10 (1999), 55–71.

62.   Elton, *Warfare in Roman Europe*, 72.

63.   Elton, *Warfare in Roman Europe*, 35–36.

64.   Elton, *Warfare in Roman Europe*, 36.

65.   Elton, *Warfare in Roman Europe*, 36–37; Nico Roymans, 'Gold, Germanic Foederati and the End of Imperial Power in the Late Roman North', in *Social Dynamics in the Northwest Frontiers of the Late Roman Empire* (Amsterdam: Amsterdam University Press, 2017), 69.

66.   Ernst Gaupp, *Die germanischen Ansiedlungen und Landteilungen in den Provinzen des römischen Weltreichs in ihrer völkerrechtlichen Eigentümlichkeit und mit Rücksicht auf verwandte Erscheinungen der Alten Welt und des späteren Mittelalters dargestellt* (Osnabrück: Otto Zeller Verlag, 1967); Hans Delbrück, *The Barbarian Invasions: History of the Art of War* (trans. Walter J. Renfoe Jr) (Lincoln: University of Nebraska Press, 1990), 284–89, 317–36; *Codex Theodosianus*, 7.8.5.

67.   Walter Goffart, *Barbarians and Romans 418–584: The Techniques of Accommodation* (Princeton: Princeton University Press, 1980), 40–55.

68.   Halsall, *Barbarian Migrations and the Roman West*, 432.

69.   Goffart, *Barbarian Tides*, 119–35; *Codex Theodosianus*, 7.4.1.

70.   Goffart, *Barbarians and Romans*, 73–80.

71.   Goffart, *Barbarians and Romans*, 80–88.

72.   Goffart, *Barbarians and Romans*, 118–23.

73.   Goffart, *Barbarians and Romans*, 137; Ferdinand Lot, 'Du régime de l'hospitalité', *Revue belge de Philologie et d'Histoire* 7 (1928), 975–1,011.

74.   Walter Goffart, 'The Technique of Barbarian Settlement in the Fifth Century: A Personal, Streamlined Account with Ten Additional Comments', *Journal of Late Antiquity* 3, no.1 (2010), 65–98; Cassiodorus, *Variae*, 2.16.5.

75.   Goffart, *Barbarian Tides*, 135–62.

76. Walter Goffart, 'Frankish Military Duty and the Fate of Roman Taxation', *Early Medieval Europe* 16, no.2 (2008), 166–90; Walter Goffart, 'Administrative Methods of Barbarian Settlement in the Fifth Century: The Definitive Account', in *Gallien in Spätantike und Frühmitterlalter: Kulturgeschichte Einer Region* (Berlin: Walter De Gruyter, 2013), 45–56.

77. Halsall, *Barbarian Migrations and the Roman West*, 432–35.

78. Halsall, *Barbarian Migrations and the Roman West*, 436–47.

79. Halsall, *Barbarian Migrations and the Roman West*, 434–35; *Chronica Gallica Anno 452*, s.a. 440 and 442.

80. Halsall, *Barbarian Migrations and the Roman West*, 439.

81. Halsall, *Barbarian Migrations and the Roman West*, 444.

82. Guy Halsall, 'The Ostrogothic Military', in *A Companion to Ostrogothic Italy* (Leiden: Brill, 2016), 188.

83. Guy Halsall, *Warfare and Society in the Barbarian West, 450–900* (London: Routledge, 2003), 60.

84. Lucas McMahon, 'Foederati, The Phoideratoi and the Symmachoi', 33–35; John Haldon, *Byzantine Praetorians: An Administrative, Institutional and Social Survey of the Opsikion and Tagmata, c. 580–900* (Bonn: Rudolf Halbelt, 1984), 100–01.

85. C.J. Simpson, '*Laeti* in the *Notitia Dignitatum*: "Regular" Soldiers vs. "Soldier-Farmers"', *Revue Belge de Philologie et d'histoire* 66.1 (1988), 80–85; Marcus Reuter, 'Studien zu den numeri des römischen Heeres in der mittleren Kaiserzeit', *Berichte der Römisch-Germanischen Kommission* 80 (1999), 359–569.

86. McMahon, 'Foederati, The Phoideratoi and the Symmachoi', 35.

87. Ian Hughes, *Patricians and Emperors: The Last Rulers of the Western Roman Empire* (Barnsley: Pen & Sword Military, 2015), 128–29.

88. Elton, *Warfare in Roman Europe*, 265.

89. Hugh Elton, 'Defence in Fifth Century Gaul', in *Fifth Century Gaul: A Crisis of Identity?* (Cambridge: Cambridge University Press, 1992), 170; Wijnendaele, 'The Early Career of Aetius', 473–74.

90. Elton, 'Defence in Fifth Century Gaul', 168; Elton's point still stands, but his claim is factually incorrect.

91. Williams and Friell, *The Rome that did not Fall*, 79.

92. Wijnenedaele, *The Last of the Romans*, 91–92; Hughes, *Aetius: Attila's Nemesis*, 82, 84.

93. Milner, *Vegetius*, 2.14; Gregory of Tours, *Decem Libri Historiarum*, 2.8; Richardot, *La Fin de l'Armee Romaine*, 271–302; for a comprehensive discussion of the 'decline of the infantry' and 'transformation of the cavalry' in the Dominate.

94. '*Hi enim adfuerunt auxiliares: Franci, Sarmatae, Armoriciani, Liticiani, Burgundiones, Saxones, Ripari, Olibriones, quondam milites Romani, tunc vero*

iam in numero auxiliarium exquisiti, aliaeque nonnulli Celticae vel Germanie nationes.' Jordanes, *De Origine Actibusque Getarum*, 36.191.

95. I do not include these two groups in the ethnographic summary since they are already well researched and what is relevant has already been or will be mentioned. See Delaplace, *La Fin de l'Empire Romain d'Occident: Rome et les Wisigoths de 382 a 531*, for a comprehensive overview of the Aquitanian Goths, or Bachrach, *A History of the Alans in the West*, for the Gallic Alans.

96. Elton, *Warfare in Roman Europe*, 132; Simpson, '*Laeti* in the *Notitia Dignitatum*', 80–85.

97. Alain Dierkins and Patrick Perin, 'The 5th-century Advance of the Franks in Belgica II: History and Archaeology', in *Essays on the Early Franks* (Eelde: Barkhuis, 2003), 166–67.

98. Dierkins and Perin, 'The 5th-century Advance of the Franks in Belgica II', 168–69.

99. Gregory of Tours, *Decem Libri Historiarum*, 2.9

100. Guy Halsall, 'Childeric's Grave, Clovis' Succession and the Origins of the Merovingian Kingdom', in *Society and Culture in Late Antique Gaul: Revisiting the Sources* (Aldershot: Ashgate Publishing, 2001), 123; Dierkins and Perin, 'The 5th-century Advance of the Franks in Belgica II', 169–70; Hughes, *Aetius: Attila's Nemesis*, 97, 133, 136; Swift, *The End of the Western Roman Empire*, 113–17.

101. Sidonius Apollinaris, *Carmina*, 5.210–11.

102. '*hic quoque monstra domat, rutili quibus arce cerebri ad frontem coma tracta iacet nudataque cervix saetarum per damna nitet, tum lumine glauco albet aquosa acies ac vultibus undique rasis pro barba tenues perarantur pectine cristae. Strictius assutae vestes procera cohercent membra virum, patet his altato tegmina poples, latus et angustam suspendit balteus alvum. Excussisse citas vastum per inane bipennes et plagae praescisse locum clipeosque rotare ludus et intortatas praecedere saltibus hastas in que hostem venisse prius; puerilibus annis est bellis maturus amor.*' Sidonius Apollinaris, *Carmina*, 5.237–50.

103. Edward James, *The Franks* (Oxford: Basil Blackwell, 1998), 57.

104. Doris Gutsmiedel-Schumann, 'Merovingian Men – Fulltime Warriors? Weapon Graves of the Continental Merovingian Period of the Munich Gravel Plain and the Social and Age Structure of the Contemporary Society – a Case Study', in *N-TAG TEN: Proceedings of the 10th Nordic TAG Conference at Stiklestad, Norway 2009* (Oxford: Archaeopress, 2012), 251–61.

105. Hans-Werner Goetz, '*Gens*, Kings, and Kingdoms: The Franks', in *Regna and Gentes: The Relationship Between Late Antique and Early Medieval Peoples and Kingdoms in the Transformation of the Roman World* (Leiden: Brill, 2003), 307–19.

106. Swift, *The End of the Western Roman Empire*, 113–17.

107. Roymans, 'Gold, Germanic Foederati and the End of Imperial Power', 60–65, 69.
108. Simpson, 'Laeti in the *Notitia Dignitatum*', 82–85.
109. Ralf Scharf, 'Ripari und Olibriones? Zwei Teilnehmer an der Schlacht auf den Katalaunischen Feldern', *MIÖG* 107 (1999), 111.
110. Léon Fleuriot, *Les Origines de la Bretagne* (Paris: Payot Publishing, 1980), 244; Christopher A. Snyder, *The Britons* (Hoboken: Wiley-Blackwell, 2003), 147.
111. Jordanes, *De Origine Actibusque Getarum*, 55.237.
112. Constantius of Lyon, *Vita Germani*, 12–18; Gildas, *De Excidio Conquestu Brittaniae*, 20–21.
113. Halsall, *Barbarian Migrations and the Roman West*, 238–39; Rob Collins, 'Brooch use in the 4th- to 5th-Century Frontier', 67.
114. Hughes, *Aetius: Attila's Nemesis*, 145; Ian Wood, 'The North-Western Provinces', in *The Cambridge Ancient History*, Vol.14 (Cambridge: Cambridge University Press, 2008), 507–09.
115. Constantius of Lyon, *Vita Germani*, 3.15–16.
116. Hughes, *Aetius: Attila's Nemesis*, 92.
117. Jordanes, *De Origine Actibusque Getarum*, 45.237.
118. Thomas Grane, *The Roman Empire and Southern Scandinavia – A Northern Connection!* (Ph.D. Diss., University of Copenhagen, 2007), 109.
119. D. Gerrets, 'The Anglo-Frisian Relationship Seen from an Archaeological Point of View', in *Friesische Studien II: Beiträge des Föhrer Symposiums zur Friesischen Philologie* (Odense: Odense University Press, 1995), 119–28.
120. *Notitia Dignitatum Pars Occidentis*, 154.20; using Ingo Maier's numbering scheme.
121. Michael Jarrett, 'Non-Legionary Troops in Roman Britain: Part One, the Units', *Britannia* 25 (1994), 60.
122. *Harold Williamson, 'The Probable Date of the Roman Occupation of Melandra', in Melandra Castle (Manchester: Manchester University Press, 1906), 122–23.*
123. Roymans, 'Gold, Germanic Foederati and the End of Imperial Power', 60–65.
124. Svante Fischer, Fernando Lopez Sanchez and Helena Victor, 'The 5th Century Hoard of Theodosian Solidi from Stora Brunneby, Oland, Sweden', *Fornvannen* 106 (2011), 189–204.
125. Ulf Nasman, 'Scandinavia and the Huns: A Source-Critical Approach to an Old Question', *Fornvannen* 103 (2008), 111–18.
126. Thomas Grane, 'Southern Scandinavian *Foederati* and *Auxiliarii*?', in *Beyond the Roman Frontier: Roman Influences on the Northern Barbaricum* (Rome: Quasar, 2008), 831–04.
127. Svante Fischer, Fernando Lopez Sanchez and Helena Victor, 'The 5th Century Hoard of Theodosian Solidi', 193.

128. Lotte Hedeager, 'Scandinavia and the Huns', *Norwegian Archaeological Review* 40 (2007), 42–58; Hedeager mostly discusses archaeological and mythological connections. See the aforementioned criticism by Nasman on the validity of his arguments.

129. Jordanes, *De Origine Actibusque Getarum*, 36.191; Sidonius, *Carmina*, 7.321–25.

130. Wolfram, *The Roman Empire and its Germanic Peoples*, 136; Maenchen-Helfen, *On the World of the Huns*, 82–84; Helfen believes the Trans-Rhenian Burgundians were separate from those of Gundicar.

131. Socrates, *Historia Ecclesiastica*, 7.30.

132. Hughes, *Aetius: Attila's Nemesis*, 97; Hydatius, *Continuatio Chronicorum*, 110.

133. *Chronica Gallica Anno 452*, s.a. 443.

134. *Lex Burgundionum*, 54.1.

135. Hydatius, *Continuatio Chronicorum*, 93; Sidonius Apollinaris, *Carmina*, 7.234.

136. Hughes, *Aetius: Attila's Nemesis*, 78

137. Hughes, *Aetius: Attila's Nemesis*, 137.

138. Drinkwater, *The Alamanni and Rome*, 327–29.

139. Drinkwater, *The Alamanni and Rome*, 330.

140. Gregory of Tours, *Decem Libri Historiarum*, 2.7; Banniard, 'L'aménagement de l'histoire chez Grégoire de Tours', 23–26; Walter Goffart, *Narrators of Barbarian History*, 14.

141. Dierkins and Perin, 'The 5th-century Advance of the Franks in Belgica II', 166.

142. *Liber Legum Novellarum Divi Theodosii Augustus*, 24.1.

143. *Liber Legum Novellarum Divi Theodosii Augustus*, 24.1; *Codex Iustinianarum* 11.60.3.

144. Eugippius, *Vita Severini*, 1.3031, 2.32–33, 4.36–37.

145. Drinkwater, *The Alamanni and Rome*, 327–28; Swift, *The End of the Western Roman Empire*, 113–17.

146. Elton, *Warfare in Roman Europe*, 99.

147. Drinkwater, *The Alamanni and Rome*, 328–29.

148. Hughes, *Aetius Attila's Nemesis*, 136; Drinkwater, *The Alamanni and Rome*, 329.

149. Jordanes, *De Origine Actibusque Getarum*, 36.191.

150. Hughes, *Aetius: Attila's Nemesis*, 155.

151. Barnish, 'Old Kaspars', 41.

152. *Liber Legum Novellarum Divi Valentiniani Augustus*, 9.1.

153. Liebeschuetz, 'The End of the Roman Army', 273.

154. Olymp. *Fragments*, 7.4; *Notitia Dignitatum in partibus Occidentis*, 7.34; *Codex Theodosianum*, 7.13.16

155. Williams and Friell, *The Rome that did not Fall*, 79; McEvoy and Meghan, 'Becoming Roman: The Not-So-Curious Case of Aspar and the Ardaburii',

Journal of Late Antiquity 9.2 (2016), 491–92; Avshalom Laniado, 'Aspar and his Phoideratoi: John Malalas on a Special Relationship', in *Governare e riformare l'impero al momento della sua divisione: Oriente, Occidente, Illirico* (Rome: Publications de l'École française de Rome, 2015), 2.

156. McEvoy, *Child Emperor Rule in the Late Roman West*, 245; Wijnendaele, 'Warlordism and the Disintegration of the Western Roman Army', 197–200.

157. Hydatius, *Continuatio Chronicorum*, 116.

158. Ian Hughes, *Aetius: Attila's Nemesis*, 190; McEvoy, *Child Emperor Rule in the Late Roman West AD 368–455*, 300; Given, *The Fragmentary History of Priscus*, 128 fr. 71; John of Antioch, 291.1

159. Claudius Claudianus, *De Bello Gildonico*, 1.415–23; Orosius, *Historiae Adversum Paganos*, 7.36.

160. Zosimus, *Nova Historiae*, 5.45.1, 3.3.4, 6.8.2.

161. Sozomenus, *Historia Ecclesiastica*, 9.8.

162. John Malalas, *Chronographia*, 3.22.2, 13.21; Ammianus, *Res Gestae*, 14.1.2.

163. Ammianus, *Res Gestae*, 18.2.2, 18.9.3, 19.2.4.

164. Coello, *Unit Sizes in the Late Roman Army*, 101–02.

165. *P. Columbia* 7.188; *P. Lond.* 5.1663.

166. C. Zuckerman, 'Legio V Macedonica in Egypt', *Tyche* 3 (1988), 279–87.

167. *P. Oxyrhynchus* 10.1261; Amin Bessiana, 'The Size of the Numerus Transtigritanorum in the Fifth Century', *ZPE* 175 (2010), 224–26.

168. Philip Rance, '*Noumera* or *Mounera*: a Parallel Philological Problem in *De Ceremoniis* and Maurice's *Strategikon*' *Jarbruch der Österreichischen Byzantinistik* 58 (2008), 121–29; for a comprehensive discussion of the terminology of *Numerus* in the sixth century. Its relation to the *Arithmos* is mentioned in footnote one.

169. Sozomen, 9.8; *P. Lond.* 5.1663. However, it is clear that '*Numerus*' was still a term used generically to mean regiment, as shown with the Perge fragments.

170. Claudian, *De Bello Gildonico*, 1.415–23; Orosius, *Historiae Adversum Paganos*, 7.39.

171. Zosimus, *Nova Historiae*, 3.3.4.

172. Fatih Onur, 'The Anastasian Military Decree from Perge in Pamphylia: Revised 2nd Edition', 197; Rance, 'Maurice's *Strategicon* and "the Ancients"', 23133; Dennis, *Maurice's Strategikon*, 140–42.

173. Ammianus, *Res Gestae*, 31.12.2; Zosimus, *Nova Historiae* 3.3.4.

174. Julian, *Letter to the Athenians* 7.24; Zosimus *Nova Historiae* 3.3.2.

175. Coello, 'Unit Sizes in the Late Roman Army', 19.

176. Synesius, *Constitutio*, 1576; Synesius, *Epistolae*, 78, 125. It should be noted that these are probably Hunnish *Foederati* enrolled at Synesius' own expense.

177. Arrian, *Taktika*, 18.

178. Luke Ueda-Sarson, 'Late Roman Shield Patterns Taken from the Notitia Dignitatum', LukeUedaSarson.com, last modified 3 January 2016, http:// lukeuedasarson.com/NotitiaPatterns.html; A.H.M. Jones, *The Later Roman Empire: 284–602*, Vol.2, Appendix II.

179. '*Contra publicam utilitatem nolumus a numeris ad alios numeros milites nos(t)ros transferri. Sciant igitur comites vel duces, quibus regendae militiae cura commissa est, non solum de comitatensibus ac palatinis numeris ad alios numeros militem transferri non licere, sed ne de ipsis quidem pseudocomitatensibus legionibus seu de ripariensibus castricianis ceterisque cuiquam eorum transferendi militem copiam adtributam, quia honoris augmentum non ambitione, sed labore ad unumquemque convenit devenire. Quod si qui contra fecerint, per singulos milites singulas auri libras a se noverint exigendas.*' *Codex Theodosianum* 7.1.18.

180. See Appendix B.

181. Zozimus, *Nova Historiae*, 5.26.4.

182. See Appendix B; this assumes legions numbered 960 men, *numeri* 640, cohorts 480, *milites* 960, *auxilia* 480, *equites* 512, *alae* 512, *cunei* 256, *comites* 512 and the unknown cavalry 512 men each, and unknown infantry 480, 640 or 960 men each depending on the circumstances in the text. This figure does not account for officers and other support personnel. However, this methodology is still highly flawed due to an incomplete understanding of the pre-*Strategikon* late Roman organization.

183. See Appendix B.

184. Halsall, *Barbarian Migrations and the Roman West*, 253. Halsall suggests the Armoricans had control of the former British forces and possibly some Gallic regiments.

185. *Liber Legum Novellarum Divi Valentiniani Augustus*, 15.1; Heather, *The Fall of the Roman Empire*, 298; Elton, *Warfare in Roman Europe*, 120–25.

186. Warren Treadgold, 'Paying the Army in the Theodosian Period', in *Production and Prosperity in the Theodosian Period* (Leuven: Peeters Publishing, 2014), 303–18.

187. *Liber Legum Novellarum Divi Valentiniani Augustus*, 6.3, 15; Hughes, *Aetius: Attila's Nemesis*, 111–13, 134–35; McEvoy, *Child Emperor Rule in the Late Roman West 368–455*, 264–65; Elton, *Warfare in Roman Europe*, 125.

188. *Liber Legum Novellarum Divi Valentiniani Augustus*, 9.1; Hydatius, *Continuatio Chronicorum*, 116, 134; *Vita Orientii*, 3; Gillett, 'The Saint as Envoy: Bishops' Lives', 139–40; Gillett remarks that the *vita Orientii* states the Roman army was largely spared, however.

189. Elton, 'Military Developments in the Fifth Century', 133–34.

190. Coello, 'Unit Sizes in the Late Roman Army', 17, 95.

191. From Drinkwater's alleged Romano-Alaman Garrisons, to Eugippius' *Foederati* in Comagenis, and then accounting for the destruction of several sites in Attila's invasion via Noricum Mediterranae in 452.

192. Wolfram, Herwig, *The Roman Empire and its Germanic Peoples*, trans. Thomas Dunlap (Berkeley: University of California Press, 1997), 104.

193. Given, *The Fragmentary History of Priscus* 169 fr. 80; Priscus does not specify if they are Romans or *Foederati*.

194. Hans Delbruck, *History of the Art of War, Volume II: The Barbarian Invasions* (Lincoln: University of Nebraska Press, 1980), 284–99.

195. Peter Heather, *The Goths* (Oxford: Blackwell Publishing, 1998), 176; That 8,000 of them were allegedly wounded or killed in 438 at *Mons Colubrarius* may be a reliable figure, and could support this estimate.

196. Rudi Paul Lindner, 'Nomadism, Horses and Huns', *Past and Present* 92 (1982) 319; see Chapter 3 for this volume's similar estimates of Hunnish capacity. The Alans of Gaul also had access to better fodder for their horses thanks to a combination of local topography, extensive agricultural development and Roman logistics.

197. Elton, *Warfare in Roman Europe*, 72.

198. Socrates, *Historia Ecclesiastica*, 7.30.

199. Hydatius, *Continuatio Chronicorum*, 110.

200. Halsall, *Barbarian Migrations and the Roman West*, 253; Jordanes, *De Origine Actibusque Getarum*, 65.237.

201. If they were using the *comes Britanniarum*'s army, then the Armoricans would have numbered about 5,312 men.

202. See Appendix B; 2,880 men, with the 70 per cent modifier applied, rounded off to 2,000.

203. Laniado, 'Aspar and his Phoideratoi', 2; Wijnendaele, *The Last of the Romans*, 10001; who, as stated, may or may not be '*olibrones*'.

Chapter 3

1.   Nic Fields, *Attila the Hun* (Oxford: Osprey Publishing, 2015), 1316; Man, *Attila*, 54–56.

2.   Florin Curta, 'The Earliest Avar-Age Stirrups, or the "Stirrup Controversy" Revisited', in *The Other Europe in the Middle Ages. Avars, Bulgars, Khazars and Cumans. East Central and Eastern Europe in the Middle Ages, 450–1450* 2 (2008), 302–10.

3.   M.C. Bishop and J.C.N. Coulston, *Roman Military Equipment: From the Punic Wars to the Fall of Rome*, 2nd ed. (Oxford: Oxbow Books, 2009), 88–89, 205–06; Michel Kazanski, 'Bowmen's Graves from the Hunnic Period in Northern Illyricum', in *'To Make a Fairy's Whistle from a Briar Rose': Studies Presented to Eszter Istvánovits on her Sixtieth Birthday* (Nyíregyháza: Jósa András Museum, 2018), 407–09.

4.   Man, *Attila*, 33; Heather, *The Fall of the Roman Empire*, 147.

5.   Charles King, 'The Veracity of Ammianus Marcellinus' Description of the Huns', *American Journal of Ancient History* 12 (1987), 77–95; Kim, *The Huns, Rome and the Birth of Europe*, 17–19; E.A. Thompson, *A History of Attila and the Huns* (Oxford: Clarendon Press, 1948), 41–43.

6.   Kim, *The Huns, Rome and the Birth of Europe*, 17–19.

7.   Thomas Barfield, 'The Hsiung-nu Imperial Confederacy: Organization and Foreign Policy', *Journal of Asian Studies* 41, no.1 (1981), 45–61; for an overview of Xiongnu organization.

8.   Nicola Di Cosmo, *Ancient China and its Enemies: The Rise of Nomadic Power in East Asian History* (Cambridge: Cambridge University Press, 2002), 169–74.

9.   Heather, 'The Huns and the End of the Roman Empire', 11; however, Heather's argument is partially misguided, as he states elsewhere that the Huns held a loose structure of confederacy similar to the migration era Germanics.

10.   Maenchen-Helfen, *On the World of the Huns*, 85–86.

11.   Atwood, 'Huns and Xiongnu', 33; Kim, *The Huns, Rome and the Birth of Europe*, 31, 59, 206.

12.   Farda Asadov, 'Ellak and Ilek: What does the Study of an Ancient Turkic Title in Eurasia Contribute to the Discussion of Khazar Ancestry?, *Acta Via Serica* 2 (2017), 113–32; Maenchen-Helfen, *On the World of the Huns*, 407; Mingarelli, *Collapse of the Hunnic Empire*, 41–43.

13.   Di Cosmo, *Ancient China and its Enemies*, 176–78. Kim, *The Huns, Rome and the Birth of Europe*, 23, 207–08.

14.   Jordanes, *De Origine Actibusque Getarum*, 5.37; Agathias, *Historiarum Libri*, 5.11.2; Kim, *The Huns, Rome and the Birth of Europe*, 58–59, 208; rendered *altziagiri* and Ούλτιζουροι. *Ulticur* may also be rendered as *Alticur*.

15.   Kim, *The Huns, Rome and the Birth of Europe*, 59; Halsall, *Warfare and Society in the Barbarian West*, 60.

16.   Given, *The Fragmentary History of Priscus*, fr. 1 and 45, 8–10; Maenchen-Helfen, *On the World of the Huns*, 438–40; Kim, *The Huns, Rome and the Birth of Europe*, 132.

17.   Maenchen-Helfen, *On the World of the Huns*, 439, 441; Peter Golden, *An Introduction to the History of the Turkic Peoples: Ethnogenesis and State Formation in Medieval and Early Modern Eurasia and the Middle East* (Wiesbaden: Otto Harrassowitz, 1992), 106–07.

18.   Kim, *The Huns, Rome and the Birth of Europe*, 60, 209.

19.   Maenchen-Helfen, *On the World of the Huns*, 439, 441; Golden, *An Introduction to the History of the Turkic Peoples*, 106–07; the Xailandur are mentioned by Armenian sources in the great raid of 395, however.

20.   Kim, *The Huns, Rome and the Birth of Europe*, 56–57.

21.   Jordanes, *De Origine Actibusque Getarum*, 53.272; Pritsak, 'The Hunnic Language of the Attila Clan', 436–37.

22. Peter Heather, *Empires and Barbarians* (Oxford: Oxford University Press, 2010), 134–41; Jordanes, *De Origine Actibusque Getarum*, 5.37.

23. Blockley, *The Fragmentary Classicizing Historians*, Vol.2, 245 fr. 11.1, 284 fr. 13; Altheim, *Geschichte Der Hunnen*, Vol.1, 27; Kim, *The Huns, Rome and the Birth of Europe*, 207–08.

24. Maenchen-Helfen, *On the World of the Huns*, 202; Dennis, *Maurice's Strategikon*, 116–17.

25. Kelly, *The End of the Roman Empire*, 37.

26. Golden, 'War and Warfare', 90.

27. Kim, *The Huns, Rome and the Birth of Europe*, 203–04; Carter Findley, *The Turks in World History* (Oxford: Oxford University Press, 2004), 38–39; Golden, 'War and Warfare', 101–102.

28. Golden, 'War and Warfare', 103.

29. Maenchen-Helfen, *On the World of the Huns*, 214–21; Fyfe, *Hunnic Warfare in the Fourth and Fifth Centuries*, 111.

30. Kelly, *The End of the Roman Empire*, 35–37; Man, *Attila*, 33.

31. Golden, 'War and Warfare', 93.

32. Golden, 'War and Warfare', 97.

33. Golden, 'War and Warfare', 92.

34. Heather, *The Fall of the Roman Empire*, 303.

35. Stephen McCotter, 'Byzantines, Avars and the Introduction of the Trebuchet', *De Rei Militari*, 9 June 2014, http://deremilitari.org/2014/06/byzantines-avars-and-the-introduction-of-the-trebuchet/.

36. Given, *The Fragmentary History of Priscus*, 14–15 fr. 1B; David Nicolle, *Attila and the Nomad Hordes* (Oxford: Osprey Publishing, 1990), 18; Golden, 'War and Warfare', 99–100.

37. Fyfe, *Hunnic Warfare in the Fourth and Fifth Centuries*, 125–33.

38. Thompson, *A History of Attila and the Huns*, 41–43; bone arrowheads are good for hunting and birding, though.

39. Nic Fields, *The Hun: Scourge of God AD 375–565* (Oxford: Osprey Publishing, 2006), 28–29; Sumner, *Roman Military Dress*, 90–92; D'Amato, *Roman Military Clothing*, 8, 12–14, 23, 46; the Romans tended to wear two tunics, a *Kamision* and a *Tunica Manicata*, even in hotter climes. Short-sleeved outer tunics may have been a Hunnish style, but this is based on very limited evidence.

40. Fields, *The Hun: Scourge of God AD 375–565*, 28–29; Sumner, *Roman Military Dress*, 90–92; D'Amato, *Roman Military Clothing*, 18–19; Kazanski and Akhmedov, 'La Tombe de Mundolsheim', 249–61.

41. Kazanski, 'Bowmen's Graves from the Hunnic Period in Northern Illyricum', 407–09; Michaela Reisinger, 'New Evidence about Composite Bows and Their Arrows in Inner Asia', *The Silk Road* 8 (2010), 42–62; Andrew Hall and Jack Farrel, 'Bows and Arrows from Miran, China', *The Journal of the Society of Archer-Antiquaries* 51 (2008), 89–98; Xenia Pauli Jensen, Lars

Jørgensen and Ulla Lund Hansen, 'The Germanic Army: Warriors, Soldiers and Officers', in *The Spoils of Victory: The North in the Shadow of the Roman Empire* (Copenhagen: Denmark National Museum, 2003), 319–22; Dennis, *Maurice's Strategikon*, 12.

42.   Dennis, *Maurice's Strategikon*, 12, 30; Vegetius, *Epitoma Rei Militaris*, 3.5.

43.   Kiss Attila, 'Huns, Romans, Byzantines? The Origins of the Narrow-Bladed Long Seaxes', *Acta Archaeological Carpathica* 59 (2014), 131–64; Christian Miks, *Studien zur römischen Schwertbewaffnung in der Kaiserzeit*, Vol.1 (Rahden: Verlag Marie Leidorf, 2007), 106, 133–34; for info on Seaxes and Asiatic-type blades.

44.   Christian Miks, 'Relikte Eines Frühmittelalterlichen Oberschichtgrabes? Überlegungen zu einem Konvolut bemerkenswerter Objekte aus dem Kunsthandel', *Jahrbuch des Römisch-Germanischen Zentralmuseums Mainz* 56 (2009), 395–538; Damien Glad, 'The Empire's Influence on Barbarian Elites From the Pontus to the Rhine (5th-7th Centuries): A Case Study of Lamellar Weapons and Segmental Helmet', in *The Pontic Danubian Realm in Late Antiquity* (Paris: ACHCByz, 2012), 356.

45.   Quintus Curtius Rufus, *Historiarum Alexandri Magni Macedonis*, 9.4.3; Arrian, *Extaktis Kata Alanon*, 3.13.4.

46.   Golden, 'War and Warfare', 110–11; Dennis, *Maurice's Strategikon*, 13–14.

47.   Lindner, *Nomadism, Horses and Huns*, 14; Dennis, *Maurice's Strategikon*, 13–14.

48.   Golden, 'War and Warfare', 90–91.

49.   Sulimirski, *The Sarmatians*, 105–06; Sulimirski remarks Hunnish gold diadems were a millenia-old practice often found in female burials on pp.194–96, however these diadems were also used by men. Bona does not mention any female weapons burials in his 1991 or 2002 studies.

50.   Procopius, *The Wars of Justinian*, 8.3.5–11; Zonaras, Plutarch, Appian and the *Historia Augusta* all mention it as well. Procopius discusses the land of the Sabir Huns (Xianbei), and claims it was the ancestral land of the Amazons. See Kaldellis, 467, footnotes.

51.   Golden, 'War and Warfare', 91.

52.   Blockley, *The Fragmentary Classicizing Historians*, Vol.2, 262–63 fr. 11.2; rendered as βασίλιδα, translating loosely to 'queen'.

53.   Given, *The Fragmentary History of Priscus*, 62–63 fr. 8.

54.   Dennis, *Maurice's Strategikon*, 65, 74, 104, 165–69; for passages on military tactics and their similarity to hunting, the latter pages specifically on how to hunt and how it compares to the Scythian drill.

55.   Vegetius, *Epitoma Rei Militaris*, 1.20; Dennis, *Maurice's Strategikon*, 38, 61–62, 116; the *Strategikon* itself states the couched lancing technique was adopted from the 'fair haired peoples', i.e. the Alans.

56.   Dennis, *Maurice's Strategikon*, 15, 62, 116.

57. Fyfe, *Hunnic Warfare in the Fourth and Fifth Centuries*, 105–06; Dennis, *Maurice's Strategikon*, 116–18; Pseudo-Maurikios classifies them with the Avars and Turks. Fyfe compares them to the Parthians.

58. Dennis, *Maurice's Strategikon*, 116.

59. Golden, 'War and Warfare', 100–01.

60. Reisinger, 'New Evidence about Composite Bows and Their Arrows in Inner Asia', 52–58.

61. Jensen, Jorgensen and Hansen, 'The Germanic Army', 319–22.

62. Man, *Attila*, 79–104.

63. Elton, *Warfare in Roman Europe*, 58–59.

64. Elton, *Warfare in Roman Europe*, 106–07.

65. Clover, 'Flavius Merobaudes', 13, Panegyric I, fr. 2B.

66. Hughes, *Aetius: Attila's Nemesis*, 96.

67. Dennis, *Maurice's Strategikon*, 52–53, 116; Agathias, *Historiarum Libri*, 4.27.4.

68. Golden, 'War and Warfare', 97.

69. Dennis, *Maurice's Strategikon*, 117.

70. Dennis, *Maurice's Strategikon*, 23.

71. Golden, 'War and Warfare', 96.

72. Ammianus Marcellinus, *Res Gestae*, 31.2.8.

73. Dennis, *Maurice's Strategikon*, 52–53, 117.

74. Dennis, *Maurice's Strategikon*, 61–62; Golden, 'War and Warfare', 95–96.

75. Dennis, *Maurice's Strategikon*, 117.

76. Agathias, *Historiarum Libri*, 3.17.5; Agathias records some Sabir Xianbei serving as heavy infantry.

77. Given, *The Fragmentary History of Priscus*, 14–15 fr. 1B.

78. Procopius, *The Wars of Justinian*, 8.11.27–31.

79. Given, *The Fragmentary History of Priscus*, 14–15 fr. 1B.

80. Gregory of Tours, *Decem Libri Historiarum*, 2.7.

81. Given, *The Fragmentary History of Priscus*, 14–15 fr. 1B.

82. Procopius, *The Wars of Justinian*, 5.21.12.

83. Procopius, *The Wars of Justinian*, 8.11.32–38.

84. Procopius, *The Wars of Justinian*, 8.14.4–5, 11.

85. Duncan B. Campbell, *Greek and Roman Siege Machinery 399 BC – AD 363* (Oxford: Osprey Publishing, 2003), 40.

86. Procopius, *The Wars of Justinian*, 5.21.3–4.

87. Sidonius Apollinaris, *Carmina*, 7.321–25; Jordanes, *De Origine Actibusque Getarum*, 37.190.

88. Sidonius Apollinaris, *Carmina*, 7.321–25; Herodotus, *Historiae*, 4.102.

89. '*Pugnacem Rugum comitante Gelono Gepida trux sequitur; Scirum Burgundio cogit; Chunus, Bellonotus, Neurus, Bastarna, Thoringus, Bructerus, ulvosa vel quem Nicer alluit unda prorumpit Francus.*' Sidonius Apollinaris, *Carmina*,

7.321–25; however, it could also be *Chunus bello notus*, or 'the Hun noted for war', although this would be conflictory with its usage in *Carmen*, 5.476.

90. Thompson, *A History of Attila and the Huns*, 136; Thompson includes the *Bructeri* too, who went on to help form the Franks. They may not be entirely fictional but are still a part of the literary tradition.

91. Mathisen, 'Catalogues of Barbarians', 23.

92. Jordanes, *De Origine Actibusque Getarum*, 37.190.

93. Goffart, *Barbarian Tides*, 197–99.

94. Sidonius Apollinaris, *Carmina*, 7.321; Jordanes, *De Origne Actibusque Getarum*, 37.190; Given, *The Fragmentary History of Priscus*, 101 fr. 64; *Chronicon Paschale*, 587.

95. Michel Kazanski, 'The Sedentary Elite in the Empire of the Huns and its Impact on the Material Civilization in Southern Russia During the Early Middle Ages', in *Cultural Transformations and Interactions in Eastern Europe* (Brookfield: Ashgate Publishing, 1993), 211–35; Anna Kharalambieva, 'Gepids in the Balkans: A Survey of the Archaeological Evidence', in *Neglected Barbarians* (Turnhout: Brepols Publishers, 2010), 245–62.

96. Kharalambieva, 'Gepids in the Balkans', 247–48.

97. Goffart, *Barbarian Tides*, 199–200.

98. Goffart, *Barbarian Tides*, 200–01; Christiensen, *Cassiodorus, Jordanes and the History of the Goths*, 335–37.

99. Kim, *The Huns, Rome and the Birth of Europe*, 9296; Harke, review of *The Huns, Rome and the Birth of Europe*, 260–62.

100. Jordanes, *De Origine Actibusque Getarum*, 38.199.

101. Theophanes, 6,032.

102. Kharalambieva, 'Gepids in the Balkans', 248–49; Kazanski, 'Bowmen's Graves from the Hunnic Period in Northern Illyricum', 408.

103. Mingarelli, *Collapse of the Hunnic Empire*, 39–40.

104. Heather, *The Goths*, 111–12.

105. Jordanes, *De Origine Actibusque Getarum*, 50.265–66; Christiansen, *Cassiodorus, Jordanes and the History of the Goths*, 85–93; Christiansen points out many problems with identifying Jordanes' ancestry and ethnicity.

106. Kim, *The Huns, Rome and the Birth of Europe*, 105–12, 118–20; Harke, review of *The Huns, Rome and the Birth of Europe*, 260–62.

107. Michel Kazanski, 'The Ostrogoths and the Princely Civilization of the Fifth Century', in *The Ostrogoths from the Migration Period to the Sixth Century: An Ethnographic Perspective* (San Marino: The Boydell Press, 2007), 90.

108. Heather, *The Goths*, 113.

109. Heather, *The Goths*, 114–15; Christiansen, *Cassiodorus, Jordanes and the History of the Goths*, 145–55.

110. Goffart, *Barbarian Tides*, 200–01; Christiensen, *Cassiodorus, Jordanes and the History of the Goths*, 335–37.

111. Heather, *The Goths*, 116.
112. Jordanes, *De Origine Actibusque Getarum*, 50.263.
113. Jordanes, *De Origine Actibusque Getarum*, 53.272; for their 'capital'.
114. Kazanski, 'The Ostrogoths and the Princely Civilization of the Fifth Century', 85–86, 89–90; his equation with Vintharius' kingdom is at best conjectural.
115. Wolfram, *The Roman Empire and its Germanic Peoples*, 183–84; Kim, *The Huns, Rome and the Birth of Europe*, 96–100; the argument of his identification is old and extensive, and Kim covers it rather thoroughly. In this case Kim's suggestion that Edica, Edekon, Edeko, etc. are probably the same figure is likely correct, despite his habit of looking for Huns in all the wrong places.
116. Maenchen-Helfen, *On the World of the Huns*, 63–66; for Scirian actions under Uldin.
117. Wolfram, *The Roman Empire and its Germanic Peoples*, 183.
118. Jordanes, *De Origine Actibusque Getarum*, 50.265, 53.272.
119. Kim, *The Huns, Rome and the Birth of Europe*, 117–18.
120. Jordanes, *De Origine Actibusque Getarum*, 46.242, 50.261.
121. Kim, *The Huns, Rome and the Birth of Europe*, 117–18.
122. Wolfram, *The Roman Empire and its Germanic Peoples*, 184.
123. Roland Steinacher, 'The Herules: Fragments of a History', in *Neglected Barbarians* (Turnhout: Brepols Publishers, 2010), 328–29.
124. Halsall, *Barbarian Migrations and the Roman West* 260, 265.
125. Hydatius, *Continuatio Chronicorum*, 171, 194.
126. Steinacher, *The Herules*, 340; Goffart, *Barbarian Tides*, 207.
127. Jordanes, *De Origine Actibusque Getarum*, 50.261; Procopiuis, *The Wars of Justinian*, 1.13.19.
128. Elton, *Warfare in Roman Europe*, 58–59.
129. Procopius, *The Wars of Justinian*, 2.25.27–28; Hydatius, *Continuatio Chronicorum*, 171.
130. Steinacher, *The Herules*, 359–60.
131. Wolfram, *The Roman Empire and its Germanic Peoples*, 187.
132. Goffart, *Barbarian Tides*, 113.
133. Peter Heather, 'Disappearing and Reappearing Tribes', in *Strategies of Distinction: The Construction of Ethnic Communities, 300–800* (Leiden: Brill, 1998), 102–03.
134. Eugippius, *Vita Severini*, 5.
135. Blockley, *The Fragmentary Classicizing Historians*, Vol.2, 228–29 fr. 4, 380.
136. Colin D. Gordon, *The Age of Attila: Fifth Century Byzantium and the Barbarians* (Ann Arbor: University of Michigan Press, 1960), 61–62.
137. Jordanes, *De Origine Actibusque Getarum*, 50.266.
138. Halsall, *Barbarian Migrations and the Roman West*, 392–93.

139. Goffart, *Barbarian Tides*, 216.
140. Jaroslav Jirik, 'Bohemian Barbarians', in *Neglected Barbarians* (Turnhout: Brepols Publishers, 2010), 263–317; for a comprehensive overview of fifth century Bohemia, its artefacts and its trade relationships.
141. Paul the Deacon, *Historia Langobardorum*, 1.16.
142. Goffart, *Barbarian Tides*, 216.
143. Jordanes, *De Origine Actibusque Getarum*, 35.182; Thompson, *A History of Attila and the Huns*, 142.
144. Given, *The Fragmentary History of Priscus*, 101 fr. 64; *Chronicon Paschale*, 587.
145. Dennis, *Maurice's Strategikon*, 102–03, 116.
146. Lindner, *Nomadism, Horses and Huns*, 3–19.
147. Dennis, *Maurice's Strategikon*, 65.
148. Lindner, *Nomadism, Horses and Huns*, 15.
149. Agathias, *Historiarum Libri*, 5.12.5; Procopius, *The Wars of Justinian*, 8.18.15.
150. Jordanes, *De Origine Actibusque Getarum*, 5.3637; Procopius, *The Wars of Justinian*, 8.5.23.
151. Socrates, *Historia Ecclesiastica*, 7.30
152. Hans Delbruck, *History of the Art of War, Volume II: The Barbarian Invasions*, 284–99.
153. Heather, *The Goths*, 151.
154. Malchus, fr. 18.4.
155. Socrates, *Historia Ecclesiatica*, 7.30.
156. Procopiuis, *The Wars of Justinian*, 7.34.42–43; Peter Heather, 'The Huns and Barbarian Europe', in *The Cambridge Companion to the Age of Attila* (Cambridge: Cambridge University Press, 2015), 225–26; Goffart, *Narrators of Barbarian History*, 84; Goffart criticizes Procopius' account.
157. Heather, *The Goths*, 173–74; Heather suggests that the contingents were not very large.
158. This includes any Sarmatians and Alans as well, although they do not appear to have been present in significant numbers.
159. Golden, 'War and Warfare', 89.
160. Golden, 'War and Warfare', 94.
161. 44,100 Germanics and Allies and 27,000 Hunnic and Iranic nomads.
162. Malchus, fr. 20.
163. Fyfe, *Hunnic Warfare in the Fourth and Fifth Centuries*, 125–33.

Chapter 4

1. Hydatius, *Continuatio Chronicorum*, 150.
2. Richard Burgess, *The Chronicle of Hydatius and the Consularia Constantino-politana* (Oxford: Clarendon Press, 1993), 5.

3.   Gregory of Tours, *Decem Libri Historiarum*, 2.6.
4.   Dennis, *Maurice's Strategikon*, 65.
5.   Barnish, 'Old Kaspars', 39.
6.   Sidonius Apollinaris, *Carmina*, 7.325–26.
7.   Given, *The Fragmentary History of Priscus*, 14–15 fr. 1B; Milner, *Vegetius*, 3.7.
8.   Caesar, *De Bello Gallico*, 4.16–18.
9.   Herodotus, *Historiae*, 7.35.
10.   Hughes, *Aetius: Attila's Nemesis*, 157.
11.   Stephen Johnson, *Late Roman Fortifications* (London: Batsford Publishing, 1983), 136–43.
12.   Drinkwater, *The Alamanni and Rome*, 328–29.
13.   Maenchen-Helfen, *On the World of the Huns*, 131; Johan Aldfelt, 'Digital Atlas of the Roman Empire', *Lund University Department of Archaeology and Ancient History*, last modified 22 May 2016, http://dare.ht.lu.se/.
14.   Man, *Attila*, 214.
15.   Kazanski and Akhmedov, 'La Tombe de Mundolsheim', 249–61.
16.   It is also possible this burial may be related to Aetius' campaign against the Burgundians in 436/37.
17.   Johan Aldfelt, 'Digital Atlas of the Roman Empire', *Lund University Department of Archaeology and Ancient History*, last modified 22 May 2016, http://dare.ht.lu.se/.
18.   Hodgkin, *Italy and Her Invaders*, 114–18.
19.   Man, *Attila*, 215; Hughes, *Aetius: Attila's Nemesis*, 157–59.
20.   Maenchen-Helfen, *On the World of the Huns*, 131.
21.   Kim, *The Huns, Rome and the Birth of Europe*, 80–83; Sidonius Apollinaris, *Carmina*, 7.321–25; Goffart, *Barbarian Tides*, 205.
22.   Gregory of Tours, *Decem Libri Historiarum*, 2.5; he calls Servatius 'Aravatius'.
23.   Hughes, *Aetius: Attila's Nemesis*, 157–59.
24.   Goffart, *Barbarian Tides*, 205.
25.   Hildinger, *Warriors of the Steppe*, 127–29; Given, *The Fragmentary History of Priscus*, 49 fr. 8.
26.   Man, *Attila*, 215–16.
27.   Johnson, *Late Roman Fortifications*, 143.
28.   Elton, *Warfare in Roman Europe*, 168; Johnson, *Late Roman Fortifications*, 143–44.
29.   '*Igitur Chuni a Pannoniis egressi, ut quidam ferunt, in ipsa sanctae paschae vigilia ad Mettinsem urbem reliqua depopulando perveniunt, tradentes urbem incendium populum in ore gladii trucidantes ipsusque sacerdotes Domini ante sacrosancta altaria perimentes. Nec remansit in ea locus inustus praeter oraturium beati Stefani primi martyres ac levitae.*' Gregory of Tours, *Decem Libri Historiarum*, 2.6.
30.   Gregory of Tours, *Decem Libri Historiarum*, 2.6.
31.   Maenchen-Helfen, *On the World of the Huns*, 131.

32. Hodgkin, *Italy and Her Invaders*, 116.

33. Johan Aldfelt, 'Digital Atlas of the Roman Empire', *Lund University Department of Archaeology and Ancient History*, last modified 22 May 2016, http://dare.ht.lu.se/.

34. Hodgkin, *Italy and Her Invaders*, 117; *Vita Genovesae*, 12.

35. *Chronica Gallica Anno 452*, s.a. 442.

36. Jordanes, *De Origine Actibuusque Getarum*, 37.194–96; *Vita Aniani*, 7; Gregory of Tours, *Decem Libri Historiarum*, 2.7.

37. Barnish, 'Old Kaspars', 38; Sidonius Apollinaris, *Epistulae*, 8.15.

38. Jordanes, *De Origine Actibusque Getarum*, 37.195.

39. *Vita Aniani*, 7.

40. Gregory of Tours, *Decem Libri Historiarum*, 2.7.

41. Elizabeth Baughman, 'The Scythian Archers: Policing Athens', in *Demos: Classical Athenian Democracy* (2003), 2–3.

42. Johnson, *Late Roman Fortifications*, 100–01, fig.33; Adrien Blanchet, *Les enceintes romaines de la Gaule* (Paris: Payot Publishing, 1907), 73–74.

43. Elton, *Warfare in Roman Europe*, 168.

44. Tadeusz Sulimirski, *The Sarmatians* (London: Thames & Hudson, 1970), 188.

45. Elton, *Warfare in Roman Europe*, 169; Johnson, *Late Roman Fortifications*, 38.

46. Elton, *Warfare in Roman Europe*, 170.

47. Johnson, *Late Roman Fortifications*, 31, 37; Vitruvius, *De Architectura*, 1.5.5.

48. Duncan Campbell, *Greek and Roman Artillery 399 BC – AD 363* (Oxford: Osprey Publishing, 2003), 3943; Richardot, *La Fin de l'Armee Romaine*, 258–61, 269; Vegetius, *Epitoma Rei Militaris*, 4.22, 29.

49. *Vita Aniani*, 7; Sidonius Apollinaris, *Epistulae*, 8.15.

50. Elton, *Warfare in Roman Europe*, 170–71.

51. Given, *The Fragmentary History of Priscus*, 14–15 fr. 1B; Gregory of Tours, *Decem Libri Historiarum*, 2.7.

52. *Vita Aniani*, 7; Gregory of Tours, *Decem Libri Historiarum*, 2.7.

53. Harries, *Sidonius Apollinaris and the Fall of Rome*, 228.

54. *Vita Aniani*, 7.

55. Barnish, 'Old Kaspars', 39; Hughes, *Aetius: Attila's Nemesis*, 100.

56. Hughes, *Aetius: Attila's Nemesis*, 154–55; Gracanin, *The Western Roman Embassy to the Court of Attila*, 7072; Given, *The Fragmentary History of Priscus*, 58–59, 68–70 fr. 8; Gregory of Tours, *Decem Libri Historiarum*, 2.5.

57. Maenchen-Helfen, *On the World of the Huns*, 130–31; Hughes, *Aetius: Attila's Nemesis*, 159; Leo, *Epistulae*, 41.

58. Leo, *Epistulae*, 41.

59. Jordanes, *De Origine Actibusque Getarum*, 36.191.

60. Sidonius Apollinaris, *Epistulae*, 7.12.3.

61. Elton, *Military Developments in the Fifth Century*, 130; Joshua the Stylite, *Chronicle*, 54; Marcellinus Comes, s.a. 499.

62. Elton, *Warfare in Roman Europe*, 76–77.
63. Jordanes, *De Origine Actibusque Getarum*, 37.194; Herodotus, *Historiae*, 7.32.
64. Sidonius Apollinaris, *Carmina*, 7.332–53.
65. Harries, *Sidonius Apollinaris and the Fall of Rome*, 6870; Gillett, 'The Hero as Envoy', 102–103.
66. Prosper, *Epitoma Chronicon*, s.a. 451; Barnish, 'Old Kaspars', 42.
67. Sidonius Apollinaris, *Carmina*, 7.333.
68. McEvoy, *Child Emperor Rule in the Late Roman West*, 294–95.
69. Sidonius Apollinaris, *Carmina*, 7.329–31.
70. Hughes, *Aetius: Attila's Nemesis*, 206.
71. Prosper, *Epitoma Chronicon*, s.a. 439; Hydatius, *Continuatio Chronicorum*, 116, 134.
72. Clover, 'Flavius Merobaudes', 13, Panegyric I, fr. 2B; Sidonius Apollinaris, *Carmina*, 5.21254.
73. Drinkwater, *The Alamanni and Rome*, 327–29.
74. MacDowall, *Catalaunian Fields AD 451*, 52–54.

Chapter 5

1.   '*campos Catalaunicos, qui et Mauriaci nominantur, centum leuvas, ut Galli vocant, in longum tenentes et septuaginta in latum.*' Jordanes, *De Origine Actibusque Getarum*, 37.192; Hughes, *Aetius: Attila's Nemesis*, 163; Bury, *History of the Later Roman Empire*, 293.
2.   Prosper, *Epitoma Chronicon*, s.a. 451; *Additamenta Altera ad Prosperi Chronicon Hauniensis*, s.a. 451; *Chronica Gallica Anno 511*, s.a. 451.
3.   Hydatius, *Continuatio Chronicorum*, 150.
4.   Gregory of Tours, *Decem Libri Historiarum*, 2.7; *Lex Burgundionum*, 17.1.
5.   Given, *The Fragmentary History of Priscus*, 101–02 fr. 64–65; *Chronicon Paschale*, 587; Theophanes, 5,943.
6.   Jordanes, *De Origine Actibusque Getarum*, 38.197, 40.208.
7.   Hodgkin, *Italy and Her Invaders*, 124; Maenchen-Helfen, *On the World of the Huns*, 131; Phillipe Richardot, *La Fin de l'armee Romaine*, 361–62.
8.   Man, *Attila*, 227.
9.   Fyfe, *Hunnic Warfare in the Fourth and Fifth Centuries*, 73–77; Miks, *Studien zur römischen Schwertbewaffnung in der Kaiserzeit*, Vol.2, 708–09, Tafel, 142, 284; Jordanes, *De Origine Actibusque Getarum*, 41.214–15.
10. Miks, *Studien zur zur römischen Schwertbewaffnung in der Kaiserzeit*, Vol.2, 191–95; Wilfried Menghin, 'Schwerter des Goldgriffespathenhorizonts im Museum für Vor-und Frügeschichte, Berlin', *Acta Praehistorica et Archaeologica* 26 (1995), 140–91; on the typology and datation of the 'Goldgriffe' Spathae.

11. Henri d'Arbois de Jubainville, 'Recherches philologiques sur l'anneau sigillaire de Pouan', in *Revue de Questions Historiques* 6 (1869).

12. Miks, *Studien zur zur römischen Schwertbewaffnung in der Kaiserzeit*, Vol.1, 99–100, 103, Vol.2, 719, Tafel 130; on the Illerup-Whyl type blades in general, and Sarry itself. The battle occurs at the end of the D2 period.

13. Miklos Erdy, 'Hun and Xiong-nu Type Cauldron Finds throughout Eurasia', in *Eurasian Studies Yearbook* 67 (1995), 17–18.

14. Johan Aldfelt, 'Digital Atlas of the Roman Empire', *Lund University Department of Archaeology and Ancient History*, last modified 22 May 2016, http://dare.ht.lu.se/.

15. Hughes, *Aetius: Attila's Nemesis*, 164; MacDowall, *Catalaunian Fields AD 451*, 56–57.

16. Johan Aldfelt, 'Digital Atlas of the Roman Empire', *Lund University Department of Archaeology and Ancient History*, last modified 22 May 2016, http://dare.ht.lu.se/.

17. M. Girard, 'Le Campus Mauriacus, Nouvelle Etude sur le Champ de Bataille d'Attila', *Revue Historique* 28, no.2 (1885).

18. Lebedensky, *La campagne d'Attila en Gaule*, 59–62.

19. *'Pugnatum est in quinto milliario de Tecis loco nuncupante Maurica in Campania.'* *Additamenta ad Chronicon Prosperi Hauniensis*, s.a. 451.

20. Macdowall, *Catalaunian Fields AD 451*, 56.

21. *Chronica Gallica Anno 511*, s.a. 451; *Lex Burgundionum* 17.1; Jordanes, *De Origine Actibusque Getarum*, 37.192; Gregory of Tours, *Decem Libri Historiarum*, 2.7.

22. *Vita Aniani*, 7; Bury, *History of the Later Roman Empire*, 293; Hodgkin, *Italy and Her Invaders*, 124; Fynes Clinton, *Fasti Romani, the Civil and Literary Chronology of Rome and Constantinople from the Death of Augustus to the Death of Justin II*, Vol.2 (Oxford: Oxford University Press, 1853), 642.

23. Hydatius, *Continuatio Chronicorum*, 150–52; Hodgkin, *Italy and Her Invaders*, 124.

24. Macdowall, *Catalaunian Fields AD 451*, 51; Elton, 'Military Developments in the Fifth Century', 138; Malchus, fr. 20; according to Malchus, an invading army of Goths in 499 had a baggage train of over 2,000 wagons. Attila's may have been almost three times larger.

25. Macdowall, *Catalaunian Fields AD 451*, 50–53.

26. Dennis, *Maurice's Strategikon*, 116–18.

27. Macdowall, *Catalaunian Fields AD 451*, 53; Vegetius, *Epitoma Rei Militaris*, 3.7.

28. Man, *Attila*, 234–35; Hydatius, *Continuatio Chronicorum*, 151.

29. Man, *Attila*, 234–35.

30. Macdowall, *Catalaunian Fields AD 451*, 52–54.

31. Dennis, *Maurice's Strategikon*, 59–60.

32.   Macdowall, *Catalaunian Fields AD 451*, 54.
33.   Barnish, 'Old Kaspars', 44.
34.   Clover, 'Flavius Merobaudes', 12, Pangeyric II, fr. 1B.
35.   Jordanes, *De Origine Actibusque Getarum*, 41.217.
36.   MacDowall, *Catalaunian Fields AD 451*, 52–53.
37.   Dennis, *Maurice's Strategikon*, 67; Vegetius, *Epitoma Rei Militaris*, 3.9.
38.   Hughes, *Aetius: Attila's Nemesis*, 120–21, 141–43; Kim, *The Huns, Rome and the Birth of Europe*, 70–71; Williams and Friell, *The Rome that did not Fall*, 79–80.
39.   A marching column of over 60,000 men would have stretched for miles.
40.   Macdowall, *Catalaunian Fields AD 451*, 53, 57–58.
41.   Dennis, *Maurice's Strategikon*, 67.
42.   Macdowall, *Catalaunian Fields AD 451*, 58–59.
43.   Macdowall, *Catalaunian Fields AD 451*, 58.
44.   Dennis, *Maurice's Strategikon*, 118.
45.   Dennis, *Maurice's Strategikon*, 70.
46.   Rance, 'Maurice's *Strategicon* and "the Ancients"', 223–51; Rance, 'Drungus, Δρούγγος and Δρουγγιστί', 106–08.
47.   MacDowall, *Catalaunian Fields AD 451*, 58.
48.   Jordanes, *De Origine Actibusque Getarum*, 37.196; MacDowall, *Catalaunian Fields AD 451*, 61. Hughes, *Aetius: Attila's Nemesis*, 165.
49.   Dennis, *Maurice's Strategikon*, 150.
50.   Leonhard Schmitz, 'Hora' in *A Dictionary of Greek and Roman Antiquities* (London: John Murray Press, 1875), 614.
51.   Vegetius, *Epitoma Rei Militaris*, 3.14.
52.   Kim, *The Huns, Rome and the Birth of Europe*, 75.
53.   Jordanes, *De Origine Actibusque Getarum*, 38.197.
54.   Hughes, *Aetius: Attila's Nemesis*, 168.
55.   Kim, 'Herodotean Allusions in Late Antiquity', 134–35.
56.   Dennis, *Maurice's Strategikon*, 23.
57.   Dennis, *Maurice's Strategikon*, 118; Constantius of Lyon, *Vita Germani*, 28; Jordanes, *De Origine Actibusque Getarum*, 50.261; Hughes, *Aetius: Attila's Nemesis*, 166.
58.   Dennis, *Maurice's Strategikon*, 144.
59.   Claudian, *De Bello Gothico*, 26.633–37; Jordanes, *De Origine Actibusque Getarum*, 38.197. Jordanes states the Alans were 'surrounded' (*concluderent*) which, disregarding his anti-Alan bias, would support this.
60.   Dennis, *Maurice's Strategikon*, 117.
61.   Dennis, *Maurice's Strategikon*, 41, 119; Halsall, *Warfare and Society in the Barbarian West*, 60; the *Strategikon* calls a regiment of *phoideratoi* a '*pagos*', latin *pagus*. Alternatively, *manus* could be used.
62.   Dennis, *Maurice's Strategikon*, 28.

63. Dennis, *Maurice's Strategikon*, 119; Ammianus Marcellinus, *Res Gestae*, 16.12.20; Philip Rance, 'The Fulcum, the Late Roman and Byzantine Testudo: The Germanization of Roman Infantry Tactics?', *Greek, Roman and Byzantine Studies* 44 (2004), 292.

64. Dennis, *Maurice's Strategikon*, 141–42, 145–46; this may also explain why fifth-century sources so often refer to three commanders over a large army, such as at the Utus.

65. Dennis, *Maurice's Strategikon*, 143–44.

66. Dennis, *Maurice's Strategikon*, 118.

67. Ian Hughes, *Belisarius: The Last Roman General* (Barnsley: Pen & Sword Military, 2009), 53–63.

68. Dennis, *Maurice's Strategikon*, 65, 117, 150.

69. '*Convenere partes, ut diximus, in campos catalaunicos. Erat autem position loci declivi tumore in editum collis excrescens. Quem uterque cupiens exercitus obtinere, quia loci opportunitas non parvum benificium confert, dextram partem hunni cum suis, sinistram romani et vesegothae cum auxiliariis occuparunt, relictoque de cacumine eius iugo certamen ineunt.*' Jordanes, *De Origine Actibusque Getarum*, 38.197.

70. MacDowall, *Catalaunian Fields AD 451*, 64.

71. Ferrill, *The Fall of the Roman Empire: The Military Explanation*, 148; MacDowall, *Catalaunian Fields AD 451*, 64.

72. Hughes, *Aetius: Attila's Nemesis*, 164.

73. Jordanes, *De Origine Actibusque Getarum*, 38.197–99; Hughes, *Aetius: Attila's Nemesis*, 167–68.

74. MacDowall, *Catalaunian Fields AD 451*, 57.

75. Dennis, *Maurice's Strategikon*, 30, 38.

76. Dennis, *Maurice's Strategikon*, 145–47.

77. Dennis, *Maurice's Strategikon*, 71, 150.

78. Dennis, *Maurice's Strategikon*, 33–34, 145–47; Elton, *Warfare in Roman Europe*, 81, 144, 253; Golden, 'War and Warfare', 96.

79. Jordanes, *De Origine Actibusque Getarum*, 39.202–06.

80. Tackholm, 'Aetius and the Battle on the Catalaunian Fields', 267; Hughes, *Aetius: Attila's Nemesis*, 164–65.

81. Tackholm, 'Aetius and the Battle on the Catalaunian Fields', 268.

82. Tackholm, 'Aetius and the Battle on the Catalaunian Fields', 268.

83. Kim, 'Herodotean Allusions in Late Antiquity', 138.

84. '*Nota vobis sunt quam sint levia Romanorum arma: primo etiam non dico vulnere, sed ipso pulvere gravantur, dum in ordine coeunt et acies testudineque conectunt.*' Jordanes, *De Origine Actibusque Getarum*, 39.204. Manuscript reading regarding 'Testudine' is uncertain; the MGH gives several iterations.

85. Brodka, 'Attila, Tyche und die Schlacht auf den Katalaunischen Feldern', 240.

86. Blockley, 'Greek Historiography in Late Antiquity', 306–308; for speeches in Priscus.

87. Whately, 'Jordanes, the Battle of the Catalaunian Fields and Constantinople', 62.

88. Whately, 'Jordanes, the Battle of the Catalaunian Fields and Constantinople', 65.

89. Dennis, *Maurice's Strategikon*, 146; it should, however, be noted that since this speech is a fabrication, gleaning any tactical details out of it is probably pointless. Nevertheless, the Romans probably did utilize the *fulcum*.

90. Jordanes, *De Origine Actibusque Getarum*, 39.204.

91. Kim, 'Herodotean Allusions in Late Antiquity', 136.

92. Jordanes, *De Origine Actibusque Getarum*, 40.207.

93. Jordanes, *De Origine Actibusque Getarum*, 38.201.

94. Jordanes, *De Origine Actibusque Getarum*, 40.209; Given, *The Fragmentary History of Priscus*, fr. 64, 101; *Chronicon Paschale*, 587. The *Chronicon Paschale* calls it a '*saggita*' while Jordanes says '*telo*'.

95. Jordanes, *De Origine Actibusque Getarum*, 40.210.

96. Kim, *The Huns, Rome and the Birth of Europe*, 77–78; Kim, 'Herodotean Allusions in Late Antiquity', 134.

97. '*Tunc vesegothae dividentes se ab alanis invadunt hunnorum caterva et pene Attilam trucidarent, nisi providus prius fugisset et se suosque ilico intra septa castrorum, quam plaustris vallatum habebat, reclusisset; quamvis fragili munimine, eo tamen quaesierunt subsidium vitae, quibus paulo ante nullus poterat muralis agger obsistere.*' Jordanes, *De Origine Actibusque Getarum*, 40.210.

98. Bachrach, *A History of the Alans in the West*, 65–67; Hughes, *Aetius: Attila's Nemesis*, 166.

99. Kim, *The Huns, Rome and the Birth of Europe*, 77; Elton, 'Defence in Fifth Century Gaul', 169, 173–74; the Goths had a habit of desertion or collapse when cooperating with the Roman army and were remarkably unsuccessful in Gaul for their entire stay in Aquitania.

100. Ammianus, *Res Gestae*, 31.2.89; Dennis, *Maurice's Strategikon*, 117–18.

101. Arrian, *Ektaxis kata Alanon*, 26–29; Arrian explicitly details the Alans' affinity for feigned retreat and how to avoid being lured in.

102. It is possible that it did, as the Huns quickly conquered the Don Alans on the Eurasian steppes upon their initial entry into Europe. This could be attributed to military factors as well as superior Hunnish organization.

103. Given, *The Fragmentary History of Priscus*, 37 fr. 5, 41 fr. 61.

104. Dennis, *Maurice's Strategikon*, 61–62.

105. Ammianus, *Res Gestae*, 31.2.89.

106. Jordanes, *De Origine Actibusque Getarum*, 43.226–28.

107. Jordanes, *De Origine Actibusque Getarum*, 40.210.

108. Hughes, *Aetius: Attila's Nemesis*, 165–66.

109. Dennis, *Maurice's Strategikon*, 48, 74, 118.

110. Golden, 'War and Warfare', 98.

111. Jordanes, *De Origine Actibusque Getarum*, 40.211.

112. Jordanes, *De Origine Actibusque Getarum*, 40.212; Clover, 'Flavius Merobaudes', 13, Panegyric I, fr. 2B.

113. Man, *Attila*, 235.

114. '*Postera die luce orta cum tumulatos cadaveribus campos aspicerent nec audere Hunnos erumpere, suam arbitrantes victoriam scientesque Attilam non nisi magna clade confossum bella confugere, cum tamen nil ageret vel prostratus abiectum, sed strepens armis, tubis canebat incursionemque minabatur, velut leo venabulis praessus speluncae aditus obambulans nec audet insurgere nec desinet fremetibus vicina terrere: sic bellicosissimus rex victores suos turbabat inclusus.*' Jordanes, *De Origine Actibusque Getarum*, 40.212.

115. Whately, 'Jordanes, The Battle of the Catalaunian Fields and Constantinople', 63.

116. Jordanes, *De Origine Actibusque Getarum*, 40.213–41.214; Dennis, *Maurice's Strategikon*, 59; according to the *Strategikon*, two regiments guarded a Roman camp, equipped with missile armaments including *ballistae*.

117. Kim, *The Huns, Rome and the Birth of Europe*, 77–78.

118. Jordanes, *De Origine Actibusque Getarum*, 40.213.

119. Dennis, *Maurice's Strategikon*, 118; Sidonius Apollinaris, *Epistulae*, 7.12.3.

120. '*Quo in conflictu quamvis neutris credentibus inaestimabilis strages commorentium factae sint, Chunos tamen eo constat victos fuisse, quod amissa proeliandi fiducia qui superfuerant ad propria reverterunt.*' Prosper, *Epitoma Chronicon*, s.a. 451; George Vernadsky, 'Der sarmatische Hintergrund der germanischen Volkerwanderung', *Saeculum* 2 (1951), 340–92; Vernadsky also suggested a tactically indecisive outcome.

121. Hydatius, *Continuatio Chronicorum*, 150.

122. *Chronica Gallica Anno 452*, s.a. 451; *Chronica Gallica Anno 511*, s.a. 451.

123. Tackholm, 'Aetius and the Battle on the Catalaunian Fields', 262–63.

124. Tackholm, 'Aetius and the Battle on the Catalaunian Fields', 263.

125. Kim, 'Herodotean Allusions in Late Antiquity', 135; Brodka, 'Attila, Tyche und die Schlacht auf den Katalaunischen Feldern', 230.

126. Hydatius, *Continuatio Chronicorum*, 150; Jordanes, *De Origine Actibusque Getarum*, 41.217; Fredegar, *Chronica Epitomata*, 2.53. However, Fredegar believes this to be from a prior battle on the Loire. This separate engagement could also reference Jordanes' alleged second Battle of Chalons in late 451 or 452.

127. '*Omnes omnino causae, quae inter Burgundiones habitae sunt et non sunt finitae usque ad pugnam Mauriacensem, habeantur abolitae.*' Lex Burgundionum, 17.1.

128. Jordanes, *De Origine Actibusque Getarum*, 40.212–41.216.

129. Fredegar, *Chronica Epitomata*, 2.53.
130. Fredegar, *Chronica Epitomata*, 2.53.
131. Jordanes, *De Origine Actibusque Getarum*, 41.216; Sid. Apol. *Carmina*, 7.344–46.
132. Sidonius Apollinaris, *Carmina*, 7.344–46.
133. Tackholm, *Aetius and the Battle of the Catalaunian Fields*, 270–71; Hughes, *Aetius: Attila's Nemesis*, 174.
134. Prosper, *Epitoma Chronicon*, s.a. 452.
135. John Michael O'Flynn, *Generalissimos of the Western Roman Empire* (Alberta: University of Alberta Press, 1983), 98.
136. Hodgkin, *Italy and Her Invaders*, 122–23; Saint Lupus' feast day, 29 July, although tantalizingly within the timeframe of Attila's invasion, is probably completely unrelated.
137. Given, *The Fragmentary History of Priscus*, 58–59 fr. 8, 99–100 fr. 16; Fredegar, *Chronica Epitomata*, 2.53; the interesting story of the plate gifted to Thorismund in the Fredegar chronicle may well be a reference to Silvanius' dinnerware.
138. Fredegar, *Chronica Epitomata*, 2.53.
139. Prosper, *Epitoma Chronicon*, s.a. 448.
140. Gillett, 'The Saint as Envoy: Bishop's Lives', 115.
141. Miklos Erdy, 'Hun and Xiong-nu Type Cauldron Finds', 17–18; Miks, *Studien zur römischen Schwertbewaffnung in der Kaiserzeit*, Vol. 2, 719.
142. Johan Aldfelt, 'Digital Atlas of the Roman Empire', *Lund University Department of Archaeology and Ancient History*, last modified 22 May 2016, http://dare.ht.lu.se/.
143. Jordanes, *De Origine Actibusque Getarum*, 41.216; Gregory of Tours, *Decem Libri Historiarum*, 2.7.
144. Kim, *The Huns, Rome and the Birth of Europe*, 78, 82, 217.
145. Tackholm, 'Aetius and the Battle on the Catalaunian Fields', 269–71.
146. Tackholm, 'Aetius and the Battle on the Catalaunian Fields', 271.
147. Gregory of Tours, *Decem Libri Historiarum*, 2.7.

Chapter 6

1. Kim, *The Huns, Rome and the Birth of Europe*, 80–83.
2. Jordanes, *De Origine Actibusque Getarum*, 43.225–28; Goffart, *Barbarian Tides*, 111, 309.
3. Gregory of Tours, *Decem Libri Historiarum*, 2.18–19.
4. Sidonius Apollinaris, *Epistulae*, 7.12.3.
5. Robert Hohlfelder, 'Marcian's Gamble: A Reassessment of Eastern Imperial Policy Towards Attila AD 450–453', *American Journal of Ancient History* 9 (1984), 54–69; Given, *The Fragmentary History of Priscus*, 98 fr. 15.
6. Barnish, 'The Battle of Vouille and the Decisive Battle Phenomenon', 19.

7.   Maenchen-Helfen, *On the World of the Huns*, 135–36; Hughes, *Aetius: Attila's Nemesis*, 177.

8.   Slavko Ciglenecki, 'Late Roman Army, *Claustra Alpium Iuliarum* and the Fortifications in the South-Eastern Alps', in *Evidence of the Roman Army in Slovenia* (Ljubljana: Narodni Muzej Slovenije, 2015), 423–24; Ciglenecki, '*Claustra Alpium Iuliarum*', 412–13; Maenchen-Helfen, *On the World of the Huns*, 136–37; however, archaeology shows that some sections of it were still fortified into the mid-fifth century and wooden fortifications existed into the sixth.

9.   Neil Christie, 'From the Danube to the Po: The Defence of Pannonia and Italy in the Fourth and Fifth Centuries AD', in *The Transition to Late Antiquity on the Danube and Beyond* (Oxford: Oxford University Press, 2007), 547–78; for an overview of the fortresses of inner Pannonia and Noricum Mediterrane.

10.   Jordanes, *De Origine Actibusque Getarum*, 52.220.

11.   Given, *The Fragmentary History of Priscus*, 39–40 fr. 5.

12.   Johnson, *Late Roman Fortifications*, 218; Elton, *Warfare in Roman Europe*, 170.

13.   Jordanes, *De Origine Actibusque Getarum*, 52.220–21; Procopius, *The Wars of Justinian*, 3.4.3035; Maenchen-Helfen, *On the World of the Huns*, 133–34.

14.   Hughes, *Aetius: Attila's Nemesis*, 179; Paul the Deacon, *Historia Romana*, 14.11; Jordanes, *De Origine Actibusque Getarum*, 52.222.

15.   Hughes, *Aetius: Attila's Nemesis*, 179.

16.   Hughes, *Aetius: Attila's Nemesis*, 179; considering both the date range in which Milan was a capital of the empire and contemporary classicizing terminology, the 'Scythians' were probably Goths.

17.   Maenchen-Helfen, *On the World of the Huns*, 138–39.

18.   Johnson, *Late Roman Fortifications*, 119–21.

19.   Maenchen-Helfen, *On the World of the Huns*, 137.

20.   Hughes, *Aetius: Attila's Nemesis*, 180.

21.   Hydatius, *Continuatio Chronicorum*, 154; *Chronicon Paschale*, 574; *Codex Theodosianum*, 15.4.1.

22.   Prosper, *Epitoma Chronicon*, s.a. 452.

23.   Given, *The Fragmentary History of Priscus*, 45 fr. 7.

24.   Gillett, 'The Saint as Envoy: Bishops' Lives', 114–15.

25.   Such as in the treaties of Margus, 443 and 448.

26.   Hughes, *Aetius: Attila's Nemesis*, 183.

27.   Prosper, *Epitoma Chronicon*, s.a. 452.

28.   Sidonius Apollinaris, *Carmina* 5.290–304; Hydatius, *Continuatio Chronicorum*, 151.

29.   Sidonius Apollinaris, *Carmina*, 5.119–274; McEvoy, *Child Emperor Rule in the Late Roman West*, 161, 180, 291; Stewart Irwin Oost, 'Aetius and Majorian', *Classical Philology* 29, no.1 (1964), 23–29.

30. *Lex Burgundionum*, 17.1.
31. *Additamenta ad Chronicon Prosperi Hauniensis*, s.a. 453; Jordanes, *De Origine Actibusque Getarum*, 43.225–28.
32. Kim, *The Huns, Rome and the Birth of Europe*, 81.
33. MacGeorge, *Late Roman Warlords*, 75–76, 109–10; Hughes, *Patricians and Emperors*, 128–29.
34. Sidonius Apollinaris, *Epistulae*, 7.12.3.
35. Sidonius Apollinaris, *Epistulae*, 7.12.3.
36. Gillett, 'The Hero as Envoy', 109.
37. Hughes, *Aetius: Attila's Nemesis*, 186.
38. Prosper, *Epitoma Chronicon*, s.a. 453; Hydatius, *Continuatio Chronicorum*, 156, 158; Jordanes, *De Origine Actibusque Getarum*, 43.228; Hughes, *Aetius: Attila's Nemesis*, 186.
39. Hydatius, *Continuatio Chronicorum*, 155, 168.
40. Given, *The Fragmentary History of Priscus*, 125–27 fr. 69; John of Antioch, fr. 293.1; Hughes, *Aetius: Attila's Nemesis*, 149, 188–90
41. McEvoy, *Child Emperor Rule in the Late Roman West*, 295–96.
42. Given, *The Fragmentary History of Priscus*, 125–27 fr. 69; John of Antioch, fr. 293.1; Hydatius, *Continuatio Chronicorum*, 160; McEvoy, *Child Emperor Rule in the Late Roman West*, 296–97.
43. Given, *The Fragmentary History of Priscus*, 128 fr. 71; John of Antioch, fr. 291.1.
44. Sidonius Apollinaris, *Carmina*, 5.306–08; Oost, 'Aetius and Majorian', 24–25.
45. Given, *The Fragmentary History of Priscus*, 128 fr. 71; John of Antioch, fr. 291.1.
46. McEvoy, *Child Emperor Rule in the Late Roman West*, 298–304.
47. Hughes, *Aetius: Attila's Nemesis*, 18990; McEvoy, *Child Emperor Rule in the Late Roman West*, 300; Given, *The Fragmentary History of Priscus*, 128–29 fr. 71; John of Antioch, fr. 291.1; Prosper, *Epitoma Chronicon*, s.a. 455.
48. MacGeorge, *Late Roman Warlords*, 41, 43, 48; Given, *The Fragmentary History of Priscus*, 136 fr. 29; Procopius, *The Wars of Justinian*, 3.6.7.
49. Sidonius Apollinaris, *Carmina*, 7.369–75.
50. Hydatius, *Continuatio Chronicorum*, 167–68.
51. Hughes, *Patricians and Emperors*, 45–48; Given, *The Fragmentary History of Priscus*, 128–29 fr. 71; John of Antioch, fr. 291.1.
52. Jordanes, *De Origine Actibusque Getarum*, 49.254–58; Theophanes, 5,946; John Malalas, 14.10.
53. Jordanes, *De Origine Actibusque Getarum*, 50.259.
54. Harke, review of '*The Huns, Rome and the Birth of Europe*', 261.
55. Kim, *The Huns, Rome and the Birth of Europe*, 89–96.
56. Mingarelli, *Collapse of the Hunnic Empire*, 56, 81–83.
57. Mingarelli, *Collapse of the Hunnic Empire*, 84.
58. Jordanes, *De Origine Actibusque Getarum*, 50.260.

59.   Jordanes, *De Origine Actibusque Getarum*, 50.261.

60.   Jordanes, *De Origine Actibusque Getarum*, 50.261.

61.   Mingarelli, *Collapse of the Hunnic Empire*, 60–68.

62.   Mingarelli, *Collapse of the Hunnic Empire*, 74–81.

63.   Heather, *The Goths*, 116, 125; Kim, *The Huns, Rome and the Birth of Europe*, 113.

64.   Jordanes, *De Origine Actibusque Getarum*, 50.265–66.

65.   Goffart, *Barbarian Tides*, 111, 309.

66.   Maenchen-Helfen, *On the World of the Huns*, 151.

67.   Williams and Friell, *The Rome that did not Fall*, 176,

68.   Given, *The Fragmentary History of Priscus*, 149 fr. 36.

69.   Given, *The Fragmentary History of Priscus*, 139 fr. 30, 150 fr. 37; Peter Golden, 'Some Notes on the Etymology of Sabir', KOINON ΔΩΡON (2013), 49–55.

70.   Kim, *The Huns, Rome and the Birth of Europe*, 131–33; Golden, 'Nomads of the Western Eurasian Steppes', 136–38.

71.   Cook, 'Megadroughts, ENSO and the Invasion of Late-Roman Europe by the Huns and Avars', 91, 100.

72.   Jordanes, *De Origine Actibusque Getarum*, 53.272.

73.   Maenchen-Helfen, *On the World of the Huns*, 164; Kim, *The Huns, Rome and the Birth of Europe*, 117–18.

74.   Given, *The Fragmentary History of Priscus*, 148 fr. 35.

75.   Jordanes, *De Origine Actibusque Getarum*, 53.273; Kim, *The Huns, Rome and the Birth of Europe*, 118.

76.   Heather, *The Goths*, 126; Kim, *The Huns, Rome and the Birth of Europe*, 84.

77.   Given, *The Fragmentary History of Priscus*, 150 fr. 37.

78.   Given, *The Fragmentary History of Priscus*, 149, 151, fr. 36 and 43; Maenchen-Helfen, *On the World of the Huns* 165–66; Williams and Friell, *The Rome that did not Fall*, 179; Heather, *The Goths*, 126; Kim, *The Huns, Rome and the Birth of Europe*, 119–20.

79.   Given, *The Fragmentary History of Priscus*, 151 fr. 38; Heather, *The Goths*, 127, 153.

80.   Given, *The Fragmentary History of Priscus*, 151 fr. 38, 152 fr. 39; Maenchen-Helfen, *On the World of the Huns*, 168.

81.   Maenchen-Helfen, *On the World of the Huns*, 168; Theophanes, 5,961.

82.   Given, *The Fragmentary History of Priscus*, 153–54 fr. 39; Heather, *The Goths*, 126; Kim, *The Huns, Rome and the Birth of Europe*, 119–20.

83.   Given, *The Fragmentary History of Priscus*, 153–54 fr. 39; *Chronicon Paschale*, 598; Kelly, *The End of Empire*, 269; Maencehn-Helfen, *On the World of the Huns*, 168.

84.   Wolfram, *The Roman Empire and its Germanic Peoples*, 184; Jordanes, *De Origine Actibusque Getarum*, 54.277–79.

85.   Heather, *The Fall of the Roman Empire*, 359–60; Man, *Attila*, 278; Kelly, *The End of Empire*, 269; Maenchen-Helfen, *On the World of the Huns*, 168.

86. Kim, *The Huns, Rome and the Birth of Europe*,132–33.
87. Golden, 'Nomads of the Western Eurasian Steppes', 143–44; Williams and Friell, *The Rome that did not Fall*, 194.
88. Kim, *The Huns, Rome and the Birth of Europe*, 139–43; Peter Golden, 'Imperial Ideology and the Sources of Political Unity Amongst the Pre-Chingissid Nomads of Western Eurasia', *Archivum Eurasiae Medii Aevi* 2 (1982), 37–76.
89. Williams and Friell, *The Rome that did not Fall*, 115; Marcellinus Comes, s.a. 493, 499.
90. Given, *The Fragmentary History of Priscus*, 136 fr. 29; Procopius, *The Wars of Justinian*, 3.6.7; Jordanes, *De Origine Actibusque Getarum*, 43.225–28; MacGeorge, *Late Roman Warlords*, 153–58.
91. Hughes, *Patricians and Emperors*, 54–55.
92. MacGeorge, *Late Roman Warlords*, 191; Hughes, *Patricians and Emperors*, 62–65.
93. Hughes, *Patricians and Emperors*, 63–64.
94. MacGeorge, *Late Roman Warlords*, 184–96; Hughes, *Patricians and Emperors*, 65–68; Halsall, *Barbarian Migrations and the Roman West*, 261; his other *magister*, Remistus, had been murdered in Ravenna.
95. Sidonius Apollinaris, *Epistulae*, 11.6; Ralph Mathisen, 'Resistance and Reconciliation: Majorian and the Gallic Aristocracy after the Fall of Avitus', *Francia* 7 (1979), 598–601; MacGeorge, *Late Roman Warlords*, 29; Hughes, *Patricians and Emperors*, 70–71.
96. Hughes, *Patricians and Emperors*, 75–76; MacGeorge, 197–201; Bruco was probably *comes Italiae*.
97. McMahon, 'The Foederati, the Phoideratoi and the Symmachoi', 36–44.
98. Sidonius Apollinaris, *Carmina*, 5.484–88; Maenchen-Helfen, *On the World of the Huns*, 161–62; Leo, *Epistulae*, 159.2, 68; Leo purchased back hostages they had taken in 452 at Aquileia.
99. Hughes, *Patricians and Emperors*, 89–90; Sidonius Apollinaris, *Carmina*, 5.471–79.
100. Hughes, *Patricians and Emperors*, 96–97.
101. MacGeorge, *Late Roman Warlords*, 83, 89–90.
102. Ralph Mathisen, *Ecclesiastical Factionalism and Religious Controversy in Fifth-Century Gaul* (Washington: Catholic University of America Press, 1989), 200, 218.
103. MacGeorge, *Late Roman Warlords*, 155–58.
104. Hughes, *Patricians and Emperors*, 90–91; MacGeorge, *Late Roman Warlords*, 203–204; Sidonius Apollinaris, *Carmina*, 5.385–442; Hydatius, *Continuatio Chronicorum*, 177; Given, *The Fragmentary History of Priscus*, 124 fr. 37.
105. Wolfram, *The Roman Empire and its Germanic Peoples*, 251; *Lex Burgundionum*, 17.1.
106. Mathisen, 'Resistance and Reconciliation', 604–07.

107. *Corpus Inscriptionum Latinarum*, XIII.23–59, XIII.23–63; Harries, *Sidonius Apollinaris and the Fall of Rome*, 46–47.

108. MacGeorge, *Late Roman Warlords*, 178–84; Hughes, *Patricians and Emperors*, 9496; he is called *comes* before his elevation to *magister militum*.

109. MacGeorge, *Late Roman Warlords*, 85–88.

110. Hughes, *Patricians and Emperors*, 96.

111. Hughes, *Patricians and Emperors*, 97–99.

112. MacGeorge, *Late Roman Warlords*, 84; Hughes, *Patricians and Emperors*, 92–93, 103, 105–06; Halsall, *Barbarian Migrations and the Roman West*, 265; MacGeorge believes Nepotianus was a Roman in the service of the Goths, but this seems unlikely. Halsall thinks he was commander of Spain, not supreme commander. Hughes thinks he was appointed to secure the support of Marcellinus via Nepotianus' marriage.

113. MacGeorge, *Late Roman Warlords*, 47–51; Hughes, *Patricians and Emperors*, 109–10; Given, *The Fragmentary History of Priscus*, 124 fr. 37.

114. Hydatius, *Continuatio Chronicorum*, 200; *Chronica Gallica Anno 511*, s.a. 460.

115. Hughes, *Patricians and Emperors*, 117–22; Halsall, *Barbarian Migrations and the Roman West*, 266.

116. Hughes, *Patricians and Emperors*, 100.

117. Halsall, *Barbarian Migrations and the Roman West*, 268–69.

118. MacGeorge, *Late Roman Warlords*, 92–93, 215–18; Halsall, *Barbarian Migrations and the Roman West*, 266–67.

119. Given, *The Fragmentary History of Priscus*, 138 fr. 30; Maenchen-Helfen, *On the World of the Huns*, 164; Kim, *The Huns, Rome and the Birth of Europe*, 117–18.

120. Elton, 'Defence in Fifth Century Gaul', 172; Mathisen, *Ecclesiastical Factionalism and Religious Controversy in Fifth-Century Gaul*, 200; MacGeorge, *Late Roman Warlords*, 91–92; Halsall, *Barbarian Migrations and the Roman West*, 268.

121. Elton, 'Defence in Fifth Century Gaul', 172.

122. Halsall, 'Childeric's Grave', 122–23.

123. James, *The Franks*, 65–67.

124. MacGeorge, *Late Roman Warlords*, 93, 98–99; James, *The Franks*, 6465; Gregory of Tours, *Decem Libri Historiarum*, 2.18; *Chronica Gallica Anno 511*, s.a. 463; Hydatius, *Chronicon*, 218.

125. MacGeorge, *Late Roman Warlords*, 100.

126. Elton, 'Defence in Fifth Century Gaul', 172; James, *The Franks*, 69; MacGeorge, *Late Roman Warlords*, 101. This was probably a group of Vandals in Spain that had been attacked by the Suebes during Aetius' time, not the Vandals in North Africa.

127. MacGeorge, *Late Roman Warlords*, 228.

128. Gregory of Tours, *Decem Libri Historiarum*, 2.18–19; Alexander Murray, *From Roman to Merovingian Gaul: A Reader* (Ontario: University of

Toronto Press, 2008), 189–91; James, *The Franks*, 69–70; MacGeorge, *Late Roman Warlords*, 10108; Kim, *The Huns, Rome and the Birth of Europe*, 8083; Halsall, *Barbarian Migrations and the Roman West*, 270–71; Murray, Halsall and MacGeorge all express doubt that *Adovacrius* is the same as *Odoacer/Odovacar*.

129. Jordanes, *De Origine Actibusque Getarum*, 45.237; Gregory of Tours, *Decem Libri Historiarum*, 2.18; Sidonius Apollinaris, *Epistulae*, 3.9; Elton, 'Defence in Fifth Century Gaul', 173–74; Elton suggests the Britons and Anthemius' battle at Arles was a two-pronged campaign.

130. Elton, 'Defence in Fifth Century Gaul', 173–74.

131. Halsall, *Barbarian Migrations and the Roman West*, 269–71; James, *The Franks*, 75.

132. Gregory of Tours, *Decem Libri Historiarum*, 2.27.

133. Barnish, 'Old Kaspars', 41–42.

Conclusion

1.   Bachrach, 'Vouille and the Decisive Battle Phenomenon', 12–14; Creasy, *Fifteen Decisive Battles of the World*, 159–60.

2.   Ferrill, *The Fall of the Roman Empire: The Military Explanation*, 147; McEvoy, *Child Emperor Rule in the Late Roman West*, 294–95; Williams and Friell, *The Rome that did not Fall*, 86–88.

3.   Geoffrey Parker, *The Cambridge Illustrated History of Warfare* (Cambridge: Cambridge University Press, 1995), 154–56.

4.   Kelly, 'Neither Conquest nor Settlement', 194–95.

5.   Whitby, 'The Balkans and Greece, 420–602', 713; Appendix B for numbers.

6.   See Appendix B for numbers; this includes forces in Pannonia Valeria and Secunda.

7.   Dennis, *Maurice's Strategikon*, 118.

8.   Whitby, 'The Balkans and Greece, 420–602', 710–11.

9.   Kim, *The Huns, Rome and the Birth of Europe*, 77.

10.   Williams and Friell, *The Rome that did not Fall*, 177.

11.   Elton, *Warfare in Roman Europe*, 133–34; Kim, *The Huns, Rome and the Birth of Europe*, 70–73, 84–85.

12.   Blockley, *The Fragmentary Classicizing Historians*, Vol.1, 61.

13.   Bachrach, 'Vouille and the Decisive Battle Phenomenon', 12–20,

14.   Bury, *History of the Later Roman Empire*, 292, 294; Bachrach, *A History of the Alans in the West*, 65–67; Hughes, *Aetius: Attila's Nemesis*, 161; Kim, *The Huns, Rome and the Birth of Europe*, 77.

15.   Bury, *History of the Later Roman Empire*, 294.

16.   Barnish, 'Old Kaspars', 41–42.

17.   Barnish, 'Old Kaspars', 45–46.

18.   Whately, 'Jordanes, The Battle of the Catalaunian Fields and Constantinople', 65–69.
19.   Barnish, 'Old Kaspars', 43–46.
20.   Wolfram, *The Roman Empire and its Germanic Peoples*, 137–38, 195.
21.   Hedeager, 'Scandinavia and the Huns', 42–58; Nasman, 'Scandinavia and the Huns', 111–18.
22.   Gildas, *De Excidio Conquestu Britanniae*, 24.

Appendix B

Tabulation of Forces in the *Notitia Dignitatum: In Partibus Orientis*

1.   Based on the research of Luke Ueda-Sarson, 'Late Roman Shield Patterns Taken from the Notitia Dignitatum', LukeUedaSarson.com, last modified *3 January 2016*, http://lukeuedasarson.com/NotitiaPatterns.html.
2.   Reduplication.
3.   Reduplication.
4.   Usually assumed destroyed in Ammianus, Res Gestae, 20.6.8; Sarson thinks it survived or was reconstituted.
5.   As stated before, Ueda-Sarson also believes that unlike Res Gestae, 20.7.1, this unit survived or was reconstituted.

Tabulation of Forces in the *Notitia Dignitatum: In Partibus Occidentis*

1.   Transferred to *magister equitum*.
2.   Transferred to *magister equitum*.
3.   Transferred to *magister equitum*.
4.   Transferred to *magister equitum*.
5.   Transferred to *magister equitum*.
6.   Transferred to *magister equitum*.
7.   Transferred to *magister equitum*.
8.   Transferred to *magister equitum*.
9.   Transferred to *magister equitum*.
10.   Transferred to *magister equitum*.
11.   Transferred to *magister equitum*.
12.   Transferred to *magister equitum*.
13.   Transferred to *magister equitum*.
14.   Transferred to *magister equitum*.
15.   Transferred to *magister equitum*.
16.   Transferred to *magister equitum*.
17.   Transferred to *comes Illyricum*.

18. Transferred to *comes Britanniarum.*
19. Transferred to *comes Britanniarum.*
20. Transferred to *comes Illyricum.*
21. Transferred to *magister equitum.*
22. Transferred to *magister equitum.*
23. Transferred to *magister equitum.*
24. Transferred to *magister equitum.*
25. Transferred to *dux Britanniarum.*
26. Transferred to *magister equitum.*
27. Transferred to *magister equitum.*
28. Transferred to *comes Illyricum.*
29. Transferred to *magister equitum.*
30. Transferred to *comes Illyricum.*
31. Transferred to *comes Africae.*
32. Transferred to *comes Africae.*
33. Transferred to *comes Africae.*
34. Transferred to *comes Africae.*
35. These five comitatenses units were destroyed in 409.
36. Transferred to *magister peditum.*
37. Transferred to *magister equitum.*
38. Transferred to *magister equitum.*
39. Transferred to *magister equitum.*
40. Transferred to *magister equitum.*
41. Placeholder unit.
42. Placeholder unit.
43. Transferred to *comes Illyricum.*
44. Transferred to *magister peditum.*
45. Transferred to *comes Illyricum.*
46. Transferred to *comes Illyricum.*

Glossary

Aedoratio	'Adoration'. A monetary donative given in place of military recruits when conscripts were requested of landowners. It was often used as an informal tax.
Agri Deserti	'Deserted fields'. Lands that had become vacant over time, often granted to *Laeti* or *Foederati*.
Akatir	The '*acatziroi*' or '*akatiroi*' of Priscus. Possibly the primary tribe in the left (eastern) wing of the Hunnic Empire.
Ala	A cavalry regiment in the Roman Army, numbering 512 men and organized into *Turmae*.
Alpidzur	A group of Oghur-speaking nomads living in a confederation on the Volga before the Hun migration.
Ämäcur	A commander of 10,000 men in the Hun decimal organization.
Amali	A group of Goths associated with the lineage of Valamir which first appear in the late 450s, who become the ruling group of the Ostrogoths.
Angisciri	A Germanic group serving Dengzich in the 460s. Presumably related to the *Sciri*.
Aniliki	The Oghuric Turkic equivalent of '*chanyu*' or 'emperor'.
Annona	A Roman unit of taxation based on the grain harvest, measuring four *Solidi* in the Theodosian period.
Antrustiones	A latinized version of the Frankish word for a warlord's personal retinue or *comitatus*.
Arithmos	Greek for '*Numerus*', usually.
Armorica	Sometimes rendered *Aremorica*, the region of modern-day Brittany in France.
Augustus	'Emperor'.

Augusta	'Empress'.
Auxilia Palatina	Roman field army forces, graded higher than the *comitatenses* and organized into *Numeri*. They are often believed to have had specialist roles.
Bacaudae	Organized rebels in the Roman state, particularly during the late third and fifth centuries.
Ballista	A powerful bolt-throwing, metal-framed, anti-personnel engine. Resembling a crossbow in appearance but working on the torsion of two springs rather than tension in the arms.
Balthi	A group of Goths associated with the lineage of Alaric, who become the ruling group of the Aquitanian Goths or Visigoths.
Bandhelm	A hemispherical helmet made by two or four plates conjoined by vertical bands with a horizontal band around the bottom.
Bandon	A 200–400-man sixth-century regiment named after the standard bearer who carried a *Bandon*, called a *Bandonarius*.
Barbaricum	The non-Roman world.
Bardor	One of the lesser Hunnic tribes in their confederation, possibly the chief group of the north or south division.
Bellonoti	A misrendering of the fictional *Balloniti* of Valerius Flaccus in Sidonius' panegyrics.
Bittugur	One of the lesser Hunnic tribes in their confederation, possibly the chief group of the north or south division.
Boisci	A group of Iranic-speaking nomads, probably related to Ptolemy's *Rhoboisci*, living on the Volga before the arrival of the Huns in Europe.
Böri	'Wolves' in Oghur. Possibly the name for the Hun royal guard.
Breones	Ostrogothic frontier forces in Raetia under the reign of Theodoric the Great.
Bucellarii	Personal bodyguard retinues hired and paid by a commander or administrator in the Roman state. Often considered 'elite' forces.
Canton	The basic division of Germanic society.

Carmen	'Song', 'Poem' or 'Panegyric'.
Centuria	The 'century', the basic infantry unit in the Roman Army above a *contubernium* (squad), numbering eighty men.
Chanyu	'Emperor', in the *Xiongnū* language.
Chernjacov Culture	An archaeological culture characterizing east-Germanic peoples from the third to fifth centuries in the Pontic, Carpathian and Danubian regions.
Claustra Iulium Alpiarum	The Roman fortifications in the Julian Alps. Part of the *tractus Italiae circa alpes*.
Cloisonné	A form of decoration utilizing gold wire and garnet inlay.
Cohors	The 'cohort'. The next level of organization above the century in the classical legion, it numbered 480 men, plus officers.
Comes rei militaris	'Count of military matters', usually the commander of a smaller mobile field army. Sometimes the commander of the garrisons in a military district.
Comes Domesticorum	'Count of the domestics', or the commander of the *Protectores Domestici* guard unit.
Comes Foederatorum	'Count of the federates'. The commander of all federate forces within the Roman Empire.
Comes Primi Ordini	'Count first order'. The highest rank in the noble order created by Constantine to honour senior officers and officials.
Comes Sacri Stabuli	'Count of the stables'. The bureaucrat in charge of horses and pack animals in the Roman Army and administration.
Comitatenses	Roman field forces, distinguished from *limitanei* by both operational role and legal and tax privileges.
Comitatus	'Retinue', a body of professional warriors paid through the gifting system that accompanied a Germanic chieftain.
Contus	'Spear' or 'lance'. *Kontos* in Greek.
Cuneus	'Wedge'. The word has two meanings: it can either refer to the 'boar's head', which was a Germanic battle formation, or a late Roman cavalry regiment, which may have numbered 256 men.

Cura Palatii	'Curator of the Palace'. Believed both to be the chief administrator of the imperial palace and commander of the palace guard.
Daylami	Persian heavy infantry from the mountainous Gilan province in Iran.
Defensorses	The shock division of a cavalry *meros* in the *Strategikon*.
Droungos	A Gallic term referring to a body of cavalry, which later developed into a term for a standardized regiment.
Dux Limitis	'Duke of borders', usually the commander of the garrison forces in a military district.
Equites	'Cavalry'.
Epistula	'Letter'.
Exercitus	A Roman field army.
Fabrica	'Factory'. In the late Roman period, usually referring to the arms factories listed in the *Notitia Dignitatum*.
Foedus	'Treaty'.
Foederati	'Federates' or more literally '[Those] bound by treaty'. People bound by treaty to the Roman state, although it usually refers to men in military service as dictated by treaty to the empire.
Francisca	The infamous Frankish axe, noted for being thrown at the enemy. Derived from the Roman military axe or *Securis*.
Fulcum	The late Roman shield wall.
Geloni	An ancient people from Herodotus related to the Scythians.
Gens	The Roman concept of 'clan', 'race' or 'nation'. The concept is not exactly the same as modern 'ethnic identity', although similar.
Gentiles	Settlements of 'soldier-farmer' militia.
Gorytos	A steppe bowcase for a strung bow. In late antiquity it typically possessed cylindrical quivers instead of an integrated arrow pouch.
Hagiography	The writing about the life of a saint or holy figure.
Historiography	The study and critical analysis of the writing of history.

Hospitalitas	A method of incorporation of *Foederati* by the preliminary allocation of tax revenues from taxable lands for their payment.
Hostes	A diplomatic 'hostage' exchanged by terms of a treaty in order to ensure peace between two polities.
Ile	Greek for '*Ala*'.
Ilik	Also rendered '*Alik*' or '*Ilek*', the title of the prince of the *Akatir* Huns, possibly the heir-apparent.
Itimari	A group of Iranic-speaking nomads living on the Volga before the Hun arrival in Europe.
Iuthungi	The foremost tribe in the *Alamanni* confederation.
Koursorses	The attack division of a cavalry *meros* in the *Strategikon*.
Kutrigur	Meaning 'seven Oghurs', the right (or west) division of the Hunnic Empire in the late fifth to mid-sixth centuries.
Laeti	Foreigners settled on land within the Roman Empire. Similar to *foederati*.
Lamellar helmet	A helmet made of lamellar plates, usually with a raised metal 'cap' on top conjoining them together. Often with a maille or quilted coif and noseguard.
Langseax	A single edged battle-knife.
Legio	The 'legion'. Originally numbering about 5,200 men, by the 450s they may have only numbered somewhere around 960 men.
Legio Palatina	Roman field army forces, graded higher than the *comitatenses* and organized into legions. They are often believed to have had specialist roles.
Limes	'Limits' or 'borders'.
Limitanei	Professional Roman garrison forces, distinguished from the *comitatenses* primarily by operational function, but also legal and tax privledges.
Liticiani	A likely corruption of *Litauiani* or *Litaui*, being Romano-British immigrants from the region of modern Caernarfon in Wales to Armorica.
Magister Equitum	'Master of the cavalry'. A predecessor command to the *magister militum* in the West, stationed in Gaul, with essentially the same function.

Magister Militum	'Master of the soldiers' of a diocese, prefecture or field army. They were divided into the *comes et magister utriusque militiae, praesentalis I, praesentalis II, per Gallias, per Hispenias, per Illyrias, per Thracias* and *per Orientem*.
Magister Officiorum	'Master of the offices'. The chief administrator of the Roman bureaucracy.
Magister Peditum	'Master of the infantry'. A predecessor command to the *magister militum* in the West, stationed in Italy, with essentially the same function.
Magister Scrinii	'Master of the secretaries'. The chief secretary of the Roman bureaucracy.
Manus	In this case, a 'band' of men, usually used to refer to a regiment of barbarian *foederati* although it can also refer to Roman forces. See also *pagus*.
Milites	'Soldiers'.
Millena	An allotment of income in the *hospitalitas* system.
Millenarii	*Foederati* paid by the allotments of the *hospitalitas* system.
Modius	An ancient Roman unit of dry measure, equivalent to about 8.73 litres.
Munifex	An unskilled Roman soldier who was required to perform regular soldiering duties.
Notararius	'Notary'.
Numerus	Late Roman regiment, originally referring to irregularly organized forces. It may have numbered about 640 men.
Oγur	A family of the Turkic languages characterized by the use of '-r' endings. Also called Lir-Turkic. Also a collective term for late fifth-century speakers of the Oghur dialect emigrating into Europe. Mistakenly rendered Ούρωγοι in Priscus.
Olibrones	An otherwise unattested group, possibly being the *Breones* of Theodoric's time, or alternatively referring to prematurely retired Roman field forces.
Onager	'Wild ass'. A late Roman torsion engine, the basis for popular conception of a 'catapult'.

Onoγur	Meaning 'ten Oghurs', one of the lesser two divisions of the Hunnic Empire of the late fifth to mid–sixth centuries.
Optimates	'Picked men'. A Roman word for nobles in barbarian societies. *Intimates* ('intimates') and *logades* ('ministers') had a similar meaning.
Pagus	A regiment of *foederati*, as said by the *Strategikon*.
Patricius	Originally one of the Roman social classes, the title became an honorific, awarded usually to important bureaucrats or generals. Aetius held the most elaborate title of *magnificus vir parens patriusque noster*.
Pedites	'Infantry'.
Plumbata	The late Roman lead-weighted throwing dart. Similar to modern lawn darts, but slightly more lethal.
Possessores	'Possessors', or the Roman landowning class.
Praefectus Praetorio	'Praetorian prefect'. The chief administrator of one of the main prefectures of the Roman Empire, those being *per Gallias*, *per Italiae, Illyrici, et Africae*, *per Illyricum* and *per Orientem*.
Praeses	'Governor'.
Protectores Domestici	The imperial guard, stationed in Rome. Originally a replacement for the praetorian guard, it became a placeholder unit for earmarked politicians.
Pseudocomitatenses	*Limitanei* grade forces withdrawn from their garrisons and placed into the field armies.
Regales	'Sub-kings'. A Roman word for greater nobles or leaders of Germanic cantons, or groups of cantons.
Ridge Helmet	A late Roman helmet characterized by a two- or four-part bowl conjoined by a central ridge-shaped metal band, with cheekpieces and a neckguard. It may or may not have a nasal or base ring, depending on the type.
Riparienses	*Limitanei*-graded riverine garrison forces.
Ripenses	*Limitanei*-graded riverine garrison forces.
Rouran	A nomadic people who dominated the Mongolian steppes during the fifth century. Also referred to as the *Juan-juan*.

Sabir	A group of Oghur-speakers who emigrated into the Pontic region in the 460s, they were likely directly related to the *Xianbei*.
Sadages	Also called the *Sadagarii*, an east Germanic, possibly Gothic, people living in the Danubian region in the 460s.
Sarayur	Meaning 'white Oghurs', a Turkic-speaking group that attacked the Huns in the 460s and also invaded Persia.
Schola Palatina	'Palatine school'. The personal cavalry field army of the emperor.
Scrinus	One of the bureaucratic secretaries of the empire.
Segment helmet	A helmet made of vertically stacked bands or segments riveted together in a conical shape. Often with a maille or quilted coif and noseguard.
Siliqua	Roman silver coin, struck at 1/1,728th of a Roman pound (or about 0.19g of silver).
Siliquaticum	A tax law passed in 444 that placed a 1/24th sales tax on all goods in order to levy funds to pay the army.
Solidus	Late Roman gold coin, struck at 1/72nd of a Roman pound (or about 4.5g of gold).
Spangenhelm	A conical helmet made of four or six plates conjoined with vertical bands, with a horizontal band running around the base. Often with cheekpieces, a noseguard and a maille or quilted coif.
Spatha	Late Roman era sword, usually with a blade length over 70cm long. Asiatic-type blades could be over 83cm in length.
Suburbanus	'Suburbs'.
Symmachi	Foreign allied troops.
Tarantiarchia	A 'half-*ala*' as described by Arrian, numbering 256 men.
Ṭarḥâns	'Tarkhans'. Possibly a name for the Hun royal guard, possibly deriving from *Xiongnū*.
Terp Tritzum	Earthenware made with mud from the 'terp' mounds in the modern Netherlands and Denmark.
Testudo	The classic 'tortoise' formation used by the Roman Army, usually during sieges.

Tieh'le	A confederation of Oghuric Turkic-speaking nomads that lived in the Altai mountains until the beginning of the fifth century AD. Also called *Gaoche*, previously called the *Tingling*.
Topos	Literary theme, trope or allusion mimicking a classical author.
Toxandria	The northernmost part of Gaul along the Rhine west of Cologne, now part of the Netherlands and Belgium.
Tribunus	'Tribune'. A title with multiple meanings, including the commander of a military regiment. Aetius held the title of *tribunus praetorianus partis militaris*, which had an unknown function.
Turma	The basic cavalry unit in the Roman Empire, consisting of 32 men.
Ulticur	The council of 'six horns', handpicked by the Hun emperor. Also rendered '*Alticur*'.
Ultzinzur	The primary Hunnic group mentioned following Dengzich. Possibly the primary tribe in the right (western) wing of the Hunnic Empire.
Utigur	Meaning 'thirty Oghurs', the left (or east) division of the Hunnic Empire in the late fifth to mid-sixth centuries.
Vexillatio	A military detachment.
Vigiles	'Watchmen'. Organized town militias, based on the original *Vigilum* in Rome and organized into cohorts.
Vir Illustris	'Illustrious man'. One of the three social rankings in the Roman Senate. Also rendered '*vir inlustris*'.
Yeniseian	A branch of the Dene-Yeniseian language family, an extinct dialect of which was probably the original *Xiongnū* language.

Bibliography

Primary Sources

Anderson, W.B., *Sidonius: Poems and Letters. With an English Translation, Introduction and Notes* (Cambridge: Harvard University Press, 1963).

Banchich, Thomas M., *The History of Zonaras: From Alexander Severus to the Death of Theodosius the Great*, trans. Thomas M. Banchich and Eugene N. Lane (London: Routledge Publishing, 2009).

Barnish, Samuel, *Cassiodorus: Variae* (Liverpool: Liverpool University Press, 1992).

Blockley, Roger C., *The Fragmentary Classicizing Historians of the Later Roman Empire: Eunapius, Olympiodorus, Priscus and Malchus*, 2 vols (Liverpool: Francis Cairns, 1981).

Blume, Fred H., *The Codex of Justinian: A New Annotated Translation with Parallel Latin and Greek Text Based on a Translation by Justice Fred H. Blume*, edited by Serena Connolly *et al* (Cambridge: Cambridge University Press, 2016).

Burgess, Richard, *'The Chronicle of Hydatius and the Consularia Constantinopolitana': Two Contemporary Accounts of the Final Years of the Roman Empire* (Oxford: Clarendon Press, 1993.)

————. 'The Gallic Chronicle of 452: A New Critical Edition with Brief Introduction', in Ralph W. Mathisen and Danuta Shanzer (eds), *Society and Culture in Late Antique Gaul: Revisiting the Sources* (Aldershot: Ashgate Publishing, 2001), pp.52–84.

————. 'The Gallic Chronicle of 511: A New Critical Edition with Brief Introduction', in Ralph W. Mathisen and Danuta Shanzer (eds), *Society and Culture in Late Antique Gaul: Revisiting the Sources* (Aldershot: Ashgate Publishing, 2001), pp.85–100.

Clover, Frank M., 'Flavius Merobaudes: A Translation and Historical Commentary', *Transactions of the American Philosophical Society* 61, no.1 (1971), pp.1–78.

Croke, Brian, *Count Comes and his Chronicle* (Oxford: Oxford University Press, 1995).

Dalton, Ormonde Maddock, *The Letters of Sidonius*, 2 vols (Oxford: Clarendon Press, 1915).

Dennis, George T., *Maurice's Strategikon: Handbook of Byzantine Military Strategy* (Philadelphia: University of Pennsylvania Press, 1984).

Devoto, James G., *Flavius Arrianus: Technè Taktika (Tactical Handbook) and Ektaxis Kata Alanon (The Expedition Against the Alans)* (Chicago: Ares Publishers, 1993).

Drew, Katherine Fisher, *The Burgundian Code: Book of Constitutions or Law of Gundobad; Additional Enactments* (Philadelphia: University of Pennsylvania Press, 1972).

————. *The Laws of the Salian Franks* (Philadelphia: University of Pennsylvania Press, 1991).

Fremantle, W.H., Lewis, G. and Martley, W.G., 'The Letters of St. Jerome', in Philip Schaff and Henry Wace (eds), *Nicene and Post Nicene Fathers, Second Series*, Vol.6 (Buffalo: Christian Literature Publishing Co., 1893).

Frendo, Joseph D., *Agathias: The Histories*, 2 vols (Berlin: Walter De Gruyter, 1975).

Given, John, *The Fragmentary History of Priscus: Attila, the Huns and the Roman Empire, AD 430–476* (Merchantville, NJ: Evolution Publishing, 2014).

Gwilt, Joseph, *The Architecture of Marcus Vitruvius Pollio* (London: Priestly and Weale, 1826).

Hartranft, Chester D., 'The Ecclesiastical History of Sozomen, Comprising a History of the Church, from A.D. 323 to A.D. 425', in Philip Schaff and Henry Wace (eds), *Nicene and Post Nicene Fathers, Second Series*, Vol.2 (Buffalo: Christian Literature Publishing Co., 1892).

Hoare, F.R., *The Western Fathers: Being the Lives of Martin of Tours, Ambrose, Augustine of Hippo, Honoratus of Arles and Germanus of Auxerre* (New York: Harper Torchbooks, 1965).

Jackson, Blomfield, 'Theodoret: Church History, Dialogues, and Letters,' in Philip Schaff and Henry Wace (eds), *Nicene and Post Nicene Fathers, Second Series*, Vol.3 (Buffalo: Christian Literature Publishing Co., 1892).

Kaldellis, Anthony, *Prokopios: The Wars of Justinian*, trans. H.B. Dewing (Indianapolis: Hackett Publishing, 2014).

Lassard, Y. and Koptev, A., 'Codex Theodosianus', *The Roman Law Library* (accessed 7 November 2017, https://droitromain.univ-grenoble-alpes.fr/).

————. 'Theodosiani Novellae', *The Roman Law Library* (accessed 7 November 2017, https://droitromain.univ-grenoble-alpes.fr/).

Mierow, Charles C., *The Origins and Deeds of the Goths* (Princeton: Princeton University Press, 1908).

Milner, N.P., *Vegetius: Epitome of Military Science*, 2nd ed. (Liverpool: Liverpool University Press, 1993).

Mommsen, Theodor, 'Iordanis Romana et Getica', in *Monumenta Germaniae Historiae*, Vol.5, Pt1 (edited by Societas Aperiendis Fontibus Rerum Germanicarum Medii Aevi) (Berlin: Weidmann, 1882).

Murray, Alexander, *From Roman to Merovingian Gaul: A Reader* (Toronto: University of Toronto Press, 2008).

'Paulus Diaconus', *The Latin Library* (accessed 7 November 2017. http://www.thelatinlibrary.com/pauldeacon.html).

Peters, Edwards, *Paul the Deacon: History of the Lombards*, trans. William Dudley Folke (Philadelphia: University of Pennsylvania Press, 1974).

Pharr, Clyde, *The Theodosian Code and Novels and the Sirmondian Constitutions: A Translation with Commentary, Glossary and Bibliography* (Princeton: Princeton University Press, 1952).

Platnauer, Maurice, *Claudian*, in *Loeb Classical Library*, 2 vols (Harvard: Harvard University Press, 1992).

Ridley, Ronald T., *Zosimus: New History* (Canberra: Australian Association for Byzantine Studies, 1982).

Strassler, Robert B., *The Landmark Herodotus: The Histories*, trans. Andrea L. Purvis (New York: Anchor Books, 2007).

Thorpe, Lewis, *Gregory of Tours: The History of the Franks* (London: Penguin Classics, 1976).

Ueda-Sarson, Luke, 'Late Roman Shield Patterns Taken from the Notitia Dignitatum', *LukeUedaSarson.com* (last modified 3 January 2016, http://lukeuedasarson.com/NotitiaPatterns.html).

Whitby, Michael and Whitby, Mary, *Chronicon Paschale 284–628 AD* (Liverpool: Liverpool University Press, 1989).

Winterbottom, M. Gildas, 'The Ruin of Britain and Other Documents', in John Morris (ed.), *Arthurian Period Sources*, Vol.7 (Felpham, West Sussex: Phillimore & Co., 1978).

Wolf, Kenneth, 'Isidore of Seville, History of the Kings of the Goths', in *Conquerors and Chroniclers of Early Medieval Spain*, 2nd ed., trans. Kenneth Wolf (Liverpool: Liverpool University Press, 2011).

Zenos, A.C., 'The Ecclesiastical History of Socrates Scholasticus', in Philip Schaff and Henry Wace (eds), *Nicene and Post Nicene Fathers, Second Series*, Vol.2 (Buffalo: Christian Literature Publishing Co., 1892).

Secondary Sources

Aldfelt, Johan, 'Digital Atlas of the Roman Empire', *Lund University Department of Archaeology and Ancient History* (last modified 22 May 2016, http://dare.ht.lu.se/).

Altheim, Franz, *Geschichte der Hunnen*, 4 vols (Berlin: Walter de Gruyter & Co., 1959).

Arbois de Jubainville, Henri d', 'Recherches philologiques sur l'anneau sigillaire de Pouan', *Revue de Questions Historiques* 6 (1869).

Asadov, Farda, 'Ellak and Ilek: What does the Study of an Ancient Turkic Title in Eurasia Contribute to the Discussion of Khazar Ancestry?', *Acta Via Serica* 2 (2017), pp.113–32.

Attila, Kiss, 'Huns, Romans, Byzantines? The Origins of the Narrow-Bladed Long Seaxes', *Acta Archaeological Carpathica* 59 (2014), pp.131–64.

Atwood, Christopher P., 'Huns and Xiongnu – New Thoughts on an Old Problem', in Brian J. Boeck, Russell E. Martin and Daniel Rowlands (eds), *Dubitando: Studies in History and Culture in Honor of David Ostrowski* (Bloomington: Slavica Publishers, 2012), pp.27–52.

———. 'The Qai, the Khongai, and the Names of the Xiōngnú', in Yu Taishan, Li Jinxiu and Bruce Doar (eds), *International Journal of Eurasian Studies*, Vol.2 (Beijing: The Commercial Press, 2015), pp.35–63.

Bachrach, Bernard S., *A History of the Alans in the West: From their First Appearance in the Sources of Classical Antiquity to the Early Middle Ages* (Minneapolis: University of Minnesota Press, 1973).

———. *Merovingian Military Organization 481–751* (Minneapolis: University of Minnesota Press, 1972).

Baldwin, Barry, 'Priscus of Panium', *Byzantion* 50 (1980), pp.18–61.

Banniard, Michel, 'L'aménagement de l'histoire chez Grégoire de Tours: à propos de l'invasion de 451', *Romanobarbarica* 3 (1978), pp.23–26.

Barfield, Thomas, 'The Hsiung-nu Imperial Confederacy: Organization and Foreign Policy', *Journal of Asian Studies* 41, no.1 (1981), pp.45–61.

Barnish, Samuel, 'Old Kaspars: Attila's Invasion of Gaul in the Literary Sources', in John Drinkwater (ed.), *Fifth Century Gaul: A Crisis of Identity?* (Cambridge: Cambridge University Press, 1992), pp.38–47.

———. 'The Battle of Vouille and the Decisive Battle Phenomenon in Late Antique Gaul', in Ralph W. Mathisen and Danuta Shanzer (eds), *The Battle of Vouille, 507: Where France Began* (Boston: Walter de Gruyter, 2012), pp.11–42.

Baughman, Elizabeth, 'The Scythian Archers: Policing Athens', in Christopher Blackwell (ed.), *Demos: Classical Athenian Democracy* (The Stoa Consortium for Electronic Publication in the Humanities, 2003), pp.1–6.

Bessiana, Amin, 'The Size of the Numerus Transtigritanorum in the Fifth Century', *ZPE* 175 (2010), pp.224–26.

Bishop, M.C. and Coulston, J.C.N., *Roman Military Equipment: From the Punic Wars to the Fall of Rome*, 2nd ed. (Oxford: Oxbow Books, 2009).

Blanchet, Adrien, *Les enceintes romaines de la Gaule* (Paris: Payot Publishing, 1907).

Blockley, Roger C., 'Dexippus and Priscus and the Thucydidean Account of the Siege of Platea', *Phoenix* 26 (1972), pp.22–26.

———. 'The Development of Greek Historiography: Priscus, Malchus, Candidus', in Gabriele Marasco (ed.), *Greek & Roman Historiography in Late Antiquity: Fourth to Sixth Century A.D.* (Leiden: Brill, 2003), pp.289–316.

Bona, Istvan, *Das Hunnenreich* (Budapest: Theiss, 1991).

———. *Les Huns: Le Grande Empire Barbare d'Europe (IVe-Ve Siecles)* (Paris: Errance, 2002).

Brodka, Dariusz, 'Attila, Tyche und die Schlacht auf den Katalaunischen Feldern: Eine Untersuchung zum Geschichtsdenken des Priskos von Panion', *Hermes* 136, no.2 (2008), pp.227–45.

Browning, Robert, 'Where was Attila's Camp?', *The Journal of Hellenic Studies* 73 (1953), pp.143–45.

Burgess, Richard, 'A New Reading for the Hydatius Chronicle 177 and the Defeat of the Huns in Italy', *Phoenix* 42 (1988), pp.357–63.

Bury, John Bagnell, *History of the Later Roman Empire* (New York: Dover Publications, 1958).

———. 'Iusta Grata Honoria', *Journal of Roman Studies* 9 (1919), pp.8–9.

Campbell, Duncan, *Greek and Roman Artillery 399 BC – AD 363* (Oxford: Osprey Publishing, 2003).

———. *Greek and Roman Siege Machinery 399 BC – AD 363* (Oxford: Osprey Publishing, 2003).

Christie, Neil, 'From the Danube to the Po: The Defence of Pannonia and Italy in the Fourth and Fifth Centuries AD', in Andrew Poulter (ed.), *The Transition to Late Antiquity on the Danube and Beyond* (Oxford: Oxford University Press, 2007), pp.547–78.

Christiensen, Arne Søby, *Cassiodorus, Jordanes and the History of the Goths: Studies in a Migration Myth* (Copenhagen: Museum Tusculanum Press, 2002).

Ciglenecki, Slavko, '*Claustra Alpium Iuliarum, tractus Italiae circa Alpes*, and the Defence of Italy in the Final Part of the Late Roman Period', *Arheoloski Vestnik* 67 (2016), pp.409–24.

———. 'Late Roman Army, *Claustra Alpium Iuliarum* and the Fortifications in the South-Eastern Alps', in Janka Istenic, Bostjan Laharanar, and Jana Horvat (eds), *Evidence of the Roman Army in Slovenia* (Ljubljana: Narodni Muzej Slovenije, 2015), pp.385–430.

Clinton, Fynes, *Fasti Romani, the Civil and Literary Chronology of Rome and Constantinople from the Death of Augustus to the Death of Justin II*, Vol.2 (Oxford: Oxford University Press, 1853).

Coello, Terence, 'Unit Sizes in the Late Roman Army', PhD diss., The Open University, 1995.

Collins, Robert, 'Brooch use in the 4th to 5th-century frontier', in Robert Collins and Lindsay Alan-Jones (eds), *Finds from the Frontier: Material Culture in the 4th–5th Centuries* (London: Council for British Archaeology, 2010), pp.64–77.

Cook, Edward R., 'Megadroughts, ENSO and the Invasion of Late-Roman Europe by the Huns and Avars', in William V. Harris (ed.), *The Ancient Mediterranean Environment: Between Science and History* (Leiden: Brill, 2013), pp.89–102.

Creasy, Edward Shepard, *Fifteen Decisive Battles of the World: From Marathon to Waterloo* (Oxford: Oxford University Press, 1915).

Curta, Florin, 'The Earliest Avar-Age Stirrups, or the "Stirrup Controversy" Revisited', in Florin Curta (ed.), *The Other Europe in the Middle Ages. Avars, Bulgars, Khazars and Cumans. East Central and Eastern Europe in the Middle Ages, 450–1450*, Vol.2 (Leiden: Brill, 2008), pp.302–10.

Delaplace, Christine, *La fin de l'Empire romain d'Occident: Rome et les Wisigoths de 382–551* (Rennes: University Press of Rennes, 2015).

de la Vassiere, Etienne, 'Huns et Xiongnu', *Central Asiatic Journal* 49 (2005), pp.3–26.

———. 'The Steppe World and the Rise of the Huns', in Michael Maas (ed.), *The Cambridge Companion to the Age of Attila* (Cambridge: Cambridge University Press, 2015), pp.175–92.

Delbrück, Hans, *The Barbarian Invasions: History of the Art of War* (trans. Walter J. Renfoe Jr) (Lincoln, Nebraska: University of Nebraska Press, 1990).

———. *The Barbarian Invasions: History of the Art of War* (trans. Walter J. Renfoe Jr) (Lincoln, Nebraska: University of Nebraska Press, 1990).

Di Cosmo, Nicola, *Ancient China and its Enemies: The Rise of Nomadic Power in East Asian History* (Cambridge: Cambridge University Press, 2002).

———. 'The Northern Frontier in Pre-Imperial China', in Michael Loewe and Edward L. Shaughnessy (eds), *The Cambridge History of Ancient China* (Cambridge: Cambridge University Press, 1999), pp.885–966.

Dierkins, Alain and Perin, Patrick, 'The 5th-century Advance of the Franks in Belgica II: History and Archaeology', in E. Taayke, O.H. Harsema, and H.R. Reinders (eds), *Essays on the Early Franks* (Eelde: Barkhuis, 2003), pp.165–93.

Dinchev, Ventzislav, 'The Fortresses of Thrace and Dacia in the Early Byzantine Period', in Andrew Poulter (ed.), *The Transition to Late Antiquity: On the Danube and Beyond* (Oxford: Oxford University Press, 2007), pp.479–546.

Elton, Hugh, 'Defence in Fifth Century Gaul', in John Drinkwater (ed.), *Fifth Century Gaul: A Crisis of Identity?* (Cambridge: Cambridge University Press, 1992), pp.167–76.

———. *Frontiers of the Roman Empire* (London: Routledge, 2012).

———. 'Military Developments in the Fifth Century', in Michael Maas (ed.), *The Cambridge Companion to the Age of Attila* (Cambridge: Cambridge University Press, 2014), pp.125–39.

———. *Warfare in Roman Europe AD 350–425* (Oxford: Clarendon Press, 1996).

Érdy, Miklós, 'Hun and Xiong-nu Type Cauldron Finds throughout Eurasia', *Eurasian Studies Yearbook* 67 (1995), pp.5–94.

Fernandez, Joaquin, 'Late Roman Belts in Hispania', *Journal of Roman Military Equipment Studies* 10 (1999), pp.55–71.

Ferrill, Arther, *The Fall of the Roman Empire: The Military Explanation* (London: Thames and Hudson, 1986).

Fields, Nic, *Attila the Hun* (Oxford: Osprey Publishing, 2015).

———. *The Hun: Scourge of God AD 375–565* (Oxford: Osprey Publishing, 2006).

Findley, Carter, *The Turks in World History* (Oxford: Oxford University Press, 2004).

Fischer, Svante and Sanchez, Fernando Lopez, 'Subsidies for the Roman West? The Flow of Constantinopolitan Solidi to the Western Empire and Barbaricum', *Opuscula* 9 (2016), pp.158–77.

————. with Victor, Helena, 'The 5th Century Hoard of Theodosian Solidi from Stora Brunneby, Oland, Sweden', *Fornvannen* 106 (2011), pp.189–204.

Fleuriot, Léon, *Les Origines de la Bretagne* (Paris: Payot Publishing, 1980).

Fyfe, Laura, *Hunnic Warfare in the Fourth and Fifth Centuries C.E.: Archery and the Collapse of the Western Roman Empire*, Master's Thesis, Trent University, 2016.

Gaupp, Ernst, *Die germanischen Ansiedlungen und Landteilungen in den Provinzen des römischen Weltreichs in ihrer völkerrechtlichen Eigentümlichkeit und mit Rücksicht auf verwandte Erscheinungen der Alten Welt und des späteren Mittelalters dargestellt* (Osnabrück: Otto Zeller Verlag, 1967).

Gerrets, Danny, 'The Anglo-Frisian Relationship Seen from an Archaeological Point of View', in Volkert F. Faltings, Alastair G.H. Walker and Ommo Wilts (eds), *Friesische Studien II: Beiträge des Föhrer Symposiums zur Friesischen Philologie* (Odense: Odense University Press, 1995), pp.119–28.

Gibbon, Edward, *The History of the Decline and Fall of the Roman Empire*, Vol.2 (New York: Modern Library, 2003).

Gillett, Andrew, *Envoys and Political Communication in the Late Antique West, 411–533* (Cambridge: Cambridge University Press, 2003).

Girard, M., 'Le Campus Mauriacus, Nouvelle Etude sur le Champ de Bataille d'Attila', *Revue Historique* 28, no.2 (1885).

Glad, Damien, 'The Empire's Influence on Barbarian Elites from the Pontus to the Rhine (5th–7th Centuries): A Case Study of Lamellar Weapons and Segmental Helmet', in Vujadin Ivanišević and Michel Kazanski (eds), *The Pontic Danubian Realm in Late Antiquity* (Paris: ACHCByz, 2012), pp.349–62.

Goetz, Hans-Werner, '*Gens*, Kings and Kingdoms: The Franks', in Hans-Werner Goetz, Jorg Jarnut and Walter Pohl (eds), *Regna and Gentes: The Relationship Between Late Antique and Early Medieval Peoples and Kingdoms in the Transformation of the Roman World* (Leiden: Brill, 2003), pp.307–19.

Goffart, Walter, 'Administrative Methods of Barbarian Settlement in the Fifth Century: The Definitive Account', in S. Diefenbach and G.M. Müller (eds), *Gallien in Spätantike und Frühmittelalter: Kulturgeschichte Einer Region* (Berlin: Walter De Gruyter, 2013), pp.45–56.

————. *Barbarian Tides: The Migration Age and the Later Roman Empire* (Philadelphia: University of Pennsylvania Press, 2006).

————. *Barbarians and Romans A.D. 418–584: The Techniques of Accommodation* (Princeton: Princeton University Press, 1980).

————. 'Frankish Military Duty and the Fate of Roman Taxation' *Early Medieval Europe* 16, no.2 (2008), pp.166–90.

————. *The Narrators of Barbarian History (A.D. 550–800): Jordanes, Gregory of Tours, Bede and Paul the Deacon* (Princeton: Princeton University Press, 1988).

————. 'The Technique of Barbarian Settlement in the Fifth Century: A Personal, Streamlined Account with Ten Additional Comments', *Journal of Late Antiquity* 3, no.1 (2010), pp.65–98.

Golden, Peter, *An Introduction to the History of the Turkic Peoples: Ethnogenesis and State Formation in Medieval and Early Modern Eurasia and the Middle East* (Wiesbaden: Otto Harrassowitz, 1992).

————. 'Imperial Ideology and the Sources of Political Unity Amongst the Pre-Chingissid Nomads of Western Eurasia', *Archivum Eurasiae Medii Aevi* 2 (1982), pp.37–76.

————. 'Nomads of the Western Eurasian Steppes: Oyurs, Onoyurs and Khazars', in Catalin Hriban (ed.), *Studies on the Peoples and Cultures of the Eurasian Steppes* (Bucharest: Editura Academiei Române, 2011), pp.135–63.

————. 'Some Notes on the Etymology of Sabir', KOINON ΔΩPON (2013), pp.49–55.

————. 'War and Warfare in the Pre-Chingissid Western Steppes of Eurasia', in Catalin Hriban (ed.), *Studies on the Peoples and Cultures of the Eurasian Steppes* (Bucharest: Editura Academiei Române, 2011), pp.65–134.

Gordon, Colin D., *The Age of Attila: Fifth Century Byzantium and the Barbarians* (Ann Arbor: University of Michigan Press, 1960).

Gracanin, Hrvoje, 'The Western Roman Embassy to the Court of Attila in A.D. 449', *Byzantinoslavica* 6 (2003), pp.53–74.

Grane, Thomas, 'Southern Scandinavian *Foederati* and *Auxiliarii*?', in Thomas Grane (ed.), *Beyond the Roman Frontier: Roman Influences on the Northern Barbaricum* (Rome: Quasar, 2008), pp.83–104.

————. *The Roman Empire and Southern Scandinavia – A Northern Connection!*, PhD Diss., University of Copenhagen, 2007.

Greatrex, G. and Greatrex, M., 'The Hunnic Invasion of the East in 395 and the Fortress of Ziatha', *Byzantion* 54 (1999), pp.66, 69.

Gutsmiedel-Schumann, Doris, 'Merovingian Men – Fulltime Warriors? Weapon Graves of the Continental Merovingian Period of the Munich Gravel Plain and the Social and Age Structure of the Contemporary Society – a Case Study', in Kalle Sognnes, Ragnhild Berge and Marek E. Jasinski (eds), *N-TAG TEN: Proceedings of the 10th Nordic TAG Conference at Stiklestad, Norway 2009* (Oxford: Archaeopress, 2012), pp.251–61.

Haldon, John, *Byzantine Praetorians: An Administrative, Institutional and Social Survey of the Opsikion and Tagmata, c. 580–900* (Bonn: Rudolf Halbelt, 1984).

Hall, Andrew and Farrel, Jack, 'Bows and Arrows from Miran, China', *The Journal of the Society of Archer-Antiquaries* 51 (2008), pp.89–98.

Halsall, Guy, *Barbarian Migrations and the Roman West* (Cambridge: Cambridge University Press, 2007).

————. 'Childeric's Grave, Clovis' Succession and the Origins of the Merovingian Kingdom', in Ralph W. Mathisen and Danuta Shanzer (eds), *Society and Culture in Late Antique Gaul: Revisiting the Sources* (Aldershot: Ashgate Publishing, 2001), pp.116–33.

————. 'The Ostrogothic Military', in Jonathan Arnold, Shane Bjornlie and Kristina Sessa (eds), *A Companion to Ostrogothic Italy* (Leiden: Brill, 2016), pp.173–200.

————. *Warfare and Society in the Barbarian West, 450–900* (London: Routledge, 2003).

Harke, Heinrich, review of *The Huns, Rome, and the Birth of Europe* by Hyun Jin Kim, *The Classical Review* 64, no.1 (2014), pp.260–62.

Harries, Jill, *Sidonius Apollinaris and the Fall of Rome AD 407–485* (Oxford: Clarendon Press, 1994).

Hayashi, Toshio, 'Huns were Xiongnu or not? From the Viewpoint of Archaeological Material', in Han Woo Choi et al. (eds), *Altay Communities: Migrations and Emergence of Nations* (Istanbul: Istanbul Esnaf ve Sanatkarlar Odalari Birligi, 2014), pp.13–26.

Heather, Peter, 'Disappearing and Reappearing Tribes', in Walter Pohl and Helmut Reimitz (eds), *Strategies of Distinction: The Construction of Ethnic Communities, 300–800* (Leiden: Brill, 1998), pp.95–112.

————. *Empires and Barbarians* (Oxford: Oxford University Press, 2009).

————. *The Fall of the Roman Empie: A New History of Rome and the Barbarians* (Oxford: Oxford University Press, 2006).

————. *The Goths* (Oxford: Blackwell Publishers, 1998).

————. 'The Huns and Barbarian Europe', in Michael Maas (ed.), *The Cambridge Companion to the Age of Attila* (Cambridge: Cambridge University Press, 2015), pp.209–29.

————. 'The Huns and the End of the Roman Empire in Western Europe', *English Historical Review* 110, no. 435 (1995), pp.4–41.

Hedeager, Lotte, 'Scandinavia and the Huns', *Norwegian Archaeological Review* 40 (2007), pp.42–58.

Hildinger, Erik, *Warriors of the Steppe: A Military History of Central Asia 500 B.C. to 1700 A.D.* (Cambridge: Da Capo Press, 2001).

Hodgkin, Thomas, *Italy and her Invaders* (Oxford: Clarendon Press, 1880).

Hohlfelder, Robert, 'Marcian's Gamble: A Reassessment of Eastern Imperial Policy Towards Attila AD 450–453', *American Journal of Ancient History* 9 (1984), pp.54–69.

Hughes, Ian, *Aetius: Attila's Nemesis* (Barnsley: Pen & Sword Military, 2012).

————. *Belisarius: The Last Roman General* (Barnsley: Pen & Sword Military, 2009).

————. *Patricians and Emperors: The Last Rulers of the Western Roman Empire* (Barnsley: Pen & Sword Military, 2015).

————. *Stilicho: The Vandal Who Saved Rome* (Barnsley: Pen & Sword Military, 2010).

Ivanisevic, Vujadin, 'The Danubian *Limes* of the Diocese of *Dacia* in the Fifth Century', in Tivadar Vida and Philip Rance (eds), *Romania Gothica II* (Budapest: Eotvos Lorand University, 2015), pp.653–65.

James, Edward, *The Franks* (Oxford: Basil Blackwell, 1998).

Jarrett, Michael, 'Non-Legionary Troops in Roman Britain: Part One, the Units', *Britannia* 25 (1994), p.60.

Jensen, Xenia Pauli, Jørgensen, Lars and Hansen, Ulla Lund, 'The Germanic Army: Warriors, Soldiers and Officers', in Lars Jørgensen, Birger Storgaard and Lone Gebauer Thomsen (eds), *The Spoils of Victory: The North in the Shadow of the Roman Empire* (Copenhagen: Denmark National Museum, 2003), pp.311–28.

Jimenez, David, 'Sidonius Apollinaris and the Fourth Punic War', in David Hernandez de la Fuuente (ed.), *New Perspectives on Late Antiquity* (Newcastle: Cambridge Scholars Publishing, 2011), pp.158–72.

Jirik, Jaroslav, 'Bohemian Barbarians', in Florin Curta (ed), *Neglected Barbarians* (Turnhout: Brepols Publishers, 2010), pp.263–317.

Johnson, Stephen, *Late Roman Fortifications* (London: Batsford Publishing, 1983).

Jones, Arnold Hugh Martin, *The Later Roman Empire: A.D. 284–602*, 2 vols (Norman: University of Oklahoma Press, 1964).

Kazanski, Michel, 'Bowmen's Graves from the Hunnic Period in Northern Illyricum', in Marta L. Nagy et al. (eds), *'To Make a Fairy's Whistle from a Briar Rose': Studies Presented to Eszter Istvánovits on her Sixtieth Birthday* (Nyíregyháza: Jósa András Museum, 2018), pp.407–17.

———. 'The Ostrogoths and the Princely Civilization of the Fifth Century', in Samuel Barnish and Fredrico Marrazzi (eds), *The Ostrogoths from the Migration Period to the Sixth Century: An Ethnographic Perspective* (San Marino: The Boydell Press, 2007), pp.81–112.

———. 'The Sedentary Elite in the Empire of the Huns and its Impact on the Material Civilization in Southern Russia During the Early Middle Ages', in John C. Chapman and Pavel Dolukhanov (eds), *Cultural Transformations and Interactions in Eastern Europe* (Brookfield: Ashgate Publishing, 1993), pp.211–35.

Kazanski, Michel and Akhmedov, Iliya, 'La Tombe de Mundolsheim (Bas-Rhin): Un chef militaire Nomade au service de Rome', *SPISY ARCHEOLOGICKEHO USTAVU AV CR BRNO* 26 (2007), pp.249–61.

Kharalambieva, Anna, 'Gepids in the Balkans: A Survey of the Archaeological Evidence', in Florin Curta (ed.), *Neglected Barbarians* (Turnhout: Brepols Publishers, 2010), pp.245–62.

Kim, Hyun Jin, 'Herodotean' Allusions in Late Antiquity: Priscus, Jordanes and the Huns', *Byzantion* 85 (2015), pp.127–42.

———. *The Huns, Rome and the Birth of Europe* (Cambridge: Cambridge University Press, 2013).

King, Charles, 'The Veracity of Ammianus Marcellinus' Description of the Huns', *American Journal of Ancient History* 12 (1987), pp.77–95.

Kos, Marjeta Sasel, 'The Embassy of Romulus to Attila: One of the Last Citations of Poetovio in Classical Literature', *Tyche* 9 (1994), p.103.

Kos, Peter, 'Barriers in the Julian Alps and the *Notitia Dignitatum*', *Arheoloski Vestnik* 65 (2014), pp.409–22.

Laniado, Avshalom, 'Aspar and his Phoideratoi: John Malalas on a Special Relationship', in Umberto Roberto and Laura Mecella (eds), *Governare e riformare l'impero al momento della sua divisione: Oriente, Occidente, Illirico* (Rome: Publications de l'École française de Rome, 2015), pp.1–18.

Lebedensky, Iaroslav, *La campagne d'Attila en Gaule 451 apr. J.-C.* (Clermont-Ferrand: Lemme Edit, 2011).

Liebeschuetz, Wolfgang, 'The End of the Roman Army in the Western Empire', in John Rich and Graham Shipley (eds), *War and Society in the Roman World* (London: Routledge, 1993), pp.265–76.

Lindner, Rudi Paul, 'Nomadism, Horses and Huns', *Past and Present* 92 (1982), pp.3–19.

Lot, Ferdinand, 'Du régime de l'hospitalité', *Revue belge de Philologie et d'Histoire* 7 (1928), pp.975–1,011.

MacDowall, Simon, *Catalaunian Fields AD 451: Rome's Last Great Battle* (Oxford: Osprey Publishing, 2015).

MacGeorge, Penny, *Late Roman Warlords* (Oxford: Oxford University Press, 2002).

Maenchen-Helfen, Otto, 'Huns and Hsiung-nu', *Byzantion* 17 (1945), pp.222–43.

———. *On the World of the Huns: Studies in their History and Culture*, edited by Max Knight (Berkeley: University of California Press, 1973).

Mathisen, Ralph, 'Catalogues of Barbarians in Late Antiquity', in Ralph Mathisen and Danuta Shanzer (eds), *Romans, Barbarians and the Transformation of the Roman World* (Burlington: Ashgate Publishing, 2011), pp.17–32.

———. *Ecclesiastical Factionalism and Religious Controversy in Fifth-Century Gaul* (Washington: Catholic University of America Press, 1989).

———. 'Resistance and Reconciliation: Majorian and the Gallic Aristocracy after the Fall of Avitus', *Francia* 7 (1979), pp.597–27.

———. 'Sidonius on the Reign of Avitus: A Study in Political Prudence', *Transactions of the American Philological Association* 109 (1979), pp.165–71.

McCotter, Stephen, 'Byzantines, Avars, and the Introduction of the Trebuchet, *De Rei Militari*, 9 June 2014, http://deremilitari.org/2014/06/byzantines-avars-and-the-introduction-of-the-trebuchet/.

McEvoy, Meghan, 'Becoming Roman: The Not-So-Curious Case of Aspar and the Ardaburii, *Journal of Late Antiquity* 9.2 (2016), pp.483–511.

———. *Child Emperor Rule in the Late Roman West, AD 367–455* (Oxford: Oxford University Press, 2013).

McMahon, Lucas, 'The Foederati, The Phoideratoi and the Symmachoi of the Late Antique East (c.a. AD 400–650), Master's Thesis, University of Ottowa, 2014.

Menghin, Wilfried, 'Schwerter des Goldgriffespathenhorizonts im Museum für Vor-und Frügeschichte, Berlin, *Acta Praehistorica et Archaeologica* 26 (1995), pp.140–91.

Miks, Christian, 'Relikte Eines Frühmittelalterlichen Oberschichtgrabes? Überlegungen zu einem Konvolut bemerkenswerter Objekte aus dem Kunsthandel' *Jahrbuch des Römisch-Germanischen Zentralmuseums Mainz* 56 (2009), pp.395–538.

———. *Studien zur römischen Schwertbewaffnung in der Kaiserzeit*, Vol.1 (Rahden: Verlag Marie Leidorf, 2007).

Milavec, Tina, 'Crossbow fibulae of the 5th and 6th centuries in the southeastern Alps', *Arheoloski Vestnik* 60 (2009), pp.223–48.

Mingarelli, Bernardo, *Collapse of the Hunnic Empire: Jordanes, Ardaric and the Battle of Nedao*, Ph.D Thesis, University of Ottowa, 2018.

Moss, J.R., 'The Effects of the Policies of Aetius on the History of the Western Empire', *Historia* 22 (1973), pp.711–33.

Nasman, Ulf, 'Scandinavia and the Huns: A Source-Critical Approach to an Old Question', *Fornvannen* 103 (2008), pp.111–18.

Nicolle, David, *Attila and the Nomad Hordes* (Oxford: Osprey Publishing, 1990).

———. *The Mongol Warlords: Ghenghis Khan, Kublai Khan, Hulegu, Tamerlane* (New York: Firebird Books, 1990).

Norwich, John Julius, *A Short History of Byzantium* (New York: Vintage Books, 1999).

O'Flynn, John Michael, *Generalissimos of the Western Roman Empire* (Alberta: University of Alberta Press, 1983).

Onur, Fatih, 'The Anastasian Military Decree from Perge in Pamphylia: Revised 2nd Edition, *GEPHYRA* 14 (2016), pp.133–212.

Oost, Stewart Irwin, 'Aetius and Majorian', *Classical Philology* 29, no.1 (1964), pp.23–29.

Parker, Geoffrey, *The Cambridge Illustrated History of Warfare* (Cambridge: Cambridge University Press, 1995).

Pritsak, Omeljan, 'The Hunnic Language of the Attila Clan', *Harvard Ukranian Studies* 6, no.4 (1982), pp.428–76.

Rance, Philip, 'Drungus, Δρούγγος and Δρουγγιστί: a Gallicism and Continuity in Roman Cavalry Tactics', *Phoenix* 58 (2004), pp.96–130.

———. 'Maurice's *Strategicon* and "the Ancients": the Late Antique Reception of Aelian and Arrian', in Philip Rance and Nicholas Sekunda (eds), *Greek Taktika: Ancient Military Writing and its Heritage* (Gdańsk: University of Gdańsk, 2017), pp.217–55.

———. '*Noumera* or *Mounera*: A Parallel Philological Problem in *De Ceremoniis* and Maurice's *Strategikon*', *Jarbruch der Österreichischen Byzantinistik* 58 (2008), pp.121–29.

————. 'The *Etymologicum Magnum* and the Fragment of Urbicius', *Greek, Roman and Byzantine Studies* 47 (2007), pp.193–224.

————. '*The Fulcum, the Late Roman and Byzantine Testudo: The Germanization of Roman Infantry Tactics?*, *Greek, Roman, and Byzantine Studies*, 44 (2004), pp.265–326.

Reisinger, Michaela, 'New Evidence about Composite Bows and Their Arrows in Inner Asia', *The Silk Road* 8 (2010), pp.42–62.

Reuter, Marcus, 'Studien zu den numeri des römischen Heeres in der mittleren Kaiserzeit', *Berichte der Römisch-Germanischen Kommission* 80 (1999), pp.359–569.

Richardot, Philippe, *La Fin de l'Armee Romaine 284–476* (Paris: Economica, 2005).

Roymans, Nico, 'Gold, Germanic Foederati, and the End of Imperial Power in the Late Roman North, in Nico Roymans, Stjin Heeren, and Wim De Clercq (eds), *Social Dynamics in the Northwest Frontiers of the Late Roman Empire* (Amsterdam: Amsterdam University Press, 2017), pp.57–80.

Scharf, Ralf, 'Ripari und Olibriones? Zwei Teilnehmer an der Schlacht auf den Katalaunischen Feldern', *MIÖG* 107 (1999), pp.1–11.

Schmitz, Leonhard, 'Hora', in William Smith ed.), *A Dictionary of Greek and Roman Antiquities* (London: John Murray Press, 1875), p.614.

Simpson, C.J., '*Laeti* in the *Notitia Dignitatum*: "Regular" Soldiers vs. "Soldier-Farmers"', *Revue Belge de Philologie et d'histoire* 66.1 (1988), pp.80–85.

Snyder, Christopher A., *The Britons* (Hoboken: Wiley-Blackwell, 2003).

Solapova, Elizabeth, *Languages, Myths and History: An Introduction to the Linguistic and Literary Background of J.R.R. Tolkien's Fiction (New York City: North Landing Books, 2009).*

Stanev, Alexander, 'Elements of the Germanic Fibula Costume South of the Danube River', in *Archaeological Data from the Balkan Provinces of the Eastern Roman Empire V-VI Century* (Ruse: Avangard Print, 2012), pp.23–32, 369–75.

Steinacher, Roland, 'The Herules: Fragments of a History', in Florin Curta (ed.), *Neglected Barbarians* (Turnhout: Brepols Publishers, 2010), pp.319–60.

Sulimirski, Tadeusz, *The Sarmatians* (London: Thames & Hudson, 1970).

Swift, Ellen, *The End of the Western Roman Empire: An Archaeological Investigation* (Stroud: The History Press, 2010).

Tackholm, Ulf, 'Aetius and the Battle on the Catalaunian Fields', *Opuscula Romana* 7, no.15 (1969), pp.259–76.

Thompson, Edward Arthur, *A History of Attila and the Huns* (Oxford: Clarendon Press, 1948).

Topalilov, Ivo, 'The Barbarians and the City: A Comparative Study of the Impact of the Barbarian Invasions in 376–378 and 442–447 on the Urbanization of Philipopolis, Thrace, in Danijel Dzino and Ken Parry (eds), *Byzantium, its Neighbours and its Cultures* (Virginia: Brisbane, 2014), pp.223–44.

Treadgold, Warren, 'Paying the Army in the Theodosian Period', in Ine Jacobs (ed.), *Production and Prosperity in the Theodosian Period* (Leuven: Peeters Publishing, 2014), pp.303–18.

Vernadsky, George, 'Der sarmatische Hintergrund der germanischen Volkerwanderung', *Saeculum* 2 (1951), pp.340–92.

Vovin, Alexander, 'Did the Xiong-nu Speak a Yeniseian Language?', *Central Asiatic Journal* 44 (2000), pp.87–104.

Wallace-Hadrill, John Michael, *The Long Haired Kings: And Other Studies in Frankish History*. (London: Methuen & Company, 1962).

Whately, Conor, 'Jordanes, the Battle of the Catalaunian Fields and Constantinople', *Dialogues d'historie ancienne* 8 (2012), pp.57–70.

Whitby, Michael, 'The Late Roman Army and the Defence of the Balkans', in Andrew Poulter (ed.), *The Transition to Late Antiquity on the Danube and Beyond* (Oxford: Oxford University Press, 2007), pp.135–62.

Wigg-Wolf, David, 'Supplying a Dying Empire? The Mint of Trier in the Late 4th Century AD, *RGZM – Tagungen* 29 (2016), pp.217–33.

Wijnendaele, Jeroen P., 'The Early Career of Aetius and the Murder of Felix (c. 425–430 CE)', *Historia* 66, no.4 (2017), pp.468–82.

———. *The Last of the Romans: Bonifatius – Warlord and Comes Africae* (London: Bloomsbuury Academic, 2016).

———. 'Warlordism and the Disintegration of the Western Roman Army', in Jeremy Armstrong (ed.), *Circum Mare: Themes in Ancient Warfare* (Leiden: Brill, 2016), pp.185–203.

Williams, Stephen and Friell, Gerard, *The Rome that did not Fall: The Survival of the East in the Fifth Century* (London: Routledge, 1999).

Williamson, Harold, 'The Probable Date of the Roman Occupation of Melandra', in R.S. Conway (ed.), *Melandra Castle* (Manchester: Manchester University Press, 1906), pp.122–28.

Wolfram, Herwig, *The Roman Empire and its Germanic Peoples*, trans. Thomas Dunlap (Berkeley: University of California Press, 1997).

Wood, Ian, 'The North-Western Provinces', in Averil Cameron, Bryan Ward-Perkins and Michael Whitby (eds), *The Cambridge Ancient History*, Vol.14 (Cambridge: Cambridge University Press, 2008), pp.497–524.

Yu, Ying-Shih, 'Trade and Expansion in Han China: A Study in the Structure of Sino-Barbarian Economic Relations' (Berkeley: University of California Press, 1967).

Zuckerman, C., 'Legio V Macedonica in Egypt', *Tyche* 3 (1988), pp.279–87.

Index